Political Parties in Revolutionary Massachusetts

# Political
# Parties
# in Revolutionary
# Massachusetts

Stephen E. Patterson

The University of Wisconsin Press

Published 1973
The University of Wisconsin Press
Box 1379, Madison, Wisconsin 53701

The University of Wisconsin Press, Ltd.
70 Great Russell Street, London

First printing

Printed in the United States of America

For LC CIP information see the colophon

ISBN 0-299-0620-0

# Contents

# Preface

Were there political parties in revolutionary America? In this study of the Revolution in Massachusetts, I seek to present the evidence that there were. Not short-lived, issue-oriented coalitions but rather established parties that produced highly consistent voting patterns on many issues over a number of years. If longevity is a criterion of party, the Massachusetts parties of the late provincial period—the Court and Country parties—lasted at least as long as the Federalist and Republican parties of a later generation. And the parties that emerged in the state during the heat of conflict, beginning in 1774—loosely termed the eastern and western parties—endured at least as long as the Free-Soil and American parties of the 1840s and 50s.

To be sure, these revolutionary parties were not highly organized, modern political machines. While they had their own structures, they were not the conscious creations of highly skilled politicians. They were nascent parties that emerged in response to the changing realities of life in America, in defiance of ideological restraints and sometimes ambiguously in contravention of their own stated ideals. They were nonetheless real for all that.

Evidence of the existence of these Massachusetts parties and of the role of partisan behavior in the development of the American Revolution has, however, often been ignored or at least obscured. There are, I believe, three main reasons why this has been so. The first is tightly interwoven with the interpretation of the Revolution itself. Ever since the eighteenth century, Whig and neo-Whig historians have argued that the Revolution was principally a constitutional struggle between colonies and mother country, that Americans were united on the lofty plane of rights, and that divisions among Americans were secondary in importance and of little consequence to the revolutionary movement. This view accepts the rhetoric of revolutionary pamphleteers at face value for, as Samuel Williams wrote in 1775, no one can conceive of the

American revolutionary cause as "the cause of a mob, of a party, or of a faction." Rather, the American cause "is the cause of self-defense, of public faith, and of the liberties of mankind." Despite the work of Carl Becker, Charles Beard and other twentieth-century historians who have attached some significance to crowds, parties, and factions, this notion has persisted to the present among many.

Second, the work of Sir Lewis Namier has convinced some students of American politics that what he says of British political behavior at the time of the Revolution is equally applicable to America. In *The Structure of Politics at the Accession of George III*, Namier wrote: "The political life of the period 1761–84 could be fully described without ever using a party denomination." Like Namier, Massachusetts scholars have sought and found ephemeral legislative coalitions formed for personal or other short-term advantage, but they have assumed that more durable coalitions simply did not exist.

Third, the ideology of the revolutionary generation has frequently been seen as an effective barrier against the creation of parties. Republicans sought unity and unanimity in their communities; they praised disinterested virtue and condemned private interest-seeking. Because they condemned party and faction as contrary to the public interest, it is often assumed that they avoided partisanship as a matter of principle. The gap between principle and reality, unfortunately, has remained a relatively uncharted valley.

That gap has been one of my chief concerns in this book. In what is in effect a political history of the American Revolution in Massachusetts, I have employed a variety of methods rather than a single method to come closer to an understanding of both political theory and political practice. I have begun in the 1750s and followed the course of events down to 1780, with particular emphasis on the years 1774 to 1780, when Massachusetts was without a settled constitution. Naturally, I hope that there is something new and of value in this book. But, at the same time, I hope that it at least begins the formidable task of synthesizing and casting in perspective the enormously rich body of monographic literature on Massachusetts that has appeared in recent years.

For the sake of clarity, I have modernized the spellings and capitalizations in most eighteenth-century quotations. Where clarity was not affected, I occasionally have retained the original to convey the flavor of the quotation.

The rules of scholarship fortunately do not require that one acknowledge every discussion with or hints from one's colleagues that have led to more accurate definition of terms, greater consistency of thought, or more thorough research. And yet without such help, a work of this sort would be impossible. Among those to whom I am indebted, I wish to thank most sincerely the following people: Merrill Jensen, my teacher and doctoral supervisor at the University of Wisconsin, to whose encouragement, guidance, and example I owe what skill I may have as an historian; Gaspare Saladino, Rupert Charles Loucks, Kenneth Bowling, Alfred Young, and Jackson T. Main, all of whom read, in its various stages, parts of my manuscript and offered numerous useful comments; Van Beck Hall, who provided me with a copy of his classification of Massachusetts towns; and Judy Wilson and Phyllis Miller, who typed and re-typed my manuscript.

In addition, I acknowledge with gratitude the invaluable research assistance I received from the directors, librarians, and staffs of the following institutions: The State Historical Society of Wisconsin (particularly director James Morton Smith, Charles Shetler, and Gerry Eggleston), the Memorial Library of the University of Wisconsin, the Massachusetts Historical Society (particularly Winifred Collins), the Massachusetts State Archives (particularly Leo and Helen Flaherty), the Boston Public Library, and the Harriet Irving Library of the University of New Brunswick. My warmest thanks are inadequate repayment for their help.

And finally I thank Linda, who realizes that being married to an historian can be worse than being married to a sailor since the historian can be at sea even when he is at home.

S.E.P.

*University of New Brunswick*
*January 1973*

Political Parties in Revolutionary Massachusetts

# Abbreviations

| | |
|---|---|
| AAS | American Antiquarian Society |
| *Acts and Resolves* | *The Acts and Resolves, Public and Private, of the Province of the Massachusetts Bay,* vols. 1, 4, 5 (Boston, 1869, 1881, 1886); *Acts and Resolves of the Province of the Massachusetts Bay,* 20 (Boston, 1918) |
| *Amer. Arch.* | Peter Force, ed., *American Archives,* 4th ser., 6 vols. (Washington, 1837–46); 5th ser., 3 vols. (Washington, 1848–53) |
| BC | *Boston Chronicle* |
| BCC | Boston Committee of Correspondence |
| BEP | *Boston Evening Post* |
| BG | *Boston Gazette* |
| 12, 14, 16, 18, 20, 26 *BTR* | Twelfth, Fourteenth, Sixteenth, Eighteenth, Twentieth, Twenty-Sixth *Report[s] of the Record Commissioners of the City of Boston* . . . (Boston, 1885, 1885, 1886, 1887, 1889, 1895) |
| CSM | Colonial Society of Massachusetts |
| EIHC | *Essex Institute Historical Collections* |
| *House Journals* | Massachusetts, *Journals of the House of Representatives* |
| Mass. Arch. | Massachusetts Archives, Archives Division, Commonwealth of Massachusetts |
| MHS | Massachusetts Historical Society |
| NEQ | *New England Quarterly* |
| WMQ | *William and Mary Quarterly* |

# 1

## Antipartisan Theory and Partisan Reality

OF ALL the participants in the American Revolution, none succeeded more than the men of Massachusetts in appropriating the Revolution and in making it their own. The Tories insisted that the Revolution began in Boston as an unprovoked attack on "government," sparked by the ambitions of sinister conspirators bent on republicanism and independence, and that it was spread by "factious demagogues" from that "Babel of Confusion" into the Massachusetts countryside until it finally set the whole continent aflame. The Whigs, for their part, argued that the "scheme" to destroy American liberty originated among a "junto" in Boston, determined "to have a revenue in America, by authority of parliament"; it had written the Stamp Act, not to provide revenue for Great Britain but to provide salaries for corrupt partisans in Massachusetts; and its intention was not only to control Massachusetts, but also "to new model the whole continent of North America" as well.[1]

Such blatant exaggeration was not the work of latter-day ptolemaists arguing, in the face of all empirical evidence, that their world was the center of the universe. These men were partisans. They argued as did partisans of a later day that the evils which had befallen them were the work of their political opponents, and they sought to justify, if not advance, their own partisan position by saying so. Their accusations illustrate two of the three propositions of this book: the politics of Massachusetts, from the late provincial period through the Revolution,

---

1. Peter Oliver, *Origin & Progress of the American Rebellion: A Tory View*, ed. Douglass Adair and John A. Schutz (San Marino, Calif., 1961), pp. 9, 27-75; John Adams and [Daniel Leonard], *Novanglus and Massachusettensis* (Boston, 1819), pp. 9-14, 17-19.

was characterized by a conflict, varying in intensity, between two political parties. The structure of party politics imposed itself on the controversy with Great Britain, defining the tactics of the Revolution, shaping its direction, and linking partisan goals with the larger assertion of rights. And, finally, new parties expressive of the variety of opinion among the revolutionaries themselves and of the plurality of Massachusetts society sprang from the ashes of the old and imposed a new pattern of partisan behavior on the politics of the state in the period from 1774 to 1780. In other words, the Revolution in Massachusetts was a dual revolution: parliamentary attempts to tax Americans and to tighten the regulation of the empire were provocative and catalytic, but the party struggle was anterior to the challenge to American liberty, it absorbed imperial issues into a partisan context from the very first, and party conflict thrived symbiotically on imperial issues until the institutions of charter government ended in 1774. Independence resolved half of the duality, but it left unanswered equally important questions about the future of Massachusetts society and government.

The terms "party," as well as the more pejorative "faction" and "junto," were used in a political sense by men of every political complexion from the late provincial period through the Revolution, with scarcely an interruption during the critical transformation from royal to republican government. Such usage clearly indicates their belief that the Massachusetts legislature was divided into two parties, that the division represented different viewpoints and often clashing "interests" in the province at large, and that sometimes this partisanship penetrated into the towns themselves, splitting families, introducing election competitions, and otherwise disturbing the "harmony" of the community. When, for example, Jonathan Edwards arrived in Northampton in the 1720s, he discovered that the town had been divided for twenty years into the "Court" party—"some of the chief men in the town, of chief authority and wealth, that have been great proprietors of their land"— and the "Country" party—"which has commonly been the greatest," and which was made up of "those who have been jealous of them [i.e., the Court party], apt to envy them, and afraid of their having too much power and influence in town and church."[2] For the most part, however, the provincial parties represented intertown rather than intratown rivalries; they sprang from two quite different kinds of towns; and they expressed themselves as legislative coalitions, fairly fluid in their composition, but stable enough to be identified with certain leaders and

2. Quoted by Perry Miller, *Jonathan Edwards* (New York, 1949), pp. 43–44.

issues from the 1750s (at least) down to the major realignments of 1774, 1775, and 1776.

Basically, the parties in their legislative form were parties of "government" and "opposition," and both of these terms were used, if not precisely as we would use them. Governor William Shirley (1741–56) fashioned a coalition of the supporters and opponents of his predecessor, Jonathan Belcher, and was accused of leaving behind a well-organized "party" more loyal to him personally than to government in general.[3] His successor, Thomas Pownall (1757–60), had already written a pamphlet in England strongly in favor of the idea of party, and he put his ideas into practice upon his arrival at the Bay.[4] Francis Bernard (1760–69), who followed in three years' time, wrote that he "found the province divided into parties so nearly equal, that it would have been madness for me to have put myself at the head of either of them," though he soon did.[5] And Thomas Hutchinson (1771–74) followed the example of all of these men when he sought, in 1771, to create his own "coalition."[6]

Men other than governors knew how the partisan game was played. They knew that often "promotions are made in gov[ernmen]t only to make tools and parties," and that even when patronage holders are laid "silently aside: that hereby the chief magistrate makes himself of a party." It was always difficult to appoint legislative agents to serve in London because "whilst we are thus in parties any but a neutral agent would be hampered and ill treated."[7] Government men continually lamented the growing power of the opposition. One of them told of a "plowman" who got elected to the General Court and, when he arrived, "he made it his business, in a low private way, to slander and abuse those of the county who were noted for supporting government or were in-

3. John A. Schutz, *William Shirley: King's Governor of Massachusetts* (Chapel Hill, N.C., 1961), pp. 41, 62, 64, 73, 84, 123–24, 133, 137, 144; William Shirley to Earl of Loudoun, 13 September 1756; Loudoun to Henry Fox, [n.d.], in Charles Henry Lincoln, ed., *Correspondence of William Shirley, Governor of Massachusetts and Military Commander in America, 1731–1760,* 2 vols. (New York, 1912), 2: 557.

4. Caroline Robbins, " 'Discordant Parties': A Study of the Acceptance of Party by Englishmen," *Political Science Quarterly* 73 (1958): 521. For Pownall's partisan behavior in Massachusetts, see Chapter 2.

5. Bernard to Lord Barrington, 1 May 1762, in Bernard Papers, 2: 189, quoted by Ellen E. Brennan, *Plural Office-Holding in Massachusetts, 1760–1780* (Chapel Hill, N.C., 1945), p. 51.

6. Hutchinson to Thomas Whately, Boston, 25 January 1771, in Mass. Arch., 27: 106–7.

7. [Israel Williams] to ———, 1759; Williams to Gov. Bernard, Hatfield, 19 August 1761; Thomas Hutchinson to Williams, Boston, 17 November 1763, in Israel Williams Papers, MHS, 2: 115, 119, 158.

trusted by it, fell in with Mr. Tyng and that party who were in the opposition." It was acknowledged that the dramatic changes in the membership of the provincial Council in the year 1766 "were carried by the interest of Otis and his party" and it was believed "that the leaders of the faction are meditating very mad, distracting measures." Thomas Hutchinson found that "the party opposed to me increases in the general court."[8]

Patriotic leaders, too, pointed to the existence of party, both before and after Independence. John Adams claimed that William Shirley was the originator of the Tory "junto," while Bernard and Hutchinson were considered the brains behind the junto in the 1760s. Mercy Warren thought that "the hopes of contending parties" were in equilibrium in early 1775. "Will not justice and freedom soon preponderate, till the partisans of corruption and venality, even backed with the weight of ministerial power, shall be made to kick the beam?"[9] By the late 1770s, men spoke of "a considerable party" centered in Essex County, opposed by another "party" centered "in Worcester, Hampshire, and Berkshire." The town of Topsfield rejected a representation act passed in 1776 as something "obtained only to serve the interest of particular parties," while men who approved the actions of a Berkshire County convention in 1779 were accused of being "actuated by party views." Theodore Sedgwick lamented "the state of party among us" while Mercy Warren believed that "the spirit of party has entered into all our departments."[10]

Their experience with partisanship in Massachusetts led men both during and after the Revolution to generalize about parties and their role in the state. "Party is inseparable from a free state," categorically wrote Tory Daniel Leonard in 1774, and he stated without qualification that "there were two parties in this province of pretty long standing."

8. Israel Williams to Gov. Bernard, Hatfield, 19 August 1761, ibid., p. 119; Thomas Hutchinson to Thomas Hutchinson, Jr., Milton, 27 May 1766; Hutchinson to William Bollan, Boston, 2 June 1767, in Mass. Arch., 26: 233, 238.

9. Adams and [Leonard], *Novanglus and Massachusettensis*, pp. 13–23; Mercy Warren to John Adams, Plymouth, 30 January 1775, in Worthington Chauncey Ford, ed., *Warren-Adams Letters*, 2 vols. (Boston, 1917–25), 1: 38.

10. Nathanael Peaslee Sargeant to Timothy Pickering, Haverhill, 28 May 1778, in Pickering Papers, MHS, 17: 153; Petition of Topsfield, in Mass. Arch., 156: 171; Theodore Sedgwick to James Sullivan, Sheffield, 16 May 1779, 10 January 1779, in Theodore Sedgwick Papers, MHS, vol. A, pp. 36, 29; Mercy Warren to John Adams, Plymouth, 29 July 1779, in Ford, ed., *Warren-Adams Letters*, 2: 114. The term "party" is, of course, used often in senses other than political. In each of the examples cited above, the context in which the term was used is unquestionably political.

"All nations, under all governments, must have parties," wrote John Adams in the 1780s, "the great secret is to control them." He believed that "the disposition to division" was apparent in all governments with democratic elements, even when balanced by aristocratic and monarchical powers. Theophilus Parsons, whose experience was entirely within Massachusetts (although he was well-read), believed that the holder of the office of house speaker "is commonly a favourite of a considerable party in the house" and that the popular election of governors (although Massachusetts had never had one) would inevitably "originate parties and factions in the state." With the experience of revolutionary congresses and legislatures fresh in his mind, he noted the particular danger of large representative gatherings. "Parties would be formed and factions engendered. The members would list under the banners of their respective leaders: address and intrigue would conduct the debates, and the result would tend only to promote the ambition or interest of a particular party. Such has always been in some degree, the course and event of debates instituted and managed by a large multitude."[11]

These were no casual statements of political theory. While they were certainly capable of a high order of political thought, Massachusetts politicians learned through practical experience that their increasingly complex society easily generated differing political viewpoints that ultimately expressed themselves in partisan form. John Adams typified this hard-headed practicality in 1817 when he wrote that "there is an overweening fondness for representing this country as a scene of liberty, equality, fraternity, union, harmony and benevolence. But let not your sons or mine deceive themselves. This country, like all others, has been a theatre of parties and feuds for near two hundred years."[12] The country to which Adams referred was Massachusetts.

Despite their realistic recognition of the fact of party, most Massachusetts politicians shared the widespread eighteenth-century suspicion of partisanship. They shrank from charges that they were partisan in their behavior; they justified their own resort to partisan tactics by claiming that they had the widest possible popular support; and they admitted more readily that their opponents were partisan than that they

11. Adams and [Leonard], *Novanglus and Massachusettensis*, p. 149; John Adams, *Defence of the Constitutions* (1787–88), in Charles Francis Adams, ed., *The Works of John Adams*, 10 vols. (Boston, 1850–56), 4: 587–88, 313; [Theophilus Parsons], "The Essex Result" (1778), in Theophilus Parsons, *Memoir of Theophilus Parsons* (Boston, 1859), pp. 388, 386, 377.

12. Adams to William Tudor, Quincy, 4 February 1817, in Adams, ed., *Works*, 9: 241–42.

were themselves. The republicans among them, particularly, interpreted the existence of partisanship as a basic weakness in their society, a symptom of the distressing condition of their country, and they hoped, in their utopian vision of the future, to see the end of all partisanship. Some men, particularly in 1774 and 1775, believed that they were witnessing the accomplishment of that vision. "Such a spirit of union, firmness, intrepidity and readiness to sacrifice every less consideration for the cause of liberty I never conceived possible, among a set of beings whose *primum mobile,* in common is self interest," wrote Reverend Samuel Stillman of Boston in November 1774. "The people through the continent are actuated by one Soul, they have laid aside every distinction of name and party, but that of Friends of Freedom. The fire has kindled, and like a shock of electricity, run through this western world."[13] The choice of words was significant. Men could have "laid aside every distinction of name and party" only if there had been parties. And the antithesis of partisanship was "the spirit of union": not, as we shall discover, a simple union of all colonies, but the republican ideal of a union of all ranks and conditions of men where harmony, virtue, and the public interest triumph over "avarice" and "self-interest."

These antipartisan principles, ironically, were embedded in the partisan schemes of republican revolutionaries, and a central goal was first to prevent, and then to control, partisanship in their "commonwealth" once the separation from Great Britain had taken place. When, for instance, in May 1776 the possibility arose that a governor might be elected to fill the void left by the recent flight of the British, John Adams, then in Philadelphia, wrote that he dreaded the consequences of electing governors "and would avoid every appearance of and tendency towards party and division, as the greatest evil." And again he asked, "Who will be your new Governor or President—Bowdoin or Winthrop or Warren? Don't divide. Let the choice be unanimous, I beg. If you divide you will split the province with factions." On any issue, Adams's sentiments were the same. When it came to forming a plan of government, he warned

13. Stillman to Mrs. Patience Wright, Boston, 13 November 1774, in Josiah Quincy, Jr., Papers, MHS, vol. 1639–1852, p. 74. The term "republican" is used here in the way it was used by English Commonwealthmen of the seventeenth and eighteenth centuries. In their usage, the "spirit" of the English constitution was republican, and it was this spirit, largely summed up in the concept of liberty, that they sought to preserve. See Caroline Robbins, *The Eighteenth-Century Commonwealthman* (Cambridge, Mass., 1959), pp. 7–8, 16, 39–40, 47–48, 121, 386; Gordon S. Wood, *The Creation of the American Republic, 1776–1787* (Chapel Hill, N.C., 1969), pp. 45, 49–65.

that the legislature should "proceed in the formation of a constitution without any hurtful divisions or altercations. Whatever the majority determine, I hope the minority will cheerfully concur in."[14] Samuel Adams even went so far as to urge his friends "to prevent unnecessary questions in the assembly which may cause contention. Now if ever Union is necessary."[15]

In all such pleas, partisanship was equated with "private interest" rather than with the "public good," and it was represented as standing in the way of the fulfillment of republican ideals. As John Adams put it after the Revolution: "The interest of the people is one thing—it is the public interest, and where the public interest governs, it is a government of laws, and not of men. The interest of a king, or of a party, is another thing—it is a private interest; and where private interest governs, it is a government of men, and not of laws."[16] Partisanship, in other words, was expressive of a self-centered individualism; parties were simply extensions of self and had as their object the promotion of what was often called "separate interest" rather than the "public interest."

Such notions extended far beyond the leadership of the revolutionary party; they were part of the everyday language of the people, and for this reason, the republican ideal of a society free of partisanship and private interest-seeking was widely accepted. "Endeavor, my friends, to overcome a vicious self-love," pleaded one opponent of the Stamp Act, "Learn to prefer the happiness of the whole to your own private advantage." And after Independence one town asserted "that a selfish view to private interest is a disqualification of the person before us" and that "social virtue and knowledge is the best and only necessary qualification of the legislator." Yet another insisted that legislators must "divest themselves of party and prejudice and seek to pursue the grand interest of the whole."[17] In theory, at least, values of "virtue," "knowledge," and consensus were asserted while partisanship, "division," and "private interest" were rejected. Even after years of partisan conflict (perhaps because of them) most men of Massachusetts would have agreed with

14. Adams to James Warren, Philadelphia, 12 May 1776, 11 June 1777, in Ford, ed., *Warren-Adams Letters*, 1: 243, 329.

15. Samuel Adams to James Warren, Philadelphia, 6 June 1776, ibid., p. 256.

16. *Defence of the Constitutions*, in Adams, ed., *Works*, 4: 404.

17. Samuel Adams to John Scollay, Philadelphia, 20 March 1777, in Harry A. Cushing, ed., *The Writings of Samuel Adams*, 4 vols. (Boston, 1904–8), 3: 365–66; "B.W. to the Inhabitants of the Province of Massachusetts-Bay," *BG*, 7 October 1765; returns of Wilbraham and Belcherstown on the constitution of 1780, in Mass. Arch., 276: 72, 40.

John Adams when he wrote in 1780 that: "There is nothing which I dread so much as a division of the republic [meaning Massachusetts] into two great parties, each arranged under its leader, and concerting measures in opposition to each other."[18]

The assertion of such antipartisan views points with singular clarity to the fact that the parties of the Revolution in Massachusetts functioned in an intellectual context that was entirely opposed to their existence. They developed without theoretical justification of any kind in response to the realities of Massachusetts life; their practical utility was seldom acknowledged; and their role was never praised. They represented, in many ways, an aberration from the prevailing value system and, in the eyes of some men, a challenge to its very existence. Thus to the revolutionary party, particularly to the republicans among them, their use of partisan forms and methods could only be justified by their overall ambition to destroy partisanship—a paradox that they were never able to resolve, and a utopian ideal that they found impossible to accomplish. With the benefit of hindsight, we can see that the behavior of the revolutionaries outstripped their theory, and that the gap between the two would only be closed when theory caught up with reality. But to the men of the time, the gap was an unbridged chasm, and its very existence created tensions that influenced both their partisan and revolutionary tactics and strategies.

To understand the nature of these revolutionary parties and their interplay with the events of the Revolution, two broad areas must be considered. First, we need to examine the intellectual context and the political theory which men used to interpret what was going on around them. And second, we need to know something about those objective social and political conditions in Massachusetts which had provided a challenge to the prevailing value system and which account for the difference between behavior and values represented by partisanship.

To consider the level of theory first, the social values of men in eighteenth-century Massachusetts were rooted in a medieval conception of society that was in part common to all men in the thirteen colonies and in England,[19] but was also in part distinctive to New England. These values seem to have sprung from three sources: the Puritanism of the founders of New England, with its European roots and its American branches; the "gothic" constitution of England, that sun around

18. John Adams to Jonathan Jackson, Amsterdam, 2 October 1780, in Adams, ed., *Works*, 9: 510–11.

19. Wood, *Creation of the American Republic*, p. 18; Robbins, *Eighteenth-Century Commonwealthman*, pp. 40–41, 45, 56–57, 379.

which all the planets of eighteenth-century political theory seemed to revolve; and the relatively new tradition of eighteenth-century English opposition thought, that "country" viewpoint which cut across Whig and Tory lines and leveled its verbal musketry at kings and administrations not only for what they had done but for what they might do. Each of these, in one way or another, promoted medieval corporate ideas, stressing the holistic values by which men must govern their relationships with other men, so that "harmony," "benevolence," "virtue," "peace," and "unity" might prevail over "selfishness," "avarice," "luxury," "anarchy," and "tyranny."

The first of these sources, Puritanism, had as its central doctrine the idea of the covenant, a contractual arrangement among the members of the church or the members of society whereby they defined their relationship with one another and with the community as a whole. In the social covenant, men agreed to subordinate themselves to a civil government which would govern according to God's law, as revealed in the Bible, and to allow "the care of the public" to prevail over their individual wishes. They were reminded by John Winthrop that men do not unite together in society as equals, since God Himself had created rich and poor, some "high and eminent" and others "mean and in subjection." But society needed all ranks of men, and their differences were meant to unite men, not to divide them: to "knit" them "more nearly together in the bond of brotherly affection." All covenanters, whether rich or poor, magistrate or ordinary man, accepted in the act of covenanting certain limitations on their liberty. They surrendered their "natural liberty," which they had in common with beasts and by which men did what they wanted without regard to their fellows, and they accepted a "civil or federal" liberty in its place. In all of their social actions they had the right thereby to do only that "which is good, just, and honest," the liberty, in short, that was congruent with the best interests of society as a whole. In all of these views, the Puritans saw themselves as a closed society, free to build their City on a Hill without outside interference, responsible to God and to each other for their actions. But most important, for our purposes, they viewed the task of making decisions for the community as a process requiring the suppression of individual opinions and private wishes. Decisions had to be in accord with God's law, not men's wishes, and the magisterial elite were best qualified to determine what the law was.[20]

Puritanism underwent many changes between the 1640s and the time

20. John Winthrop, "A Model of Christian Charity," in Perry Miller, ed., *The American Puritans* (New York, 1956), pp. 82–83, 79–80; John Winthrop, "Speech to the General Court," ibid., pp. 90–93; John Cotton, "Limitation of Government,"

of the American Revolution, but many of its social values persisted, its rhetoric was understood in every town in Massachusetts, and there were clergy and laity alike who interpreted events in terms of its grand design. Such pamphlets as Jonathan Edwards's *The Nature of True Virtue,* published posthumously in 1765, reinforced that tendency. Edwards saw society ideally as a harmonious, organic whole, its members each with a function but subordinate to the working of the whole. "There is a beauty of order in society," he wrote of his ideal community. "As when the different members of society have all their appointed office, place, and station, according to their several capacities and talents, and every one keeps his place, and continues in his proper business. In this there is a beauty, not of a different kind from the regularity of a beautiful building, or piece of skilfull architecture." To Edwards, this structured society must be governed by disinterested virtue that placed the good of the whole society (or, as he called it, "being in general") above the good of any individual. He believed that the individual was important, and that the "virtuous benevolence" which should govern society "will seek the good of every individual being unless it be conceived as not consistent with the highest good of being in general."[21] But his emphasis on "the highest good of being in general" was the key to his and to all Puritan views of decision-making. He believed that society, from its inception, was governed by laws, God's laws. A legislator's task was not to inquire of his constituents' wishes, but to consult the higher law: his task was to fashion man's law as closely after God's law as possible, and only by doing so would "the highest good of being in general" be achieved.

Edwards spoke of ideals, but he was practical enough (and conscious as well of the partisanship in his own society) to admit that some men attach themselves "to a particular person, or private system" rather than to the public interest. "Such a determination, disposition, or affection of mind," he wrote quite bluntly, "is not of the nature of true virtue." The course which society must take was therefore plain. "If there be any being [read "party" or "partisan"] statedly and irreclaimably opposite, and an enemy of being in general, then consent and adherence to being in general will induce the truly virtuous heart to forsake the enemy and to oppose it."[22] Such statements as this could alone have provided revolutionaries with justification for their antipartisan views, but it was a

ibid., pp. 85–88. See also Perry Miller, *Errand into the Wilderness* (Cambridge, Mass., 1956), pp. 141–52.

21. Jonathan Edwards, *The Nature of True Virtue,* ed. William K. Frankena (Ann Arbor, Mich., 1960), pp. 35, 8–9.

22. Ibid., pp. 18, 104.

thread in a larger fabric reinforced by the tough strands of English constitutionalism.

The English constitution, like a medieval tapestry, was at once a work of amazing complexity and singular unity. Two of its ideas are central to this discussion of party: its idea of "the people" and its concept of the common law. From the fourteenth century onward, "the people" had a role in English government as one of the three estates into which men imagined their society was divided—kings, nobility, and commons. Despite the fact that the commons consisted of knights, burgesses, rich men, and poor men, it was imagined that their "interest" was a single interest, and that they were to function in society and government as a unitary body. In fact, of course, rivalries existed among ranks and classes, but these rivalries were given no recognition in theory and assigned no role in the political process as long as medieval notions of corporate unity prevailed. Although challenged by some men in the eighteenth century, these notions still dominated both in England and America, and men in revolutionary Massachusetts were largely agreed that class conflict, separate interest-seeking, or even the conscious identification of separate group interests ought ideally to be swallowed up in the larger pursuit of the "public interest."[23]

The achievement of consensus was not, in the structure of English constitutionalism, a hopelessly utopian ideal forever out of reach, but rather a practical accomplishment realized in the law itself. And this brings us to a consideration of the special meaning Englishmen, and more particularly the men of Massachusetts, attached to the law in the seventeenth and eighteenth centuries, a fundamental matter if we are to understand what a legislator's task was thought to be, and why he could not be partisan. Basically, these men agreed with the speaker of the first Parliament in the reign of James I that "the laws, whereby the ark of this government hath been ever steered, are of three kinds: the first, the Common Law, grounded or drawn from the Law of God, the Law of Reason, and the Law of Nature, not mutable; the second, the positive Law, founded, changed, and altered by and through the occasions and politics of times; the third, Customs and Usages, practiced and allowed with time's approbations, without known beginnings."[24]

23. Wood, *Creation of the American Republic*, pp. 18–20, 22; F. W. Maitland, *The Constitutional History of England*, 3d ed. (Cambridge, 1961), pp. 85–90; George L. Haskins, *The Growth of English Representative Government* (Philadelphia, 1948), pp. 67–88.

24. Quoted in J. W. Gough, *Fundamental Law in English Constitutional History* (London, 1955), p. 30.

Significantly, he began with the common law, that amazing corpus of decisions of the king's courts which applied to all men in common, in contradistinction to the much narrower jurisdictions of admiralty courts, or bishops' courts, or manorial courts, and which was inextricably bound up with the great unwritten code of "natural" law. How much of the written common law was brought from England to America in the early days of colonization is a subject of controversy, but this is far less important a matter than men's understanding of the concept of common law, for it was the principles of "equity" that lay behind judicial decisions rather than the details of the decisions themselves that constituted the "fundamental" law, and to Englishmen and American colonists alike, those fundamentals were immutable. They were fundamentals of "the Law of God, the Law of Reason, and the Law of Nature," and hence the same whether applied in England or in America.[25]

It followed naturally that a jurist was not called upon to "make" law, but rather to apply the grand principles of "natural law" to the specific circumstances of the cause before him. It may not be so apparent, but the same limitations rested upon the legislator in Parliament, for it was simply presumed that "positive," or man-made laws, though they could be altered over time to satisfy changing circumstances, must nonetheless conform to the "equity" of the common law. The law, in other words, was of a piece: it could not mean one thing in the king's courts, and another in Parliament. Sir Edward Coke put it plainly: "And it appears in our books that in many cases the common law will control acts of parliament and sometimes adjudge them to be utterly void: for when an act of parliament is against common right and reason, or repugnant, or impossible to be performed, the common law will control it, and adjudge such act to be void."[26] The principle, of course, is the operative principle in the American concept of judicial review, and although English courts did not have the right to lay aside acts of Parliament which they believed to be contrary to "equity," the courts did have the right to interpret the laws, and to assume that their application must conform to "fundamental law."[27]

25. Mark DeWolfe Howe, "The Sources and Nature of Law in Colonial Massachusetts," in George Athan Billias, ed., *Selected Essays: Law and Authority in Colonial America* (Barre, Mass., 1965), pp. 1–16; George L. Haskins, "Reception of the Common Law in Seventeenth-Century Massachusetts: A Case Study," ibid., pp. 17–31; George L. Haskins, *Law and Authority in Early Massachusetts: A Study in Tradition and Design* (New York, 1960), pp. 4–6, 123–40, 164, 186–87.

26. Quoted by Gough, *Fundamental Law,* pp. 31–32. See also Charles Howard McIlwain, *The High Court of Parliament and Its Supremacy* (New Haven, Conn., 1910).

27. Gough, *Fundamental Law,* pp. 17–22.

This medieval conception of the law, unlike our modern conception of a law dynamic and changing to reflect men's shifting values and circumstances, was the concept held by men of Massachusetts at the time of the Revolution. In fact, it was basic to their quarrel with Great Britain. James Otis argued in 1761 that the Writs of Assistance were "against the fundamental principles of law," and in 1764 that the limited power of Parliament and the sanctity of private property were "fundamental maxims of the British constitution." John Adams's "Dissertation on the Canon and Feudal Law" (1765) was an extended argument against the arbitrariness of old divine right and feudal theories of law which ran counter to fundamental law, and which now (figuratively) were rearing their heads again in America. Men would find "the foundations of British laws and government in the frame of human nature, in the constitution of the intellectual and moral world," said Adams. It was this fundamental law which served as the essential limitation on Parliament's exercise of power, and which defined men's rights, which were "inherent and essential, agreed on as maxims, and established as preliminaries, even before parliament existed."[28]

With this view of the law, we can now understand better in what context a Massachusetts legislator functioned. First, he was not called upon to "make" law, but rather to affirm the principles of the common law in the positive law of the province. In other words, his task was essentially that of the judge, and his exercise of delegated power was limited in the same way a judge was limited by the principles of equity or of fundamental law which were anterior to all written law. Such a view of the legislator's task sounds foreign to us only because we have become accustomed to thinking of a legislature as separate and apart from the other functions of government, that is, to the doctrine of the "separation of powers" as laid down in the constitution of 1787. But men in Massachusetts made no such distinction before the Revolution. They shared with Englishmen the medieval tradition of a legislature that interchangeably exercised legislative, judicial, and executive powers.[29] The

28. Ibid., p. 192; James Otis, *The Rights of the British Colonies Asserted and Proved* (Boston, 1764), in Charles F. Mullett, ed., *Some Political Writings of James Otis, The University of Missouri Studies,* vol. 4 (Columbia, Mo., 1929), pp. 52, 55, 62–63, 69, 72; John Adams, "A Dissertation on the Canon and Feudal Law" (1765), in Adams, ed., *Works,* 3: 463. The proceedings of the town of Boston, November 20, 1772, refer to the "fundamental maxims of the common law," and state that "all positive and civil laws, should conform as far as possible, to the Law of natural reason and equity." 18 *BTR,* pp. 95, 98. See also Charles F. Mullett, *Fundamental Law and the American Revolution, 1760–1776* (New York, 1933).

29. Haskins, *Growth of English Representative Government,* pp. 94, 98.

judicial role, particularly, was considerable. Known as the "Great and General Court," the Massachusetts legislature frequently functioned as a common law court in adjudicating the boundaries between towns, determining the proprietorship of rivers and streams, settling numerous other cases in civil law that seemed to spill over the jurisdictional limits of the lesser courts, or recommending action in other more suitable courts. The legislator, in short, was a judge in fact as well as in theory; no clear distinction was made among his several functions; and he was circumscribed in the performance of his duties by a rich tradition of common law in which the liberties of the people were rooted.

The second, and salient, feature of this theoretical context emerges logically from the first. It was a commonplace among Englishmen of the seventeenth and eighteenth centuries that no man could be judge in his own cause; or, to say it another way, no man could be both judge and party.[30] And here we have a substantial clue as to the probable origin and early usage of the term "party" in its political sense. In the "High Court of Parliament," as in any court, the jurist must be detached from the case, a disinterested representative of the whole people, called upon to exercise reason and morality in his interpretation of the fundamental law. Because he could not be "party" to the cause, he did not, in fact theoretically could not, represent the "interests" of his constituents or any privileged group of them, but rather he must represent the whole people. The General Court of Massachusetts maintained that tradition.[31]

Despite its medieval roots, fundamental law was perceived by eighteenth-century theoreticians in a peculiarly "enlightened" way. God's universe presented no mysteries, as if hidden obscurely in the interstices and vaults of a gothic cathedral, but was as plain as a New England meetinghouse. As John Adams explained it, the founders of New England "knew that government was a plain, simple, intelligible thing, founded in nature and reason, and quite comprehensible by common sense." Government and the law were "simple" because they reflected the "simplicity" of the universe, and the keys to understanding that simplicity were the principles of "knowledge and virtue." Knowledge led men, whether legislators or rank and file, to see the harmonies of natural law; virtue or disinterestedness allowed them to apply those harmonious principles in man's law. Knowledge likewise gave men the ability to judge

30. Gough, *Fundamental Law*, p. 10.

31. Considerable controversy resulted from McIlwain's argument (in *High Court of Parliament*) that Parliament was still thought of primarily as a court in the seventeenth and eighteenth centuries. The validity of the concept in the case of Massachusetts, however, is indisputable. See Haskins, *Growth of English Representative Government*, p. 94.

whether the laws proclaimed by their rulers were "within the limits of equity and reason." Knowledge was a check against tyranny, or, as John Adams put it, "wherever a general knowledge and sensibility have prevailed among the people, arbitrary government and every kind of oppression have lessened and disappeared in proportion."[32] Knowledge was, in one sense, the antithesis of party: it directed men's minds upward and outward towards those principles of equity and reason upon which all law must rest, while party directed men's attention inward upon their selfish and interested wishes in the matter. Knowledge, as many Massachusetts revolutionaries never tired of saying, would be the salvation of America.[33]

The concept of a unitary people governed by laws conforming to absolute principles of morality and reason represented a significant persistence of the medieval in the political theory of eighteenth-century men of Massachusetts. But in our discussion of Coke's belief that men's laws could be bad, and of the American revolutionaries' concern that knowledge prevail over arbitrary government, we have already embarked on a consideration of ideas that were essentially seventeenth- and eighteenth-century in origin; this brings us to the third source of ideas which constituted the political theory of the revolutionary generation. The term "opposition" or "Country" tradition defines better than "Whig" the rich theory developed in England from the 1640s onward, which was embodied in the Glorious Revolution of 1689, and which by the eighteenth century cut across "Tory" and "Whig" lines in its warnings on behalf of liberty. "Country" men held that the independence of Parliament was

---

32. "Dissertation on the Canon and Feudal Law," in Adams, ed., *Works*, 3: 454, 448. The theory behind the need for "simplicity" in understanding was widely held among republican thinkers. John Trenchard and Thomas Gordon argued that both leaders and followers alike must have understandings that were not "perverted by subtleties and distinctions." *Cato's Letters*, 4 vols. (London, 1723–24), 1: 181–82. Rousseau believed that the principles of corporatism were the "enemies of political subtleties" and that simplicity was inherent in the corporate order: "So long as several men unite and consider themselves as one body . . . all the springs of the State will be vigorous and simple, the maxims by which they are regulated will be clear and comprehensible; and there will be no jarring opposing interests; the common good will be everywhere evident, and nothing will be necessary but a sound understanding to perceive it." Jean Jacques Rousseau, *The Social Contract*, ed. Charles Frankel (New York, 1947), p. xviii.

33. See, for example, Samuel Adams as "Valerius Poplicola," *BG*, 5 October 1772; Thomas Young to Hugh Hughes, Boston, 21 December 1772, in MHS Miscellaneous Bound Papers, vol. 14; the Constitution of 1780, chapter V, section II, in Robert J. Taylor, ed., *Massachusetts, Colony to Commonwealth: Documents on the Formation of Its Constitution, 1775–1780* (Chapel Hill, N.C., 1961), pp. 127–46: 142–43.

the mainspring of British liberty, and that administration must be entirely separate from the legislative body, in contrast to the "Court" view that the king's interest required active support for his administration within Parliament itself.[34] Two works in the "Country" tradition—*Cato's Letters* (1723–24) by John Trenchard and Thomas Gordon, and Lord Bolingbroke's *A Dissertation Upon Parties* (1733–34)—can usefully be considered here for a number of reasons: first, they were widely read and quoted by men of the revolutionary generation in Massachusetts; secondly, they both spoke directly to the problem of party; and thirdly, they represented different political persuasions among the opposition, "radical Whig" in the case of Trenchard and Gordon, "Tory" in the case of Bolingbroke.

Trenchard and Gordon were convinced that parties were signs of weakness in the system and the result of man's natural depravity, but they found it impossible to discuss the politics of their time without reference to them. Parties were the creatures of private ambition and greed and seldom, if ever, subordinated their separate interests to the public good. They seem to have arisen from two separate sources. The first were created by the Stuart kings as the instruments of oppression and tyranny, a means of dividing the people in order to control them. In fact, the practice of oppressors "will always be to form parties, and blow up factions to mutual animosities, that they may find protection in those animosities," a clear indication that when partisanship runs high, the potential for tyranny is great. It was understood as well that the "instruments and accomplices" of the tyrant's oppression would be given "separate and unequal privileges" above the people, another clear indicator of the tyrant's intentions.[35] But aside from these monarchical factions, other leaders formed parties by appealing to the passions of the people, by raising mobs, and by parlaying their popularity into power. The radicals were convinced that the great bulk of the people had the sense and judgment upon which a virtuous state could be erected, but people in crowds they distrusted as being susceptible to the blandishments of

34. J. G. A. Pocock, "Machiavelli, Harrington, and English Political Ideologies in the Eighteenth Century," *WMQ*, 3d ser., 22 (1965): 571. See also Bernard Bailyn, *The Ideological Origins of the American Revolution* (Cambridge, Mass., 1967), pp. 34–35; Wood, *Creation of the American Republic*, pp. 14–15. Although they overlook the country-court dichotomy, two other excellent studies of opposition thought and its acceptance in America are Robbins, *Eighteenth-Century Commonwealthman*, pp. 8, 56–87, 115–25; and H. Trevor Colbourn, *The Lamp of Experience: Whig History and the Intellectual Origins of the American Revolution* (Chapel Hill, N.C., 1965), pp. 49–53, 59–106.
35. *Cato's Letters*, 1: iv–v, 109; 3: 214–15.

haranguing demagogues. "In raising parties and factions, inflaming goes a thousand times further than reasoning and teaching." Where "sobriety and capacity" are the qualities one expects of a public man, they "are not talents that recommend to the Crowd, who are always taken with shallow pomp and sound."[36] In sum, the radicals feared equally an oppressive king and an unvirtuous people, and they believed that either might express themselves in partisan form, a notion that deeply impressed their American readers.

The radicals, however, lived in an age when reason (and John Locke) taught that men differ in their opinions, and that these differences must be tolerated. The notion challenged consensual politics, but the radicals acknowledged that a forced "uniformity of thoughts" was "a thing tyrannical and impossible!"[37] Still, they did not see the need for toleration as a justification for party, and, in the end, wrestled in vain with the conflict apparent between the individual's wishes and the public good. It was a conflict between the medieval and the modern that was common to the eighteenth century, and in this case the medieval won out: the radicals paid lip-service to individual differences of opinion, but they held that the end result must be a uniform acceptance of what was best for all, whether or not it was thought best by the individual. What they sought was disinterested passion: "Every passion, every view that men have, is selfish in some degree; but when it does good to the public in its operation and consequence, it may be justly called disinterested in the usual meaning of the word: so that when we call any man disinterested, we should intend no more by it, than that the turn of his mind is towards the public, and that he has placed his own personal glory and pleasure in serving it." In effect, the radicals anticipated Rousseau. They believed that the public interest is not incompatible with self-interest, and that it would only seem so to the man who is so narrow and so wrapped up in himself that he cannot see how his own interest and the public interest coincide.[38]

This question of the role of the individual in the political order is central to our understanding of the radical view of party, for the radicals emphasized the individual's public responsibilities rather than his private rights or opinions. Men must exercise their independent judgments, but in a disinterested way. Parties served to impair that judgment by placing

36. Ibid., 2: 311; 4: 251.
37. Ibid., 2: 235–37.
38. Ibid., 2: 240–41; 4: 4–6. It was Locke's psychology that gave *Cato* particular difficulty, and although he undertook to examine it, he found it difficult to know what to do about the diversity of opinion among men. Ibid., 4: 185–86. For Rousseau's solution, see *Social Contract,* ed. Frankel, p. 18.

the interests of the partisans above the public interest. The same was true of all combinations based on private interest, these men believed, and they denounced the great joint stock companies equally with political parties as combinations with "bodies but no souls, nor consequently consciences." The only answer was for men to preserve their individuality, but to subordinate it to the general welfare. "Let neither private acquaintance, personal alliance, or party combination, stand between us and our duty to our country."[39]

The radicals were joined in their analysis of partisanship by Lord Bolingbroke, the foremost writer of his time on the subject, and as widely read in America as the radicals. Bolingbroke agreed that partisanship as it had revealed itself in England had invariably preceded tyranny and corruption: it was a premalignancy with an unfavorable prognosis. Before the Glorious Revolution, the "court fomented our national divisions," because arbitrary rulers "must divide and incense parties one against another, that they may be always able to bribe the passions of one side, and so usurp on both." Such divisions are not inherent in society, Bolingbroke believed, but are the result of a conscious design, a conspiracy, to undermine the liberty of the people. To carry out the division, "or to maintain and renew the division of parties in a state, a system of seduction and fraud is necessary to be carried on." Like the radicals, he affirmed that "a wise and brave people will neither be cozen'd, nor bully'd out of their liberty; but a wise and brave people may cease to be such; they may degenerate; they may sink into sloth and luxury; they may resign themselves to treacherous conduct." And thus the combination of designing king and a debauched people result in division, in partisanship, the vehicle by which liberty will be destroyed.[40]

Bolingbroke, however, became more precise in his analysis of the source of partisanship in his own time, and what he said had particular application to Massachusetts in the 1750s and 1760s. The king, he believed, by relying on Robert Walpole as a kind of "prime minister," had created a party of his own for the purpose of controlling Parliament. "Parliaments are the true guardians of liberty," Bolingbroke asserted. "By the corruption of parliament, and the absolute influence of the king, or his minister, on the two houses, we return into that state to deliver or secure us from which parliaments were instituted, and are really governed by the arbitrary will of one man."[41] He imagined that in the future an ideal "national" or "country" party might exist which would be

39. Cato's Letters, 3: 172; 1: 111, 281.

40. Henry St. John, First Viscount Bolingbroke, A Dissertation Upon Parties, 8th ed. (London, 1754), pp. xxiv, 2–3, 180, xxv–vi.

41. Ibid., pp. 151, 40–41.

"formed on principles of common interest" rather than "directed to the particular interests of any set of men whatsoever." And in this case, it would be permissible for the crown to "adopt" or support such a party since it had not created it. But he saw no evidence in his own time that parties were prepared to speak only in the national interest, while "luxury" had permeated the whole people, presaging disaster.[42]

Both Bolingbroke and *Cato* found ready acceptance among men in Massachusetts because their society too, the latter believed, was succumbing to "luxury," and the partisanship they saw in their legislature seemed likewise to have sprung from the ambitions of tyrants (represented by the governor) and the corresponding decline in the virtue of the people. But more than this, the appeal of "Country" political theory to Massachusetts people sprang from its application of well-known and deeply seated beliefs about the nature of society and the processes of government. It reaffirmed their heritage of Puritan and English constitutional principles: it promoted a politics of consensus based on reason and morality, a government of law and not of men, and the suppression of private interests in favor of the public interest. It added vitality to these principles by suggesting how they might be undermined and how protected.

But it failed to cope with the dilemma which confronted both Englishmen and Americans in the shape of an increasing social pluralism and a diversity of political opinion seemingly intent upon imposing themselves on the political order. Because neither "Country" men nor any other significant body of political thinkers were able to close the gap between theory and reality, there could be parties in the prerevolutionary era, but no party "system," no open recognition of the value of parties, nor any institutional procedure by which one party might succeed another as the wishes and values of the people shifted. The belief that law and its formation were relative, dependent on the wishes and opinions of the people rather than on immutable principles, was the thought of a later time—a response to modern, liberal notions which were in their infancy in the eighteenth century, which were increasingly appealed to during the Revolution, and which set in motion the process by which partisanship would eventually be accepted in theory as well as fact. But antipartisan theory prevailed through all the period we are considering here.

One must add, moreover, that the same political theory which denied

---

42. Ibid., pp. 56, 161, 300–302. Bolingbroke's notion of a "country party," dedicated to the common interest, seems to have been in John Adams's mind when he sought to justify the partisan activity of the Whigs in his famous *Novanglus* letters. Adams and [Leonard], *Novanglus and Massachusettensis*, pp. 73–74, 76–77.

the legitimacy of party and stood in the way of a party system stood likewise in the path of democracy, as we understand it, and of a democratic system. And in saying this, one simply acknowledges the close relationship that exists between democracy and partisanship, at least as the terms are used in western, liberal democracies.[43] Both recognize the legitimacy of diversity in the values and opinions of the people. Together they provide the mechanism for translating that diversity of values and opinion into law: democracy, by providing that the wishes of a simple majority of the people shall determine legislation; partisanship, by providing the majorities or potential majorities, which democracy demands. In an important sense, modern democracy represents a complete reversal of the principles inherent in the medieval political theory of consensus. For we now hold not only that government derives its authority from the people (the doctrine of popular sovereignty so widely accepted among the American revolutionaries), but also that the law itself derives from the people, something no revolutionary theoretician argued. Since the wishes of the people are the sources of law, it follows that the many interests of the people must be represented in the legislative process and that the public good, still an important goal, can only be reached by compromising or synthesizing the many voices with which the public speaks. It is here that parties serve democracy, for by "pork-barrelling," "horse-trading," and compromise, partisanship has made possible the rational control of conflicting values and built a system of accommodation out of what eighteenth-century thinkers believed would be the anarchy of interest politics. The emergence of a politics of accommodation naturally left some men displeased, particularly those who be-

43. The role of the people in eighteenth-century Massachusetts government might best be described as "predemocratic." A number of the features we associate with democratic government were already present: there was widespread suffrage among adult males; there was a significant role for the people in local government; and all institutions of government accepted a simple majority as an adequate, if not desirable, sanction for law. But theory idealized unanimity and rejected diversity and plurality, while the concept of "fundamental law" stood directly in the path of any belief in "government of the people" as we understand it. I am thus in fundamental disagreement with Robert E. Brown's argument that property ownership and a widespread suffrage made colonial Massachusetts a middle-class democracy. See *Middle-Class Democracy and the Revolution in Massachusetts, 1691–1780* (Ithaca, N.Y., 1955). Richard Buel, Jr., likewise argues against the existence of democracy on the basis of the prevalence of undemocratic theory in "Democracy and the American Revolution: A Frame of Reference," *WMQ*, 3d ser., 21 (1964): 165–90. Michael Zuckerman shows how the belief in consensus acted as a constraint on the people in town government in "The Social Context of Democracy in Massachusetts," ibid., 25 (1968): 523–44.

lieved they were witnessing the divorce of politics from morality,[44] but it was the essence of the liberal democracy developing in America.

The full potential of partisanship was not realized until the 1830s,[45] but the "party system" which emerged then rested on a broad base of experience that stretched back into the eighteenth century, and which, in its origins in such colonies as Massachusetts, was a response to practical necessity rather than to political theory. Before turning to a consideration of those objective social and political conditions which stood behind the emergence of partisanship in eighteenth-century Massachusetts, however, we should consider in what way political theory was objectively applied. The divergence between behavior and ideals was never so great as to render theory meaningless, after all, and any discussion of the departure of one from the other must be balanced against the understanding that men took their beliefs seriously, and that corporate values found concrete expression in the institutions and in many of the practices that ordered men's lives.

By the eighteenth century, the chief repository of traditional values was unquestionably the town, and the town meeting paralleled the structure of corporate thought.[46] The town meeting called upon every qualified member of the community to assume the responsibility for attending meetings, acquainting himself with community matters, and finally of voting to promote or protect the public good. Even men who did not possess the necessary property qualifications were often permitted to vote, but this was because both the qualified voters and the unqualified were subject to social controls that prevented, to a very considerable extent, individualistic or partisan expressions of opinion.

One of these controls was the practice of "seating the meetinghouse."

44. The New England abolitionists are excellent examples of the persistence into the nineteenth century of corporate ideals, antipartisanship, and the belief in fundamental law. See, for example, Walter M. Merrill, *Against Wind and Tide: A Biography of Wm. Lloyd Garrison* (Cambridge, Mass., 1963), pp. 200–205.

45. The best historical discussion of the development of the party system in America is Richard Hofstadter, *The Idea of a Party System: The Rise of Legitimate Opposition in the United States, 1780–1840* (Berkeley, Calif., 1969). He places little emphasis, however, on Americans' experience with partisanship in the colonial period, and no emphasis on the influence of the Revolution on the idea of party.

46. Michael Zuckerman, *Peaceable Kingdoms: New England Towns in the Eighteenth Century* (New York, 1970), pp. 50–84; Kenneth A. Lockridge, *A New England Town, the First Hundred Years: Dedham, Massachusetts, 1636–1736* (New York, 1970), pp. 18–21. Zuckerman sees the structure of the New England town as a response to environment as well as theory; Lockridge chooses the anthropological approach and argues that Dedham had much in common with all "Closed Corporate Peasant Communities."

Even as late as the revolutionary period, many towns followed the seventeenth-century custom of ranking the community "according to age, estate, and qualifications," and although the practice was far from universal by the revolutionary period, the fact that it persisted at all suggests that "knowing one's place" was still taken seriously.[47] Further, leadership roles generally went to front-pew men, men whose wealth and education presumably entitled them to make those judgments in reason and morality that were the essence of law. These men did not constitute oligarchies, in any rigid sense of the term, but one seriously misrepresents eighteenth-century Massachusetts towns if he fails to recognize the elitism that characterized local politics, particularly the politics of the older, wealthier, more diversified communities. "Go into every village in New England," John Adams wrote in the 1780s, "and you will find that the office of justice of the peace, and even the place of representative, which has ever depended only on the freest election of the people, have generally descended from generation to generation, in three or four families at most." Adams was, of course, too sweeping in his generalization, but there was a measure of truth in what he said. Jonathan Jackson was closer to the mark when he claimed that most of the larger town meetings in Massachusetts "must depend upon a few to guide and manage the whole."[48]

The domination of an elite in decision-making did not, however, render nugatory the role of the people. Any decision had to stand the test of the peoples' knowledge and understanding, the measure of reason and morality, and that frequently meant a rigorous intellectual review

47. Ezra S. Stearns, *History of Ashburnham* (Ashburnham, Mass., 1887), p. 557; Carpenter and Morehouse, *The History of the Town of Amherst* (Amherst, Mass., 1896), p. 78; Benjamin and William Cutter, *History of Arlington* (Boston, 1880), pp. 94–95; *Worcester Town Records from 1753 to 1783*, ed. Franklin P. Rice, *Worcester Society of Antiquity Collections*, vol. 4 (Worcester, Mass., 1882), pp. 92–95.

48. Adams, *Defence of the Constitutions*, in Adams, ed., *Works*, 4: 392–93; Jonathan Jackson, *Thoughts Upon the Political Situation of the United States of America* ... (Worcester, Mass., 1788), p. 109. Michael Zuckerman disputes Adams's statement in *Peaceable Kingdoms*, p. 203. Probably no present-day historian would argue that there were town "oligarchies," as Zuckerman rigidly defines them, while many would agree that elitism—the concentration of power in the hands of a few— was common, particularly in coastal and Connecticut Valley communities. See Robert J. Taylor, *Western Massachusetts in the Revolution* (Providence, 1954), pp. 11–26, 33; John J. Waters, Jr., *The Otis Family in Provincial and Revolutionary Massachusetts* (Chapel Hill, N.C., 1968), pp. 61–75; James A. Henretta, "Economic Development and Social Structure in Colonial Boston," *WMQ*, 3d ser., 22 (1965): 75–92; Benjamin W. Labaree, *Patriots and Partisans: The Merchants of Newburyport, 1764–1815* (Cambridge, Mass., 1962), pp. 1–15.

of the problem so that the rightness of the elite's decision could be confirmed and everyone thereby satisfied that the public good was being served. Given the obligation to "inform," the leadership inevitably saw its responsibility to draw the lines clearly between the "right" solution and other "wrong" solutions. In practice, this meant that the leadership presented its examination of the problem, and its solution, in such simple terms, with such clear delineation of right and wrong, that even the least educated could understand, an approach that continued to characterize the political writings of both sides during the Revolution. With the full range of positive consequences ranked so starkly and simply on one side, towns "concurred unanimously" in the decisions of their leaders with remarkable frequency right down to the Revolution. Furthermore, the intolerance with which they greeted implacable resistance to "right" decisions simply confirms the assertion that the towns, to a very considerable degree, represented medieval corporate ideals in practice in the eighteenth century.[49]

No system ever works perfectly, however, and the behavior of Massachusetts townsmen throughout the eighteenth century frequently placed considerable strain on the ideals of union, harmony, and benevolence. Examples abound of communities split into opposing factions—sometimes on purely local matters, sometimes on issues of provincial importance. The eastern town of Dedham was rent with "great heat of spirit and party zeal . . . great jars and contentions and animosity" when it chose its selectmen in 1727.[50] Jonathan Edwards found that "contention and party strife were 'the old iniquity' of Northampton" when he returned to the Connecticut Valley in the 1720s, and he deplored the fact that contention, "so evil a thing among neighbours," had even divided families.[51] The town of Boston split into hard-money and soft-money proponents in the 1740s and finally rejected the hard-money champion, Thomas Hutchinson, as its representative in the legislature, even though Hutchinsons had been front-pew men for generations.[52] Numerous towns divided over church matters, others over questions of land, while Newbury petitioned the legislature in the 1760s to have the farming end of the community separated from the commercial end since the interests of

49. For an example of the unanimity of towns, see the votes on the Constitution of 1778 in Mass. Arch., 156: 304–428; 160: 1–31.
50. Kenneth A. Lockridge and Alan Kreider, "The Evolution of Massachusetts Town Government, 1640–1740," WMQ, 3d ser., 23 (1966): 561.
51. Quoted by Perry Miller, *Jonathan Edwards*, p. 101.
52. Thomas Hutchinson to Israel Williams, Boston, 19 May 1749, in Israel Williams Papers, 2: 140.

the two were irreconcilable.[53] While the sources of contention were various, three forces seem to stand out as major challenges to the ideals of harmony and consensus in the period before and during the Revolution: an intensified consciousness of class and of economic interest, a nascent but developing sense of democracy, and the intrusion of royal authority.

The experience of Newbury reflects an increasingly common phenomenon in eighteenth-century Massachusetts: the realization that society in many towns, and even more so in the province at large, was not a homogeneous entity; that there were fundamental differences of opinion based on divergent economic interests; and that those divergent interests often dominated men's thinking in spite of the most earnest pleas on behalf of the "public." This consciousness of "separate interest" was not new to the eighteenth century: it had been present from the first settlements in the 1630s, largely among the merchants, whose desire to turn profits at home, and establish useful contacts abroad, ran counter to the very principles John Winthrop sought to establish. The history of the rise of commerce in colonial Massachusetts is the continuing story of conflict between a rationalist and pragmatic merchant class and the medieval values of closed corporatism.[54] Where merchants did accommodate themselves to the value structure of corporatism, they did so by assuming the old roles of the Puritan magistrates, that is, by becoming the governing elites in that band of coastal towns that stretched in the 1760s from Newburyport on the North Shore to the old town of Plymouth in the south. In Boston, in the early 1760s, merchants dominated every town office of importance, from town representative to selectman to overseer of the poor, and the same was true to a greater or lesser extent in every commercial port. A political satirist writing in 1763 claimed that the great merchants and traders "rule with ir'n in every public meeting, / Make men and women do what they think fitting, / Are magistrates in all great sea port towns, / Where men do nothing but wear tawdry gowns."[55]

53. Taylor, *Western Massachusetts*, pp. 38–40, 44–51; Lockridge, *New England Town*, pp. 79–90, 117–18, 135, 147–48; Labaree, *Patriots and Partisans*, pp. 2–3.

54. Darrett B. Rutman, *Winthrop's Boston: Portrait of a Puritan Town, 1630–1649* (Chapel Hill, N.C., 1965), pp. vii, viii, 182–201, 249–52, 274–79; Bernard Bailyn, *The New England Merchants in the Seventeenth Century* (Cambridge, Mass., 1955), pp. 16, 39–44, 75–76, 103–4, 112–97.

55. Labaree, *Patriots and Partisans*, p. 14; Henretta, "Economic Development and Social Structure in Colonial Boston," pp. 75–92; Stephen Everett Patterson, "Boston Merchants and the American Revolution" (M.A. thesis, Univ. of Wis., 1961), pp. 14–15; *BG*, 14 March 1763.

Despite the practice of intermarriage, and the creation of great merchant families like the Hutchinsons, the Faneuils, and the Bowdoins,[56] the influence of the merchants was less oligarchic than economic. Shipbuilders, mast-riggers, cordwainers, wharfingers, laborers—all realized that commerce buttered their bread, and that their life and livelihood depended on a flourishing trade. The tentacles of commerce, moreover, reached far inland, linking the fortunes of commercial farmers and lumbermen, like the prospects of coastal producers, the fishermen, and the distillers, with the success of Yankee voyages to the West Indies, to Spain, to Africa, or to the other colonies. As John Adams was to put it, even the farmers were "addicted to commerce."[57]

But the pervasiveness of commerce among men of many ranks and callings did not, as one might have expected, guarantee harmony. Trade within the colony, after all, was governed by principles not unlike those mercantilist principles which governed trade at the imperial level, and merchants, playing the role of the mother country, sought to sell more than they bought, or to put it another way, to buy cheap and sell dear. Likewise, the interests of producers and merchants diverged on the question of money supply: the producer hoping for a plentiful, perhaps even inflationary, currency, to ensure high prices for produce and easy repayment of debts; the merchant (once established in trade) expecting a stable medium of exchange to protect his savings or facilitate his overseas transactions. Furthermore, farmers in the eastern agricultural areas of Massachusetts had special problems of their own—problems of overpopulation, land scarcity, and poverty (which will be explored more fully in the next chapter), all of which accentuated the differences among economic and social groups rather than their common interests.

From the second decade of the eighteenth century, men spoke quite self-consciously of their interests as "farmers" or as "merchants," and each blamed the other for adverse fluctuations in the business cycle which neither fully understood. Numerous pamphleteers openly espoused the interest of one or the other. From 1714 onward, men spoke specifically of a "Landed Interest" as opposed to "the Trading Party." And for thirty-five years, controversy raged between farmers and small merchants on the one hand, and the "rich men" and "the Court" on the other over the respective merits of land banks and silver banks, of paper currency and coin.[58]

56. Bailyn, *New England Merchants*, pp. 196–97.
57. John Adams to Mercy Warren [Philadelphia], 16 April 1776, in Ford, ed., *Warren-Adams Letters*, 1: 222–23.
58. John Colman, *The Distressed State of the Town of Boston Once More Con-*

This is not to suggest that farmers and merchants represented two clearly defined, homogeneous groups, for they were neither. There were always farmers whose interests and inclinations were inseparable from lumber kings and other exporters, just as there were always merchants (often the younger and less well-established) who saw the accumulated wealth of the great merchants as a threat to their own advance.[59] There was, in fact, a plurality of interests in the Massachusetts of the eighteenth century, but, more important, it was a plurality that expressed itself consciously, and ultimately in partisan form.

A second challenge to prevailing values—a challenge that grew out of the consciousness of "separate interest" but also in turn contributed to it—was the demand for increased democracy, both at the town and provincial level. While sufficient studies have not been done to allow generalization, it is clear that in the towns of Watertown and Dedham the result of partisanship in town meetings was a shifting of power from the selectmen to the meeting itself, allowing it to originate, rather than merely to review and approve, policy.[60] In Northampton, where old leaders held on until much later, the democratic bias (and class consciousness) of upstart opponents like Timothy Root was obvious. "I won't worship a wig," he said, slamming clergy and gentlemen. "They are nothing but men moulded up of a little dirt; I don't care a turd, or I don't care a fart for any of them."[61] In the 1750s, a Southampton democrat got himself elected to the legislature by consciously splitting the town into factions, and by appealing to the lower class. He gave speeches in public houses and throughout the town, "declaiming against the conduct of the great men (as he called 'em) at the General Court, representing them as destroyers of their country with lucrative views to their

sidered . . . (Boston, 1720), in Andrew McFarland Davis, ed., *Colonial Currency Reprints, 1682–1751,* 4 vols. (Boston, 1910–11), 2: 70; [John Wise as] Amicus Patriae, *A Word of Comfort to a Melancholy Country or the Bank of Credit erected in the Massachusetts-Bay Fairly Defended* . . . (Boston, 1721), ibid., pp. 159–223; Paul Dudley, *Objections of the Bank of Credit Lately Projected at Boston* . . . (Boston, 1714), in Andrew McFarland Davis, ed., *Tracts Relating to the Currency of the Massachusetts Bay, 1682–1720* (Boston, 1902), pp. 85–109; F——l B——t, *A Letter from one in Boston to his Friend in the Country* . . . (Boston, 1714), ibid., pp. 111–45; John Colman, *The Distressed State of the Town of Boston, etc. Considered* . . . (Boston, 1720), ibid., pp. 233–46. See also Joseph B. Felt, *An Historical Account of Massachusetts Currency* (Boston, 1839), pp. 64–137.

59. Taylor, *Western Massachusetts,* pp. 52–54; Colman, *Distressed State of* . . . *Boston,* in Davis, ed., *Tracts,* p. 244.

60. Lockridge and Kreider, "Evolution of Town Government," pp. 549–74.

61. Quoted by Miller, *Jonathan Edwards,* pp. 43–44.

own emolument." Since such men could not be trusted, "the only way to remedy these inconveniences was for the town to send honest plow-men to represent them at court, and further to effect his own election, told the people at Southampton to induce them to vote for him he would get them made a district, and obtain for 'em a grant of a large tract of unappropriated land, adjoining to that place." In this way, the democrat intimidated the regular representative, who refused to stand for office, and won election for two years running.[62]

Theoretical justifications for democracy were few indeed in the period before the Revolution,[63] but the pressures were there and they occasion-ally expressed themselves in political form, as these examples indicate. During the 1760s, these pressures grew, particularly among urban crowds. But it was not until 1774, as succeeding chapters will show, that democratic pressures became a major determinant of party.

The third challenge to traditional values was the royal charter itself, both in terms of the institutions it established and the theoretical struc-ture it placed on Massachusetts society. Established in 1691 in the after-math of the Glorious Revolution, the new charter differed from the original charter of 1629 in a number of ways, not the least of which was the creation of strong lines of authority connecting the province with imperial administrative agencies, principally through the person of the royal governor. The veto power of governor and king over the laws of Massachusetts, as well as the requirement that its laws "be not repug-nant" to the laws of England destroyed whatever semblance of closed corporateness Massachusetts had enjoyed as a colony in the seventeenth century, and turned the collective mind outward in the same way that commerce was doing. Massachusetts was part of an empire, a small spoke in a great wheel, and not the City on a Hill that its founders had hoped it would be.

The powers of the governor strengthened this imperial view, at least among a favored few, for the governor's patronage attached to him a string of judicial officers whose influence was felt in every county, and whose support of the prerogative was demonstrated in the Council and even in the popularly elected House. The charter, in other words, made possible the creation of a governor's party, an extension of "the Court"

62. Israel Williams to Gov. Bernard, Hatfield, 19 August 1761, in Israel Williams Papers, 2: 119.

63. One such was John Wise, A Vindication of the Government of New-England Churches (1717), reprinted with an introduction by Perry Miller (Gainesville, Fla., 1958), pp. 42–43, 47–51, 60–65. Wise's primary concern was to promote democracy in church government, although many of his arguments referred specifically to the benefits of democracy in the state.

into the community and into all the institutions of central government. It likewise provided an opportunity for wealthy merchants or large land-owners to link their interests with those of the prerogative, exchanging their support for the court's protection of their wealth and position in society.[64]

Royal government thereby challenged the basic assumptions of cor-poratism: it denied the unitary interest of the people, and seemed to promote the creation of a privileged "aristocracy." As a result, the cor-porate view retreated to the towns in the eighteenth century. As long as the town remained the primary focus of men's political attention, which it did well into the century, the challenge of imperial and prerogative views mattered little. As the Revolution approached, however, and pro-vincial and imperial issues forced themselves upon men's consciousness, the divergence between corporate values and provincial practices be-came more and more apparent, and ultimately evoked opposition to the "special privilege," "separate interest," and "aggrandizement" that pro-vincial politics seemed to represent.

Partisanship in revolutionary Massachusetts rested on these realities: on a process of change that undermined corporate values and created a social pluralism and a consciousness of economic interest, on a growing demand for democracy, on a prerogative politics introduced with the royal charter, and on an opposition to the power and privileges of the governor's men. Naturally, as royal government ended in 1774, the em-phasis shifted among these factors. But whether before 1774 or after, Massachusetts parties sprang principally from internal rather than ex-ternal causes. In the broadest sense, the parties represented divergent views of how society should develop and how it should be governed. More precisely, to anticipate the following chapters, parties represented a divergence among Massachusetts towns.

But they were also from the first—and this is the irony of their exist-ence—clothed in the rhetoric and ideology of antipartisanship. Both government and opposition parties believed themselves to be the "natural leaders" of the community whose goals were designed to promote its best interest, and in this respect both presumed to speak for the public,

64. The original charter of 1629 similarly required the conformity of Massa-chusetts laws to the laws of England, but without the mechanisms of enforcement provided by the charter of 1691 and subsequent instructions to royal governors. "The Charter of the Massachusetts Bay Company" (4 March 1629), in Merrill Jensen, ed., *American Colonial Documents to 1776*, vol. 9 in *English Historical Documents* (New York, 1955), p. 83; "The Charter of the Province of the Massa-chusetts-Bay" (1691), *Acts and Resolves*, 1: 16. For a discussion of the Court party, see chapter 2.

often without troubling themselves too greatly to learn what the public felt. Each felt that their opposition represented the only "party," the only attempt to establish principles contrary to the "public good" and the only challenge to the ideal, united, and cohesive society. In this sense, partisanship always represented corruption, but it was the other fellow who was corrupt. Israel Williams expressed precisely such a point of view in 1760 when the Court party (representing, he believed, the public good) had won over the new governor, Bernard. "Now being so wonderfully delivered from our enemies," he wrote, "may all intestine [broils], animosities, and dissensions forever cease and universal love and harmony prevail with men of every character."[65] His wish was essentially no different from that of John and Sam Adams in 1776.

This is the paradox of the Revolution in Massachusetts: that it should be shaped by political parties whose goals, in part, were the eradication of partisanship. But it was a paradox that was larger than either the place or the event; it was the paradox of an age. It was the result of that ideational collision of the traditional with the modern which characterized the great revolutions of the eighteenth century and which led ultimately to the complete acceptance of diversity and partisanship in western civilization. In Massachusetts, the first glimpses of the potential of partisanship, and the first substantial adjustments in theory to justify the idea of party, were formulated during the Revolution (see Chapter 10). This theorizing began the long process by which the chasm between ideals and reality would be closed.

But the bulk of the Whigs, particularly the leadership circle of John and Sam Adams, James and Joseph Warren, Elbridge Gerry, and Thomas Young (to name only some), saw partisanship as a symptom of the evils that had befallen their country. Like Cato and Bolingbroke, they saw parties as instruments of tyranny and private interest, and their comments throughout the Revolution indicate that they believed they were rooting out a corrupting influence from their society, and that from the upheaval there would result a united and harmonious society in which partisanship—and the material greed that was at its base—would be swept away. The Revolution to them was a sort of moral purge. Society was already in decline when the intrusion of parliamentary taxation added urgency to the need for reform, but reform was needed on two fronts, the imperial and the provincial, and it was the provincial that was the focus of their dreams. Their own society must undergo a reformation, partisanship must cease, and the old and tested corporate

65. Williams to Hutchinson, Hatfield, 3 December 1760, in Israel Williams Papers, 2: 119.

ethic must be restored over the corpse of a new, and unwanted intruder. It was this faith in the efficacy of the traditional corporate principles upon which their society was founded that shaped the revolutionary ideals of these leaders. "After all," wrote Samuel Adams to Elbridge Gerry in 1775, "virtue is the surest means of securing the public liberty. I hope you will improve the golden opportunity of restoring the ancient purity of principles and manners in our country. Every thing that we do, or ought to esteem valuable, depends upon it." John Adams warned that "every man must seriously set himself to root out his passions, prejudices, and attachments, and to get the better of his private interest. The only reputable principle and doctrine must be that all things must give way to the public." And similarly, the constitution of 1780 warned, just as John Winthrop had in the colony's first years, that "Government is instituted for the common good; for the protection, safety, prosperity, and happiness of the people; and not for the profit, honor, or private interest of any one man, family, or class of men."[66]

The republican leaders of the Revolution saw clearly the gulf that lay between theory and behavior in the politics of Massachusetts, and they chose to alter behavior. They chose the more difficult, in fact an impossible, task. For once the cohesive force of their opposition role was removed with the defeat of the governor's party, the great variety and diversity of goals among the Whig partisans suddenly surfaced. By the time of Independence, the state was dividing into two new political parties which were expressive of the ineluctable plurality of Massachusetts society. Leaders could, and would, continue to speak with the rhetoric of corporatism, seeking first to prevent and then to minimize the effects of partisanship. But history was to prove that it was theory, rather than behavior, that must change. How the parties of the early Revolution—the Court and the Country—gave way to a new division after Independence is the focus of this book. How Americans began to alter their political theory to conform with their increasingly conscious attempts to secure legislative majorities is a necessary adjunct. Both fact and theory demonstrate the extent to which the Revolution in Massachusetts, despite the ideals of its leaders, was part of a larger movement towards partisan democracy in America.

66. Samuel Adams to Gerry, Philadelphia, 29 October 1775, in Cushing, ed., *Writings of Samuel Adams,* 3: 229–31; John Adams to Mercy Warren, Philadelphia, 16 April 1776, in Ford, ed., *Warren-Adams Letters,* 1: 222-23; Taylor, ed., *Massachusetts: Colony to Commonwealth,* p. 129.

# 2

# Partisanship in Provincial Massachusetts

AS FAR back as John Adams's memory could take him into the political history of prerevolutionary Massachusetts, "there [had] always [been] a court and country party in the province." His "always" was vague, but other evidence shows that the terms "court" and "country" were used from the early eighteenth century, that the parties assumed some cohesion from the Land Bank controversy of 1740 onwards, that they matured during the governorships of William Shirley (1741–56) and Thomas Pownall (1757–60), and that they were the major determinants of political behavior from the late provincial period until 1774.[1] The parties were not simply legislative factions, nor were they short-lived, issue-oriented coalitions. Rather they were expressions of a divergence among politically active Massachusetts towns which cannot be explained by any single set of circumstances but which was entangled in a complex web of economic, social, political, and ideological conditions in the towns themselves. By the late 1750s, the divergence showed itself both inside the legislature and out: inside, in the remarkably consistent voting behavior of 102 of 122 politically active towns (see table 1, Appendix A); outside, by a sometimes subtle and sometimes plainly obvi-

1. Charles Francis Adams, ed., *The Works of John Adams*, 10 vols. (Boston, 1850–56), 10: 241–44; "A Letter from one in Boston to his Friend in the Country . . ." (Boston, 1714), in Andrew McFarland Davis, ed., *Tracts Relating to the Currency of the Massachusetts Bay, 1682–1720* (Boston, 1902), pp. 111–45. For one view of Shirley's "coalition," with particular emphasis on the role of James Otis, Sr., see John J. Waters, Jr., *The Otis Family in Provincial and Revolutionary Massachusetts* (Chapel Hill, N.C., 1968), pp. 76–109. See also John A. Schutz, *William Shirley: King's Governor of Massachusetts* (Chapel Hill, N.C., 1961); John A. Schutz, *Thomas Pownall, British Defender of American Liberty: A Study of Anglo-American Relations in the Eighteenth Century* (Glendale, Calif., 1951).

ius difference in attitude towards the world and the processes of change
at work in it. What were these processes and how did they produce a
partisan division among Massachusetts towns?

The differences between the two groups of party towns can best be
seen when set against a backdrop of their similarities. In many ways,
both groups responded to the same environmental stimuli; towns on
each side faced similar internal and external challenges, and both were
caught up in the flow of change that can best be described as the modernization process,[2] a process which neither fully (nor perhaps even
partially) understood.

They were, to begin with, only a part of the total number of Massachusetts towns. Out of a total of 204 towns listed in a 1761 tax list, only
about 120 were represented in the legislature in any year in the late
provincial period, while a high rate of absenteeism after the first few
days of a new session cut the numbers actively engaged in legislative
work even further. The average number of towns responding in each
of six roll call votes taken between 1757 and 1764 was 84, while the total
number of towns participating in the six roll calls combined was only
122.[3] Generalizations about these politically active towns, one must
therefore caution, cannot necessarily be extended to all Massachusetts
towns, nor vice versa.

In terms of population, rate of taxation, and tenure of representatives
(which are general indicators, at least, of the degree of urbanization,
community wealth, and political stability) the two groups were very
much alike. Excluding Boston, which because of its size and complexity
represents an anomaly in any comparison, the median size of a Court
party town in 1765 was 1,090. Excluding those second and sometimes
third towns which shared the representative of a larger town (something more common among Court than among Country party towns),
the median population was 1,308 (Newton, in Middlesex County). The
median size of the Country party towns was 1,313 (Framingham, also

2. The term "modernization," as used here, denotes the process whereby relatively simple, closed, farming societies have evolved into more complex, interdependent communities as a result of the application of knowledge gained from the
scientific revolution. See C. E. Black, *The Dynamics of Modernization: A Study in
Comparative History* (New York, 1966), pp. 1–34. I am greatly indebted to Rupert
Charles Loucks, who permitted me to read his provocative study of Connecticut's
transition to modernity, a doctoral dissertation in preparation for the University of
Wisconsin. His application of Black's scheme to late eighteenth- and early nine-
teenth-century Connecticut gives new meaning and significance to the idea of republicanism, which he sees as a transitional ideology.

3. *House Journals,* 9 July 1761; 9 December 1757; 12 October 1758; 9 October
1759; 3 February, 20 April 1762; 1 February 1764.

in Middlesex County). By way of comparison, the median population of all Massachusetts towns was only 840,[4] a clear indication that political activity was a function of size while partisanship was not.

The rate of taxation also touched each party equally. Dividing a 1761 tax list into the heavily taxed (group a), the moderately taxed (group b), and the lightly taxed (group c), one finds that each party had almost equal numbers of towns from the respective tax groups. The contrast comes again not between the parties, but between the politically active and the politically inactive towns. All towns in group a were active; 52 of 55 group b towns were active; but only 53 of 127 group c towns played active legislative roles (see table 1, Appendix A).

The legislative tenures of the representatives from each party were comparable. Court party adherents who sat in the legislative session of 1763–64 had served an average of 5.8 years each, while Country party adherents had served slightly longer, 6.3 years on the average. Figured over a 20-year period, Court party members served an average of 4.2 years each against 4.0 years for Country party members.[5] While either set of figures demonstrates a measure of political stability, the figures for 1764 indicate, if anything, a growing tendency in both parties to rely on political experience in the choice of legislators. Doing so was not novel in many towns of both persuasions, however. Such towns as Cambridge, Charlestown, Newton, Groton, and Plymouth in the Court party, for example, had chosen representatives for 15-, 14-, 12-, 17-, and 15-year tenures, respectively, while the average for single long tenures in the Court party was 8.3 years. Country party tenures matched those of the Court party closely and long terms were experienced in Salisbury, Bradford, Marlborough, Framingham, Waltham, and Sturbridge. The average long term in the Country party was 7.8 years (see table 1, Appendix A).

Averages, of course, tend to blur the processes of political change and the evidence of political upheaval, but the point is made nonetheless that both parties functioned in what was in many ways a common environment. Examined more closely in relation to political, social, and economic processes of change at work in the eighteenth-century towns of Massachusetts, the similarities continue.

While all politically active towns did not experience change to the

4. Population statistics for the year 1765 are from Evarts B. Greene and Virginia D. Harrington, *American Population before the Federal Census of 1790* (New York, 1932), pp. 21–30. See also Michael Zuckerman's Reply to David Grayson Allen, "The Zuckerman Thesis and the Process of Legal Rationalization in Provincial Massachusetts," *WMQ*, 3d ser., 29 (1972): 464.

5. *House Journals*, 1744–45 to 1763–64.

same degree, nor did they all react in the same way, the processes of change were pervasive enough to touch all. The processes may be described under five major headings: population growth, the division or partition of towns, the spread of religious diversity, the extension of economic (principally commercial) interaction, the decline of agricultural opportunity and an accompanying economic diversification. Each of these points merits comment.

The population of Massachusetts tripled in the period from 1701 to 1765,[6] and while the availability of considerable land in the central and western regions as well as in the District of Maine made growth in these areas phenomenal, numerous towns in the first-established eastern areas experienced rapid growth, often with little emigration to reduce the pressures of greatly increased population densities. Such towns as Brookfield, Dudley, Oxford, and Southborough in Worcester County, in the central to western part of the province, tripled and in some cases quadrupled in size over 30- and sometimes 20-year periods, if one may judge from the number of births recorded between 1720 and 1759. Such northeastern towns as Gloucester and Middleton in Essex County experienced more modest, but nonetheless substantial rates of growth, while Norton, Dedham, and Watertown in the southeastern part of the province had passed from the small village to the substantial town stage, complete with growth pains, by the end of the colonial period.[7]

The effect of rapid population growth was to erode the harmony and homogeneity of many towns. Towns with large land areas found themselves developing with several nuclei, usually geographically determined, and the propensity towards internal conflict steadily rose until legislative petitions produced partitioning and the establishment of new towns. During the eighteenth century, close to 65 percent of all new towns were created by dividing older ones.[8] In some cases, divisions were accomplished harmoniously and with little challenge from the parent town, often because geographic necessity—the distance of some

6. Greene and Harrington, *American Population*, pp. 14–17.

7. Robert Higgs and H. Louis Stettler, III, "Colonial New England Demography: A Sampling Approach," *WMQ*, 3d ser., 27 (1970): 293. J. M. Bumsted, "Religion, Finance, and Democracy in Massachusetts: The Town of Norton as a Case Study," *Journal of American History* 57 (1970–71): 819–20; Kenneth A. Lockridge, "The Population of Dedham, Massachusetts, 1636 to 1736," *Economic History Review*, 3d ser., 19 (1966): 318–44; Edward M. Cook, Jr., "Social Behavior and Changing Values in Dedham, Massachusetts, 1700 to 1775," *WMQ*, 3d ser., 27 (1970): 547–48; Kenneth A. Lockridge and Alan Kreider, "The Evolution of Massachusetts Town Government, 1640–1740," ibid., 23 (1966): 572.

8. Allen, "Zuckerman Thesis," 453.

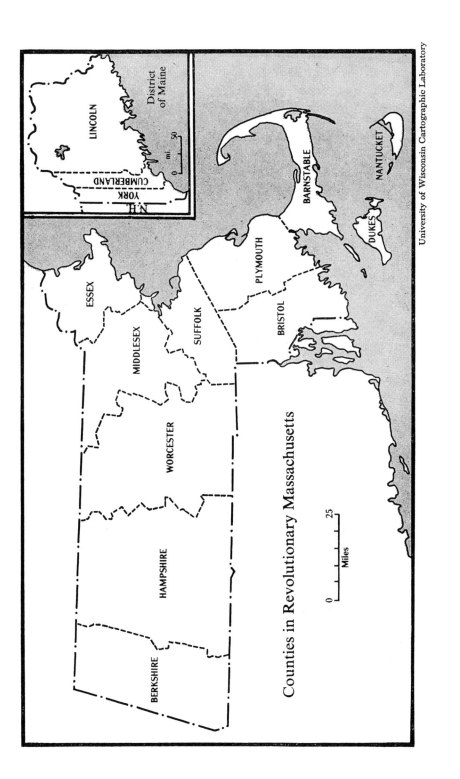

Counties in Revolutionary Massachusetts

settlements from the meetinghouse—made division a reasonable means of maintaining social order and cohesion. But there were numerous towns which bitterly resented the loss of population and tax revenues, particularly those such as Stoughton in Suffolk County which seemed constantly bombarded by the requests of small groups to be "set off to the next town." Stoughton experienced 17 divisions in the eighteenth century.[9]

As significant as the bifurcation of towns was the internal subdivision of towns into precincts. Newbury and Bridgewater were each divided into five precincts by the late provincial period, Dedham into four, and the practice was widespread. In Dedham the creation of precincts was the result of bitter disputes over where meetinghouses should be located and with their establishment the power of the town selectmen diminished, the range of their authority narrowed, and many of their earlier concerns either passed to the precincts or back to the townsmen themselves. As one author put it, "the sum of the parts was less than the former whole, and the weakening of social control allowed more scope for the actions of the individual."[10]

The process equally provided more scope for the interference of the provincial legislature in town affairs. By the mid-eighteenth century, virtually dozens of petitions for partitioning or "setting off" had to be disposed of, and the fact that the province could and did throw the onus onto the parent town to show cause why the petition should not be granted meant that numerous committees of selectmen frequently found themselves on the defensive.[11] The notion that the town was a stable and enduring entity inevitably suffered, and the concept of the closed corporate peasant community increasingly appeared more as an ideal than as a reality.

The twin processes of growth and fragmentation often expressed themselves in matters of religion. Precinct divisions were frequently the result of splits in congregations, arguments over ministers, or the location of meetinghouses. The Great Awakening, by dividing many com-

9. Ibid., p. 452n. The town of Watertown petitioned to have an earlier decision, annexing part of the town to Cambridge, reversed in order to improve tax revenues. *House Journals*, 19 April 1757.

10. *House Journals*, 15 February 1763; "A Description of Bridgewater, 1818," in *MHS Collections*, 2d ser., 7 (1818): 168; Cook, "Social Behavior and Changing Values in Dedham," pp. 555–59.

11. See, for example, material on Stoughton in *House Journals*, 5 June 1752, 8 June, 7 September 1753, 7 December 1757. In some cases, the legislature circumvented the town clerk and selectmen by referring a petition to the precinct clerk, further undermining the central authority of the town.

munities into Old Lights and New, weakened the homogenizing power of the Congregational Church, while in many towns Anglicans and Baptists succeeded in establishing small congregations, further diversifying the community.[12]

Where the growth of religious diversity tended to make men look inwards and to think of themselves as members of social groupings that were smaller than the town, a countervailing tendency developed in men's economic relationships. By the end of the provincial period, almost all of the politically active towns had ceased to be insular, agricultural communities with simple, intratown economic relationships. Almost all of them were already, or were in the process of becoming, commercially oriented, with a varying degree of economic relationships with other towns. The changing nature of civil litigation illustrates. Where in the early eighteenth century, litigation was generally between inhabitants of the same town, principally in larger urban centers such as Boston, Charlestown, or Cambridge, by mid-century the bulk of litigation involved parties from different communities, and where the first party came from Boston, Charlestown, or Cambridge, the second party usually came from the more rural towns.[13] In other words, economic relationships were transcending town boundaries and in the process were creating a broader, more interdependent pattern to men's economic lives than had prevailed in the closed corporate peasant community. The development of commercial centers in every county, including the westernmost, the Maine counties, and the small island counties shows that the growth of economic interaction was not confined to any one particular part of the colony.[14]

The extension of men's economic relationships was linked closely to internal pressures on the practice of agriculture. While these pressures exhibited themselves chiefly in the eastern agricultural towns, most areas of the province were influenced in one way or another. The problem, simply put, was that there was not enough land in many towns to

12. Cook, "Social Behavior and Changing Values in Dedham," pp. 559–65; Lockridge and Kreider, "Massachusetts Town Government," p. 570; Bumsted, "Religion, Finance, and Democracy," pp. 819, 820. See also Richard L. Bushman, *From Puritan to Yankee: Character and the Social Order in Connecticut, 1690–1765* (Cambridge, Mass., 1967), pp. 220, 221–32, 235–66.

13. Appendix A, table 1, lists the politically active towns and shows how they rated on Van Beck Hall's commercial-cosmopolitan scale. See his *Politics Without Parties: Massachusetts, 1780–1791* (Pittsburgh, 1972), pp. 3–22. Records of civil suits are used to indicate economic interaction by Allen, "Zuckerman Thesis," pp. 456–58.

14. Hall, *Politics Without Parties*, pp. 9–11.

support their burgeoning populations. The towns of Dedham in Suffolk County and Norton in Bristol County were typical of a number of eastern farming towns which, by the mid-eighteenth century, were experiencing rising land prices, a diminution of the average landholding, and a dwindling proportion of landowners. As populations continued to climb and young men resisted breaking close family ties by seeking opportunities in less populated areas further west or in Maine, the incidence of poverty rose and the range between the well-to-do and the less wealthy broadened. In Dedham the number and proportion of relief recipients increased as the eighteenth century progressed. In numerous towns, not only those in the east where land depletion was greatest, the practice of "warning out" increased. Worcester County towns "warned out" more than four times as many indigents in the 14-year period from 1754 to 1767 than they had in the previous 17 years.[15]

The decline of agricultural opportunities, however, should not necessarily be read as a decline of economic opportunity.[16] Under the pressure of declining landholdings and increased land shortages, many men chose to pursue other economic endeavors. By 1740, as one account shows, the town of Norton had seen the number of husbandmen decline to 37 percent of the working population and the number of laborers and artisans increase to 58 percent. The inhabitants of the town of Dedham may not have experienced the relative economic equality of earlier years, but by the end of the Revolution a significant number of them had branched out sufficiently into commercial, industrial, and other pursuits to make the town one of the leading commercial-cosmopolitan towns in the new state.[17] Also, the declining land values experienced in Dedham by the time of the Revolution[18] may well be an indicator that the demand for agricultural opportunities was declining in the face of a growing diversification of economic activity.

15. Kenneth Lockridge, "Land, Population, and the Evolution of New England Society, 1630–1790," *Past and Present*, no. 39 (April 1968), pp. 62–80; Cook, "Social Behavior and Changing Values in Dedham," pp. 566–73; Allen, "Zuckerman Thesis," p. 454.

16. Both Cook and Lockridge tend to do this. Lockridge, "Land, Population, and Society," pp. 62–80; Cook, "Social Behavior and Changing Values in Dedham," pp. 546–80. We need a closer analysis of the number of men involved in nonagricultural pursuits and of the variety of nonagricultural opportunities before equating agricultural decline with economic decline.

17. Bumsted, "Religion, Finance, and Democracy," p. 823; Hall, *Politics Without Parties*, p. 10.

18. Cook, "Social Behavior and Changing Values in Dedham," p. 570. Note also that land values in the most highly commercial-cosmopolitan towns were, at the end of the Revolution, lower than in those towns in the middle range. Dedham ranked in the former. See Hall, *Politics Without Parties*, p. 17.

The point to be made, however, is not that Dedham's experience was typical of the experience of all Massachusetts towns by the time of the Revolution, but only that the dual processes of population growth and declining agricultural opportunities in some parts of the province set off a chain reaction that was felt throughout much of Massachusetts. They reinforced the tendency toward diversification, they accelerated the process of social stratification, and in large measure contributed to the development of a social pluralism that challenged the uniformity and homogeneity which had formed the basis of the closed corporate peasant community. Most important, all of these processes of growth, fragmentation, and diversification were processes that chiefly touched the politically active towns of the province. Least touched were small farming communities and these, at the end of the provincial period, played little or no part in the political life of the province. The parties, as we shall now see, were drawn from the medium and large towns as measured by their commercial, administrative, and cultural activity.[19]

Of the 122 politically active towns, 50 voted together with great regularity as members of the Court party, a party that was noted for its close support of the royal governor and that was intimately connected with every function of provincial government—executive, legislative, and judicial. Geographically, the 50 towns took the shape of a somewhat stylized capital H superimposed on a map of the province. The right vertical line of towns ran along the coast from Almsbury, Salem, Ipswich, and Marblehead in Essex County, through populous Plymouth

19. Appendix A, table 1. An excellent study of Massachusetts political life from 1739 to 1756 by Robert Zemsky argues that legislative behavior was not characterized by partisanship. He writes that "alliances among politicians did exist, but they were invariably small, close-knit, and ephemeral . . . . In the Assembly the people's representatives went about their tasks unfettered by party responsibilities, without a party position to cleave to." *Merchants, Farmers, and River Gods: An Essay on Eighteenth-Century American Politics* (Boston, 1971), p. 22. Elsewhere, he demonstrates that the assembly could be divided into "leaders" and "rank and file," that leaders tended to come from east coast and Connecticut Valley towns, and that the "rank and file" did not always follow the lead of their ostensible "leaders" (pp. 286–308). This would suggest that Zemsky and I differ more in our choice of terminology than in substance. His "leaders," with some exceptions, correspond to my "Court party," the "rank and file" (again with exceptions) to my "Country party." Zemsky chooses to ignore the use of the term party at the time, but it should be noted that the roll call votes used by Zemsky (1740–56) do not seem to reveal the same high level of voting consistency as those I have used (1757–64). A partisan typology of Massachusetts towns, therefore, appears most applicable after 1757, although the roots of the parties certainly run back much further than that. One must remember that parties historically have seldom been fixed entities but rather processes in a constant state of flux and development.

County, to Nantucket in the south. The party included all of the towns of maritime Barnstable County until 1760, when all but one of the towns defected to the opposition with the politically dominant Otis family. The left vertical line corresponded to the Connecticut River Valley and comprehended a wide swath on either side of the river including all of the towns of Hampshire and (after 1761) Berkshire counties, with the exception of a single town—Brimfield, on the Worcester County line. Connecting the two verticals was an irregular horizontal line that ran west from Boston roughly along the road to Worcester and that included a number of central Middlesex County towns, along with the town of Worcester and several of its neighbors.[20]

A distinct majority of the Court party towns—28 of the 50—ranked among the commercial-cosmopolitan centers of the province. That is, measured on a scale ranging from subsistence level farming communities on the one side to most economically diversified and culturally active on the other, the Court party towns typically rated high. By the late provincial period they were, or were in the process of becoming, the administrative and judicial centers of Massachusetts. They were centers of newspaper publishing, legal practice, and commerce, and, as a result, they were the wealthiest towns in the province.[21]

The marks of the leading Court party towns were economic diversity, social pluralism, and a considerable openness and toleration in matters of religion. There was, in other words, a developing individualism of the sort one associates with modern, urbanized society. The processes of growth were changing men's behavior whether or not their values were keeping pace. The town of Bridgewater in Plymouth County provides an example. Located in the northwestern corner of Plymouth County only 30 miles from Boston, Bridgewater had a population of nearly 4,000 by 1764. A variety of soil conditions made possible the development of an extensive and diversified agriculture featuring field crops of corn, rye, oats, and flax, and ideal hay fields permitting considerable cattle raising. In addition, great natural stands of both hard and soft woods, especially white pine, made possible a large-scale production of

20. Appendix A, table 1. Note that the Barnstable County towns are listed as outside the party structure because of their equally divided voting records in the years 1757 to 1764. The significant point, however, is that (with the exception of Yarmouth) the towns in this group voted perfectly consistently with the Court party, before 1760, and equally consistently with the Country party thereafter.

21. Appendix A, table 1. Van Beck Hall's classification of towns is used here as a general rather than a precise measure of the differences between groups of towns. In some cases, I realize, towns would not have achieved by the 1760s those rankings which Hall gives them in the 1780s. See *Politics Without Parties*, pp. 3–22.

"timber, planks, boards, shingles, wood and coals," which were shipped for the most part southward by way of Taunton or Plymouth. The town exploited its forest resources with a number of saw mills and in addition had an iron slitting mill and a nail manufactory. The economic diversity meant, of course, that a rising population could easily be absorbed into the economy and Bridgewater thus seems to have been free of the frustrations experienced by such towns as Watertown, only 20 miles away.[22]

In addition, Bridgewater appears to have been relatively free of the contention and acrimony accompanying the division of churches and of the town itself into precincts. By the time of the Revolution, the town had five precincts with as many Congregational churches plus a small Episcopal church and a Baptist meetinghouse. Not only did the division of town and churches appear amicable, but the clergy were almost without exception kept in their posts for life, with the result that four of them served their congregations in the eighteenth century for 62-, 63-, 60-, and 62-year terms.[23]

The combination of economic diversity and adaptability on the one hand with a cautious, accommodative approach to social intercourse on the other produced a politics in Court party towns that steadily moved from a relatively open to an elitist system as the century progressed. Eleven different men served Bridgewater as representatives in the first quarter of the eighteenth century. Each served on the average for 2.2 years and left office at the rate of every 1.6 years. In the second quarter, however, the number of representatives dropped to nine, who served an average of 3 years each, while in the third quarter, only four served as representatives for an average of 6.5 years each.[24] In Boston, which provided support for both the Court and Country parties, elitism expressed itself as a concentration of political power in the hands of the wealthiest 7 percent of the town's property owners.[25]

Rooted in towns which were diversified, open, and relatively tolerant at the same time that they were politically cautious and increasingly elitist, the legislative faction of the Court party assumed a parallel stance that was pragmatic and undogmatic and yet unabashedly elitist. Its first goal was to control the legislature. Established by charter in 1691, the

22. "Description of Bridgewater," pp. 173–76.
23. Ibid., pp. 161–68.
24. Ibid., pp. 159–60. The turnover rate in the second quarter was 1.4 years, in the third, 2.8 years. It has been shown earlier that towns of both parties were tending to leave power longer in the same hands by the 1760s. What gave the Court party towns uniqueness was that their elites tended also to be the provincial elite.
25. James A. Henretta, "Economic Development and Social Structure in Colonial Boston," *WMQ*, 3d ser., 22 (1965): 90.

Great and General Court consisted of two houses, a House of Representatives and a Council, the first elected annually by 40-shilling freeholders, and the second by the House and the retiring Council sitting together. The Court party's control of the House was essentially managerial: it invariably elected the speaker and through him established procedures and dominated committees. As popularly elected representatives, however, Court party members had a dual allegiance—to their constituents and to the prerogative—although there were few occasions before the Revolution when any Court party townsman found the one incompatible with the other. The potential issue was kept submerged by occasional concessions to popular demands, but that was a small price to pay for the public esteem upon which the exercise of power depended.

Control of the Council, on the other hand, was absolute and far less conciliatory. Twenty-eight retiring councilors voting with Court party supporters in the House easily overawed, if they did not overwhelm, newly elected representatives when both houses sat to choose a new Council. The Council was thus in many ways a self-perpetuating entity until the Revolution, a reward for faithful Court party adherents in the House, and a haven, free from the shifting tides of popular sentiment, for the province's political elite. When, for example, Governor Shirley's "principal ministers of State," Thomas Hutchinson and Andrew Oliver, failed to win favor with Boston voters after 1749, the Court party simply promoted them to the Council, where they sat until the Revolution.[26]

Outside the General Court, legislative members of the Court party displayed the same double loyalties that they did within it. They were leading men in their towns and enjoyed the respect due them as members of the local elite. At the same time, they were tied tightly to the central government of the province by administrative and judicial offices, dispensed to them as leaders of the province's chief towns by the governor. Of the Court party legislators identified from the roll call votes of the 1750s, about 80 percent held or were soon to hold office as justice of the peace or judge of the inferior court. Even with the governor's usually futile attempts to win over opposition members by offering them similar posts, only 36 percent of Country party legislators held judicial offices (see table 2, Appendix A). Thus, while patronage was not a first cause of partisanship, its handling by royal governors helped to sharpen the distinction between the two parties in the legislature and to heighten the elitist propensities of the Court party.

Its elitism to the contrary, this party out of which most future Massa-

26. "Novanglus," 30 January 1775, in John Adams and [Daniel Leonard], *Novanglus and Massachusettensis* (Boston, 1819), p. 15; *House Journals*, 31 May 1749.

chusetts Tories were to come was not narrowly "conservative" in any philosophical sense, committed neither to the defense of a traditional social order nor to a return to a simpler way of life. On the contrary, in practice the Court party stood furthest from the ideal closed corporate, peasant community. It stood in the vanguard of modernization in its practical, nondoctrinaire, day-to-day adaptation to the processes of growth and change and, until the Revolution isolated some of its men and hardened them in their support of external authority (whether parliamentary or monarchic), the Court party was the party of a still dimly perceived modern, pluralistic order.

The Country party, on the other hand, responded quite differently to the processes and pressures of change. For most of the late provincial period, it served as an opposition party, and out of its organization and its experience grew the revolutionary movement. The 52 towns of the Country party geographically assumed the shape of a giant crescent, beginning in the northeastern corner of the province in the town of Salisbury, sweeping in a widening curve back through Middlesex and into Worcester counties and then forward through Suffolk and Bristol counties to the southeastern coast at Dartmouth. After 1760, most of the towns of peninsular Barnstable County were also included (see table 1, Appendix A). But to lay stress on the typical, the Country party was a party of eastern, inland towns. Its strength came from large clusters of inland towns spread like a fan within a 40-mile radius of Boston.

Despite variations in size and character, the typical Country party town ranked in the middle range on the commercial-cosmopolitan scale (see table 1, Appendix A). That is, it was less wealthy than its Court party counterpart, less involved in governmental administration and cultural activity. It was commercially active but did not rank as a major trade center. More important, it was still strongly committed to agriculture and thus most strongly felt the pressure of population growth and its attendant demands on a limited land supply. It is here that it differed most sharply from the Court party town: in its commitment to agriculture, it resisted diversification and thus forced up land values. By the end of the Revolution, the highest land values in the province were recorded by these towns in the middle range of commercial-cosmopolitan activity.[27] The typical Country party town, it would appear, was by necessity or choice less able to cope with the economic challenges of the times.

There were notable exceptions to these generalizations. Three of Boston's four representatives voted with (in fact, provided leadership

27. Hall, *Politics Without Parties*, pp. 17, 58.

for) the Country party, but because of Boston's size and dominant influence in provincial politics, it inevitably provided support for both parties.[28] Besides Boston, 19 other towns were either already or would soon become ranked with the leading commercial-cosmopolitan towns in Massachusetts, although by far the greater number of such towns was to be found in the Court party. Also in the Country party were a number of coastal communities such as Chilmark and Tisbury in Dukes County and York and Kittery in York County, Maine, along with some 6 small towns devoted to subsistence agriculture and very little commercial or cultural activity. Despite the adherence of these few small farming communities, however, none of the Country party towns could be called a frontier town by the 1760s.[29] The frontier had passed them by while the pressures of population growth and commercialization were mounting. Cut off from the safety valves of unlimited cheap land or in most cases from the open sea with its variety of exploitative possibilities, the Country party towns found a vent for their frustrations in opposition politics.

The Country party did not, however, rise up phoenix-like at some easily discernible point in time. It evolved over the late provincial period and by the 1760s was still in the process of growth and change. But it seems clear that an early and important influence on its development was the Land Bank controversy of 1740. The Land Bank was both a symbolic and a realistic attempt to cope with the problems of towns in transition from purely agricultural to partly agricultural and partly commercial economies: symbolic, because it asserted (as closed corporate peasant communities always had) that land was the prime unit of wealth; realistic, because it sought to provide a circulating medium of exchange to facilitate the increasing commercial activity in which Land Bank investors and their towns were engaged. By issuing paper currency in exchange for land mortgages, the Land Bank nicely joined the two. But after an initial challenge from a rival Silver Bank headed by prosperous coastal merchants, the Land Bankers were finally put out of business by a British government order extending the Bubble Act of 1720 to the colonies.[30]

28. Rather than count Boston twice, it has been listed as a Country party town although one of its four votes was, with only one exception, regularly cast with the Court party. Appendix A, table 1.

29. Many of the Country party towns were frontier towns in the 1690s and early 1700s. See Frederick Jackson Turner, "The First Official Frontier of the Massachusetts Bay," *CSM Publications* 17 (1915): 250–71.

30. The best discussion of the Land Bank is George Athan Billias, *The Massachusetts Land Bankers of 1740*, in *Univ. of Maine Studies*, 2d ser., no. 74 (April

The patterns of Land Bank support and Country party involvement are strikingly similar. Boston provided some leadership for the bank but most of its directors came from towns within a 40-mile radius of Boston. They were all men who had economic interests that were divided between land and business[31] so that they themselves, along with many of the investors in the bank, epitomized the transitional nature of their communities. The towns of most directors eventually became prominent Country party towns, while the incidence of Land Bank investment was significantly higher in towns that supported the Country party in the late provincial period as compared with those that supported the Court party.[32] Geographically, the areas of Land Bank investment and Country party support were almost identical. There was very little investment from towns along the Plymouth or Barnstable County coast and virtually none from Hampshire County in the west except for the town of Brimfield on the Worcester County line, the only Hampshire town to support the Country party (see table 1, Appendix A). In other words, areas involved in Land Bank investment provided strong support for the Country party; areas rejecting the Land Bank tended to support the Court party.

The Country party, one must therefore conclude, was not a party of farmers nor a party of frontier radicalism. It was a party of towns caught up in the processes of rapid growth and change. If they lay on a frontier, it was on the frontier of modernization, for what they were experiencing was the cutting edge of an open, competitive, diversified, pluralistic order slicing its way into once homogeneous, tradition-rooted, closed corporate peasant communities. Their reaction was understandably contradictory. They clung tenaciously to agriculture and to the social values of a simpler past at the same time that they realistically formed a political

---

1959). See also John C. Miller, *Sam Adams: Pioneer in Propaganda* (Boston, 1936), pp. 10–15; Thomas Hutchinson, *The History of the Colony and Province of Massachusetts-Bay,* ed. Lawrence Shaw Mayo, 3 vols. (Cambridge, Mass., 1936), 2: 298–301.

31. Billias, *Massachusetts Land Bankers,* pp. 17–31.

32. Andrew McFarland Davis, "List of Partners in the Land Bank of 1740," *CSM Collections* 4 (1910): 165–94. Direct comparisons of the number of land bankers in various towns are meaningless because of wide variations in population. A more meaningful figure is the number of investors per 100 of population. This Land Bank multiplier appears in Appendix A, table 1. The Court party mean was 0.379 investors per 100 of population. The Country party figure, excluding Boston, was 0.471. The figures must be viewed as approximate since the earliest census of the towns was taken in 1765. Greene and Harrington, *American Population,* pp. 21–30.

party to promote their interests. They looked both backwards and for-
wards, and finally they espoused a republican ideology that held out the
hope that men's behavior could be altered and society reformed. Country
party towns provided a fertile seedbed for such ideas: they lay, in effect,
on the republican frontier.

How the Country party became a party of revolution now becomes our
chief concern. Its dynamic, to generalize first, was a desire to overcome
the enormous problems created by the processes of growth and change,
a desire to explain those processes in intelligible terms, and to counteract, rather than adapt to, the unacceptable manifestations of change:
the fragmentation of society, the political disharmony, the economic
competitiveness, and the undermining of consensual ideals. With very
imperfect tools of analysis, Country party members groped towards a
rationalization of their dilemma and an appropriate course of action
which in many ways presaged their revolutionary republicanism. Their
concern focused on three areas: the corruption of the patronage system,
the insularity of the commercial classes, and the growth of a propertyless
working class. In each case, the Country party saw an undesirable consciousness of separate interest, and in each case, the party's answer was
the same: society must be pulled together, separate interests must be
subordinated to the public good, a new consensus must be found. As
early as the 1750s, these ideas began to take shape.

Patronage was an early concern, one which typified the eighteenth-
century tendency to personalize the forces of change and to blame men
as individuals for the unsettled conditions of the time. To members of
the Country party, patronage was a sign of corruption since it created
in the minds of the recipients a second allegiance (to the governor)
conflicting with their prior, and only legitimate, allegiance to the public.
As John Adams was to put it in 1774, "the office of a justice of the peace
is a great acquisition in the country, and such a distinction to a man
among his neighbours as is enough to purchase and corrupt almost any
man." The dispensing of county offices represented an intrusion upon
the self-contained structure of the Massachusetts town, in Adams's view,
and it created "a dependence in the minds of the principal gentlemen
of the place upon the court" with the result that even men without
judicial offices, such as clergymen and doctors, since they associated
with the "principal gentlemen," likewise identified themselves as "governor's men."[33] In his search for the original cause of this corruption,

33. Adams to Abigail Adams, York [Maine], 30 June 1774, in Lyman H. Butterfield, ed., *Adams Family Correspondence*, 2 vols. (Cambridge, Mass., 1963), 1: 116.

Adams hit upon Governor Shirley, who, he said, "was a crafty, busy, ambitious, intriguing, enterprising man; and having mounted . . . to the chair of this province, he saw in a young growing country, vast prospects of ambition opening before his eyes, and conceived great designs of aggrandizing himself, his family and his friends."[34]

Similar sentiments were expressed at the time of Shirley's governorship. The town of Watertown, for example, was one in which the pressures of change were clearly in evidence throughout the early eighteenth century. It was represented in the General Court in the early 1750s by a Court party adherent, John Hunt, a Harvard graduate who owned a general store and tavern. Hunt's patronage benefits were many: he was appointed justice of the peace and a collector of taxes for Middlesex County. When he bid for the collectorship of the liquor excise in Essex and Worcester counties as well, however, a considerable number of his townsmen turned against him, opposed his reelection in 1756, and petitioned the legislature that his appointment as an exciseman was "against the law." By 1757, the town was split down the middle and Hunt's reelection was immediately challenged by his opponents. When the General Court ordered a new election, the vote was so close that the selectmen returned two names and asked the House to determine the choice. Throughout the crisis, however, the selectmen favored Hunt and, according to the opposition, did everything in their power to prevent qualified supporters of Daniel Whitney, the challenger, from voting. The affair dragged on until finally, in 1758, Daniel Whitney was seated as Watertown's representative. Whitney immediately carried Watertown into the ranks of the Country party and power in the town shifted to the opposition.[35] In effect, Watertown experienced its revolution in the 1750s.

The town of Stoughton in Suffolk County similarly disposed of a representative, John Shepard, whose patronage posts, it was believed, had corrupted him. Shepard had been appointed a guardian of Stoughton's Indians, which gave him control over vast acreages of land set aside for their upkeep. In a land-hungry area, Shepard's honesty was essential, but he provocatively stripped the lands of their wood and timber, shocking the townsmen, who demanded his removal. The evi-

34. "Novanglus," 30 January 1775, in Adams and [Leonard], *Novanglus and Massachusettensis,* p. 15.

35. *House Journals,* 8 June 1756; 26 May, 31 May, 1 June, 16 August, 26 August, 6 December 1757; 1 June, 6 June 1758; 8 March, 14 March, 17 March, 5 June 1759. See also Clifford K. Shipton, *Biographical Sketches of those Who Attended Harvard College* [*Sibley's Harvard Graduates*], vols. 6–13 (Boston, 1942–65), 9: 414–18.

dence was so overwhelmingly against Shepard that the General Court was obliged to deny him his seat, while his successor, Joseph Hewens, became a strong and consistent supporter of the Country party.[36]

There was truth, of course, to the charge that the Court party was patronage-ridden and to the belief that William Shirley wielded his patronage powers for political advantage. When Shirley was placed in command of colonial forces at Ticonderoga in 1755, he so lavishly rewarded his Court party friends with supply contracts and so undiplomatically interfered in the administration of northern New York that other royal officials, including the Earl of Loudoun, commander of his majesty's forces in America, readily accepted the charge of the Massachusetts opposition that Shirley had created a party of plunder.[37] Where all of them erred, however, was in their belief that patronage was a cause of partisanship rather than a result. Shirley had created a party, wrote the Earl of Loudoun to Henry Fox in England, "by two methods, by enriching his friends, by lavishing the public treasure, and by imposing on the people, that he is the only man entrusted in American affairs, by the King or his servants."[38] Whether perfectly accurate or not, however, the charge clinched the case against Shirley and he was removed.

The appointment of Shirley's successor, Thomas Pownall, added a new and unique twist to the patronage issue. Pownall, like Shirley, believed in working with a faction of government supporters. A governor, he wrote, must "at his first accession . . . be cautious how he proceeds till he has had time to connect together and form such good men as will act in concert with his administration."[39] What shocked the Court party, however, was the governor's apparent unwillingness to cast them in their traditional role. He sought advice from Thomas Hutchinson and Andrew Oliver, but as often he would consult with the acknowledged leaders of the Country party, the Boston representatives Benjamin Prat and John Tyng. According to John Adams, Hutchinson and Oliver "could not bear the competition of Prat and Tyng, much less be overruled and supplanted by them."[40] As a result, a political revolution—

36. *House Journals*, 30 May, 16 November, 18 November 1754, 5 February 1755.
37. Schutz, *Pownall*, pp. 65–66; William Otis Sawtelle, "Thomas Pownall, Colonial Governor, and Some of His Activities in the American Colonies," *MHS Proceedings* 63 (1931): 237.
38. William Shirley to Earl of Loudoun, 13 September 1756; Loudoun to Henry Fox, in Charles Henry Lincoln, ed., *Correspondence of William Shirley, Governor of Massachusetts and Military Commander in America, 1731–1760*, 2 vols. (New York, 1912), 2: 557.
39. Pownall to Loudoun, 15 December 1757, Loudoun Papers, 5014, quoted by Schutz, *Pownall*, pp. 116–17.
40. Adams, ed., *Works*, 10: 242.

albeit temporary—took place in the province. "In a short time," wrote Hutchinson, "most of the chief friends of Mr. Shirley became opposers of Mr. Pownall, and most of Mr. Shirley's enemies became Mr. Pownall's friends."[41] In a curious reversal of roles, the Court party then openly mounted a campaign against the governor and determined, according to John Adams, "by propagating slanders against the governor among the people, and especially among the clergy, to raise discontents, and make him [Pownall] uneasy in his seat."[42] In Hutchinson's view, on the other hand, "it was not possible for me as a member of the legislature [i.e., of the Council] to agree with every measure [of Pownall] without being a mere machine, and having no judgment of my own."[43] Ironically, the Court party made its own contribution to the development of anti-prerogative attitudes in Massachusetts.

Equally ironic was the role of the royally appointed governor, Pownall. In his first speech to the legislature, he vowed to maintain the powers of the governor but also, at the same time, "always religiously [to] observe your ever valuable charter rights and privileges." According to later revolutionaries, he seemed "to have been a friend to liberty and to our constitution, and to have had an aversion to all plots against either."[44] But most important, he strengthened the legislative power and organizational cohesiveness of the Country party when he appointed many of its leading men "to places of honour and trust and made them his confidants."[45] He won over James Bowdoin, a newly appointed councilor, and Thomas Hancock, another of Boston's wealthiest merchants, who managed to get elected to the Council during Pownall's governorship. In his appointments to judicial posts Pownall strongly favored the

41. Hutchinson, *History*, ed. Mayo, 3: 42. For another account, with less emphasis on "parties," see John J. Waters and John A. Schutz, "Patterns of Massachusetts Colonial Politics: The Writs of Assistance and the Rivalry between the Otis and Hutchinson Families," *WMQ*, 3d ser., 24 (1967): 555–57. See also John Francis Burns, *Controversies between Royal Governors and Their Assemblies in the Northern American Colonies* (Villanova, Pa., 1923), pp. 142–43.

42. "Novanglus" [No. 2], 30 January 1775, in Adams and [Leonard], *Novanglus and Massachusettensis*, p. 17.

43. Hutchinson to ———, 8 November 1764, in *Jasper Mauduit: Agent in London for the Province of Massachusetts-Bay, 1762–1765, MHS Collections* 74 (1917): 166n.

44. 16 August 1757, Journals of the Council of Massachusetts, original in Archives Division, Commonwealth of Massachusetts, microfilm copy reel 8, Records of the States of the United States, in State Historical Society of Wisconsin; "Novanglus" [No. 2], 30 January 1775, in Adams and [Leonard], *Novanglus and Massachusettensis*, p. 17. See also Adams to William Tudor, 4 February 1817, in Adams, ed., *Works*, 10: 243.

45. Hutchinson, *History*, ed. Mayo, 3: 41n.

Country party, and it was his appointments that raised the percentage of office-holders in the party to 36 percent. Without his appointments, only 22 percent of Country party legislators held judicial offices.[46] Pownall even challenged the supremacy of the Court party in Hampshire County with a justice of the peace appointment that, in the words of the county elite, "put us into such company as we never inclined to keep." Only the patient solicitations of Thomas Hutchinson averted a mass resignation of the leading judicial officers of the county. Hutchinson himself believed that he was "really of less consequence than I have been these twenty years," and that "many things which use to fall to me go into other hands."[47] Hutchinson therefore determined to adopt a stoical outlook and wait for better days, and he urged his friends to do likewise.

Hutchinson's patience was well calculated, for it must have been obvious to him that Thomas Pownall disliked the factionalism of Massachusetts politics, and would not willingly remain much longer. He did not. After a long and fruitless struggle to replace the colonial agent, William Bollan—William Shirley's son-in-law and agent more for the Court party than for the General Court—Pownall asked to be relieved of his post, and in the summer of 1760 he sailed for England.[48] Before Hutchinson had even had time to form an opinion of the new governor, Francis Bernard, he wrote candidly to Israel Williams that "it will not be saying a great deal to tell you that we have not made a bad exchange."[49] As it turned out, however, Bernard began his administration with as much caution as Pownall. "I found the province divided into parties so nearly equal," wrote Bernard of his arrival, "that it would have been madness for me to have put myself at the head of either of them. I had therefore nothing to do but to keep to myself and maintain my own dignity."[50]

46. Pownall to Bowdoin, 14, 21 July 1770, in *MHS Collections*, 6th ser., 9 (1897): 199, 205; Appendix A, table 2. Samuel Niles, Joseph Gerrish, and Humphrey Hobson are examples of Country party supporters with consistent voting records who received Pownall appointments.

47. Joseph Dwight *et al.* to Governor Thomas Pownall, Springfield, 19 May 1759; [Israel Williams to ?] [1759]; Hutchinson to Israel Williams, Milton, 2 July 1759; Hutchinson to Dwight *et al.*, Boston, 2 June 1759; Dwight to Israel Williams *et al.*, Sheffield, 5 June 1759; John Worthington to [Israel Williams], Springfield, July 1759; Hutchinson to Williams, Boston, 5 August 1759; Hutchinson to Williams, Milton, 17 July 1758, all in Israel Williams Papers, MHS, 2: 114, 115, 150, 149, 115, 116, 151, 142.

48. Thomas Hutchinson to Israel Williams, Boston, 10 February 1759; Hutchinson to Williams, 12 July 1760, ibid., pp. 146, 155.

49. Hutchinson to Williams, Boston, 25 August 1760, ibid., p. 156.

50. Bernard to Barrington, 1 May 1762, Bernard Papers, 2: 189, quoted by Ellen

The parties were equally cautious. Thomas Hutchinson admitted that he had to be wary because he did not know what Pownall had told Bernard before his arrival, and could therefore not be sure of his prejudices. But, he noted with satisfaction, "If he has shown any greater regard to T[y]ng and his adherents than to any other persons it is not generally known."[51] Within a month, however, the chief justice of the province died, and Bernard was confronted with the task of appointing a successor. The Otises of Barnstable County promptly let the governor know that Pownall had promised a justiceship to James Otis, Sr., a member of the Council, when the first vacancy occurred in the Superior Court. That would mean elevating one of the incumbent justices to make room for Otis. Members of the Court party, however, felt that Lieutenant Governor Hutchinson should also be chief justice, and two of Hutchinson's closest friends, Andrew Oliver and Israel Williams, urged Bernard to appoint him.[52] When Bernard accepted their recommendation, his action convinced both parties that he had thrown in his lot with the Court party. Bernard, wrote James Otis, Jr., "fell into some of the worst hands upon his first arrival."[53] But the Court party, into whose hands Bernard had presumably fallen, believed itself "wonderfully delivered from our enemies." "I . . . wish such wise and benevolent measures may run through his whole administration," wrote Israel Williams.[54]

Bernard's appointment of Hutchinson not only changed the political allegiance of the two parties—the Court party now became once again the staunch upholder of the royal prerogative while the Country party became the opposition—but it also changed the internal nature of the Country party itself, introducing new policies, new leadership, and new followers, gradually transforming it into the revolutionary party it was to become. Its new policy was to attack such increasingly unpopular imperial agencies as the customs house and the admiralty court, which

E. Brennan, *Plural Office-Holding in Massachusetts 1760–1780* (Chapel Hill, N.C., 1945), p. 51.

51. Hutchinson to Williams, Boston, 25 August 1760, in Williams Papers, 2: 156.

52. See Leslie J. Thomas, "Partisan Politics in Massachusetts during Governor Bernard's Administration, 1760–1770" (Ph.D. Diss., Univ. of Wis., 1960), pp. 1–18; Andrew Oliver to Williams, Boston, 30 September 1760, in Williams Papers, 2: 103.

53. Bernard to Lord Halifax, 17 November 1760, Bernard Papers, 1: 283, reproduced in Josiah Quincy, Jr., *Reports of Cases Argued and Adjudged in the Superior Court of Judicature of the Province of Massachusetts-Bay Between 1761 and 1772*, ed. Samuel M. Quincy (Boston, 1876), p. 410; Otis to Jasper Mauduit, Boston, 23 April 1762, in *Jasper Mauduit*, p. 29.

54. Williams to Hutchinson, Hatfield, 3 December 1760, in Williams Papers, 2: 119.

had recently cracked down on mechants engaged in smuggling and had resorted to the use of much hated writs of assistance (general search warrants) to aid in making arrests. The consequence of this policy was the political alliance of the Country party towns with a sizable part of Boston's merchant community, an alliance that well suited the Country party's second major concern: to draw the merchants into a new consensus and thereby overcome the undesirable results of social pluralism.

By happy coincidence, key men from both the customs house and the admiralty court left their jobs in 1760 and went over to the opposition. Benjamin Barons, the collector of customs, was suspended after a dispute with his fellow customs officials, and in his pique "he procured a meeting of merchants, in which he was considered as principal, to act against the Court of Admiralty."[55] The other defector was James Otis, Jr., advocate general in the admiralty court, son of the disappointed Supreme Court aspirant, who angrily "swore revenge" against the successful Thomas Hutchinson and immediately fell in with the scheme of Barons and the merchants. With information provided by Barons, about 60 Boston merchants petitioned the General Court that the province had been cheated out of its one-third of the revenue from confiscated cargoes and urged the legislature to sue for recovery of the money.[56] And at the same time, the merchants, with Otis as their advocate, petitioned the Superior Court of Massachusetts asking to be heard on the question of writs of assistance.[57]

The court cases that resulted propelled Otis and his fellow lawyer, Oxenbridge Thacher, into the leadership of the Country party. The legislature, prodded on by the Country party, sued the surveyor of customs for the province's share of seizures, and won two actions in inferior courts only to have both judgments reversed by the Superior Court under Thomas Hutchinson's direction.[58] In the writs of assistance case, Hutchinson feared for awhile that the brilliant oratory of Otis had convinced the court. "But," he wrote later, "I prevailed with my brethren to continue the cause until the next term, and in the meantime wrote to England, and procured a copy of the writ, and sufficient evidence of the practice of the Exchequer there," so that he could prove the legality of

55. Quincy, *Superior Court,* p. 424; James Otis, as "Hampden," *BG, September* 1769.

56. Hutchinson to Israel Williams, Boston, 21 January 1761, in Williams Papers, 2: 156; Quincy, *Superior Court,* pp. 541–42.

57. Quincy, *Superior Court,* pp. 412–13.

58. *Gray* v. *Paxton,* and *Province of Massachusetts-Bay* v. *Paxton,* in Quincy, *Superior Court,* pp. 541 *et seq.*

the writs and thereby defeat Otis at the next session.[59] But Otis an(
Thacher only lost in a technical sense, for the *Boston Gazette* reportec
that their arguments had done them great honor "and nothing could
have induced one to believe they were not conclusive."[60] Bostonians
elected Otis and three merchants to represent them in the legislature in
1761, and in 1763 they added Thacher to the group. Otis and Thacher
stepped into the vacated positions of Prat and Tyng as leaders of the
Country party, or as Otis began to call them, the "friends of liberty."[61]

"The town of Boston," according to John Adams, "had been, almost
invariably, at the head of the opposition, that is of the country party,"[62]
and by the early 1760s, the party's activities increasingly focused on that
town. With Otis and Thacher as leaders, the party in Boston represented
a coalition between part of the merchant community and politicians
whose legislative ties ran out into the republican frontier. Each had
their organizations for formulating plans of action and for maintaining
contact with each other.

A merchant society with 146 members was operating in Boston by
early 1763. In their constitution the merchants stated that "care shall
be taken to avoid, as much as possible, all party disputes,"[63] but, as John
Adams explained, the society cooperated closely with Otis and other
popular leaders. The politicians, on the other hand, had what they called
the Caucus Club, and they met regularly at the home of a merchant and
local politician, Thomas Dawes, to discuss both town and provincial
politics. There, as John Adams reported, "they smoke tobacco till you
cannot see from one end of the garret to the other. There they drink flip,
I suppose, and there they choose a moderator, who puts questions to
the vote regularly; and selectmen, assessors, collectors, wardens, fire-
wards, and representatives, are regularly chosen before they are chosen
in the town." Though the politicians curried popularity among the

59. Hutchinson, *History*, ed. Mayo, 3: 68; Hutchinson to Conway, 1 October
1765, in Mass. Arch., 26: 155. See also John Adams's minutes and abstract as well
as the editorial note in *Legal Papers of John Adams,* ed. L. Kinvin Wroth and
Hiller B. Zobel, 3 vols. (Cambridge, Mass., 1965), 2: 123–34, 134–44, 106–23.

60. *BG,* 23 November 1761.

61. 16 *BTR,* pp. 57, 88; Otis to Jasper Mauduit, Boston, 23 April 1762, in *Jasper
Mauduit,* p. 30. See also Lawrence Henry Gipson, "Aspects of the Beginning of the
American Revolution in Massachusetts Bay, 1760–1762," *AAS Proceedings* 67
(1958): 11–32; Waters and Schutz, "Patterns of Massachusetts Colonial Politics,"
pp. 563–67.

62. Adams, ed., *Works,* 10: 241–44.

63. "The Society for Encouraging Trade and Commerce within the Province of
the Massachusetts Bay," constitution and list of subscribers in Ezekiel Price Manu-
scripts, MHS.

townspeople, they did not challenge the political pre-eminence of the merchant class, at least during the early 1760s. "They send committees to wait on the merchants' club," explained John Adams, "and to propose and join in the choice of men and measures,"[64] with the result that merchants continued to dominate important town offices in the early 1760s.[65] At this point, at least, there was no apparent challenge to commercial supremacy in Boston.

Outside of Boston, the organization of the Country party was probably less extensive. Before he left Massachusetts in 1761 to become chief justice of New York (on Pownall's recommendation), Benjamin Prat met with members of the party at Dedham and advised them to remain united "and forsake not the assembling yourselves together." But by 1762, Thacher was advising Prat that problems had arisen and the "brotherhood" was not so united as before. "Come yourself and dispell all clouds. Whatever other variant and inconsistent interest and factions are among us, we shall unite on your return and make you the head of the union as you were the former of it."[66] The chief cause for the split, Thacher implied, was James Otis, Jr., who had temporarily defected from the Country party when his father was offered a patronage post (justice of the quorum) by Bernard and who was now meeting with Bernard periodically, as Prat and Tyng had with Pownall when he was governor. But the Otises stayed "bought" for a very short time only, and thereafter patronage did little to alter the coalition of urban merchants and Country party towns that formed the essence of the developing revolutionary movement.

Whether by conscious design or not, the political union of Boston merchants and Country party towns corresponded with that ideal goal of the Country party to draw Massachusetts society together in a classless assertion of the public welfare. The same goal encouraged the party to expand itself again in 1765, when opposition to the Stamp Act drew the Boston street crowds, and with them a new group of "popular" leaders, into an attack on the stamp agent and other royal officials, and ultimately into the political forum of the province. The combination of country

64. Adams, ed., *Works*, 2: 144.

65. In 1767, for instance, all seven selectmen were merchants: Joseph Jackson, Samuel Sewall, John Ruddock, John Hancock, William Phillips, Timothy Newell, John Rowe, 16 *BTR*, p. 197. See also Stephen Everett Patterson, "Boston Merchants and the American Revolution" (M.A. thesis, Univ. of Wis., 1961), passim; and Henretta, "Economic Development and Social Structure in Colonial Boston," p. 90.

66. Shipton, *Biographical Sketches*, 10: 233; Thacher to Prat, 1762, in Thacher Papers, MHS, vol. 1667–1790.

towns with a new urban wing transformed the Country party into a "Popular party"—and this is what it was called thereafter, at least by Bernard, Hutchinson, and their supporters.

Chief among the architects of this coalition was Samuel Adams. Born the son of a small merchant and maltster, educated at Harvard, Adams had dabbled in business and journalism, but at age 43 he was a man with no real profession and was singularly undistinguished. His great interest, in an age when the professional politician was still unheard of, was politics. He talked politics in Boston taverns, in the Fire Clubs, and the "singing clubs" that he organized among the common people, and even with the clerics of the Congregational Church, of which he was an active member. His partisan bias was doubtless inherited from his father, who invested in the Land Bank scheme of the early 1740s and lost heavily when the governor defeated it. He was motivated by no thoughts of personal aggrandizement: in a materialistic age he spurned the opportunity to get ahead at the public expense, cared little about his personal appearance, and left to his devoted wife the difficult task of managing their domestic economy on the meager income he did receive. His apparent source of income was his part-time position as one of Boston's tax-collectors, but his sympathy for the human predicament far outweighed his sense of duty to his office with the result that he fell far behind in his collections—and, of course, made lasting friends in the process. His Puritan background, combined with a developing republicanism, provided him with a frame of reference within which he spoke and wrote, in a rhetorical and exaggerated way, of a world torn between forces of good and forces of evil. And they provided him with the language and common assumptions that explain the appeal of his writings among his New England neighbors.[67]

Samuel Adams added a new dimension to the Popular party in Boston. He brought into its ranks two new types of politicians whose presence greatly altered the methods used by the party and who account in no small way for its ultimate success. Of the first group, William Mollineux and Ebenezer MacIntosh provided contact with the lower classes in Boston. They were strictly local politicians who could pack the town meeting, organize public demonstrations, or coordinate popular action with party policy. The second group, on the other hand, consisted of men of wealth or talent or both, men capable of playing a role on the provincial or even the intercolonial stage. These men were assiduously

67. Ralph Volney Harlow, *Samuel Adams: Promoter of the American Revolution* (New York, 1923); Miller, *Sam Adams,* passim.

groomed by Sam Adams to provide leadership for the party and, if in no other respect than as a patron of political genius, Sam Adams would deserve a foremost place in the history of the American Revolution.

John Adams stands at the head of the list. A distant cousin of Sam Adams, born in Braintree not far from Boston, John Adams attracted notice as a brilliant student at Harvard and thereafter in the law firm of James Putnam. Never "popular" in the sense that James Otis and Sam Adams were, John Adams provided ingenuity, a gift for raising even minor grievances to the highest level of principle, and a "largeness of view" without which the "thirteen clocks," to use his own analogy, would never have struck as one. John Adams provided a link with other non-Bostonians such as James Warren of Plymouth (who was married to James Otis's sister, Mercy) and Elbridge Gerry of Essex County.

Second of Sam Adams's protegés was John Hancock, noted less for his ability—which was meager at best in the early years though more considerable after Independence—than for his inherited wealth which he put at the disposal of the Popular party. As a backcountry farmer was to put it directly to Hancock years later: "I remember we used to say that you found the money and Sam Adams the brains."[68] Hancock inherited the prospering importing-exporting business of his uncle, Thomas Hancock, and as a leading Boston merchant he found it much easier than did Sam Adams to mix with the social elite of the community. Like Thomas Cushing, another merchant-politician, he sometimes found himself torn between Adams's "radical" methods (which stressed the involvement of crowds but not their predominance) and the more moderate wishes of the merchant community, which, as we shall see, eventually, and perhaps inevitably, produced serious stresses and strains within the revolutionary party.

The role of street people in the revolutionary movement was, and is, a matter of interpretation.[69] To Bernard, future Tories, and many mer-

68. William Gordon to John Adams, Jamaica Plain, 19 October 1780, in "Letters of the Reverend William Gordon," *MHS Proceedings* 63 (1931): 445.

69. Interest in the role of "the inarticulate" in the American Revolution has been generated largely by the work of Jesse Lemisch: "The American Revolution Seen from the Bottom Up," *Towards a New Past: Dissenting Essays in American History,* ed. Barton J. Bernstein (New York, 1968), pp. 3–45; "Jack Tar in the Streets: Merchant Seamen in the Politics of Revolutionary America," *WMQ*, 3d ser., 25 (1968): 371–407; and "Listening to the Inarticulate," *Journal of Social History* 3 (1969): 1–29. Useful counterweights to Lemisch's class consciousness and social struggle themes are Pauline Maier, "Popular Uprisings and Civil Authority in Eighteenth-Century America," *WMQ*, 3d ser., 27 (1970): 3–35, and James H. Hutson, "An Investigation of the Inarticulate: Philadelphia's White Oaks," ibid., 28 (1971): 3–25, who stress the often conservative and law-abiding character of

chants, the urban crowd was a mob, violent and irrational in its behavior, and to be controlled in any orderly society. In Boston during the Revolution, they cynically believed that the "mob" must be directed, and they easily assumed that popular politicians were its directors.

According to Bernard, the merchants' nonimportation agreement of 1765, drawn up in opposition to the Stamp Act, was not a spontaneous thing. Rather, certain members of the "faction," as he called the Popular party, were "obliged to use the greatest threats, even to marking houses in the day time for nightly ruin, before they could get many respectable merchants in this town to sign the engagement not to send to Great Britain for goods."[70] When a similar agreement was formed in March 1768 to combat the Townshend Acts, Bernard again insisted that "the merchants were dragged into the cause, their intercourse and connections with the politicians, and the fear of opposing the stream of the people, have at length brought it about against the sense of an undoubted majority both of numbers, property, and weight." He explained that some merchants "were told they would be obnoxious to the lower sort of people[,] some were threatened with the resentment of the higher: some were made afraid for their persons and houses: others for their trade and credit." Even at that, many merchants refused to sign and "it can never be carried into execution without the interposition of the mob."[71] Thus, in Bernard's view, the Popular party was a coalition of "mobs"and "politicians," a class movement which no respectable merchant would willingly join.

But Bernard's picture of a polarized society was grossly exaggerated. Most merchants did not have to be coerced to sign the nonimportation plan of 1765, and the few "respectable"ones who were, were the friends of Thomas Hutchinson.[72] In 1767 and 1768, it was much more difficult

---

America's colonial inarticulate. All of these authors, however, tend to overemphasize the role of urban crowds. My study of Massachusetts suggests that the Boston crowd, while it possessed an identity, was unable to rationalize its purpose or to separate itself wholly from the ideas and goals of republican leaders. Rural people, however, as Chapter 4 indicates, were able to formalize and synthesize their revolutionary purpose, and to establish a direction different from, if not contrary to, that of the early revolutionary leadership. See also George Rudé, *The Crowd in the French Revolution* (Oxford, 1959), particularly chapter XV.

70. Bernard to Shelburne, 31 August 1767, in Bernard Papers, 6: 236–37, quoted by Thomas, "Partisan Politics in Massachusetts," p. 388.

71. Bernard to Shelburne, 21 March 1768, in *Letters to the Ministry from Governor Bernard . . .* (Boston, 1769), pp. 23–25.

72. Arthur Meier Schlesinger, *The Colonial Merchants and the American Revolution, 1763–1776* (New York, 1957), p. 80.

to get an agreement and Popular leaders had to settle at first for a half-way, nonconsumption agreement. But the fact that such prominent merchants as John Rowe, Henderson Inches, Edward Payne, Ezekiel Price, William Phillips, John Hancock, Thomas Boylston, and John Erving, Jr., consented to sit on committees to draw up nonconsumption and, later, nonimportation plans,[73] is clear proof that the Popular party was not an instrument of the lower classes with class struggle its goal.

What Bernard failed to realize was that the Popular party had won the support of the Boston crowd only by default. There was nothing in the rhetoric of James Otis or Samuel Adams to suggest that a redistribution of wealth and power was a goal, nothing to suggest that society should fragment and pursue class struggle. Quite to the contrary, the Popular leaders stressed the need for a union of all interests in the defense of liberty.

From the point of view of the Popular leaders, the urban crowd was a fact of life. The Boston crowd had been active for years,[74] and its progressive exclusion from town politics[75] may have been reason enough for its apparent wish to become more actively engaged in the issues of the day. The question therefore for Popular leaders was not whether to involve the crowd, but how to involve it. To a traditionalist of Samuel Adams's makeup, the crowd had to be absorbed into a general, consensual approach to politics. He sought less to foment class conflict than to overcome it, and his constant pleas were for a revolutionary force that would combine the efforts of the merchant and lower classes in a common endeavor.[76] That is not to say that merchants and lower classes necessarily agreed, for in fact, they became increasingly uncomfortable bed-fellows. But social cohesion was becoming central to the emerging republican ideology of the revolutionary leaders, and disharmony within the Popular party simply added particular cogency to the idea.

73. *BEP*, 23 November 1767; *BG*, 30 November 1767, 4 January 1768; 16 *BTR*, pp. 221, 223–24; Anne Rowe Cunningham, ed., *Letters and Diary of John Rowe* (Boston, 1903), pp. 144–45, 152; Charles M. Andrews, "The Boston Merchants and the Non-Importation Movement," *CSM Publications* 19 (1918): 201.

74. Maier, "Popular Uprisings," pp. 5–6.

75. Henretta, "Economic Development and Social Structure in Colonial Boston," p. 90.

76. See, for example, Instructions of the Town of Boston to its Representatives in the General Court, May 1764; Town of Boston to Dennys De Berdt, 22 October 1766; "Determinatus" [*BG*, 8 August 1768], in Harry A. Cushing, ed., *The Writings of Samuel Adams*, 4 vols. (New York, 1904–8), 1: 1–6, 89–99, 236–40. See also the disapproval of the riots of August 1765, expressed by two later Sons of Liberty: "Diary of John Quincy, Jun.," *MHS Proceedings* 4 (1860): 47–49; "Diary of John Rowe," ibid., 2d ser., 10 (1896): 61.

Popular party activity in Boston, however, should not be allowed to obscure the larger and more significant pattern of party politics at the provincial level. Under the catalytic influence of imperial attempts to tighten trade regulations and to tax Americans, the opposition party in Massachusetts broadened its base and placed Boston, an atypical opposition town, in the leading role. But the point to be made is that many Massachusetts towns—the towns of the prerevolutionary Country party —were long used to dealing with external threats to their self-sufficiency. They came together as a party to cope with the encroachments of an external world on their closed corporate values. The challenge of Parliament appeared as another of those encroachments, and it was easy to imagine the complicity of the Massachusetts Court party. Thus they translated Parliament's acts into familiar terms: they blamed Thomas Hutchinson for writing the Stamp Act and the Court party for promoting it, and used the issue to unseat numerous Court party legislators in the election of 1766. They drummed Hutchinson out of the Council, using their newly won majority in the House, and thereafter enjoyed a command over Massachusetts political life that exceeded the bright days of the Pownall administration.[77]

By the end of the provincial period, then, Massachusetts politics had assumed a structure that imposed itself on the developing revolutionary movement. It was characterized, first, by a partisan division of the province's large and middle-sized towns along lines that corresponded to the extent of their economic and cultural diversity. The parties represented conflicting values and sometimes conflicting interests, but not in any simple farmer-merchant dichotomy. Secondly, partisanship was supported (not created) by royal governors whose patronage powers allied them with leading men in the province's commercial, administrative, and cultural centers. Thirdly, a very considerable number of small, mostly agricultural towns with no cultural or administrative roles, lay completely outside the party structure and played no part whatever in the early years of the Revolution, although, by the 1780s they were to become the most numerous group of towns involved in state politics.

77. Henry Bass to Samuel P. Savage, 19 December 1765, in "Samuel Phillips Savage Papers, 1703–1779," *MHS Proceedings* 44 (1911): 683–702; Edmund S. and Helen M. Morgan, *The Stamp Act Crisis* (Chapel Hill, N.C., 1953), pp. 121–22; Brennan, *Plural Office-Holding*, p. 78. Thirty-two legislators were named in *BG*, 31 March 1766, as plural office-holders and supporters of the Stamp Act, with the recommendation that electors reject them. Of the 32, 25 came from towns designated in Appendix A as Court party towns, four came from towns not clearly aligned, two came from Country party towns, and one from a new town not listed in the Appendix.

The emergence of these towns in the period after 1774 transformed the Revolution, as we shall see, and in so doing, they raised issues and shaped goals that fell outside the republican framework of the early Revolution, while they articulated thoughts that had remained inchoate among the urban crowd.

Until 1774, however, the Revolution in Massachusetts sprang from a partisan conflict, extending back into the provincial period, between towns that were at different stages of the modernization process. Neither "radical" nor "conservative" in any latter-day sense, the parties were divided in their response to an intensive process of growth and change. Court party towns were the more elitist, but also the more adapted to economic diversification and social pluralism, and to the competition and conflict engendered by them. The Country party towns, on the other hand, believed that their lost world could be regained, that society and its values could be reformed, and the modern world could be forced to conform to their traditional concepts of order.

# 3

## The Popular Party in Boston:
## An Uneasy Coalition

FOR THE leaders of the Popular party, the town of Boston presented the greatest challenge to, and the severest test of, their republican notion that a fragmented and diversified society could be reintegrated. It was the largest town in New England, the commercial and cosmopolitan center of the region, a major port in the British imperial system, and thus the most heterogeneous of New England towns. Boston was unique.

Yet it posed problems that seemed central to the task of creating a new consensus in Massachusetts. It had a large and self-conscious commercial community that (at least in the late provincial period) dominated local politics. It had as well an active urban working class, experienced in the ways of street politics and eager to play an expanded role in local, provincial, or even imperial affairs. Both had their leaders and both their own distinctive political styles. The problem for such nascent republicans as Samuel and John Adams, who were committed politically to neither group, was how to unite these sometimes disparate forces in a common endeavor, so that the republican ideals of unity and consensus might inform their methods as well as shape their goals. An examination of Popular party activity in Boston from 1769 to 1774 explains, at least in part, why the republican dream failed in Massachusetts, and how new parties could begin to take shape so quickly upon the decline of the old.

In the most general sense, republicans believed that the rapid change taking place in their society represented decay, and that it was the result of "luxury" and "avarice" among the people.[1] But more specifically, and

1. For a discussion of the fear of American corruption, see Gordon S. Wood, *The Creation of the American Republic, 1776–1787* (Chapel Hill, N.C., 1969), pp. 107–14.

with greater accuracy, they saw the rise of commerce and the spread of commercial values throughout society as a primary cause of changing behavior. They retained the traditional, Puritan suspicion of men who profited, sometimes usuriously, from trade.[2] And their suspicions were reinforced by their reading of *Cato*'s radical Whig assertion that "there is a sort of men found almost every where, who having got a set of gainful and favourite speculations, are always ready to spread and enforce them, and call their doing so *Public Spirit*."[3] *Cato* went further than his American readers were prepared to follow when he claimed that "a free people are kept so, by no other means, but an equal distribution of property,"[4] but they agreed with him that man's propensity to seek wealth stood in the way of the ideals of unity and cohesiveness in society and, if left unchecked, led directly to anarchy and tyranny.

It was in this republican sense that Popular party leaders gave an economic interpretation to the events of their time. They did not advocate economic leveling or class conflict, but they were convinced that commerce had fragmented their society into "private attachments" and "separate interests" and therefore that commerce and those involved in it must be the focus of their reformation efforts. "The spirit of commerce corrupts the morals of families," lamented John Adams at the height of the Revolution, and he called on every American "to root out his passions, prejudices, and attachments, and to get the better of his private interest." There was the belief that honest poverty promised the brightest hope for America. "For my own part," wrote Samuel Adams, "I have been wont to converse with poverty; and however disagreeable a companion she may be thought to be by the affluent and luxurious who never were acquainted with her, I can live happily with her the remainder of my days, if I can thereby contribute to the redemption of my Country."[5]

2. The acceptance of medieval views of usury in seventeenth-century Massachusetts is indicated by Bernard Bailyn in his introduction to "The Apologia of Robert Keayne," *CSM Publications* 42 (1964): 243–48. The changing position of the merchant in New England society is discussed in Bailyn, *The New England Merchants in the Seventeenth Century* (Cambridge, Mass., 1955), pp. 21–22, 40–44, 139, 189. See also Edmund Morgan's suggestive article on the persistence of Puritan values among revolutionaries: "The Puritan Ethic and the American Revolution," *WMQ*, 3d ser., 24 (1967): 3–43.

3. [John Trenchard and Thomas Gordon], *Cato's Letters*, 4 vols. (London, 1723–24), 1: 25, 11–12, 282.

4. Ibid., 3: 172; 1: 32, 11.

5. John Adams to Mercy Warren, Philadelphia, 16 April 1776, in Worthington Chauncey Ford, ed., *Warren-Adams Letters*, 2 vols. (Boston, 1917–25), 1: 222–23; Samuel Adams to William Checkley, Boston, 1 June 1774, in Harry A. Cushing, ed., *The Writings of Samuel Adams*, 4 vols. (New York, 1904–8), 3: 128.

To curb luxury and avarice, the Adamses believed, the men most infected by them must be educated to their public duty. Merchants must deny themselves their profits; they must be reintegrated into society; they must prove to the world that their love of liberty and virtue exceeded their love of gain.

Commercial boycotts against Great Britain thus became a favorite tactic of republican leaders, for they thrust merchants into the forefront of the revolutionary movement and forced them to put patriotism before profits. In fact, nonimportation agreements, as they were called, epitomize the dual nature of the Revolution in Massachusetts, since they combined in a single act the colonial rejection of Britain's right to tax them and the republican determination to reform their own society. To the merchants, however, most of whom shared the revolutionary abhorrence of British interference, the emphasis on nonimportation raised serious questions: were not merchants carrying more than their share of the burden of protest? were not their positions of importance in seacoast towns being threatened by demagogues and a new leveling spirit? did not the public good depend upon commerce and the maintenance of commercial ties with the mother country? These were questions which, in the asking, placed serious strains on the solidarity of the revolutionary movement. Increasing dissatisfaction among merchants in the late 1760s and early 1770s, together with the brilliant exploitation of that dissatisfaction by leaders of the Court party, made the Popular party in its last few years before Independence an uneasy coalition indeed.

The Court party, though considerably weakened in the aftermath of the Stamp Act, still sood as a competitor for the support of Boston's merchants and served as a constant reminder that the revolutionary party did not speak for all people in the province. When the legislature, under the direction of Popular leaders, prepared a circular letter urging all colonies to join in resisting the Townshend Revenue Acts, Court party adherents strongly objected, even though their objections were struck from the journals. When the British ministry ordered the letter rescinded, 17 Court party legislators were willing to comply.[6] Subsequently, when Boston called for a convention of towns to protest the arrival of British troops in the capital, numerous towns in Hampshire, Berkshire, and Essex counties, still attached to the Court party, refused to send delegates.[7] Thus the Court party, in addition to reluctant mer-

6. Merrill Jensen, *The Founding of a Nation: A History of the American Revolution, 1763–1776* (New York, 1968), pp. 249–50, 255–56, 265–71.

7. Richard D. Brown, "The Massachusetts Convention of Towns, 1768," *WMQ*, 3d ser., 26 (1969): 94–104.

chants, stood as a constant challenge to the republican wish to confront Great Britain with a commercial boycott. A relatively weak nonconsumption agreement was the best Popular leaders could muster in the first few months of the Townshend duties.

It took until August 1, 1768, for an operative nonimportation agreement to be drawn up in Boston, and another year of strong-arm methods to coerce holdouts into joining the plan. A committee of six merchants—each of them a staunch "Son of Liberty"—theoretically provided enforcement of the agreement, but in actual fact, street crowds played a major role. Governor Bernard, of course, believed that the merchants, left to their own devices, would never have instituted nonimportation as a means of combating parliamentary taxation.[8] A hard core of about 80 merchants, however, worked closely with Popular leaders, even though most of the others among Boston's 200-odd merchants had to be "persuaded" to cease importing prohibited goods. The plan called for a boycott of most goods, including the duties articles (lead, glass, painters' colors, and tea), from January 1, 1769, to January 1, 1770, and it was subscribed to in all of the coastal towns after similar popular pressures.[9]

Popular action did not go unchallenged, however. In Boston, a small group of determined Tory merchants, including the sons of Thomas Hutchinson, continued to import until they were publicly black-listed by "the well disposed" majority.[10] One of those black-listed was the editor of the *Boston Chronicle,* a dour Scot named John Mein, whose response was a skillful campaign through the pages of his newspaper to expose the contrived unanimity of the merchant community. To explode the fiction that nonimportation was working, he went to the customs officials, who quite willingly allowed him to copy from their records the list of articles that had been imported since January 1, and by whom. Then he simply published them in his paper. If they were correct, they demonstrated the duplicity of many subscribers, including some who

8. Leslie J. Thomas, "Partisan Politics in Massachusetts during Governor Bernard's Administration, 1760–1770" (Ph.D. Diss., Univ. of Wis., 1960), pp. 430–32, 747–58; Thomas Hutchinson to [Richard] Jackson, 23 March 1768, in Mass. Arch., 26: 296; Anne Rowe Cunningham, ed., *Letters and Diary of John Rowe* (Boston, 1903), p. 190; *BG,* 21 August 1769; Bernard to Shelburne, 21 March 1768, in Bernard Papers, 6: 291–92, quoted by Thomas, "Partisan Politics in Massachusetts," pp. 750–51. The merchants on the committee were Thomas Cushing, John Hancock, William Phillips, Edward Payne, John Rowe, and John Barrett.

9. Eighty-five merchants belonged to the Sons of Liberty in 1769. See *MHS Proceedings* 11 (1871): 140–42. Compare with the list of Boston merchants of the revolutionary period in Stephen Everett Patterson, "Boston Merchants and the American Revolution" (M.A. thesis, Univ. of Wis., 1961), Appendix, pp. 165–71.

10. *BC,* 17 August 1769; *BG,* 21 August 1769.

were well-known Sons of Liberty. Samuel Adams naturally responded with the charge that Mein had been made a "tool by the band of placemen and pensioners here," but Mein simply replied that nonimportation could be interpreted as a scheme of the big merchants, well stocked before the boycott began, to squeeze out their small competitors by cutting off their source of supply.[11]

Mein's charges caused great dissension in the ranks of the merchants, but in the final analysis, his campaign had the opposite effect from that intended. Mein himself was mobbed in the streets and so threatened that he fled from town for his life. Moreover, instead of destroying the nonimportation agreement, the campaign simply weakened the merchants' part in it and increased the activity of the crowd, who were determined to hold the merchants to their word. In October, under pressure, the merchants agreed that they would extend their boycott until all revenue duties (not just the Townshend duties) were removed, if New York and Philadelphia would agree to do likewise. When the latter refused to go this far, Popular leaders decided that Boston must continue the boycott into 1770, at least until the Townshend duties were removed.[12]

By December 1769, merchants were losing even the theoretical control they had exercised over the nonimportation movement. The merchants' committee of inspection, which in the summer of 1769 had consisted of six reputable merchants, met at the Coffee House in Boston on December 18 with 12 persons present. Among the new members were William Mollineux (considered a street leader), Isaac Smith, Samuel Dashwood, William Whitwell, and Jonathan Mason—some of whom were not merchants at all, while others were small traders of little consequence.[13]

Such increasing interference in merchant affairs was naturally resented. As one Bostonian wrote to his English correspondent, "By what I can learn, there is a greater opposition to [nonimportation] in Boston

11. *BC*, September–October 1769, passim. Adams wrote as "Populus" in *BG*, 28 August 1769; Cushing, ed., *Writings of Samuel Adams*, 1: 378–80. Mein's reply to Adams and to others was entitled "Catechism of the Well Disposed," *BC*, 13, 19, 26 October 1769.

12. Cunningham, ed., *Diary of John Rowe*, p. 194; "A Tory," *BEP*, 6 November 1769; *BC*, 9 November 1769; Thomas Hutchinson to Hillsborough, 11 November 1769, Sparks Mss., vol. 10, New England Papers, pp. 52–53, cited by Clifford K. Shipton, *Biographical Sketches of Those Who Attended Harvard College* [*Sibley's Harvard Graduates*], vols. 6–13 (Boston, 1942–65), 8: 183; Thomas, "Partisan Politics in Massachusetts," pp. 767–68.

13. Cunningham, ed., *Diary of John Rowe*, p. 195.

than there is in any of the provinces that have come into the agreement." Many of the merchants who had been forced to subscribe in 1768 now refused to agree to an extension of the agreement beyond the original deadline. Some of these men had already imported goods, although they had been forced to store them under the supervision of the merchants' committee. But, said Andrew Eliot, "When the first of January arrives, the owners will insist upon it, that the engagement is at an end—and seem determined to expose their commodities for sale. This will occasion warm debates and much altercation."[14]

His prediction was correct. When eight or nine merchants broke the agreement and began selling in January, Popular leaders took over completely. They began by throwing open the merchants' meetings to the entire populace, so that each was in "every way a town meeting except in the mode of calling it." This "Body," as it was called, met almost daily, and its committee, made up of hundreds of people, systematically visited each of the uncooperative merchants, forcing them to give up all goods imported contrary to the agreement. Lieutenant Governor Hutchinson, now acting governor since the departure of Bernard, found himself in the uncomfortable position of having to surrender the tea imported by his sons, while he reported to his superiors in Britain that there was nothing he could do to control the mobs.[15]

Only a crisis of the first order made possible the reassertion of royal authority. After days of crowd activity and frequent skirmishes with the British regulars stationed in Boston, the fatal clash of March 5 gave the Revolution its first "martyrs." The Boston Massacre might have sparked a major conflict had not cool heads prevailed on both sides.[16] As it was, it marked the beginning of a steady decline in revolutionary ardor; it drained off the energies of the Boston crowd, and made people in the rural areas wonder if perhaps urban crowds were not the primary

14. Andrew Eliot to Thomas Hollis, Boston, 25 December 1769, in "Letters from Andrew Eliot to Thomas Hollis," MHS Collections, 4th ser., 4 (1858): 446–47.

15. Hutchinson to Sir Francis Bernard, Boston, 17 January 1770, in Mass. Arch., 26: 434; Cunningham, ed., Diary of John Rowe, p. 196; Nathaniel Rogers to Hutchinson, Boston, 19 January 1770, in Mass. Arch., 25: 351; Shipton, Biographical Sketches, 8: 185; Thomas Hutchinson, The History of the Colony and Province of Massachusetts-Bay, ed. Lawrence Shaw Mayo, 3 vols. (Cambridge, Mass., 1936), 3: 192–93.

16. Hutchinson to ———, Boston, March 1770, in Mass. Arch., 26: 452; Hutchinson to [Hillsborough], March 1770, ibid., 25: 376–79; Cunningham, ed., Diary of John Rowe, pp. 197–98. The most recent account of the Boston Massacre is Hiller B. Zobel, The Boston Massacre (New York, 1970), which leans heavily towards the Tory view of events.

cause of much of the trouble with Britain and royal authority.[17] Hutchinson skillfully delayed the massacre trials until tempers had cooled, while during the summer of 1770 authoritative reports from England that the Massachusetts charter would be suspended confirmed many men in their moderate tendencies.[18] These factors, together with Parliament's decision to remove all of the Townshend duties except that on tea, prepared the way for the final breakdown of nonimportation.

New York merchants led the way by concluding nonimportation in July 1770, but such Popular leaders as Samuel Adams were determined that there must be no compromise with parliamentary taxation and were convinced that continuing provocations (the Crown ordered the seizure of Castle William in Boston harbor as a garrison headquarters) would hold Boston merchants to their agreement. But by September, large numbers of merchants were meeting almost daily apart from the "Body" and Popular leaders, and by mid-month, when the "Body" met for three days, the merchants felt ready to challenge Adams directly. As Hutchinson wrote: "There happened during this time to be a very grand meeting of merchants and tradesmen upon the subject of importation where Adams made an attempt to inflame them, declaring I had given up the castle and would give up the charter. But some of the merchants declared that was not the business of the meeting and repeatedly stopped him from going on. This my friends thought was a sort of trial of the strength of the faction and that this incendiary would not be able to accomplish his purposes."[19] Hutchinson's report proved correct. The meeting decided to invite Philadelphia merchants to a congress to discuss nonimportation, something Adams had opposed a few months before.

17. Joseph Hawley reflected this change in attitude towards Boston in a speech before the General Court in November. See Henry Young Brown to Hutchinson, Portsmouth, 28 November 1770, in Mass. Arch., 25: 453-54.

18. Hutchinson to Thomas Gage, Boston, 18 March, 13 April 1770, in "Correspondence . . . Relative to the Boston Massacre . . . ," AAS Proceedings, n. ser., 47 (1938): 287, 303; Thomas Pownall to the Committee of the Town of Boston, London, June 1770; Pownall to James Bowdoin, 14, 21 July 1770, in The Bowdoin and Temple Papers, MHS Collections, 6th ser., 9 (1897): 189-93, 197-98, 205-8.

19. By May, even "Sons of Liberty" were among the merchants defecting from the nonimportation movement. Cunningham, ed., Diary of John Rowe, pp. 201, 204-5; Hutchinson to ———, Boston, 26 July 1770, in Mass. Arch., 26: 523; Samuel Prince to ———, Boston, 26 July 1770, in MHS Miscellaneous Bound Papers, vol. 13 (1761-70). Both Hutchinson and Prince, writing separately, said that nine-tenths of the merchants wished to end nonimportation of all goods except tea. On events in September, see Cunningham, ed., Diary of John Rowe, p. 207; Hutchinson to Bernard, 15 September 1770, in Mass. Arch., 27: 1-3.

But when Philadelphia joined New York merchants in ending the boycott, Boston merchants simply pushed Adams aside. On October 17, 72 merchants met in the British Coffee House and voted to follow New York's and Philadelphia's example. Immediately preceding this meeting, one should note, several British men-of-war sailed into Boston harbor. John Rowe, former member of the merchants' committee of inspection, "inspected" the man-of-war *Rose* on October 9 and dined with Commodore Hood on the *Romney*. On October 12, the day after nonimportation officially ended, Commodore Hood and his lady dined at Rowe's home, with other British officials and Boston merchants present.[20]

By the end of 1770, revolutionary passion had pretty much abated and the Popular party in Boston itself stood in disarray. Moderate merchants dissociated themselves completely from the party, and though they were not ready to acquiesce in Parliament's claim of supremacy, neither were they prepared to accept the leadership and methods of Samuel Adams nor the interference of masses of the people in their affairs. To Thomas Hutchinson, the time seemed ripe for a new coalition of moderate merchants and old "friends of government," and the social life generated by the presence of the military provided him with the occasion. At a "very full assembly of gentlemen and ladies" held in January 1771, Hutchinson observed that "the civil and military were mingled together, commissioners of the customs and heads of the Sons of Liberty are subscribers upon the same paper." Hutchinson feared that he had assumed the government of Massachusetts "rather too late in life for the sake of a coalition," but he was determined "to make it last as long as I can."[21]

Thomas Hutchinson is the most underrated of the participants in the events of his time. The fact that he was on the losing side is, of course, largely responsible, but beyond that, he has been seen as an inflexible, obdurate, rather unimaginative colonial official, who failed to provide the leadership he might have for the disorganized American Tories.[22] What is too often overlooked is that he was caught between a British government with an almost unerring capacity for blunder in its dealings

20. Arthur Meier Schlesinger, *The Colonial Merchants and the American Revolution, 1763–1776* (New York, 1957), p. 233; Hutchinson to Thomas Whately, Boston, 3 October 1770, in Mass. Arch., 27: 12; Cunningham, ed., *Diary of John Rowe*, p. 208.

21. Hutchinson to Thomas Whately, Boston, 25 January 1771, in Mass. Arch., 27: 106–7.

22. See for example William H. Nelson, *The American Tory* (New York, 1961), pp. 22–39.

with Americans and, on the other side, an established opposition which, despite its fluctuating fortunes, controlled the Massachusetts legislature after 1766. Popular propagandists placed him with Julius Caesar, Judas Iscariot, and the Roman popes on the lowest level of hell, but the ferocity of their exaggeration is a measure of his stature in their eyes. John Adams denounced his politics long after most Americans had forgotten who Hutchinson was, but he believed that no American in the eighteenth century knew more about the subject of money than Hutchinson.[23]

Hutchinson came to the governorship of his native province in 1771 after a long career in which he had held almost every official post of importance, and his governorship, for all of the pressures on two sides, was in many ways a success. He failed in his attempt to fashion a new coalition in support of his administration, but his attempt made it impossible for the revolutionary leaders ever to regain the cohesiveness of the early and mid-1760s.

Hutchinson's goal, as Shirley's had been, was to win over key men from the ranks of the opposition party. At first, the prospect seemed bright. When Hutchinson's commission arrived in March 1771, a large meeting of Boston's merchants gathered at the British Coffee House, prepared a congratulatory message, and then marched, 106 strong, to present their address in person. Several members of the "Sons of Liberty," including John Rowe and John Erving, were among the group.[24] Soon afterwards, John Adams retired temporarily from Boston politics, leaving his seat in the legislature to James Otis, who seemed to have recovered from his mental illness. To everyone's surprise, however, Otis spoke in the legislature with great moderation and in support of the governor's right to call the General Court outside of Boston, until finally he slipped back into his "frenzy" and had to be carried away, bound.[25] But Hutchinson's most promising prospect was John Hancock.

The flirtation with Hancock began almost by accident. Hutchinson wanted a close supporter, Thomas Flucker, elected to the Council and

---

23. Adams referred to Hutchinson's leadership in bringing an end to paper money in Massachusetts in 1749. See Malcolm Freiberg, "Thomas Hutchinson and the Province Currency," *NEQ* 30 (1957): 190.

24. Cunningham, ed., *Diary of John Rowe*, p. 213; Mass. Arch., 25: 468. John Erving was a councilor who was probably the first prominent member of the Popular party to defect to Hutchinson. See Hutchinson to ———, Boston, 4 August 1770, ibid., 26: 530.

25. Hutchinson to ———, Boston, 24 May 1771; Hutchinson to ———, Boston, June 1771; Hutchinson to ———, Boston, 5 June 1771; Hutchinson to Francis Bernard, Boston, 3 December 1771, ibid., 27: 171–73, 178–79, 180–81, 260–61.

therefore bargained with Popular party members in the House to elect
him, in return for which he promised to withhold his veto of their choice
of John Hancock. The deal fell through when Flucker failed to be
elected, but soon after a number of men approached the governor with
the proposal that Hancock receive his support in future. They assured
Hutchinson that Hancock "wished to be separated from Mr. Adams, another representative of the town, an incendiary equal to any at present
in London, and, if I would admit him to the Council, they had no doubt
there would be an end to the influence he now has by means of his
property in the town of Boston." By December, the rift between Adams
and Hancock was in the open and "Hancock has declared he will never
again connect himself with Adams." By 1772, Hancock had ceased to
attend meetings of the Popular leaders, had chosen an envoy to deal
with Hutchinson, and had convinced Hutchinson that he would never
rejoin the Popular party. Hancock's "coming over," wrote Hutchinson
to Francis Bernard, "will be a great loss to them as they support themselves with his money." By April, Hancock and Adams were voting on
opposite sides in the legislature, and Hancock was a leading voice of
moderation. But the flirtation was not altogether in Hutchinson's control: he had found Hancock "pliable" and had "made great use of him,"
but when the chance came for Hutchinson to show his approval by accepting Hancock into the Council, Hancock declined the nomination.[26]

Hancock has always been something of an enigma, but his actions in
the early 1770s reveal a shrewdness that should not be underestimated.
Where Adams stuck with old methods and continued to hammer away
at old themes in his letters to the *Boston Gazette*, Hancock tacked with
the prevailing winds. In the legislative elections of 1772, Adams won
reelection as a Boston representative by a bare margin and ran 175 votes
behind the top three choices.[27] Hancock undoubtedly saw the prospect
of replacing Adams as a House leader, and hence his decision to pass up
the offer of a Council seat. In fact, with his close friend and confidant,
Thomas Cushing, another Boston merchant who was both moderately
wealthy and moderate in his politics, Hancock continued to deal with

26. Hutchinson to John Pownall, Boston, 30 May 1771; Hutchinson to Hillsborough, Boston, 4 June 1771; Hutchinson to ——, Boston, 5 June 1771;
Hutchinson to Gage, Boston, 1 December 1771; Hutchinson to ——, Boston,
24 January 1772; Hutchinson to Francis Bernard, Boston, 29 January 1772, ibid.,
pp. 174, 176–77, 180–81, 258, 284–85, 286–87; Hutchinson to James Gambier,
7 May 1772, quoted by William V. Wells, *The Life and Public Services of Samuel
Adams,* 3 vols. (Boston, 1866), 1: 467; Hutchinson to John Pownall, Boston, 5 June
1772, in Mass. Arch., 27: 342–43.
27. 18 *BTR*, p. 78.

Hutchinson, secretly arranging the procedure by which they would bring the General Court back to its traditional seat in Boston, while circumventing the uncompromising Adams.[28]

Hutchinson was not the author of trouble in the Popular party, but he was clearly the beneficiary. In January 1772, at the same time that Hancock was "coming over," another key member of the Popular party, Dr. Benjamin Church, became a secret "writer on the side of government." Church remained in the North End Caucus Club, that manipulator of Boston politics, where he had first-hand knowledge of the plans of Adams and his friends, but he provided Hutchinson and his successor, Thomas Gage, with invaluable information until his exposure as a spy in 1775.[29] Hancock and Church gave Hutchinson's administration its sunniest moments.

Samuel Adams, on the other hand, provided the roughest storms. Determined to stir his countrymen from their lethargy, he grasped at anything that might restore the enthusiasm and the unity of the revolutionary movement. When the British ministry decided, in 1772, to make the judges of the superior court independent of the legislature by paying their salaries, he and the other "liberty men" pushed in the Boston town meeting for a new assertion of American rights and the creation of a Committee of Correspondence that would coordinate the exchange of political sentiment among the Massachusetts towns. The plan succeeded in spreading revolutionary rhetoric among the people, and it prepared them for important leadership roles in the future. Furthermore, it provoked Hutchinson into making a highly ill-conceived speech to the legislature in support of parliamentary supremacy, thereby weakening his ties with Massachusetts moderates. A much-publicized exposure of a series of letters, written by Hutchinson privately to London merchant and parliamentarian Thomas Whately, further tarnished his image, and Hutchinson's effectiveness as governor diminished considerably in his final months in office.[30]

28. Hutchinson to John Pownall, 5 June 1772, in Mass. Arch., 27: 342–43. Hutchinson's discussion with Hancock and Cushing may have been the one he referred to in his conversation with George III on July 1, 1774. See Peter Orlando Hutchinson, ed., *The Diary and Letters of His Excellency Thomas Hutchinson,* 2 vols. (Boston, 1884–86), 1: 167.

29. Hutchinson to Francis Bernard, Boston, 29 January 1772, in Mass. Arch., 27: 286–87.

30. Hutchinson to Bernard, Boston, October 1772, ibid., pp. 391–92; "Valerius Poplicola," *BG,* 5 October 1772; 18 *BTR,* pp. 88–108; Thomas Young to Hugh Hughes, Boston, 21 December 1772, in MHS Miscellaneous Bound Papers, vol. 14 (1771–75); Hutchinson to Dartmouth, Boston, 20 December 1772; Hutchinson

But the agency of Hutchinson's undoing, and the catalyst that revived the revolutionary movement was the British government and its Tea Act. Popular leaders in Boston were slow to see the potential of the Tea Act as an issue to arouse the people, but when the Philadelphians took the lead, Boston quickly followed. The act, Popular leaders believed, was a trick to get Americans to pay the Townshend tax on tea since, by shipping its product directly to America, the East India Company would be able to undersell even smuggled tea. In Boston, the tea consignees were treated like the old stamp distributors or like black-listed merchants of 1769: the "Body" was revived, and its power was soon considerable.[31] Once again, merchants were expected to close ranks with their countrymen, but this time, they determined to resist.

The story of the Boston tea party is well known. Its impact on the fortunes of the Popular party is what must concern us, and that was shaped in part by the response of the British government. Parliament was practically unanimous in its approval of the Boston Port Act, passed on March 31, 1774, the first of the "coercive acts." The port of Boston would be closed to all inward traffic on June 1, to all outgoing traffic on June 15. The customs house would be moved to Marblehead and the capital to Salem. These conditions would continue until the destroyed tea had been paid for in full. In addition, Thomas Hutchinson was replaced by General Thomas Gage, commander of his Majesty's forces in North America, who would become governor and "captain general" of Massachusetts. The news reached Boston on May 10.[32]

Samuel Adams and other Popular leaders believed that a commercial boycott was the only answer. That, really, is what they wanted when the town of Boston met on May 13 and elected Adams moderator and then chairman of a committee to prepare a circular letter to the other colonies as well as to decide on a course of action "relative to the late edict of a British parliament." But Adams and his friends seriously hoped that the merchants would come into a nonimportation agreement themselves.

As an indicator of their wish to reintegrate the merchants with the

---

to ———, Boston, 7 January 1773; Hutchinson to Dartmouth, Boston, 7 January, 22 February 1773, in Mass. Arch., 27: 431, 438–39, 436–37, 451–52; John Andrews to William Barrell, Boston, 4 June 1773, in Andrews-Eliot Papers, MHS, p. 21. For a full discussion of these matters, with special emphasis on the formation of the Committee of Correspondence, see Richard D. Brown, *Revolutionary Politics in Massachusetts: The Boston Committee of Correspondence and the Towns, 1772–1774* (Cambridge, Mass., 1970), pp. 38–91, 143–48.

31. The best account of the events surrounding the Boston tea party is Benjamin Labaree, *The Boston Tea Party* (New York, 1964).

32. Ibid., pp. 183–89; Hutchinson, *History*, ed. Mayo, 3: 329.

revolutionary movement, they directed the choice of Adams's committee so that 6 of the 11 members were merchants, including John Rowe, the owner of one of the tea ships. More merchants were named to a committee to go to Salem and Marblehead (the two ports that would benefit from Boston's plight) to tell them of the town meeting's sentiments. The Committee of Correspondence was ordered to send letters throughout the colonies and to the other towns in the province. And then came the most important vote of all: "It is the opinion of this town that if the other colonies come into a joint resolution to stop all importations from Great Britain and exportations to Great Britain, and every part of the West Indies, till the act for blocking up this harbor be repealed, the same will prove the salvation of North America and her liberties." To continue importing, however, would lead to the triumph of oppression over freedom. Every gentleman who had correspondents in the other seaports was then asked to write to them, urging their "coming into the measures" of the town's vote.[33] But, significantly, the town did not actually vote to enter into a nonimportation agreement, and when Sam Adams's Committee of Correspondence later that day drew up a circular letter asking whether the Bostonians may not "rely on your suspending trade with Great Britain at least," it did so on its own account.[34] The letter went out to all of the colonies.

Sam Adams did not have to conduct a poll of Boston's merchants to see if they would support nonimportation, for the town was full of controversy and many merchants—so far were they from Adams's line of thought—were determined to pay for the tea. One of the Adams men, in fact, readily admitted that "the present dispute seems confined to these two sentiments: either to pay, or not to pay for the tea."[35] Merchants who had long supported royal authority jumped at the chance to urge their fellows to join with them in a plan to raise the necessary funds, and they imagined that their only opposition was from men in the lower classes. As one of them wrote, "the merchants who either will not or cannot make remittances, the smugglers, the mechanics, and those

33. 18 BTR, pp. 172–74. Sam Adams's assurance that the meeting would go as he and his friends planned, led him, on May 12, to write to Elbridge Gerry, informing him of the "results" of the meeting. He said that Oliver Wendell headed a committee to go to Marblehead and Salem, and the next day Wendell was elected, just as Adams had assumed he would be. Cushing, ed., *Writings of Samuel Adams*, 3: 105–6.

34. Boston Committee of Correspondence to Philadelphia Committee of Correspondence, 13 May 1774, in Cushing, ed., *Writings of Samuel Adams*, 3: 109–11; "Town of Boston to the Colonies," 13 May 1774, ibid., pp. 107–9.

35. *Amer. Arch.*, 4th ser., 1: 487–89.

who are fascinated with the extravagant notion of independency, all join to counteract the majority of the merchants, and the lovers of peace and good order."[36] Even John Rowe, who was sitting with the committee appointed to determine the town's response to the Port Act, believed that the wisest course of action would be to pay for the tea, while two other merchant members of the committee (Thomas Boylston and Nathaniel Appleton) avoided its meetings altogether.[37] By May 18, several of the merchants who were "for compromising matters" began circulating a subscription to pay for the tea. One of the first subscribers was George Erving, son of the councilor and former Son of Liberty John Erving, and he declared after signing "that if it should be promoted, he is ready to put down two thousand pounds sterling towards it, and will take it upon himself to wait on Governor Gage and know what his demands upon us are." Another merchant, John Amory, bravely got up at the town meeting on the same day and urged that Erving's example be followed. But his plea was "in general rejected," while clerk William Cooper made certain that no mention of the speech got into the minutes of the meeting.[38] Such were Sam Adams's problems.

But Adams was a master, and his handling of the town meeting of May 18 proved it. Naturally enough, the committee appointed at the previous meeting to prepare a circular letter and to consider what should be done, was asked to report. A spokesman replied orally that it had received several proposals, but that they were still under consideration. The town clerk was then directed to summon Thomas Cushing to read a written report of the activities of the committee. But Cushing appeared and said he had no such written report. When other prodding questions were asked about the contents of the circular letter, Sam Adams volunteered the information that the votes of the last town meeting had been included.[39] In short, direct questions received nothing but evasive answers and the reason for this is abundantly clear. The circular letter, already sent out to the other colonies, had not been written by the committee appointed for that purpose at all, but had been secretly prepared by the old Committee of Correspondence and immediately sent southward in the trusty hands of Paul Revere. The committee with the six merchant members so painstakingly chosen at the previous meeting, was before the end of this meeting being referred to as "the committee

36. Ibid., pp. 506–8.

37. Cunningham, ed., *Diary of John Rowe*, pp. 269–70, 278.

38. John Andrews to William Barrell, Boston, 18 May 1774, in Andrews-Eliot Papers, p. 32; 18 *BTR*, pp. 174–75.

39. 18 *BTR*, pp. 174–75.

to receive proposals and plans and to consult [on] ways and means for the relief of the poor." In short, the efforts of Sam Adams and clerk William Cooper (who jotted down only what he thought proper) completely twisted the original purpose of the committee, leaving Adams and his own Committee of Correspondence in unlimited control of the situation.[40]

Meanwhile, the tea subscription was still circulating about the town. Had the subscription attracted the signatures of both moderate merchants and the supporters of the governor's party, it would, in effect, have created that coalition that Thomas Hutchinson had made the goal of his administration. But the subscription did not, and its failure resulted largely because it was addressed to Hutchinson himself. Hutchinson would soon be departing for England and the promoters of the subscription hoped that since he "know[s] our condition and [has] at all times displayed the most benevolent disposition towards us," he would act as their unofficial agent "and make such favorable representations of our case as that we may hope to obtain speedy and effectual relief."[41] The promoters thus erred greatly, for though they could expect to get considerable sympathy from the moderate merchants, they could never get them to commit the political blunder of addressing Hutchinson and requesting that he be their agent. The extent of their blunder became obvious on May 24, when a large group of merchants met at the town house to discuss the subscription. There were very few present in sympathy with Hutchinson and his party, and no one would offer a copy of the subscription for the meeting's perusal. The meeting therefore concluded by protesting against the subscription, and "apprehending said address is intended to justify the administration of Mr. Hutchinson, when governor of this province, we hereby utterly disclaim said address, and disavow a measure so clandestinely conducted, and so injurious in its tendency."[42]

40. Sam Adams was covering up the fact that the Committee of Correspondence was implying in its letters that Boston had formally adopted nonimportation. The trouble began when Adams, confident of success in the town meeting, wrote to correspondents on the day before the meeting, telling them that the town had already adopted nonimportation. The meeting of May 13, as I have noted above, fell short of his expectations. See Adams to Gerry and Adams to Portsmouth [New Hampshire] Committee of Correspondence, Boston, 12 May 1774, in Cushing, ed., *Writings of Samuel Adams*, 3: 105–7. Also, compare with Labaree, *Boston Tea Party*, p. 220.

41. "Address of Merchants and Others of Boston to Governor Hutchinson," 28 May 1774, in *Amer. Arch.*, 4th ser., 1: 361–62.

42. Cunningham, ed, *Diary of John Rowe*, p. 271; "Protest of the Merchants and Traders of Boston," in *Amer. Arch.*, 4th ser., 1: 362–63.

When the address was finally presented to Hutchinson (now at Castle William) towards the end of May, it was, as the moderate merchants suspected, a justification of Hutchinson's administration, and it was signed only by merchants and others who had long supported the Court party. The address expressed "the entire satisfaction we feel at your wise, zealous, and faithful administration, during the few years you have presided at the head of this province." The addressers greatly deplored the calamities that would soon fall on Boston as a result of the operation of the Port Act. Without criticizing the justice of Parliament, "we could humbly wish that this act had been couched with less rigor" and that its execution might have been delayed to allow time to comply with its conditions. But the addressers acknowledged the justice of "making restitution for damage done to the property of the East India Company," and they promised to "bear our proportions of those damages whenever the sum and manner of laying it can be ascertained." Following the request that Hutchinson act as their agent, the names of 123 "merchants and others" appeared.[43] Among them were the Selkrigs, Winslows, Greenes, Theophilus Lillie, and Jonathan Simpson, who had been among the most recalcitrant adherents to nonimportation in 1769 and 1770. There, too, were the names of tea merchants Winslow and Clarke. The only important person in the list to have defected from the Sons of Liberty was John Erving; all the others had either been attached to Hutchinson politically and socially or had shown no political tendencies of note.

Within a very short time, broadsides appeared all over Boston listing the "addressers" and demonstrating that of the total of 123, only 27 were actually merchants, another 36 were traders (that is, retailers rather than wholesalers), and the other 60 were not directly connected with trade. The broadside, without doubt, was the product of the Popular party; in fact, the members of the Committee of Correspondence were later sworn to complete secrecy not to reveal who had played a role in "characterizing the addressers to Governor Hutchinson."[44] As part of

---

43. "Address of Merchants and Others of Boston to Governor Hutchinson," 28 May 1774, in *Amer. Arch.*, 4th ser., 1: 361–62. James H. Stark gives the date of the address as May 30, 1774, in *The Loyalists of Massachusetts* (Boston, 1907), pp. 123–25.

44. Ten men classified as "factors" could also be considered as merchants, which would bring the total to 37. The broadside appears in *MHS Proceedings* 11 (1871): 392–94. The Committee of Correspondence action is dated July 5, 1770, and is recorded in BCC Letters and Minutes, George Bancroft Collection, New York Public Library (microfilm copy courtesy of Merrill Jensen, Univ. of Wisconsin), p. 770.

the Popular party's protest against the addressers, the broadside served an important function: it showed that Boston's merchant class, as a unit, had not defected to Hutchinson. And there certainly was considerable justice in the claim, for there were over 200 importing-exporting merchants in Boston at the time, of whom the 27 addressers were but a fraction. The point is important, for, after Independence, very few Boston merchants other than the 27 addressers were considered Tories.[45]

Sam Adams, however, was less interested in the doings of "the tools of Hutchinson" than he was in pushing the rest of the merchants into a nonimportation agreement. On May 21, his Committee of Correspondence adopted nonimportation as its policy, and it determined to get the bulk of the merchant class to agree.[46] But the merchants were just as determined to avoid it and when, on May 30, the town met once again, 200 to 300 merchants and traders attended to speak and vote against it. Even some of Hutchinson's addressers appeared, not only to speak against nonimportation but to continue their effort to get payment for the tea. But, as the provincial treasurer Harrison Gray later reported, "the principal heads of the opposition to government" were standing at the doors to greet the merchants as they entered, telling them "that now was the time to save our country. That if they gave their voice in favor of paying for the tea, we should be undone, and the chains of slavery riveted upon us! which so terrified many honest, well meaning persons, that they thought it prudent not to act at all in the affair."[47]

Before the meeting had actually accomplished anything, someone moved that it be adjourned to June 17. But Sam Adams had come to get importation stopped and he would not be put off. If the merchants would not enter into a nonimportation agreement, the people themselves must simply determine to stop buying and consuming British goods. The committee "to receive proposals and consider ways and means" was thereupon directed to prepare a paper "to be carried to each family in the town" for their signature and their promise "that they will purchase nothing of, but totally desert those who shall counterwork the salutary measures of the town." And while the merchants looked on helplessly,

45. The question as to how many of Boston's merchants became Loyalists has been a subject of controversy. But the notion that most of them did so was corrected by Robert A. East, *Business Enterprise in the American Revolutionary Era* (New York, 1938), pp. 219–20.

46. Schlesinger, *Colonial Merchants*, p. 315 and n; BCC Letters and Minutes, p. 759.

47. H. Gray, "A Few Remarks upon Some of the Votes and Resolutions of the Continental Congress . . ." (Boston, 1775), pp. 6–7, quoted by Schlesinger, *Colonial Merchants*, p. 316.

the Adams-controlled meeting directed the Committee of Correspondence to communicate to the other towns in the province its decision to form the nonconsumption agreement.[48]

Adams and his friends were disgusted with the merchants who, as Boston clergyman Charles Chauncy said, "are so mercenary as to find within themselves a readiness to become slaves themselves, as well as to be accessory to the slavery of others." But the merchants could be got around, thought Chauncy. "Our dependence, under God, is upon the landed interest, upon our freeholders and yeomanry. By not buying of the merchants what they may as well do without, they may keep in their own pockets two or three millions sterling a year, which would otherwise be exported to Great Britain." Surely, thought Chauncy, the "barbarous Port Act" would move the farmers to agree to nonconsumption.[49]

Such, at least, was the hope of Sam Adams and his Committee of Correspondence when in early June it drew up what it called a "Solemn League and Covenant," an agreement to cease the importation and consumption of all British and West Indian goods, and sent it out to all the towns in Massachusetts. And though the Covenant was clearly the work of the Adams faction alone, the Committee of Correspondence was soon declaring that "this effectual plan has been originated and been thus carried through by the two venerable orders of men styled mechanics and husbandmen, the strength of every community."[50]

The merchants, however, were not idle. On June 2, both moderates and "friends of government" met at the west side of the court house and while they debated and discussed what should be done, a messenger broke into their midst. A Captain Williamson had just arrived at Marblehead from Bristol with news of "another act of parliament for the better regulating the province of the Massachusetts Bay." The act, by destroying the old elected Council and replacing it with a royally appointed one, and by prohibiting more than one town meeting a year, struck, as the merchants realized, at "the very charter granted to this province by King William and Queen Mary."[51] What could they do? The horror of

48. 18 BTR, pp. 175–76.

49. Chauncy to Richard Price, Boston, 30 May 1774, in "The Price Letters," MHS Proceedings, 2d ser., 18 (1903): 266–68.

50. A subcommittee was appointed on June 3 to draw up the Solemn League. BCC Letters and Minutes, pp. 763–64. See also Schlesinger, Colonial Merchants, p. 319n. The Solemn League and Covenant appears in Amer. Arch., 4th scr., 1: 397–98. For a frank admission that the Solemn League was created after the failure to get Boston merchants to act, see BCC to Westborough, 24 June 1774, BCC Letters and Minutes, pp. 822–23.

51. Cunningham, ed., Diary of John Rowe, pp. 273–74; The Massachusetts Gov-

impending disaster could not be avoided by a nonimportation agreement which, it was now clear, would not attract support in Philadelphia
and New York. The only choice remaining had to be taken, and the
merchants resolved to take it. "The trading part promised themselves a
general compliance [by] which the tenor of the act [i.e., the Port Act]
would have been readily come into, i.e., making compensation for the
tea."[52] Tories and moderates, so it seemed, had united.

But would it last? Within days, the town was in an uproar when the
news leaked out about the secretly devised Solemn League and Covenant. Some moderate merchants were livid with rage. John Andrews, for
instance, who had opposed Hutchinson most consistently, now lashed
out at the Adams group. "Our committee of correspondence, not content
with the calamities already come upon us, have issued out letters to
every town in the province (without consulting the town in regard to
the expediency of such a measure) accompanied with a Solemn League
and Covenant so styled." To Andrews, the Committee of Correspondence
was preventing unity, not promoting it. "Animosities are higher than
ever, each party charging the other as bringing ruin upon their country—
that unless some expediency is adopted to get the port open, by paying
for the tea, (which seems to be the only one), am afraid we shall experience the worst of evils, a civil war, which God avert!" The merchants
were now ready to pay for the tea, he wrote, "but instead of that, those
who have governed the town for years past, and were in a great measure
the authors of all our evils, by their injudicious conduct, are grown more
obstinate than ever, and seem determined to bring total destruction
upon us, which may be sufficiently evinced by all their conduct." It
was bad enough, thought Andrews, to have one's port closed up, but
now the Solemn League would "stop the little inland trade we expected."
Andrews was determined to hold out against the pressures of the Adams
faction, and many other moderate merchants were prepared to stand
with him.[53] But agonizing indecision haunted many counting-houses.

Boston presented a sorry sight when the merchants met again, on
June 15, with the retail traders. The wharves stood deserted, "not one
topsail merchantman to be seen"; out in the harbor, the big troop trans-
ports and men-of-war rode quietly at anchor, while on Boston Common
the tents of His Majesty's Fourth and Forty-Third Regiments had just

---

ernment Act, 20 May 1774, in Merrill Jensen, ed., *American Colonial Documents
to 1776*, vol. 9, *English Historical Documents* (New York, 1955), pp. 781–83.
  52. John Andrews to William Barrell, Boston, 12 June 1774, in Andrews-Eliot
papers, p. 33.
  53. Ibid.

been pitched beside those of two other regiments to blot out the green.[54] With four regiments now in town, the threat of the crowd must have seemed slim, but the merchants who were determined to pay for the tea could take small comfort in this. The obstacles to their success seemed overwhelming.

Towards the end of May, for example, five of them privately had visited Governor Gage to find out the value of tea destroyed and to whom they might apply to make payment. Gage, however, knowing that they were not responsible for the tea's destruction refused to give them any information and replied that they would "not be able to know anything with certainty, till either this town, as a town, or the General Court apply to him." Furthermore, when 127 "merchants and others" addressed Gage on June 8, offering, as they had to Hutchinson, to assume their share of the damages, Gage replied that he had no discretionary power to deal with the situation. He simply expressed the hope that "those in whose hands power is vested" would speedily determine upon a method for indemnifying the East India Company. But now, at the meeting on June 15, new opposition to the merchants' paying for the tea was expressed, in all probability by the small traders present, many of whom were friends of Sam Adams. In the end, as John Rowe jotted in his diary, the meeting "did nothing, being much divided in sentiment."[55]

Meanwhile, the Boston newspapers began carrying letters both for and against the Solemn League. For the merchants, the *Massachusetts Gazette and Post-Boy* spoke out against nonimportation as a measure that would ruin two-thirds of the traders in the seaports.[56] But Edes's and Gill's *Boston Gazette,* as faithful as ever to the Adams faction, warned that people in "divers parts of the country," "having become quite impatient by not hearing a non-importation agreement has yet been come into by the merchants, are now taking the good work into their own hands."[57] Criticism began to be voiced, too, about the activities of the Committee of Correspondence, but when the town met once

54. Cunningham, ed., *Diary of John Rowe,* p. 275; Andrews to Barrell, 12 June 1774, in Andrews-Eliot Papers, p. 33.

55. "Extract of a letter received in Philadelphia," Boston, 2 June 1774, in *Amer. Arch.,* 4th ser., 1: 380; "Address of Merchants and Others of the Town of Boston, to Governor Gage," 8 June 1774; Gage's answer to address of merchants, Salem, 8 June 1774, ibid., p. 399; Cunningham, ed., *Diary of John Rowe,* p. 275. Similar divisions appeared among Marblehead and Salem merchants as well. See *Amer. Arch.,* 4th ser., 1: 358, 391, 401–2, 424–25.

56. "Zach Freeman," *Massachusetts Gazette and Post-Boy* (Boston), 18 July 1774.

57. *BG,* 13 June 1774.

again on June 17, the Adams faction maneuvered events to attempt to cover up the fact that the Committee had originated the League. Though Sam Adams himself was attending the General Court in Salem, John Adams took the chair, and Adams men secured a vote empowering the Committee of Correspondence to write to all the colonies, informing them "that our brethren the landed interest of the province, with an unexampled spirit and unanimity, are entering into a non-consumption agreement." Then, when the meeting resumed in the afternoon, it voted (William Cooper wrote "unanimously") that the thanks of the town be given the Committee of Correspondence for "their faithfulness in the discharge of their trust, and that they be desired to continue their vigilance and activity in that service."[58] But Bostonians were far from unanimous and there were many who agreed with one writer's charges that the committee was illegal, that it had no one's permission to create a Solemn League, and that in so doing it was as tyrannical as it imagined Parliament to be.[59]

The great bulk of the merchants, whether of moderate or Tory persuasion, thereupon determined that they must intervene to bring a halt to the Solemn League. For many, this meant that the Committee of Correspondence must be destroyed, while for others, less drastic measures could be taken. But both groups agreed that the Adams faction must be faced in the town meeting, and when it assembled in Faneuil Hall on June 27, there were probably more merchants present than there had been for years. But, of course, the mechanics and tradesmen, whose participation Sam Adams refused to reject, were also there, swelling the crowd to such an extent that the meeting had to reassemble at the Old South meetinghouse.

The barrage against the Committee of Correspondence began immediately, and it was ordered to read to the meeting all letters it had sent to other towns, together with their replies. A simmering rage must have grown among the addressers of Hutchinson as they heard themselves maligned in letters to New York and Philadelphia. Then the town requested that the Solemn League be read along with letters that accompanied it. Before these letters were fully read, one angry "friend of government" arose and moved that the Committee of Correspondence be censured and dissolved. Some of the moderate merchants were surprised. "For my own part," wrote John Andrews, "I did not expect the vote would have been put as it was, i.e., to censure and dismiss the

58. "P.R.," *Massachusetts Gazette*, 13 June 1774; 18 *BTR*, pp. 176–77; Cunningham, ed., *Diary of John Rowe*, pp. 275–76.
59. "Y.Z.," *Massachusetts Gazette*, 27 June 1774.

committee, but rather expected it would tend only to order them to suspend the covenant till the Congress should meet." But, he went on, the letters to New York and Philadelphia had so angered the addressers "that nothing less than the committee's being annihilated would satisfy them."[60]

The impetuosity of the addressers may have lost them some support, but not much. The moderate Samuel Eliot jumped to his feet and delivered a long and vigorous speech "in so masterly a style and manner as to gain the plaudit of perhaps the largest assembly ever convened here, by an almost universal clap." Eliot reasoned with the crowd, explaining that he would receive a shipment of goods from England because goods were also being shipped to New York, Philadelphia, and Rhode Island. The other ports would continue to import, and Boston could not be expected to stand alone. In attacking the Solemn League and the Committee of Correspondence, Eliot was joined by Treasurer Harrison Gray and merchants Thomas Gray, Samuel Barrett, John Amory, Edward Payne, Francis Greene, and Ezekiel Goldthwait.

But they did not go unanswered. Moderator Samuel Adams relinquished the chair so that he could defend the Committee of Correspondence and he was joined in the rebuttal by Dr. Joseph Warren, William Mollineux, Josiah Quincy, Jr., Dr. Thomas Young, and Benjamin Kent— the principal members, in short, of the North End Caucus Club. It grew dark, but the debate showed no signs of ending so the meeting adjourned until the morning of the next day. The debate was just as heated when it resumed, and such merchants as John Rowe were convinced that they had put the Committee in the wrong. But when the vote on the censure motion came, the opponents of the Committee were defeated by a majority of four to one. Then, as if to rub salt in an open wound, the Adams faction succeeded in getting a vote expressing the town's complete satisfaction with "the upright intentions" and the "zeal" of the Committee, and asking it to "persevere with their usual activity and firmness." The defeated merchants filed out grim-faced and saddened. "This affair will cause much evil one against the other," wrote John Rowe. "I wish for peace in this town; I fear the consequences."[61]

Even after the town meeting, the Committee of Correspondence maintained the fiction that the Solemn League and Covenant "originated altogether from the country without any of their advice or interposi-

60. Cunningham, ed., *Diary of John Rowe*, p. 276; 18 *BTR*, pp. 177–78; John Andrews to William Barrell, Boston, 22 July 1774, in Andrews-Eliot Papers, p. 34.
61. Andrews to Barrell, 24 July 1774, in Andrews-Eliot Papers, p. 34; 18 *BTR*, p. 178; *Amer. Arch.*, 4th ser., 1: 489; Cunningham, ed., *Diary of John Rowe*, p. 276.

tion."[62] But many merchants, determined at least to end this falsehood, willingly signed one or the other of two protests against the Committee and the League that circulated towards the end of June. One hundred and twenty-nine men protested that the Solemn League would ruin many merchants and shopkeepers by ending trade with Spain and Portugal as well as with Great Britain, and that shipbuilders would suffer as well. The Committee of Correspondence therefore had simply increased the difficulties of Americans rather than lessened them, and in so doing it had abused the characters of all those who had disagreed with it. They protested, likewise, against the proceedings of the town "so far as they have adopted the illegal proceedings of the said committee." John Andrews was one of eight merchants who signed a second protest, so that they might express themselves in slightly different terms.[63]

Had the merchants been satisfied with their protests, they might have accomplished the modest ends they sought and thereby exposed the Committee. But within days, the "high friends to government" were spreading the story that the principal leaders of the people would soon be arrested and sent to England.[64] And then some of them convinced Governor Gage to make the stupidest blunder of all. On June 29, he issued a proclamation forbidding any person in the province to sign the Solemn League or to enter into "such unlawful, hostile and traitorous combinations," and he ordered magistrates and other officers to arrest any person who signed or offered such a covenant to be signed by others.[65] The Adams faction could have asked for nothing more perfect to popularize the idea of nonconsumption.[66]

---

62. Andrews to Barrell, 22 July 1774, in Andrews-Eliot Papers, p. 34; "Candidus" [Samuel Adams], BG, 27 June 1774.

63. "Protest Against the Proceedings of the Town Meeting in Boston on the 27th of June 1774," Boston, 29 June 1774, in *Amer. Arch.*, 4th ser., 1: 490–91; John Andrews to William Barrell, Boston, 22 July 1774, in Andrews-Eliot Papers, p. 34; *BEP*, 4 July 1774.

64. Andrews to Barrell, 22 July 1774, in Andrews-Eliot Papers, p. 34.

65. "A Proclamation for Discouraging Certain Illegal Combinations," Salem, 29 June 1774, in *Amer. Arch.*, 4th ser., 1: 491–92.

66. For a discussion of the reaction of Massachusetts towns to the Solemn League and Covenant, see Brown, *Revolutionary Politics*, pp. 200–209. Brown believes that although at least half of the towns responding to Boston's appeal "endorsed" the idea of nonconsumption, only seven actually entered the Solemn League (pp. 200–201). Arthur M. Schlesinger, however, suggests that most towns found the wording of the Worcester covenant more satisfactory, and so followed it rather than Boston's covenant. *Colonial Merchants*, p. 323. In any event, it would seem that nonconsumption was widely accepted in principle, whether or not it was adopted in "covenant" form.

The struggle between Sam Adams and the merchants in Boston was not the only challenge Adams had to face at this time, for New York and Philadelphia also resisted Adams's nonimportation proposals. Adams and his friends had determined by the spring of 1774 that the Tea Act and the ensuing events should bring about not just a union within Massachusetts but a united protest of all the colonies. Thus, after several meetings in early May involving the Committees of Correspondence of the towns surrounding Boston, letters went out to New York and Philadelphia proposing collective action in the form of a suspension of trade with Britain. The New York Committee agreed that unity was desirable, but it sidestepped a trade stoppage by proposing "a Congress of Deputies from the colonies in general," and the Philadelphians grasped at the New York suggestion as a means to avoid any disruption in trade.[67] Faced with such widespread opposition to his kind of "union," Adams had to change his tactics, and he did so with considerable success in the new session of the legislature.

The General Court met at Salem in late May, but its removal from Boston gave the prerogative no advantage. Using a committee which met in secret both from the governor and from Tory members in the House, Samuel Adams and his friends completely arranged the plans for Massachusetts to join with other colonies in a Continental Congress and then got the plans accepted before the governor could dissolve them. In the dying moments of charter government the Popular party gained the legislature's support of nonconsumption, while Governor Gage's agent, Secretary Flucker, read the terse proclamation of dissolution outside the chamber's locked doors. As the patriots within smiled their smiles of satisfaction, the proclamation's final, and rather fitting prayer, rang through the halls: "God Save the King!"[68]

The Tea Act had thus supplied republicans with the most perfect issue imaginable for advancing their political plans and for arousing the people to a sense of their rights. "The ministry," Sam Adams had written to James Warren in December 1773, "could not have devised a more effectual measure to unite the colonies."[69] As the people began forming

67. Samuel Adams to James Warren, 31 March 1774, in Cushing, ed., *Writings of Samuel Adams*, 3: 92–94; BCC Letters and Minutes, pp. 753–59, 871–74.

68. *House Journals*, 25 May–17 June 1774; *Amer. Arch.*, 4th ser., 1: 421–22; *BG*, 20 June 1774. See also the fascinating account of how Adams and his friends outfoxed Daniel Leonard, the only Tory member of the secret committee. The account was written by Robert Treat Paine and is in the Robert Treat Paine Papers, MHS, Box 1766–1776.

69. Adams to Warren, Boston, 28 December 1773, in Ford, ed., *Warren-Adams Letters*, 1: 19–20.

their Committees of Correspondence, Adams imagined that his long-sought union was coming about, and by April of 1774, he was writing, "The body of the people are now in council. Their opposition grows into a system. They are united and resolute."[70]

But were they? The events of May and June show clearly that they were not. Try as he might, Adams could not regain the support of the bulk of the merchant community, which he had alienated by 1770. And throughout the tea crisis, John Hancock trimmed between moderate merchants and an inflamed populace, but always dissociated from Adams.[71] If any real "union" was developing in Massachusetts, it was not a union of all classes, but a union of mechanics and husbandmen, of town workers and farmers, who, moved by Sam Adams's Solemn League and Covenant, were beginning to organize, not just against Parliament's coercive acts, but against their fellow countrymen, the merchants. Far from being united, the people were, as Ann Hulton observed, "divided into several parties, at variance, and quarreling with each other. Some appear desponding, others full of rage. The people of property, of best sense and characters, feel the tyranny of the leaders, and foresee[ing] the consequences of their proceedings, would gladly extricate themselves from the difficulties and distress they are involved in by making their peace with Great Britain, and speedily submitting to the conditions and penalties required."[72]

Did this then mean that the merchants had defected, that they were willing to give up the struggle for American rights? It meant nothing of the kind. "We don't mean to oppose any general measure that may be adopted by the Congress," wrote John Andrews after the showdown with Adams in the town meeting, "but are as well disposed in the cause of freedom as any of our opponents and would equally detest and oppose tyranny exercised either in England or America."[73] Andrews' remarks were typical of the sentiments of moderate merchants and the very fact that some, such as John Rowe, continued to hold positions in the town meeting, sitting on committees with Adams men, shows that the moderate merchants were neither ready to defect nor willing to give up the

70. Adams to Arthur Lee, Boston, 4 April 1774, in *Amer. Arch.*, 4th ser., 1: 239.

71. For evidence of the open hostility between Hancock and Adams, see the account of the Boston town meeting of November 5, 1773, in 18 *BTR*, p. 146. Hancock's continuing role as a Popular leader, however, is discussed by Hutchinson in a letter to an unnamed correspondent, Boston, 3 December 1773, in Mass. Arch., 27: 581–82.

72. Ann Hulton to ——, Boston, 8 July 1774, in *Letters of a Loyalist Lady* (Cambridge, Mass., 1927), p. 73.

73. Andrews to William Barrell, Boston, 22 July 1774, in Andrews-Eliot Papers, p. 34.

struggle for American rights. But they differed from Adams markedly
as to the means by which the struggle should be carried on. They
opposed the Solemn League because they believed, as Ann Hulton did,
that it was a plan "in opposition to the merchants" and, if it succeeded,
"must be attended with the ruin of most of 'em here [in Boston]."[74]
They opposed Adams, too, because of his acceptance of the "democracy,"
that is, his belief that the urban crowd must be included in his republican consensus. Also, clearly, they stood opposed to any idea of independence or separation from Great Britain, upon which their trade and
livelihood so greatly depended.

But it would be a mistake to think that Sam Adams alone represented
the Popular party in Boston and that his ideas prevailed throughout it.
The opinions of the moderate merchants were, after all, well represented
in the top ranks of Popular party leadership. John Hancock, Thomas
Cushing, John Rowe, Samuel Barrett, and Edward Payne were some of
the more prominent merchants who continued to play important roles
in the revolutionary movement, but apart from Samuel Adams and his
men. Thomas Hutchinson recognized the cleavage in the Popular party
and, although his exploitation of it was successful only in the short run,
he took some satisfaction in the leaders' failure to span the breach. "The
conductors of the people are divided in sentiment," wrote Hutchinson
in the fall of 1773, "some of them professing that they only aim to remove
the innovations since the date of the Stamp Act . . . and though they
don't think parliament has a just authority, yet they are willing to acquiesce, seeing it had been so long submitted to. Others declare they will
be altogether independent." Among the moderates, Hutchinson included
Thomas Cushing, speaker of the House, a clergyman from Boston "who
has such influence in our political measures" (probably Dr. Samuel
Cooper), and "some of the Council who have most influence there"[75]
(which would include James Bowdoin).

In his assessment, Hutchinson was perceptive. Thomas Cushing wrote
to Arthur Lee at about the same time, expressing his hope that nothing
would happen to cause "a rupture fatal to both countries." If Parliament
would let the issue of its supremacy "fall asleep" and give up the attempt
to raise a revenue in America, "I should think Great Britain would regain the affections of the people in America, retrieve her commerce, and
recall that confidence in her wisdom and justice, which is so necessary
for the mutual interest of both countries."[76] Cushing's views were typical

74. Ann Hulton to ———, Boston, 8 July 1774, in *Letters*, p. 74.
75. Hutchinson to Lord Dartmouth, Boston, 9 October 1773, in Mass. Arch., 27:
549–51.
76. Cushing to Lee, Boston, September and October 1773, in "Letters of Thomas

of the moderate merchants of Boston: they rejected parliamentary supremacy, but they wanted an end to the agitation of the issue by both sides in order to preserve the empire and their favorable position in Massachusetts society. Cushing, however, as Hutchinson noted, was representative of only one wing of the Popular party.

The other wing—"republicans" would be the best label, though Hutchinson used none—had "for their head one of the members of Boston who was the first person that openly and in any public assembly declared for a total independence and who from a natural obstinacy of temper and from many years practice in politics is perhaps as well qualified to excite the people to any extravagance in theory or practice as any person in America." Hutchinson, of course, referred to Sam Adams and, the political prejudice stripped away, there can be no doubt the governor was paying Adams the supreme compliment. Adams was a genius. Without accepting the view of Hutchinson and other Tories that Adams was a puppeteer and the crowd his puppet, one is obliged to recognize Adams's talent for understanding crowd psychology, and his remarkable ability to shape the crowd's purpose to his own.

Adams never committed to writing his ideas on Independence, and we have only Hutchinson's word for it that he actually called for Independence in town meetings. But there can be no doubt, regardless of what he said, that his actions seemed to point in that direction. He had risen to importance only in the last seven years, said Hutchinson, but his influence "has been gradually increasing until he has obtained such an ascendancy as to direct the t[own] of B[oston] and the H[ouse] of R[epresentatives] and consequently the C[ouncil] just as he pleases." His one principle, said Hutchinson (thinking it a bad one), was "that in political matters the public good is above all other considerations." Such a principle had led Adams to abandon every rule of morality in his political conduct, the governor thought. He has always been opposed to "conciliating measures" whether advanced in the councils of the party or in the House of Representatives. "But his chief dependency is upon a Boston town meeting where he originates his measures, which are followed by the rest of the towns and of course are adopted or justified by the assembly." Adams, concluded Hutchinson (again complimenting him), could never be bought off with an appointment to some public position for he would simply use it to "increase his abilities if not his disposition to do mischief."[77]

Thus, the goal to reform society and to unify the people socially and

Cushing from 1767 to 1775," *MHS Collections*, 4th ser., 4 (1858): 360, 363.

77. Hutchinson to Dartmouth, Boston, 9 October 1773, in Mass. Arch., 27: 549–51.

politically fell short of accomplishment even within the revolutionary party itself. By the spring of 1774, moreover, the patriot leaders were forced to face the reality of their own and the people's disunity. Where the desire to destroy avarice and luxury had led them to seek out the merchants and to cast them in leading roles in the struggle against "tyranny," the experience of May and June 1774 convinced the Adams faction, at least, that the "virtue" that would save American rights must be found elsewhere. "The trade will forever be divided when a sacrifice of their interest is called for," wrote Samuel Adams. Is it not therefore necessary, he asked, to suspend trade with Great Britain, and "let the yeomanry (whose virtue must finally save this country) resolve to desert those altogether who will not come into the measure?" And again: "Let the yeomanry of the continent, who only, under God, must finally save this country, break off all commercial connection whatever with those who will not come into it [i.e., a commercial boycott]."[78] This change in attitude had a profound impact on the Revolution in Massachusetts, for in calling on the "yeomanry" to save American liberties, Adams and his friends left the clear impression that merchants could not be entrusted with the task. And by so doing, they not only threw the ball to the rural wing of their party, but also encouraged the political awakening of dozens of small farming communities that had never before played an active role in provincial politics.

78. Adams to Charles Thomson, Boston, 30 May 1774; Adams to Silas Deane, Boston, 31 May 1774, in Cushing, ed., *Writings of Samuel Adams*, 3: 123, 125–27.

# 4

---

# The Backcountry Awakens, 1774-1775

QUITE APART from the revolutionary leadership, the Massachusetts people themselves played a significant role in shaping the Revolution, sometimes leaping ideologically far ahead of the leaders, sometimes dividing bitterly among themselves, and sometimes even defying the leadership and setting goals many leaders considered of dubious merit. The leaders, in other words, were unable to establish a single direction for the Revolution, but were forced constantly to cope with pressures of an active and seldom united population. As a result, their success as leaders was in many ways dependent on their flexibility and endurance, on their ability to follow in order to lead; consequently the direction of the Revolution in Massachusetts is best described as the vector among several forces rather than the result of any single force.[1] The followers or "the people" merit attention as one of those forces.

Still, writing the history of the common man is a difficult task. In Boston, as has been seen, the crowd played a significant role in shaping the Revolution, but it was never able to fasten its control on government nor to express through the town meetings ideas which diverged in any way from those of the elite. In the countryside, however, there were some towns where popular forces took control. Their instructions to representatives, votes in town meetings, and reports of mass gatherings,

1. My interpretation of the role of the Massachusetts people, and of the relationship between leaders and people, differs markedly from the view presented in Oscar and Mary F. Handlin, "Radicals and Conservatives in Massachusetts after Independence,"*NEQ* 17 (1944): 343–55. The Handlins tend to equate consistency of leadership with unanimity among the people, and to assume that leaders and people (Tories excepted) spoke with the same voice. Both this and subsequent chapters demonstrate, I believe, the falsity of these notions.

coupled with those actions that invariably speak louder than words anyway, reveal the emergence in 1774 of a predominantly rural, popular wing of the Revolution, independent of the old leadership, determined to direct the Revolution into more democratic channels. Their underlying assumptions, sometimes explicitly stated, were that the people were sovereign, the ultimate source of all authority on earth, that the delegation of power to government was only partial, and that the exercise of power must always be subject to popular checks and control. More than a general tendency among the people, the new movement assumed coherence as a bloc in the provincial congresses, recognizably if loosely defined by men at the time as the "western" or "country" towns. And it evoked a reaction among "eastern" or "mercantile" towns that called into question not only the new movement's revolutionary methods, but its basic assumptions as well, thereby laying the groundwork for a new partisanship representing fundamental divisions among the people themselves even before the break with Britain occurred.[2]

The British ministry, ironically, unintentionally contributed to the rise of the rural movement by clamping the lid on the town of Boston (as Thomas Hutchinson had frequently urged) in the "Intolerable Acts" of 1774. The transfer of the capital to Salem meant that Boston was no longer the focal point of political activity, and it did not become so again until 1776. The closing of the port, even to small coastal or river craft, greatly reduced commercial activity, caused scarcities, and drove up prices, forcing people to place the fulfillment of their material needs ahead of participation in politics. The arrival of General Thomas Gage as governor gave fresh importance to the presence of troops in Boston, making political agitation difficult if not impossible. The dismissal of the old Council, many of whom were Bostonians or residents of towns close by, further decreased the influence of the town politically, while some individual Popular party leaders consciously chose quieter pursuits. James Bowdoin, for instance, in bad health, retired into the country.

2. Provided one recognizes the limitations of these categories, the terms "western," "country," "eastern," and "mercantile" are useful: they were terms used at the time of the Revolution and they indicate the general character of each political group. Without recorded roll call votes, however, for the provincial congresses or the early state legislatures, it is impossible to define the groups with precision. Still, as subsequent chapters, particularly Chapters 9 and 10, will show, there was strong support for the western position among some eastern, chiefly agricultural, towns. Using Van Beck Hall's commercial-cosmopolitan scale, it appears that the least commercial-cosmopolitan towns were coalescing into a new political force, with some help from such larger, more commercial towns as Worcester. *Politics Without Parties: Massachusetts, 1780–1791* (Pittsburgh, 1972), pp. 3–22.

John Hancock, influenced by the moderation of fellow merchants, did nothing of note for several months. This left Sam Adams, and naturally there were designs against him. As one writer reported, "The ultimate wish and aim of the high government party is to get Samuel Adams out of the way, when they think they may accomplish every [one] of their aim[s]."[3] The patriots themselves, however, fulfilled this wish by appointing Adams a delegate to the Continental Congress, in effect reducing the leadership of the party in Boston to the second tier, probably headed by Dr. Joseph Warren.

The reduction of Boston's influence did not have the tranquilizing effect expected by Hutchinson and Parliament. For one thing, before Adams and his fellow delegates set out for Philadelphia on August 10, he succeeded in convincing many people throughout the rural part of the province that they were responsible for the Solemn League, and that upon them depended its success. Adams's Committee of Correspondence played upon latent antagonism between farmers and Boston merchants by informing country towns of importers "so sordid as to prefer their private advancement to the safety of the Community" and by urging them to cease consumption of imported goods. To overcome the fear of one town that the Solemn League was really a trick of the never-to-be-trusted Boston merchants, Adams wrote frankly, "that the merchants importing goods from England, a few [ex]cepted, were totally against the Covenant. They complained of it in our town meeting as a measure destructive of their interests."[4] As a result of Adams's prodding, the country towns took it upon themselves to force Boston's merchants into line, and in doing so they soon found themselves outdistancing the old revolutionary leaders. Certain of these rural towns became, in effect, the real leaders of the revolutionary movement, for a short time at least.

The most vigorous and the most radical of the country towns was Worcester, the commercial and administrative center of an agricultural area but not strictly speaking an agricultural town itself. When the town met (illegally) on August 22, it drew up its own Solemn League, making Sam Adams's look moderate by comparison. Where Adams had called for

3. The two acts were the so-called Boston Port Act and the Massachusetts Government Act: 14 Geo. II, c. 19, and 14 Geo. III, c. 45. On Samuel Adams, see John Andrews to William Barrell, Boston, 11 August 1774, in Andrews-Eliot Papers, MHS, p. 37.

4. Boston Committee of Correspondence to Westborough, 24 June 1774, BCC Minutes, George Bancroft Coll., New York Public Library, pp. 822–23; Samuel Adams for Committee of Correspondence of Boston to Committee of Correspondence of Colrain, in Harry A. Cushing, ed., The Writings of Samuel Adams, 4 vols. (New York, 1904–8), 3: 145.

an end to importation by October 1, the Worcester articles moved the date up to September 1. The subscribers agreed to buy only from persons who would "sign and swear an oath that all articles offered for sale by them were imported before 1 Sept." The agreement would continue until the port of Boston was opened, the troops withdrawn, the castle restored, all revenue acts annulled, and all pensions to governors and judges ended. Other country towns followed Worcester's rather than Boston's Solemn League. Numerous eastern towns, however, particularly in coastal Essex County, either ignored the proposal or promised only to enter into any agreement settled on by the Continental Congress. Such maritime towns as Marblehead and Salem openly refused to accept the covenant, reminding their fellows that Boston itself had not actually adopted it.[5] As a result, the Solemn League gained its greatest impetus from inland towns—towns that were furthest from the orbit of royal authority and thus had the least to fear.

The actions of Parliament were thus in a sense self-defeating. They reduced the influence of the Popular party in Boston but at the same time, by forcing a shift of provocative activity elsewhere, they also cancelled out the moderating influence of the merchant community in Boston, which had done so much to prevent the early success of the nonimportation plan. And by reducing the opportunity for moderates directly to oppose extremist activities, Parliament's actions actually encouraged more radical action on the part of country towns, which by now were the only ones able to act without fear of reprisal. Thus when Governor Gage met with his new Council, appointed by mandamus, at the end of August, and called upon the councilors for reports on their respective counties, he learned to his discomfort "that the frenzy had spread in a greater or less degree through all."[6]

5. Minutes of Worcester meeting of August 22 are reproduced in William Lincoln, *History of Worcester, Massachusetts* (Worcester, 1862), pp. 84–85. Towns following the Worcester plan included Mendon, Brimfield, and Rehoboth. Examples of towns deferring to the Continental Congress include Brookline, Newbury, and Haverhill. John G. Metcalf, *Annals of the Town of Mendon* (Providence, 1880), pp. 320–21; Charles M. Hyde, *Historical Celebration of the Town of Brimfield* (Springfield, Mass., 1879), pp. 309–10; Leonard Bliss, *The History of Rehoboth* (Boston, 1836), p. 145; *Muddy River and Brookline Records, 1634–1838* (Brookline, Mass., 1875), p. 247; Joshua Coffin, *A Sketch of the History of Newbury, Newburyport, and West Newbury* (Boston, 1845), p. 244; George Wingate Chase, *The History of Haverhill* (Haverhill, Mass., 1861), pp. 371–72; Arthur M. Schlesinger, *The Colonial Merchants and the American Revolution, 1773–1776* (New York, 1957), pp. 323–24 and n.

6. Gage to Dartmouth, Salem, 27 August 1774, in Albert Matthews, ed., "Documents Relating to the . . . Massachusetts Royal Council, 1774–1776," *CSM Publications* 32 (1937): 471.

What British officials did not recognize, and therefore failed to exploit, was the growing polarization among Massachusetts people as they faced a number of important issues in the fall of 1774. Such questions as what to do about courts of law, mandamus councilors, Tories, military prep- arations, and, most important, the form of government provided the catalyst to separate Massachusetts society into two opposing groups and to lay the foundation for fundamentally opposite views of the nature and purpose of the Revolution. While the groups were always somewhat amorphous, the western faction included most of Berkshire, Hampshire, and Worcester counties, many towns in Middlesex, and some from Bristol and Suffolk as well. The eastern faction, on the other hand, in- cluded most of Essex, Plymouth, Barnstable, Dukes, the Maine counties, Suffolk (Boston's leaders vacillating), and parts of Bristol and Middle- sex. Varying in the intensity of their convictions, Worcester and later Berkshire were most radical of the western counties; Essex, both in influence and in the rationalization of its position, led the eastern faction.

The polarization of opinion developed gradually among Massachu- setts people in conjunction with an enormous upsurge in their political activity during the summer and fall of 1774. The increase in practical democracy was common to all counties, whether maritime or inland, and was in evidence in the numerous county conventions that sprang up to fill the need for collective action after the General Court's dissolution. Significantly, the three western counties took the lead in calling these conventions, and it was here that the popular role began to receive definition, not only in terms of the practical needs of the moment, but as an idealistic guide for future reformist action.

The first conventions were in Berkshire:  on June 6 and 7 to adopt a variation of Samuel Adams's Solemn League and Covenant, and again on August 4 to determine what should be done about the courts of law. After a moderate beginning, the Berkshire delegates moved progessively towards more radical views. In July they agreed "that we will observe the most strict obedience to all constitutional laws and authority" and inveighed against "all licentiousness" and "disorderly mobs and riots." By August, however, if the town of Pittsfield is typical, they believed it "highly necessary that no business be transacted in the law, but that the courts of justice immediately cease, and the people of this province fall into a state of nature until our grievances are fully redressed."[7]

Hampshire County, however, was torn by opposing views. The old Connecticut River towns were not ready for the state of nature, and the

7. [David Dudley Field], *A History of the County of Berkshire, Massachusetts* (Pittsfield, 1829), pp. 114–18; J. E. A. Smith, *The History of Pittsfield, 1734–1800* (Boston 1869), pp. 191–92, 194–95.

convention that met on August 26 voted not to prevent the sitting of the courts. But there was "great zeal in the west," according to one observer, and he doubted that the convention could hold down the people.[8]

Worcester County leaped ahead of the others by voting on August 9 to seek a meeting of Worcester, Middlesex, and Boston representatives for the purpose of planning cooperative action. The Bostonians took the liberty of balancing off the preponderance of rural representatives by inviting representatives from Salem and Marblehead, and together they sat down in Faneuil Hall on August 26. Here they voted that all judges and other judicial officers were "rendered unconstitutional" by the Massachusetts Government Act. They decided a provincial congress was necessary "for counteracting the system of despotism" and also for substituting referee committees that would function in place of the unconstitutional law courts. They encouraged each county to choose delegates to the congress, to oppose the sitting of law courts, to oppose the execution of Parliament's coercive acts, and to promote military training.[9] Most significantly, the group conducted themselves as if the province had been reduced to a state of nature, and as if the people themselves, meeting at the county level, should take the lead in providing themselves with some form of interim government. But when it came to implementing these ideas in subsequent conventions, the counties diverged markedly.

Worcester, first among the counties to dispense altogether with the traditional vote of allegiance to George III, assumed the most radical posture. Not only did its convention resolve "to prevent the sitting of the respective courts," but also "by the best ways and means," which was for "the inhabitants of this county to attend, in person, the next inferior court." The people themselves must take matters into their own hands. Realizing that constitutional forms would soon be dispensed with

8. From the diary of Jonathan Judd, in James Russell Trumbull, *History of Northampton Massachusetts from Its Settlement in 1654*, 2 vols. (Northampton, 1902), 2: 345.

9. Harry A. Cushing, *History of the Transition from Provincial to Commonwealth Government in Massachusetts* (New York, 1896), pp. 102–3; John Sweetser, Jr., for Boston Committee of Correspondence to Committee of Correspondence of Charlestown, Boston, 19 August 1774, in MHS Miscellaneous Bound Papers, vol. 14 (1771–75); BCC Minutes, pp. 783–84; Minutes of "a meeting of delegates from the Counties of Worcester, Middlesex, and Essex with the Committee of Correspondence of the Town of Boston in behalf of the County of Suffolk," Boston, 26 August 1774, in MHS Miscellaneous Bound Papers, vol. 14; Thomas Young to Sam Adams, Boston, 19 August 1774, in Cushing, *History of the Transition*, pp. 102–3n, 72–73 and n.

altogether, both the Worcester and Middlesex conventions called for a general congress to meet at Concord in October.[10]

The contrast between the actions of Worcester and Essex was remarkable. Essex County, which met in early September at Ipswich, voted that "the judges, justices and the other civil officers in this county, appointed agreeable to the charter and the laws of the province, are the only civil officers in the county whom we may lawfully obey." While it was the duty of these officers to ignore the new act of Parliament, as long as they abided by the charter they should be supported and "their lawful doings" obeyed. More specifically, the next court due to sit at Newbury-port should sit and its judgments should be sustained by the county.[11]

The divergent tendencies among the county conventions did not, of course, represent a fully developed cleavage in Massachusetts society. In the heat of crisis, most people did not know which way to move, or how quickly they should do so. Most conventions revealed conflicting tendencies and the most famous, the Suffolk Convention, was in many ways typical.

In fact the Suffolk Resolves, considered so daring by members of the First Continental Congress, reflected many of the conflicting sentiments of Americans generally. They were cautious in their acknowledgment of George III as their rightful sovereign. They were radical in calling for a complete boycott of the courts of law and resistance to all officials who might try to execute acts contrary to the charter of the province. But at the same time they attempted to mitigate social conflict by recommending "that all creditors exercise forbearance to their debtors" and by urging debtors to pay their debts and submit disputes to arbitration. Beyond this, the resolves demanded that mandamus councilors resign their seats before September 20 or be considered enemies of the colony; they called for nonimportation, the encouragement of home manufactures, military training under officers with "sufficient capacity for that purpose," and the meeting of a provincial congress in Concord on the second Tuesday of October. The resolves emphasized the people's determination to act only on the defensive, but warned also that if popular leaders were arrested, "every servant of the tyrannical and unconstitutional government should be likewise arrested." Finally a committee of the convention was appointed to visit Governor Gage and inform him of the country's alarm at the fortifications springing up around Boston, while at the same time Paul Revere was entrusted with the task of

10. Lucius R. Paige, *History of Hardwick* (Boston, 1883), p. 84.
11. *Essex Gazette*, 6–13 September 1774; Mrs. E. Vale Smith [Blake], *History of Newburyport* (Newburyport, Mass., 1854), p. 80.

delivering a copy of the resolves to the Continental Congress in Philadelphia.[12]

Though the resolves were no more remarkable than those of other conventions meeting at the time in Massachusetts, they arrived in Congress at a moment when Sam Adams, confronted by moderation even more formidable than what he had encountered in Boston, could use them to great advantage. "They were read with great applause," wrote Adams, and were followed by resolutions that gave new spirit to the actions of Congress.[13]

Conventions continued in almost every county in Massachusetts during the fall of 1774. Some, such as the Cumberland Convention, urged social moderation, calling upon the people to "suppress, at all times, riots, mobs, and all licentiousness," and reminding them that God "loveth order, not confusion." But other meetings, such as those in Worcester, resulted in huge popular demonstrations against mandamus councilors, courts of law, and anyone who supported royal government.[14] On the whole, the conventions represented the first, and one of the most significant, examples of increased democracy in revolutionary Massachusetts. Uninhibited by the traditions of the town meeting or the controls of the provincial legislature, the county conventions represented the almost complete assumption of all government by the people themselves. Where huge throngs assembled to witness the proceedings of their representatives, the results were even more likely to be expressions of the will of ordinary people.

A second area of increased democratic activity—and a major contributor to the growing divergence of opinion—was in popular actions against the courts of law. Here again the western counties took the lead. By early August Governor Gage was receiving reports that in Berkshire mobs were "rising in many places" with the intention of preventing the holding of the courts at their next term, and that the people were rising in Hampshire and Worcester as well.[15]

---

12. "Suffolk Resolves," *The Journals of Each Provincial Congress of Massachusetts in 1774 and 1775,* ed. William Lincoln (Boston, 1838), pp. 601–9. See also John Andrews to William Barrell, Boston, 3 September 1774, in Andrews-Eliot Papers, p. 42.

13. Adams to Charles Chauncy, Philadelphia, 19 September 1774, in Cushing, ed., *Writings of Samuel Adams,* 3: 155–56.

14. Cushing, *History of the Transition,* pp. 107–8; Metcalf, *Annals of Mendon,* pp. 328–29; Paige, *Hardwick,* p. 85.

15. Letter to Gage from Hampshire County, 10 August 1774, in Matthews, ed., "Documents Relating to the . . . Massachusetts Royal Council," pp. 472–73; Gage to Earl of Dartmouth, Salem, 27 August 1774, in *Amer. Arch.,* 4th ser., 1: 742–43.

When the court sat at Great Barrington, in Berkshire County, in mid-August about 1500 people (some from Connecticut) crowded in and around the court house so that there was room in the building for neither judge nor jury. The judge thereupon was forced to adjourn. But the town's legislative representative, a lawyer who vowed he would see Parliament's acts executed, found himself greased, feathered, and placed down a well overnight to cool off.[16]

At Springfield, in Hampshire County, the court was similarly intimidated when it met on August 30. Here a great concourse of people (3000–4000, according to one report) gathered outside the courthouse and sent a delegation inside, demanding that all court officials present themselves. When they did so, they were forced to sign a statement solemnly promising not to execute any office, in accordance with the recent Massachusetts Government Act. "The people to their honor behaved with the greatest order and regularity," wrote one observer, who noted that the people drew themselves up into military formation and "marched with staves and music." But a less sympathetic writer declared that "Now we are reduced to a state of anarchy" and are without law "except the law of nature which [is] much vitiated and darkened to go by." Everybody at Springfield, he lamented, "submitted to our Sovereign Lord the Mob."[17]

In the rural areas, large numbers of people could rely on intimidation of the judges to prevent the sitting of the courts, but in Boston intimidation was impossible. Here, when the Superior Court met on August 30, it was the courage of the jurors, who collectively refused to serve, that prevented the court's carrying on in the usual way. The matter was complicated by the fact that Peter Oliver, the impeached chief justice, took his place at the bench with several other Superior Court justices. The grand jurors listed Oliver's presence as the first and chief reason why they would not serve. He had been charged with high crimes and misdemeanors, they said, and had not been acquitted. Furthermore, they complained that judges, under the new act, were now chosen at the pleasure of the king; that three of the judges had taken oaths to serve as mandamus councilors; and that they would be betraying their native rights should they serve. The petit jurors presented a similar statement, adding that the Massachusetts Government Act was an infringement of the charter rights of the province. The court could there-

16. John Andrews to William Barrell, Boston, 13, 17 August 1774, in Andrews-Eliot Papers, pp. 37–39; Smith, *Pittsfield*, p. 196.

17. *Amer. Arch.*, 4th ser., 1: 747; letter of Joseph Clarke, Springfield, 30 August 1774, and diary of Jonathan Judd, in Trumbull, *Northampton*, 2: 346–48, 345–46.

fore do nothing more than adjourn, and when it met the next day to transact business that did not require juries, Chief Justice Oliver was not present.[18]

By September, all normal judicial procedures were brought to a halt. In Plymouth and Bristol counties, the county courts were prevented from sitting. The Superior Court was adjourned by proclamation in Suffolk and Bristol counties in September while no attempt was made to hold it in Middlesex in October "by reason of the difficulty of the times." In Worcester, where the crowds were always demonstrative, the justices of the court of common pleas, together with lawyers and the sheriff, had to walk between rows of the crowd, estimated at 6000 people, chanting a promise not to hold courts under the new acts of Parliament. When Gage consulted with his Council on the subject, they advised him not to send troops to enforce the sitting of courts since the people could defeat them by simply refusing to serve as jurors. Royal justice had ended.[19]

But in many places, courts created by the people sprang up to fill the void. The town of South Brimfield "voted to choose twelve men as a court of justice and honour, to judge and determine all controversies that may hereafter arise in said district." Other towns followed, while the county conventions urged the creation of semijudicial arbitration boards that would settle civil disputes without recourse to the law. But popular justice was sporadic at best, while the lack of it could easily stir up class resentments. Creditors were bound to suffer, while the indebted could easily escape their obligations. Almost at once, the demand began to come from certain merchants for a common court system. "Your congress must substitute something for us in the place of our vitiated courts of justice," wrote Joseph Greenleaf to Robert Treat Paine.[20] And similar comments were increasingly voiced throughout the commercial areas of the province.

For the time being, however, the Revolution was in the hands of the people, and they showed it not only in the tone of their county conven-

18. *Amer. Arch.*, 4th ser., 1: 744–45, 747–49; jurors' resignation, Boston, 30 August 1774, in MHS Miscellaneous Bound Papers, vol. 14; John Andrews to Wm. Barrell, Boston, 30 August 1774, in Andrews-Eliot Papers, p. 41.

19. Cushing, *History of the Transition*, pp. 88–89; Eunice Paine to R. T. Paine, Taunton, 16 September 1774, in Robert Treat Paine Papers, MHS, vol. 2 (1766–76); Gage to Dartmouth, 2 September 1774, in Matthews, ed., "Documents Relating to the . . . Massachusetts Royal Council," pp. 474–75; Paige, *Hardwick*, p. 85.

20. Cushing, *History of the Transition*, p. 91; see also vote of Malden, 20 September 1774, in Deloraine Pendre Corey, *The History of Malden* (Malden, Mass., 1899), pp. 763–64; Greenleaf to Paine, Boston, 16 October 1774, in Robert Treat Paine Papers, vol. 2.

tions and their demonstrations against the courts of law, but also in their treatment of Tories. Chief amongst these in the eyes of the people were the 36 men named as mandamus councilors in an order received by Governor Gage on August 6. For the most part, the councilors were the friends and relatives of Thomas Hutchinson. There were three Olivers and two Hutchinsons plus old political allies like Israel Williams, Daniel Leonard, John Worthington, and Timothy Ruggles, the conservative president of the Stamp Act Congress. Others, such as Thomas Flucker and Harrison Gray, had held royal appointments in the past. The only notable persons from outside the old Court party were John Erving, Sr., and his son, who had been Sons of Liberty in the 1760s, but who had drifted away with other disenchanted Boston merchants by 1770. Of the 36 men appointed, however, only 10 were sworn in when Governor Gage met with them at Danvers on August 8. Others either did not attend, refused to accept the office, or wanted time to think it over. By the end of the month, 24 had accepted, even though a considerable number of them had been intimidated by crowds.[21]

Rural towns took the lead in dealing with the councilors. As John Andrews wrote, "The inhabitants of the country towns (where many of them belong) are prodigiously vexed, and it's my opinion (if we may judge from the tenor of all their conduct) that they won't suffer anyone [of the councilors] to live among 'em." Timothy Ruggles, riding eastward from his home in Hardwick, found the road near Worcester blocked by people who wanted his resignation in advance. He made his way through them and accepted the office once he reached Salem, but warnings from his friends followed quickly. From Hardwick, one of the Olivers wrote "that the spirits of the people in this and the neighboring towns, especially New Braintree and Greenwich, are worked up to such a pitch of resentment and rage against you that you must not attribute it to pusillanimity in me when I advise you, if you value the preservation of your life, not to return home at present." A few days later, Ruggles was warned out of Bristol County, where 3000 people assembled to demand that Colonel Gilbert of Freetown not accept the position of sheriff. "Such is the spirit of this country," wrote a resident of Taunton. "They seem to be quite awake, and to have awoke in a passion. It is more dangerous being a Tory here than at Boston, even if no troops were there."[22]

21. John Andrews to William Barrell, Boston, 6 August 1774, in Andrews-Eliot Papers, p. 37; Matthews, ed., "Documents Relating to the . . . Massachusetts Royal Council," pp. 461n, 465–66, 472.

22. John Andrews to William Barrell, Boston, 18 August 1774, in Andrews-Eliot Papers, p. 39; Gage to Dartmouth, Salem, 27 August 1774, in Matthews, ed., "Doc-

Popular sovereignty thus received a real boost throughout rural Massachusetts. The people had never had the right to participate in the election of councilors or county officials, but now they assumed the right to demand the resignations of these men. And they did so with the strength of numbers. Two thousand persons assembled on Worcester common to demand the resignation of Timothy Paine and to hear him beg their forgiveness for having accepted in the first place. Worcester followed up its action by instructing its legislative representative (who never got the opportunity to sit) to demand the impeachment of every mandamus councilor who accepted his post. One thousand people assembled before the court house steps in Cambridge to hear Samuel Danforth and Joseph Lee read their unqualified resignations, while only a few days later, a mob of 4000 surrounded Lieutenant Governor Thomas Oliver's Cambridge house to make similar demands. But Oliver, fearing that the mob would become unmanageable, slipped away, leaving the crowd unsatisfied. The mob, he wrote, was "of the lower class."[23]

The stories of popular action against mandamus councilors and other Tories could be multiplied a dozen times. From rural towns in Suffolk County (where Joshua Loring was forced to flee his home by men armed with cutlasses) to the Connecticut Valley (where Israel Williams was mobbed and later smoked in a smokehouse to encourage his political conversion), the common yeoman, who had to this point played no significant part in the revolutionary movement, now took it upon himself to deal with royal appointees and other Tories. His new and spirited activity did not go unnoticed. "The country people," wrote John Andrews of Boston, "being vastly more vigilant and spirited than the town, did not fail to visit Brattle and Sewall's house last evening, but not finding either of 'em at home, they quietly went off."[24] Sometimes quietly, and sometimes not so quietly, rural Massachusetts was assuming a significant role in the revolutionary movement.

uments Relating to the . . . Massachusetts Royal Council," p. 471; Daniel Oliver to Timothy Ruggles, Hardwick, 19 August 1774, ibid., p. 476; Extract of a Letter from Taunton, Massachusetts, 25 August 1774, in *Amer. Arch.*, 4th ser., 1: 732.

23. Gage to Dartmouth, 25 August 1774; Timothy Paine to Gage, Worcester, 27 August 1774; Lieut.-Gov. Oliver to Dartmouth, Cambridge, 3 September 1774, all in Matthews, ed., "Documents Relating to the . . . Massachusetts Royal Council," pp. 476–77, 473–74, 485–86; Declaration of Samuel Danforth and Resignation of Joseph Lee, in *Amer. Arch.*, 4th ser., 1: 763.

24. Mr. Loring's Narrative, 31 August 1774, in Matthews, ed., "Documents Relating to the . . . Massachusetts Royal Council," p. 480; Robert J. Taylor, *Western Massachusetts in the Revolution* (Providence, 1954), p. 66; John Andrews to William Barrell, Boston, 30 August 1774, in Andrews-Eliot Papers, p. 41.

Was the increase of democracy that attended popular activity in the rural areas simply a consequence of the collapse of royal government, or was it the expression of an underlying principle? Were the people actually trying to replace old forms with new, reformed, more democratic ones? In one area of their activity at this time, they obviously were. This was in the formation of new militia organizations—the beginnings of a people's army.

Plans for a militia grew out of a spontaneous call to arms that nearly plunged the colonists into war in early September 1774. Early on the morning of September 1, under cover of darkness, a party of British regulars in 13 boats pulled out into the Mystic River from Boston and headed for Charlestown on the other side. There, as day broke, they emptied a provincial arsenal of its contents, loaded guns and powder aboard their boats, and slipped back to Boston undetected and without incident. The discovery of what had happened understandably caused a certain irritation among the people of Charlestown and the surrounding area since it seemed part of a well-designed plan to disarm the people. As reports spread westward, however, irritation gave way to open hostility for in the re-telling, the story was sufficiently embroidered to make it appear that the troops had met resistance, that a skirmish had followed, and that six townsmen had been killed. Before the day was out, the rumor rather than the facts had reached 40 miles westward and, within five days, to Connecticut and New York. In the full flush of anger, men everywhere reached for their weapons and headed east. One man said that "he never saw such a scene before—all along were armed men rushing forward, some on foot, some on horseback, at every house women and children making cartridges, running bullets, making wallets, baking biscuit, crying and bemoaning and at the same time, animating their husbands and sons to fight for their liberties, tho' not knowing whether they should ever see them again." Thousands of men went all the way to Cambridge before learning the truth; thousands more turned back as word gradually reached them. The actual number of men involved could not, of course, have been ascertained even at the time; but the most reliable estimate was that 60,000 men had sprung to arms —almost every able-bodied man in some towns—and while large numbers flocked eastward from Connecticut and New Hampshire, the great bulk of the men came from western Massachusetts.[25]

25. It was Ezra Stiles, then a minister in Newport, Rhode Island, and later president of Yale, whose interest in the uprising led him to gather reports from as many sources as possible as to the course taken by the rumor and the reaction of the people to it. He recorded a full account of his findings in his diary under date of

There was spirit in the western towns, but that spirit needed harnessing; military organization was needed and the continued activity of General Gage and the army in Boston finally made this clear. "The governor is making all kinds of warlike preparations," wrote Abigail Adams to her husband in mid-September, "such as mounting cannon upon Beacon Hill, digging entrenchments upon the neck, placing cannon there, encamping a regiment there, throwing up breast works, etc., etc." Such leading steps produced varied reactions. Highly incensed, people in the rural areas met Gage's challenge with military preparations of their own. "Our people in the country are busy making carriages for cannon, etc., etc., so that preparations for war are carrying on as if the last reason of states was soon to be tried," wrote Joseph Palmer of Boston. "The country people, as 'tis said, have turned Paddock's Field . . . into dung and have carried them into their fields; what crop they will produce is only written in the prophecies."[26]

In contrast to the irate reaction of rural people, Boston moderates feared lest Gage's actions precipitate a crisis at a time when rural tempers were short. "General Gage continues fortifying the south entrance of the town," wrote Joseph Greenleaf to Congressional delegate Robert Treat Paine; "I fear if he doth not desist, he will get himself into trouble. The spirits of the people want calming. Tis difficult to keep the country back." Only the fact that Congress was in session was preventing the people from forming a formidable army, added Greenleaf. "I hope we shall not be too impatient."[27]

Even as Greenleaf hoped his moderate hopes, however, rural people, encouraged by their county conventions, were consolidating and formalizing their military organization. Worcester, for instance (so it was reported in Boston), had by October an army of seven regiments of a thousand men each, which turned out twice weekly "to perfect them-

---

November 17, 1774. *The Literary Diary of Ezra Stiles,* ed. Franklin Bowditch Dexter, 3 vols. (New York, 1901), 1: 476–85. See also John Adams's references to the episode, dated September 6 and November 6, 1774, in Lyman H. Butterfield, ed., *Diary and Autobiography of John Adams,* 4 vols. (Cambridge, Mass., 1961), 2: 124, 160; and also Israel Putnam to Aaron Cleveland, Oxford, [3] September 1774, in Mary deWitt Freeland, *The Records of Oxford, Mass.* (Albany, N.Y., 1894), pp. 362ff.

26. Abigail Adams to John Adams, Braintree, 14 September 1774, in Lyman H. Butterfield, ed., *Adams Family Correspondence,* 2 vols. (Cambridge, Mass., 1963), 1: 151; Joseph Palmer to Robert Treat Paine, Boston, 15 September 1774, in Robert Treat Paine Papers, vol. 2.

27. Joseph Greenleaf to Robert Treat Paine, Boston, 13 September 1774, Robert Treat Paine Papers, vol. 2.

selves in the military art." The men "are called minute men, i.e., to be ready at a minutes warning with a fortnight's provision and ammunition and arms." Significantly, they sought to embody democratic principles in their militia organization. The Worcester County convention specifically suggested that old officers be cast aside and that the men themselves elect from their own numbers suitable officers to lead them. This popular army thus quickly became an important democratizing agent. Men from the age of 18 could join, and vote, without restrictions of any kind; they could determine themselves who among them would be given important posts, and the results could—and often did—leave the socially prominent in the ranks with the yeoman farmer. "The country towns in general," noted one writer, "have chose their own officers and muster for exercise once a week at least, when the parson as well as the squire stands in the ranks with a firelock."[28] Such a combination of the sense of power with experience in a new, more democratic way of doing things influenced the revolutionary thinking of people in backcountry Massachusetts, and they, in turn, did much to alter the shape of the American Revolution as it developed in the province.

Emboldened by a new and increasingly clearer understanding of their revolutionary purpose, several deputations from county conventions sought direct confrontations with Governor Gage during September and October. Joseph Palmer was a member of the committee sent by the Suffolk County Convention. He reported that, "after several fruitless attempts," the committee received a curt reply from the governor to the effect that he had been addressed several times on the subject and wished to be "excused" from hearing any more. Even when it came to deputations, it seems the people of rural areas were more persistent than Bostonians, and they sorely tried the governor's patience. "The dispositions of the people in the country are in general so restless," wrote John Andrews, "that they are continually sending committees down upon one errand or another—which has caused the Governor to say that he can do very well with the Boston selectmen, but the damned country committees plague his soul out, as they are very obstinate and hard to be satisfied." Andrews went on to tell of the arrival in Boston of a deputation of twelve men from Worcester County whose tempers, one might guess, were rather frayed when, well over a week later, they finally got the opportunity of presenting their address to the governor. The fortifications on Boston neck, the bringing of cannon into the city, and the

28. The "minute men" were apparently an invention of the Worcester County Convention of September 20, 1774. Paige, *Hardwick*, pp. 85–86; John Andrews to William Barrell, Boston, 1, 5 October 1774, in Andrews-Eliot Papers, p. 45.

further reinforcement of troops, stated the address, all strongly indicated "some dangerous design."[29]

The fact that Governor Gage found the country committees more persistent, and therefore more trying, than the Boston committees is an indication of the gradual shifting of the balance of power that was developing within the revolutionary movement in Massachusetts. Where before, Boston had led both tactically and in the articulation of republican ideals, now the awakened backcountry, involving numerous towns previously inactive in provincial politics (as Chapter 10 will show), was assuming leadership, urging more radical measures, and expressing ideals that transcended the republican framework of the early Revolution. In late September, an episode illustrated the shift in the power structure. At that time, Gage ordered the construction in Boston of barracks to house the growing number of troops. Many in town, including the selectmen, felt that, if the troops had to be there, barracks would be of benefit to the town since, with their construction, the troops all would be housed in one place instead of scattered throughout the community. The rural areas, however, vigorously objected; they determined not to sell lumber, or allow it to be sold for such a purpose, and they called upon the Boston Committee of Correspondence to prevent Boston workers from working on the barracks. To persist, the Bostonians were warned, might "not only incur blame from our sister colonies, but essentially affect the union now subsisting between town and country." The Boston Committee thereupon voted that it was not prudent for workers to go on with the work "as they might thereby give offence to their country brethren." When questioned by Gage on the subject, the committeemen replied that "it was not in their power to influence the country."[30]

The growing importance of the backcountry to the revolutionary movement had, in one sense, a psychological explanation. Rural people felt important. They had a new sense of their own power—a sense that arose from their mass gatherings (a phenomenon hitherto confined almost exclusively to urban settings), from their forcing the end to royal justice and the resignations of royally appointed officials, and from their treat-

29. Joseph Palmer to Robert Treat Paine, Boston, 15 September 1774, ibid.; John Andrews to William Barrell, Boston, 5 October 1774, in Andrews-Eliot Papers, p. 45; Address from the County of Worcester, Presented to his Excellency the Governor, 14 October 1774, in *Amer. Arch.*, 4th ser., 1: 868–69.

30. Boston Committee of Correspondence to Berkshire, Boston, 24 September 1774, in BCC Minutes, pp. 793–94; John Andrews to William Barrell, Boston, 25 September 1774, in Andrews-Eliot Papers, p. 45; "Meeting of Several Committees . . . ," Boston, 27 September 1774, in *Amer. Arch.*, 4th ser., 1: 897.

ment of Tories. But at the same time, the increased importance of the rural areas stemmed from their readiness to institutionalize and formalize their power in novel and more democratic ways. County conventions, for example, represented a unique challenge to the primacy of the town in local government, while militia organizations exemplified a tangible and increasingly conscious application of democratic principles.

There was, of course, popular participation in the actions of commercial towns such as Boston and the coastal towns of Essex County. But it was tempered with a sense of caution. In the backcountry, town meetings continued as a matter of course and were simply the first step towards far more daring projects that often involved mass demonstrations and intimidation of Tories. In the commercial towns, where royal authority had the support of armed force, the holding of town meetings was in itself a "radical" act. In Boston, the town got around the strict letter of the Massachusetts Government Act (which prohibited all but annual meetings without the consent of the governor) by adopting the simple expedient of meeting by adjournment. Their meeting, claimed the Bostonians, began in May and could continue from time to time until it was dissolved. But there was timidity. In early August, the town met at Faneuil Hall to discuss the distribution of donations that were pouring in from "our sympathetic brethren in the other colonies," but it met "not without some apprehensions that government would have interposed and dispersed them, by virtue of the new acts."[31]

But Gage did nothing to interfere this time. Rather, he chose Salem as the place to stand firm. In late August, a Salem town meeting was announced. Gage responded by issuing a proclamation strictly prohibiting all persons from attending.[32] On the day of the meeting, he called the Salem Committee of Correspondence before him and demanded to know if they had called it. When they admitted they had, he ordered them to disperse it. But they refused, leaving the governor no choice but to arrest them and call out the troops to break up the meeting. The Salemites, however, concluded their business (the election of delegates to a county convention) while the troops were mustering, and thus conflict was avoided. The next day, Gage reaped the consequences of his action when 3000 men from towns close by came into Salem, sent a delegation to the governor, and warned him that no bail would be paid for the Committee

31. Gage to Dartmouth, Salem, 27 August 1774, in Matthews, ed., "Documents Relating to the . . . Massachusetts Royal Council," p. 471; John Andrews to William Barrell, Boston, 9, 13 August 1774, in Andrews-Eliot Papers, p. 37.

32. Proclamation of Gage, Salem, 23 August 1774, in *Amer. Arch.*, 4th ser., 1: 729.

of Correspondence. Gage dropped the prosecution rather than push matters to the extreme.[33] Thus in their own way the commercial towns stood firm.

Relatively speaking, however, the commercial towns could not (or, at least, did not) go as far as their country cousins. When, for example, Gage demanded that John Hancock disband the Governor's Cadets and return the flag he had presented them, Hancock did so. The company contented itself with the presentation of a rather impolite address to the governor.[34] By October, moreover, the spirit had so far gone from Boston that the town meeting willingly appointed a committee to meet with Gage and "produce some plan to preserve peace and harmony among the soldiers and inhabitants." Moderates applauded Gage's skill in quieting the town. "I think it a degree of condescension we could not have expected from the governor," wrote John Andrews, "as he not only permits the meeting, contrary to the express letter of the act, but rather promotes it by holding a conference with them when assembled in that capacity." To be sure, the spirit of Sam Adams was still in a segment of the population, and when Gage's proposal was later submitted to the town meeting, "a discontented few, who make it their principle to keep up the ball, by their influence among the popularity, raised a party, and caused the whole day to be passed in altercation." James Otis, in a sane interval, spoke against cooperation with the governor while Dr. Benjamin Church, the still undetected Tory spy, urged acceptance of Gage's proposals. To old Popular party supporters, "this proceeding has had too much the air of coalescence with the idea of a garrisoned town, and wounded the delicacy which had hitherto been observed upon that head."[35] The Popular leaders won to the extent of getting the moderate committee replaced, but by mid-November the new committee had met with Gage and worked out a new plan to prevent incidents between townspeople and troops.[36] Without Sam Adams, clearly, Boston's revolutionary ardor had significantly diminished.

Thus by the fall of 1774, the revolutionary movement in Massachusetts had developed three significant characteristics: first, an awakened back-

33. Report of Salem Town Meeting, 24 August 1774, ibid., p. 730; John Andrews to William Barrell, Boston, 25, 26 August 1774, in Andrews-Eliot Papers, p. 40.

34. *Amer. Arch.*, 4th ser., 1: 709; John Andrews to William Barrell, Boston, 16, 17 August 1774, in Andrews-Eliot Papers, pp. 37–38, 39.

35. John Andrews to William Barrell, Boston, 31 October, 1 November 1774, in Andrews-Eliot Papers, p. 46; James Lovell to Josiah Quincy, Jr., Boston, 3 November 1774, in Josiah Quincy, Jr., Papers, MHS, vol. 1639–1852, p. 69.

36. John Andrews to William Barrell, Boston, 3, 17 November 1774, in Andrews-Eliot Papers, p. 46.

country had begun to take an important part in shaping the movement; second, both the course of events and the attitudes of the people, particularly in rural areas, had contributed to an increase in the practice of democracy; and third, from a relative standpoint, the activities of rural towns and some western commercial centers tended to be more radical and daring than those of the eastern commercial towns. In such an atmosphere, representatives from every county in the province came together in an extralegal provincial congress.

Thomas Gage inadvertently provided time and place for the congress when, on September 1, he issued precepts for an election of legislative representatives. The Great and General Court would meet in Salem on October 5, said the election writs.[37] But by September 14, it was clear that Gage had changed his mind for, not only had he ordered all provincial records transported into Boston, but he had cleared Salem of troops and ordered barracks and hospitals constructed for them there to be torn down. Resolves of several counties proposed, however, that if no legislature were convened, the assembled delegates form themselves into a provincial congress. And this is the idea that prevailed throughout the province when, in the ensuing elections, instructions were given for delegates to meet regardless of the action of the governor. By September 22, in Boston it was "generally supposed they [the representatives] will adjourn themselves to Concord, where it is intended that the Provincial Congress shall meet and resolve themselves into such a body." Many towns elected two sets of representatives, one to go to Salem, the other to Concord. Similarly, many towns made it practically impossible for Gage to allow a General Court meeting by forbidding their representatives to work with any councilors but the ones elected by the legislature the previous spring. Governor Gage, therefore, had little choice when he issued a proclamation on September 28 discharging all elected representatives and declaring his intention not to meet them.[38]

But on October 5, 90 representatives gathered in Salem. For three days they waited patiently for the governor to appear and then, laying the responsibility for their action on him, they voted a series of resolves condemning the governor's proclamation of September 28 as unconsti-

37. A copy of the writ was entered in the journal of the Provincial Congress when it met. Lincoln, ed., *Journals of Each Provincial Congress*, p. 4.

38. Joseph Warren to Massachusetts Members of the First Continental Congress, Boston, 12 September 1774, in Autograph Letters of Joseph Warren, New York Public Library; John Andrews to William Barrell, Boston, 14, 22 September 1774, in Andrews-Eliot Papers, p. 44; Proclamation of Gage, 28 September 1774, in *Amer. Arch.*, 4th ser., 1: 809–10.

tutional and his remarks on the state of the province as "injurious and unkind." They resolved themselves into a provincial congress, to be joined by others elected for that purpose, and they then adjourned to Concord.[39]

For two reasons, the number of delegates that assembled in Concord on October 11 was extraordinarily large. For one thing, no limitations upon representation were in effect, and many towns sent more delegates than they normally could have sent to the General Court. In the second place, many towns had elected separate delegations to the legislature and to the congress while the men at Salem decided that both should sit. Thus, where a normal General Court had around 150 members, the First Provincial Congress had 293, almost double. But of greater significance, the representation from the eastern coastal counties was near normal while delegations from the predominantly agricultural inland counties were enormous. (See Appendix C, columns 1 and 2 for county-by-county figures.) Available population statistics, as presented in Table 1, show that western counties were experiencing a much higher rate of growth than eastern counties and thus were entitled to increased representation. But comparing the data in Table 1 and columns 1 and 2 in Appendix C,

Table 1. Population Figures, Massachusetts Counties Listed from West to East, with Three Maine Counties Last (whites only)

| County | 1765 | 1776 |
|---|---|---|
| Berkshire | 2,911 | 17,952 |
| Hampshire | 18,472 | 32,701 |
| Worcester | 31,239 | 45,031 |
| Middlesex | 32,710 | 40,121 |
| Bristol | 20,900 | 24,916 |
| Suffolk | 34,997 | 27,419[a] |
| Essex | 42,706 | 50,923 |
| Plymouth | 20,733 | 26,906 |
| Barnstable | 11,691 | 12,936 |
| Nantucket | 2,820 | 4,412 |
| Dukes | 2,180 | 2,822 |
| York | 10,465 | 17,623 |
| Cumberland | 7,366 | 14,110 |
| Lincoln | 2,623 | 15,546 |

SOURCE: Evarts B. Greene and Virginia D. Harrington, *American Population Before the Federal Census of 1790* (New York, 1932), pp. 21–40.

[a] Figures are distorted by the fact that Boston was still under the impact of occupation and its population was listed as 2,719 whites as compared with a pre-war figure of 15,720.

39. John Andrews to William Barrell, Boston, 6 October 1774, in Andrews-Eliot Papers, p. 45; Cushing, *History of the Transition*, p. 82.

we find that four inland counties—Middlesex, Worcester, Hampshire, and Berkshire—had a total population of 135,805, or 40.5 percent of the total, while they sent to the First Provincial Congress 177 delegates, or 60 percent of the total.

As this first of three provincial congresses got underway, it became increasingly obvious that spirited backcountrymen expected their ideas to dominate. Coastal moderates like John Andrews were greatly disturbed by the Congresses, "as they are principally composed of spirited, obstinate countrymen, who have very little patience to boast of." Andrews feared that the Congresses would adopt measures that would impede the adjustment of differences with Great Britain, "as the more prudent among 'em bear but a small proportion." Some leaders of the Popular party, however, attempted to control events by siding with rural representatives on many occasions, and by impressing upon their friends not present the order with which proceedings were conducted. "You would have thought yourself in an assembly of Spartans or ancient Romans," wrote Dr. Joseph Warren to Josiah "Wilkes" Quincy of the First Congress, "had you been a witness to the order which inspired those who spoke upon the important business which they were transacting."[40]

Most proceedings of the Congress were conducted in strict secrecy, and the journals, of course, did not record the substance of debates. But bits and pieces of information leaked out in sufficient quantity to suggest the general train of events. Not at all secret was the appointment of "a committee to take into consideration the state of the province"—the same sort of committee used in the past by Sam Adams to manage all affairs of the legislature. But there is no indication it had as much power in the Congress. John Hancock, Joseph Hawley of Hampshire County, Elbridge Gerry of Essex, Artemas Ward of Worcester, James Warren of Plymouth, and Joseph Warren of Boston were among the initial 15 members, joined at the end of November by the returned members of the Continental Congress, including Sam Adams. Just as open was the appointment of a committee directed to visit Governor Gage. The committee found Gage polite and willing at least to accept their address for later perusal. Also, there was no secrecy in the appointment of Henry Gardner of Stow (Middlesex) as Receiver-General to replace the royally appointed Harrison Gray. The Congress ordered all towns to cease payments of taxes to Gray and to forward them henceforth to Gardner. When Governor Gage heard this, however, he could no longer remain

40. John Andrews to William Barrell, Boston, 20 October 1774, in Andrews-Eliot Papers, p. 46; Joseph Warren to Josiah Quincy, Jr., Boston, 21 November 1774, in Josiah Quincy, Jr., Papers, vol. 1639–1852, p. 76.

passive. On November 10, he issued a proclamation prohibiting subjects of the king from complying with the resolves or directions of the unlawful assembly.[41]

Even though the important issues confronting Congress were discussed in secret, rumors that were heard without echoed a recurring theme: radical countrymen were carrying the ball, often contrary to the wishes of moderate coastal representatives. "The town of Boston is by far the most moderate part of the province," wrote Joseph Warren. "Boston seems to be put out of the question in most of the proceedings of our [Provincial] Congress," echoed James Lovell, adding that "all the sea-ports" were without influence in some matters.[42]

The matters of importance were three in number: what to do about fortified Boston, how to make the Continental Congress's Association (in part, a boycott of British goods) work, and whether to form a provincial army in anticipation of war. There were two sides to each issue. Rural extremists wanted Boston sacrificed to American liberty, and therefore demanded that patriotic Bostonians leave the city at once. Moderates in Boston found the idea "as absurd as it is impracticable" but some Popular party members fell into line with rural thinking. "I think the inhabitants of this town are distracted to remain in it with such formidable fortifications at its entrance," wrote Samuel Cooper to John Adams. But mass emigration was, in the end, "found to be an unpracticable measure." Gage reported to England that "many individuals are gone, and others going through fear . . . of being apprehended." But, he added, those who were moving were "the most obnoxious," implying that Boston would become even more moderate in the future.[43]

When it came to trade with Great Britain, the delegates of commercial towns were completely without influence. On October 21, for instance, a committee was appointed to report a nonconsumption agreement, a realistic step since the Congress could organize a consumers' boycott of

41. Lincoln, ed., *Journals of Each Provincial Congress*, pp. 16, 17, 49, 58; John Andrews to William Barrell, Boston, 14 October 1774, in Andrews-Eliot Papers, p. 45; Proclamation by Gage, 10 November 1774, in *Amer. Arch.*, 4th ser., 1: 973–74.

42. Joseph Warren to Josiah Quincy, Jr., Boston, 21 November 1774, in Josiah Quincy, Jr., Papers, vol. 1639–1852, p. 76; James Lovell to Joseph Trumbull, 26 December 1774, in Joseph Trumbull Papers, Connecticut Historical Society.

43. James Lovell to Josiah Quincy, Jr., Boston, 10–25–28 October 1774, in Josiah Quincy, Jr., Papers, vol. 1639–1852, p. 66; John Andrews to William Barrell, Boston, 20 October 1774, in Andrews-Eliot Papers, p. 46; Samuel Cooper to John Adams, 16 October 1774, in *Amer. Arch.*, 4th ser., 1: 878; Gage to Dartmouth, Boston, 30 October 1774, ibid., p. 950.

merchants importing goods, whereas it could not create a nonimportation plan by simple legislation. When the committee dragged its heels, a new one was appointed a week later, and its report congratulated "those patriotic merchants" who had ceased to import after the "commencement of the cruel Boston port bill," but it "reflect[ed] with pain on the conduct of those who sordidly preferred their private interest to the salvation of their suffering country, by continuing to import as usual." The report urged a complete boycott of such merchants.[44]

Moderates outside of the First Provincial Congress had placed high hopes in the proceedings of the Continental Congress, hoping that they would "have some influence upon the councils of the provincial one, and check their impetuous zeal." But in Philadelphia, the decision was reached to end all import trade with Great Britain beginning December 1, 1774. And when word reached Massachusetts of this, farmers determined that merchants would not cheat as in the past. Enforcement, they resolved in the Provincial Congress, would be rigid.[45]

Merchants, the Congress determined on December 3, might have until the following October to sell goods brought in before the deadline. But beginning at once, the activities of merchants would be placed under the scrutiny of committees of inspection in every town. The committees would see that the association was "strictly executed," and if necessary, they would even take a full inventory of all merchants' goods to ensure that no imports from Britain, Ireland, the British West Indies, or the wine islands (which might ship by way of Britain) were sold after October 10, 1775. Rural delegates were adamant on this point not, wrote James Lovell of Boston, because of "cool political principles," but rather because of their "anger and resentment" towards Massachusetts merchants. There was overwhelming "evidence of mercantile chicanery in our former non-importation," wrote Lovell, while there was already "the appearance of an inclination to relax in the manner of executing what relates to arrivals [of ships] between December and February, now." As a result, Boston merchants and those in all other seaports were simply told that, from now on, the farmer was in control. "The country knows what it can do in inland places, and seems determined to let England

44. Lincoln, ed., *Journals of Each Provincial Congress*, pp. 25, 40–41.

45. John Andrews to William Barrell, Boston, 19 October 1774, in Andrews-Eliot Papers, p. 46. The provisions of the Continental Association are reproduced in Merrill Jensen, ed., *American Colonial Documents to 1776*, vol. 9, *English Historical Documents* (New York, 1955), pp. 813–16. Besides providing for the beginning of nonimportation on December 1, 1774, they required nonexportation of American goods to British ports, from September 10, 1775, and the nonconsumption of British goods imported contrary to the Association.

know that in the present struggle, commerce has lost all the temptations of a bait to catch the American farmer."[46]

The hottest issue, however, was whether the province should form an army of its own and press Gage and his redcoats into open conflict at the earliest possible time. It took all of the efforts of moderates in the Provincial Congress "to confine the inland spirit solely to the defensive." "Nothing, I think," wrote James Lovell in October, "but speedy knowledge of a change of measures in England can prevent a capital winter stroke." The danger of conflict was greater in November when Joseph Warren wrote that "it will . . . require a very masterly policy to keep the province for any considerable time longer in its present state."[47] Every movement of British troops was the occasion for a new protest to Gage. "I do not believe the ministry have signified an intention to oblige us to take the field," wrote James Lovell in December. "But while such is my belief, I assure you the general current is otherwise, and especially in the Provincial Congress now sitting."[48]

For the rural delegates, the course that must be followed was clear. "We must fight," wrote Joseph Hawley, the best known of the westerners. "There is not heat enough yet for battle," he realized, and "there is not military skill enough," but "that is improving, and must be encouraged and improved." From the very beginning of the Congress, therefore, the westerners urged the establishment of "a standing army to be composed of fifteen thousand men." Moderates in the Congress and without were opposed. The scheme, wrote John Andrews of Boston, was "not only ridiculous, but fraught with a degree of madness, just at this juncture." But the idea fitted in very closely with the plans of Sam Adams who, by October, had written to his friends urging them "to provide themselves without delay with arms and ammunition, get well instructed in the military art, embody themselves and prepare a complete set of

46. Lincoln, ed., *Journals of Each Provincial Congress*, pp. 57–58; Lovell to Joseph Trumbull, 26 December 1774, in Trumbull Papers. The harsh feelings between inland customers and coastal merchants are exemplified by the spirited report adopted by the Worcester town meeting on March 7, 1774. They charged that "the mercantile part of this Province" continued to import tea "while the merchants and traders in the other governments desisted." But worse, they raised prices not only of tea but of coffee, chocolate, and other commodities, "an extortion that is sufficient to put them to the blush, if they are not lost to every sentiment, except that of self interest." *Worcester Town Records*, ed. Franklin P. Rice, *Worcester Society of Antiquity Collections* 4 (1882): 216.

47. Lovell to Josiah Quincy, Jr., Boston, 25 October 1774; Warren to Josiah Quincy, Jr., Boston, 21 November 1774, both in Josiah Quincy, Jr., Papers, vol. 1639–1852, pp. 66, 76.

48. Lovell to Josiah Quincy, Jr., Boston, 9 December 1774, ibid., p. 83.

rules that they may be ready in case they are called to defend themselves against the violent attacks of despotism." Adams's entreaties were not enough, however, for moderate opposition within the First Provincial Congress was strong enough to prevent the irreversible decision to create an extralegal provincial army. Rather, on October 26, after considerable debate and amendment, the Congress resolved to create a committee of safety whose task was the arming and organizing of militia units through-out the province,[49] a simple recognition and extension of the minute men. The compromise was an admission that a resort to arms might be-come necessary, but it fell short of the wishes of rural and Popular party activists.

Sam Adams and other delegates to the Continental Congress had re-turned from Philadelphia and taken seats in the Provincial Congress, when, on December 10, "it was moved . . . that arms be immediately taken up against the king's troops." Reports of the proceeding are sketchy, but a letter from Boston reported that, on the last day of the Congress, after the resolution calling for armed conflict, "one of the members got up and told them such a move was infamous, when at the same time, the members knew that neither Connecticut nor any of the southern colonies meant to oppose his Majesty's arms; on which account the Congress immediately dissolved, and a new one is to be chosen."[50]

Gossip about the abrupt dissolution spread widely, and the report that circulated in Philadelphia filled in the names of the principal de-baters. It said that Samuel Adams made the motion and then was violently opposed by another member of the Continental Congress, the moderate Thomas Cushing. Cushing, went the report, strongly warned the delegates that "the southern colonies would not approve of it, nor stand by you." But Adams replied that "he well knew you would have the support and assistance of all the colonies; on which T. Cushing gave him the lie, with saying, 'that is a lie, Mr. Adams, and I know it, and you know that I know it'—which occasioned much altercation and de-bate." The Congress had dissolved itself and called for new elections, the Philadelphia report agreed, because of the impasse reached in

49. Joseph Hawley, "Broken Hints to be communicated to the committee of con-gress for the Massachusetts" [fall 1774], in Hezekiah Niles, ed., *Principles and Acts of the Revolution in America* (Baltimore, 1822), pp. 107–8; John Andrews to William Barrell, Boston, 20 October 1774, in Andrews-Eliot Papers, p. 46; Sam Adams to Thomas Young, Philadelphia, 17 October 1774, in Cushing, ed., *Writings of Samuel Adams*, 3: 162–63; Lincoln, ed., *Journals of Each Provincial Congress*, pp. 31–34.

50. Extract of a letter from a Gentleman in Boston to his friend in New York, 12 December 1774, in *Amer. Arch.*, 4th ser., 1: 1039.

debate.[51] Samuel Adams and other Popular party leaders naturally denied that there was a serious split among the leadership. But the split between moderates and activists had been there for some time, as the previous chapter indicated, and even now Adams did not pretend that he and Cushing saw eye to eye.

More important than the split in Popular party leadership, however, was the division developing between radical agrarians and moderate representatives of coastal commercial areas. One writer interpreted the Congress as a fruitless battle between the upper and lower classes of representatives. "The late Provincial Congress, distracted and divided by a variety of views and opinions, separated without doing anything more than you see in the resolves. The principal object of their meeting was to cajole the men of property, but no impression could be made on them." In the next Congress, he said, "republican leaders" would again attempt to "levy a sum of money for raising, clothing, and paying an army to take the field against the King's troops in the ensuing spring." But, he added, "the moneyed men are convinced that acts of rebellion will be punished with confiscation of their estates, and that is a penalty they do not feel bold enough to experience."[52]

The journals of the Second Provincial Congress (which met from February to May 1775) do not record any such split between "moneyed men" and "republicans." In fact, they reveal, at least at first glance, a rather single-minded pursuit of a common objective—complete military preparedness. The Congress appointed a commissary to take charge of acquiring provisions and ordnance; it sent out requests for information on the state of the militia; it sent directions to every town for making saltpeter; it took steps to link up the military forces of Massachusetts with those of its neighbors; it prepared the rules for a "constitutional army," and finally it decided to set up its own army (apart from local militia units). All the while, it issued public decrees warning the people not to relax in their military preparations and predicting an early resort to arms. But the journals projected a false sense of unanimity. They showed, for instance, in a rare recorded vote, that 96 of 103 members present on April 8 favored the establishment of a provincial army. But representatives of commercial towns, according to another report, adamantly resisted. "[I]n Essex County," wrote William Pynchon of Salem in his diary, "so many delegates dissented that the project, as is supposed,

51. Stephen Collins to Robert Treat Paine, Philadelphia, 14 January 1775, in Robert Treat Paine Papers, vol. 2.

52. Extract of a letter from Boston to a Gentleman of New York, 19 February 1775, in *Amer. Arch.*, 4th ser., 1: 1248.

must be laid aside, or referred to the Continental Congress." The recorded vote may have been accurate, of course, but it did not indicate how many opponents of the plan absented themselves while the vote was being taken. In other areas, moreover, there are subtle indications in the journals of rural distrust of eastern towns. When the Congress appointed 11 men as the provincial committee of safety, for instance, it voted that five should constitute a quorum "provided always that not more than one of the said five shall be an inhabitant of the town of Boston."[53] Despite tension and disunity in the Congress, the issue of military preparedness was, of course, resolved at Lexington. The division that had made it an issue, however, was not, and the intensity of that division revealed itself ultimately on the question of a constitution.

Massachusetts, the leader of revolutionary activity, was the last of the original 13 states to settle upon a fixed constitution. It did not do so until 1780. This is a fact that much current historiography tends to ignore. If the people of Massachusetts, supposedly middle class landowners, were as united in their revolutionary goals as some historians suggest,[54] why did they not quickly settle upon a form of government to replace the one destroyed by the Massachusetts Government Act in 1774? The answer, quite simply, is that from the very beginning of discussions on this subject, the people of Massachusetts could not agree upon a form of government. Rural westerners wanted farreaching and immediate reforms of a democratic nature. Moderate easterners, less sure of what they wanted—and much more concerned with the still undetermined relationship between the colonies and Great Britain— at first united chiefly in their desire for caution and then, taking a cue from the Tories whom they resembled in many ways, they looked outside of Massachusetts for a solution to the problem, in this case, as we shall see, to the Continental Congress.

Even before the First Provincial Congress met in October 1774, Popular leaders in Boston began reporting to Sam Adams and his colleagues at Philadelphia that there was a fundamental division in the province on the constitutional question. "By all our advices from the westward," wrote Thomas Young, "the body of the people are for resuming the old

53. Lincoln, ed., *Journals of Each Provincial Congress*, pp. 97, 99, 100, 105, 111, 120–29, 135, 110, 89–90; entry of 16 April 1775, in Fitch Edward Oliver, ed., *The Diary of William Pynchon of Salem* (Boston, 1890), p. 43.

54. Robert E. Brown suggests that the matter of a constitution was not an issue in Massachusetts since people were satisfied that they enjoyed "democracy" under the charter of 1691. *Middle-Class Democracy and the Revolution in Massachusetts, 1691–1780* (Ithaca, N.Y., 1955), pp. 368–70, 387–90, 399.

charter, and organizing a government immediately."[55] This idea of taking up the first charter of Massachusetts again—the charter of 1629—appealed to many, doubtless because it gave to the province almost virtual independence. Joseph Warren, who some suspect replaced Sam Adams as the chief leader of the Popular party,[56] echoed Young's statement and developed it further. "Many among us," he wrote to the Massachusetts delegation in Philadelphia, "and almost all in the western counties, are for taking up the old form of government according to the first charter. It is exceedingly disagreeable to them to think of being obligated to contend with their rulers, quarrel for their rights every year or two. They think this must always be the case in a government of so heterogeneous a kind as that under which they have lived."[57]

The real intent of the westerners is obvious from their votes in county conventions and town meetings: every officer of government must be directly elected by the people. The purpose of a provincial congress, said a Worcester convention, must be "to devise proper ways and means to resume our original mode of government, whereby the most dignified servants were, as they ever ought to be, dependent on the people for their existence as such." The town of Worcester told its delegate to the First Provincial Congress that, if all infractions of their rights were not redressed, then the people should be considered absolved from their charter obligations, and, from a state of nature a new constitution should be prepared. The new form, they said, must provide that "all officers shall be dependent on the suffrages of the people for their existence as such, whatever unfavorable constructions our enemies may put upon such a procedure."[58] The town of Leicester, also in Worcester County, argued that "charters have been bubbles,—empty shadows, without any certain stability or security." For that reason, their representative was told that he must oppose any motion "for patching up that under King William and Queen Mary." A new form of government must be provided as well as courts of law such "as may be best adapted to our present circumstances." By January, the Leicester instructions called even more urgently for "an immediate assumption of government, as the only means

55. Thomas Young to Sam Adams, Boston, 4 September 1774, quoted by Cushing, *History of the Transition*, p. 80.

56. John Cary, *Joseph Warren: Physician, Politician, Patriot* (Urbana, Ill., 1961).

57. Joseph Warren to Massachusetts Members of the First Continental Congress, Boston, 12 September 1774, in Autograph Letters of Joseph Warren.

58. Votes of Worcester Convention, 31 August 1774, in Paige, *Hardwick*, pp. 84–85; Instructions to Worcester representatives, October 1774, in Lincoln, *History of Worcester*, pp. 91–92.

by which we may be reduced to order, and the laws of the province have their usual and uninterrupted course."[59]

In contrast to the westerners, "other persons, more especially in the eastern counties, think that it will be trifling to resume the old charter," as Joseph Warren wrote to Philadelphia. Warren wrote in mid-September 1774 and, at that time, easterners were not united on any plan, but Warren believed that even those who wanted a new constitution wished to maintain some connection with Great Britain. They believed, according to Warren, that the people of Massachusetts should "make such proposals of a certain limited subjection to the King as they judge convenient, which he may accept or reject as he pleases." Others wanted no change whatever and the instructions of some towns to their congressional delegates reflected their moderation. Brookline admonished its representative to "adhere to the Charter of the Province," while Topsfield in Essex County told its delegate to "use your endeavours that King George the 3rd be acknowledged as our rightful sovereign." Topsfield similarly urged that "all our constitutional and charter rights and privileges be kept good and inviolable to the latest posterity," though the Provincial Congress must do nothing that would be "repugnant to what the Continental Congress may resolve."[60] Samuel Locke of Sherburne, hoping that the form of government as laid down in the charter of 1691 would be continued as closely as possible, wrote to the Boston Committee of Correspondence urging it to call publicly for a continuation of the legally elected Council, whether the governor would work with it or not.[61] Clearly, the easterners wanted no basic changes in the internal structure of government.

Many Popular leaders in Boston found themselves agreeing with the western position, not because they subscribed to rural pleas for democratic reform, but because they now avidly sought independence and

59. Instructions of Leicester, 10 October 1774 and 9 January 1775, in Emory Washburn, *Historical Sketches of the Town of Leicester, Massachusetts* (Boston, 1860), Appendix, pp. 451–54.

60. Warren to Massachusetts Members of First Continental Congress, Boston, 12 September 1774, in Autograph Letters of Joseph Warren; Brookline Instructions to its Representatives, 27 September 1774, in *Muddy River and Brookline Records*, p. 249; Topsfield Instructions, 11 October 1774, in *Town Records of Topsfield, Massachusetts*, 2 vols. (Topsfield, 1917–20), 2: 335–36.

61. Samuel Locke to Boston Committee, Sherburne, 26 September 1774, in Cushing, *History of the Transition*, p. 81n. A number of towns agreed with Locke that the old Council should participate. See, for example, instructions of Malden, in Corey, *Malden*, p. 739.

they saw the resumption of the first charter as a means to that end. Joseph Warren agreed that the first charter should be resumed and for precisely this reason, for in November he wrote to Josiah Quincy, Jr., that, "if the late acts of Parliament are not to be repealed, the wisest step for both countries is fairly to separate and not spend their blood and treasure in destroying each other."[62] Likewise, Benjamin Kent, a member of the North End Caucus Club, wrote to Robert Treat Paine that he looked "back with detestation on the state of government of Massachusetts Province ever since our last charter's [establishment]. It is impossible that the interests or advantages of Great Britain should not frequently interfere with the interests and advantages of the colonies, while she sets governors, etc., over us." For this reason, Kent was "glad King William's charter is annihilated by Great Britain, and it will now be our own fault, yes and an unpardonable fault in us, if we take up with anything short of our old charter."[63]

It is impossible to outline, in full detail, the conflicting positions of reformers and moderates on the constitutional question as of the fall of 1774 for the simple reason that the two positions were not developed in detail. What we see are the roots of a conflict that continued until 1780, but roots, nonetheless, that were clearly visible to men at the time and that caused considerable alarm to such men as Samuel Adams for whom union—both social and intercolonial—was a primary goal. One might expect that Adams would side with fellow members of the Popular party and with westerners in urging an immediate rejection of the charter of 1691, thereby producing the almost virtual independence towards which he seemed to be working. But Adams was too clever for that, and he was idealistic enough to believe, as John Adams did, that the result of revolutionary activity must be a reformed society free from the party strife of the previous years—a society in which men must be "influenced not by partial or private motives, but altogether with a view of promoting the public welfare." He therefore knew, as he read Joseph Warren's letter to the Massachusetts delegation in Congress, that eastern moderates must be drawn gradually towards the desired goal. And his reply to Warren proposed a solution that epitomized his republican principles.

"The eastern and western counties appear to differ in sentiment with regard to the two measures mentioned in your letter," he began. "This difference of sentiment might produce opposition, in case either part should be taken. You know the vast importance of union. That union is

62. Joseph Warren to Josiah Quincy, Jr., Boston, 21 November 1774, in Josiah Quincy, Memoir of the Life of Josiah Quincy Jun. (Boston, 1825), p. 208.
63. Benjamin Kent to Robert Treat Paine, Boston, 15 September 1774, in Robert Treat Paine Papers, vol. 2.

most likely to be obtained by a consultation of deputies from the several towns, either in a house of representatives or a Provincial Congress. But the question still remains, which measure to adopt." In answering this question, Adams might well have been influenced by his surroundings, for his task in Philadelphia was constantly to prod and push along a Congress that was for the most part considerably more moderate than he. "It is probable," he decided, "that the people would be most united, as they would think it safest, to abide by the present form of government,—I mean according to the charter." Then he presented his reasoning, displaying his manipulative genius at its best. "The governor has been appointed by the crown according to the charter," he noted, "but he has placed himself at the head of a different constitution. If the only constitutional council, chosen last May, have honesty and courage enough to meet with the representatives chosen by the people by virtue of the last writ, and jointly proceed to the public business, would it not bring the governor to such an explicit conduct as either to restore the general assembly, or give the two houses a fair occasion to declare the chair vacant? In which case, the council would hold it till another governor should be appointed." Such steps, thought Adams, "would immediately reduce the government proscribed in the charter; and the people would be united in what they would easily see to be a constitutional opposition to tyranny. You know," he concluded, "there is a charm in the word 'constitutional.' "[64]

Adams wrote at the end of September 1774 and his letter arrived after the General Court, meeting at Salem, resolved itself into the First Provincial Congress—too late to have any particular influence. But he held to the principle of his plan, and even though he encouraged extreme steps in other matters during the winter of 1774–75, he maintained his belief that a "constitutional opposition to tyranny" would unite the people more than any other course of action.

By spring, the constitutional crisis was reaching its apex, now influ-

64. In a series of letters written in 1774 and 1775, Adams showed how his great practical ability was backed up by solid idealism—unless, of course, he lied to his best friends. On the importance of union, see Adams to James Warren, Philadelphia, 25 September 1774, in Cushing, ed., *Writings of Samuel Adams*, 3: 157–59. For opposition to partisanship, see Adams to Arthur Lee, Boston, 29 January 1775, ibid., pp. 169–72; Adams to Elbridge Gerry, Philadelphia, 26 September 1775, ibid., pp. 226–27; Adams to Gerry, Philadelphia, 29 October 1775, ibid., pp. 229–31. In this last letter, Adams concluded: "After all, virtue is the surest means of securing public liberty. I hope you will improve the golden opportunity of restoring the ancient purity of principles and manners in our country. Everything that we do, or ought to esteem valuable, depends upon it." His specific suggestions on the constitutional question were in his letter to Joseph Warren, Philadelphia, September 1774, ibid., pp. 156–57.

enced by two factors. First, the governor, according to the constitution of 1691, had to issue writs for a new election of a House of Representatives to meet the last Wednesday in May. The Provincial Congress, therefore, had to decide what it would do if the governor did as the charter ordered or, on the other hand, what it would do if he did not obey the charter. Secondly, Lexington and Concord—though considered minor skirmishes by some Tories and moderates—clearly indicated the probability of all-out war, in which event the people of Massachusetts must act to provide themselves with a proper form of government. The Provincial Congress, before Lexington, resolved that the people should obey writs of election if the governor issued them, and that the House should meet as it had always done, though it should refuse to work with the mandamus council. Otherwise, the people should elect new delegates to a third provincial congress. By early May, however, all chances for a General Court had passed and the Provincial Congress therefore recommended that each town "elect and depute as many members as to them shall seem necessary and expedient" to meet at Watertown on May 31, and thereafter for up to six months.[65]

But these are the steps the Provincial Congress took publicly. Behind closed doors a fierce controversy raged. Eastern moderates had by now adopted the position that the Congress itself must act as the government until the Continental Congress—and it alone—had chosen a new form of government for the province. They believed, obviously, that the voices of moderation were stronger in Philadelphia. They undoubtedly were, for in early May, the Provincial Congress began "digesting a plan of government and mean to put into execution immediately without consent of the Congress at Philadelphia, which," noted David Cobb of Taunton, "has given some little uneasiness to the moderate Whigs of the province." These moderates, Cobb went on, "suppose the province Congress will be sufficient for all the purposes of government until the Continental Congress had given their sanction to a form of government for us. The uneasiness just mentioned," he concluded, "is not known out of doors."[66]

But the atmosphere in the Provincial Congress really just reflected the attitudes of people out of doors. Eastern moderates were simply reacting to the widespread upsurge in democratic feeling that was sweeping the rural areas. Even some Popular leaders thought it had gone too far and

65. Lincoln, ed., *Journals of Each Provincial Congress,* 1 April, 5 May 1775, pp. 116–17, 195–96.

66. David Cobb to Robert Treat Paine, Taunton, 12 May 1775, in Robert Treat Paine Papers, vol. 2.

they pleaded with their colleagues in Philadelphia to provide Massachusetts with a form of government that would rescue the province from the chaos they thought prevailed. "Government is so essential that it cannot be too soon adopted," wrote Elbridge Gerry to the Massachusetts delegates. "The people are fully possessed of their dignity from the frequent delineation of their rights, which have been published to defeat the ministerial party in their attempt to impress them with high notions of government." The trouble, thought Gerry, was that the people were now assuming too much power. "They now feel rather too much their own importance, and it requires great skill to produce such subordination as is necessary." The people, thought Gerry, also were placing the army on too lofty a plane. "They have affected to hold the military too high, but the civil must be first supported; and unless an established form of government is provided, it will be productive of injury. Every day's delay," he continued, "will make the task more arduous." Even Joseph Hawley, a westerner himself and a man sympathetic in many ways with the democratic aspirations of his neighbors, believed that the bickering in the Provincial Congress must be brought to a conclusion. "[E]very affair is amazing[ly] retarded and done to irrepressible disadvantage for want of civil government and the efforts of this colony must soon be [under]mined unless your Congress either give us a plan of civil government or countenance our adopting one according to our best discretion."[67]

By the time Gerry and Hawley wrote in June, Congress, under the inevitable direction of Samuel Adams, had acted to solve the Massachusetts crisis. On June 9, it recommended that the people of Massachusetts revert to the charter of 1691 by considering the governor and lieutenant-governor absent. A House of Representatives should be elected by the people "as near as may be to the spirit and substance of the charter" and it should then choose a Council which, together with the House, would exercise all the powers of government. Sent over the signature of John Hancock, president of the Congress, the resolve made an immediate impression on the Provincial Congress at Watertown. By June 20, the delegates took action to dissolve themselves and to provide for constitutional elections—that is, elections in which franchise limitations would apply and which would permit each town to choose only as many representatives as provincial law allowed.[68]

67. Elbridge Gerry to Massachusetts delegates in the Continental Congress, Watertown, 4 June 1775, in *Amer. Arch.*, 4th ser., 2: 905; Joseph Hawley to Robert Treat Paine, Watertown, 12 June 1775, in Robert Treat Paine Papers, vol. 2.
68. Resolve of Continental Congress, 9 June 1775, in Lincoln, ed., *Journals of*

Thus the charter of 1691 was resumed not, as some historians suggest, because it was acceptable to the great bulk of the people but rather because its resumption was the clearest way out of an extremely difficult situation. On the surface, perhaps, it would appear that the decision to carry on with established forms of government was a victory for the moderates who, in their conservatism, wanted no basic changes in the internal power structure of Massachusetts government and society, but the victory was tactical rather than strategic. In reality, the reconstituted General Court simply became another battleground for the new contending forces in revolutionary politics—the eastern moderates and the western reformers.

---

*Each Provincial Congress,* 20 June 1775, p. 359; John Hancock to Massachusetts Provincial Congress, Philadelphia, 10 June 1775, in *Amer. Arch.,* 4th ser., 2: 955; Letter of Provincial Congress to Massachusetts towns, 20 June 1775, in Lincoln, ed., *Journals of Each Provincial Congress,* pp. 359–60.

# 5

# Partisanship and Independence

IN THE summer of 1775, with a resolution of the Continental Congress pointing the way, Massachusetts again took up its charter of 1691. Towns throughout the colony conducted "constitutional" elections and on July 19, General Court representatives gathered in Watertown to pick up where the General Court at Salem had left off just over a year before.[1] There were significant changes, however, which meant from the beginning that government would not function as it had prior to 1774. Governor Gage, as commander of British troops in Boston, could not be accepted as a "constitutional" governor, and the governor's chair was therefore considered temporarily vacant. The Council, in the governor's absence, was to serve in both an executive and a legislative capacity: it assumed the governor's right to appoint executive and judicial officers—such as sheriffs, justices of the peace, justices of the Superior Court—while at the same time it sat as the upper house of the legislature.[2] Beyond this change, however, even the nature of the lower house was significantly different from that of 1774. In 1774, as generally in times past, the coastal counties had predominated numerically, with the result that the rural west had never taken the lead in legislative matters. But the fall and winter of 1774–75 had taught farmers that they possessed considerable power if they chose to use it, and it had awakened their interest in more democratic ways of doing things. Thus, when the General Court replaced the Provincial Congress, the awakened back-

1. William Lincoln, ed., *The Journals of Each Provincial Congress of Massachusetts in 1774 and 1775* (Boston, 1838), p. 359; *House Journals,* 19 July 1775.
2. Harry A. Cushing, *History of the Transition from Provincial to Commonwealth Government in Massachusetts* (New York, 1896), pp. 175–76.

country was determined to continue its leading role in the revolutionary movement. The backcountry, of course, could not send the mammoth delegations that it had to the Provincial Congresses. But it could send, according to provincial law, considerably more representatives than it had ever chosen to do up to 1774, and the fact that it exercised its rights resulted in a General Court that could be dominated by the agricultural towns, if they chose to vote as a bloc.[3] (Compare columns 1 and 3 in Appendix C for a view of the relative increase in representation from the predominantly small-town, agricultural counties such as Worcester, at the expense of the predominantly commercial-cosmopolitan such as Plymouth.)

The very purpose of reverting to the charter, however—at least as Sam Adams saw it—was to put an end to the factiousness that had split the Provincial Congresses into radical and moderate groups, and to substitute for it union that Adams and his friends sought as one of their revolutionary goals. It was the course of appeasement that Adams and his friends had determined to follow, but they faced the nearly impossible task of appeasing moderates by providing stable government while at the same time maintaining the revolutionary ardor of the western reformers. And to make matters worse, some of the best patriot heads were in Philadelphia, both Adamses included. The task fell to Joseph Hawley of Northampton. It was apparently Hawley's decision that, since the House was in western hands, the Council should go to eastern moderates. Thus, although when the session began the legislators were "much divided as to their test for the gentlemen to be councilors," within a few days Hawley had found support for the election of several moderate men of social position and wealth, including congressional delegate Thomas Cushing, who had opposed the creation of a colonial army the previous winter.[4] Of the 28 men finally elected,

3. It is clear from the chapters that follow that there were several towns in the eastern counties of Essex, Suffolk, Bristol, and Plymouth whose representatives sided with the western reformers. These towns were generally small agricultural communities which ranked in group C on Van Beck Hall's commercial-cosmopolitan scale. See his tables and maps in *Politics Without Parties: Massachusetts, 1780–1791* (Pittsburgh, 1972), pp. 9–12. Since the votes on particular issues are not given in the journals, however, it is impossible to be perfectly accurate in determining the numerical strength of each "party" in the legislature.

4. John Pitts to Samuel Adams, 20 July 1775, in Samuel Adams Papers, New York Public Library; James Warren to John Adams, Watertown, 20 July 1775, ibid; James Warren to Samuel Adams, Watertown, 20 July 1775, in Worthington Chauncey Ford, ed., *Warren-Adams Letters*, 2 vols. (Boston, 1917–25), 2: 415–16. Cushing, of course, was away at Congress, as were the Adamses and Paine, who were also elected councilors.

only 6 came from towns west of Watertown and even 1 of these 6, Moses Gill, had moved west from Boston just the year before.[5] One cannot conclude, of course, that men who came from east of Watertown necessarily all thought alike, but the very fact that they came from eastern areas that had traditionally dominated the Council shows the extent to which the resumption of charter government was meant as a concession to moderates.

But reformers were willing to make concessions in form only. Once the General Court had settled down to business, the House turned its attention to internal reforms that reflected the predominance of reformist westerners and that epitomized their wish to bring government closer to the people. One of the first acts passed declared null and void all previous acts that had denied to any town or district with fewer than 30 freeholders the right to representation in the legislature.[6] A tax act apportioned a £46,000 levy among the several counties, with the heaviest burden falling on Essex County.[7] Though the apportionment was probably done fairly, it brought the rather significant complaint from one newspaper writer that it amounted to an "oppressive taxation of the trading and monied interests."[8] The legislature, however, was willing to make reforms that would benefit merchants as well, as it did when it provided for the establishment of new admiralty courts, unlike the detested British courts in that they were to have juries.[9] Still, the reform impulse was confined to the lower house.

The Council, by contrast, was perfectly willing to fit itself into old molds. Its first chance was provided, probably unwittingly, by Joseph Hawley and the lower house when they passed an act "which Hawley calls a roller. It is designed to vacate all the offices civil and military and clear the stage for the council to bring on again who they please."[10] The Council was pleased to fill offices of Superior Court justices, justices of the peace, and sheriffs with merchants, well-off lawyers, and old Popular

5. *House Journals*, 21 July 1775. The six were Jedediah Foster (Brookfield, Worcester), Jabez Fisher (Wrentham, Suffolk), James Prescott (Groton, Middlesex), Moses Gill (Princeton, Worcester), Dr. John Taylor (Lunenburg, Worcester), Eldad Taylor (Westfield, Hampshire).

6. 23 August 1775, *Acts and Resolves*, 5: 419–20.

7. 31 October 1775, ibid., pp. 423–36.

8. "O.P.Q." in *Massachusetts Spy* (Worcester), 18 May 1776, reproduced by Robert J. Taylor, ed., *Massachusetts, Colony to Commonwealth: Documents on the Formation of its Constitution, 1775–1780* (Chapel Hill, N.C., 1961), pp. 29–30.

9. James Warren to Samuel Adams, Watertown, 23 October 1775, in Ford, ed., *Warren-Adams Letters*, 2: 423.

10. James Warren to Robert Treat Paine, Watertown, 7 August 1775, in Robert Treat Paine Papers, MHS, vol. 2.

party members. And it was not averse to handing out several offices to single persons, even though plural office-holding had been roundly condemned by the Popular party when practiced by William Shirley, Francis Bernard, and Thomas Hutchinson.[11] Reformist members of the House did not forget, however, and while they had no legal power to disapprove the appointments, they could, and did, take action "to prevent persons holding places incompatible." By mid-October, James Warren was warning Sam Adams in Congress that both of them were going to be forced to relinquish several of their offices.[12] And with a speed that reflected the seriousness of the business, Adams wrote back to Elbridge Gerry that "it is in your power . . . to prevent a plurality of places incompatible with each other being vested in the same person. This our patriots have loudly and very justly complained of in time past, and it will be an everlasting disgrace to them if they suffer the practice to continue."[13] Thus Adams lived up to earlier ideals though his fellow delegate, John Adams, accepted the position of chief justice in the same month.[14]

By the fall of 1775, it had become apparent that the Council, like Councils in the prerevolutionary period, was little interested in promoting basic internal social or political reforms and had, in fact, identified itself with the moderate faction that had been evident ever since the late 1760s, particularly in Boston and other coastal areas. The House, on the other hand, though voting records do not exist to show who was responsible for reform legislation, seemed to be influenced by the large western representation and to be considerably more radical than the Council. Thus the attempt by certain Popular party leaders to heal the breach between moderate and reform factions in the revolutionary movement appeared, by the fall of 1775 to have been completely frustrated, so much so that the next issue to divide moderates and reformers also drove old Popular leaders themselves into alien camps and ended forever the loose coalition that had been the Popular party.

On the surface, the issue seemed trivial enough:  would the Council

11. Ellen E. Brennan, *Plural Office-Holding in Massachusetts 1760–1780* (Chapel Hill, N.C., 1945), p. 112.

12. James Warren to Samuel Adams, Watertown, 23 October 1775, in Ford, ed., *Warren-Adams Letters*, 2: 423.

13. Samuel Adams to Elbridge Gerry, Philadelphia, 29 October 1775, quoted by William V. Wells, *The Life and Public Services of Samuel Adams*, 3 vols. (Boston, 1866), 2: 332.

14. John Adams to Perez Morton, secretary of the Council, Philadelphia, 24 November 1775, in Adams Papers, original in MHS, microfilm copy in State Historical Society of Wisconsin, reel 345.

or the House appoint high militia officers? But it involved social, political, and constitutional questions that went to the very heart of the controversy between moderates and reformers. The House accepted literally a resolution of the Continental Congress in July that "assemblies" throughout the continent appoint militia officers. The Council, on the other hand, argued that the Continental Congress had called for the restoration of the charter government of Massachusetts, that the province had accepted its advice, and that they were therefore bound constitutionally to allow the Council to maintain the governor's prerogatives, which included the right to appoint militia officers.[15] When the General Court adjourned on November 11, the battle lines between House and Council were clearly drawn. "The two houses have not parted in the best humor," wrote James Warren, "a poor time to altercate." The Council, continued Warren, had "lost much of the respect and confidence of the people by their behavior on this occasion. Though the occasion is melancholy, it excites ridicule in the gravest among us to see more especially some individuals among them contending for the prerogative of the governor with all the zeal of Bernard and Hutchinson, the hauteur and pomp of Majesty."[16]

The Council, like moderates generally the year before, wanted the backing of the Continental Congress for their position, and for this purpose Paul Revere was promptly sent dashing off to Philadelphia with a letter to the members of the Massachusetts delegation signed by James Otis, president of the Council. The letter pointed to the inconsistencies in the two resolves of the Continental Congress—the one calling for a resumption of the Massachusetts charter, the other concerning militia appointments—and it stressed the Council's desire to abide by the charter.[17] But personal letters that also went to Philadelphia from Massachusetts pointed out that this was no ordinary dispute between House and Council. The House, wrote John Pitts, claimed the right to participate in militia appointments as "the indispensable right of the people w[h]ich they will not relinquish." Pitts, a close ally of Sam Adams, sided with the House though he believed that unity was more important than the issue. "Surely this is not a time for the Council to contend for prerogative when the safety of the whole depends upon our union." Far

15. Joseph Hawley to Samuel Adams, Watertown, 12 November 1775, in Samuel Adams Papers; Elbridge Gerry to John Adams, Watertown, 11 November 1775, in Adams Papers, reel 345.

16. James Warren to Samuel Adams, Watertown, 12 November 1775, in Ford, ed., *Warren-Adams Letters*, 2: 426–27.

17. Council of Massachusetts to their Delegates in the Continental Congress, Watertown, 11 November 1775, in *Amer. Arch.*, 4th ser., 3: 1531.

better, he thought, to renounce the old charter "which can be of no consequence now." The issue, thought Pitts, was being used by the Council to preserve intact the old form of government, and they therefore had "discovered as great an attachment to what they call their prerogative in this respect as they could if they were sure it would be permanent."[18] Joseph Hawley, writing to John Adams, was certain that the people would not tolerate a loss of their new privileges. If Congress sided with the Council, it would, he believed, "throw the colony into the utmost confusion, and end in the destruction of the Council."[19] Elbridge Gerry agreed, adding that, though the members of the House were not certain what form they wanted their new government to take, they "abhor the thoughts of ever having the appointment of militia officers revert to the governor" and "they conceive that once the mode of appointment is confirmed to and practiced by the assemblies and people throughout the continent, it never will revert to the governor."[20]

What Elbridge Gerry feared most, however, was that the Council would get some support from Congress, for he knew that the Massachusetts delegation did not see eye to eye on all matters concerning Massachusetts politics, and he knew that the Council was banking on this. He knew, in other words, that the Council could rely on the sympathy of Thomas Cushing, at least, and perhaps even of others, such as the ever unpredictable John Hancock—who had courted moderates and even flirted with Thomas Hutchinson's prerogative politics in the early 1770s[21]—and the cautious Robert Treat Paine. Gerry's fears were well-founded. When John Adams talked to his colleagues, he found, as he explained in his private reply to the Council, that they were "not unanimous," while privately he admitted that open hostility among members of the Massachusetts delegation prevented their making a collective reply. Such trouble had happened a thousand times before, Adams frankly admitted to Joseph Hawley, and Thomas Cushing would neither agree to a joint letter nor would he "say what opinion he would give if it was moved in Congress." To Adams, who had long contended with

18. John Pitts to Samuel Adams, Watertown, 12 November 1775, in Samuel Adams Papers. James Warren also wrote at this time: "can an adherence to the old rotten charter be a balance for having the militia in the hands of the people?" To Samuel Adams, 12 November 1775, in Ford, ed., *Warren-Adams Letters*, 2: 426–27.

19. Hawley to Adams, Brookfield, 14 November 1775, in Charles Francis Adams, ed., *The Works of John Adams*, 10 vols. (Boston, 1850–56), 9: 364.

20. Gerry to John Adams, Watertown, 11 November 1775, in Adams Papers, reel 345.

21. See Chapter 3.

Cushing's complete opposition to separation of the American colonies from Great Britain, Cushing's animosity was exasperating and humiliating. "[I]t is very hard to be linked and yoked eternally with people who have either no opinions or opposite opinions," he complained, "and to be plagued with the opposition of our own colony to the most necessary measures, at the same time that you have all the monarchical superstition and the aristocratical domination of nine other colonies to contend with."[22]

To the Council's request for advice, John and Sam Adams replied independently while Cushing and Hancock acted jointly. Both Adamses advised the Council to concede the militia matter to the House. "The point was so plain," wrote John Adams, "I did not see the least occasion for laying the controversy before Congress." But he admitted that he was also influenced by the desire to avoid revealing the split that existed between the two "branches of our new government,"[23] and one might guess also that he did not care to show Congress the split that existed within the Massachusetts delegation. Hancock and Cushing, on the other hand, were at first determined to lay the whole affair before Congress and in a first, noncommittal letter back to Massachusetts they avoided expressing their personal opinions. Within a week, however, doubtless prompted by intelligence from Massachusetts such as the Adamses were receiving, the two replied with a tactfully worded statement to the effect that they, and all congressional delegates they had talked with, thought the Council in the right, but that at such a critical time, the Council might "gratify the house of representatives in this claim, but not by any means further to deviate from the charter."[24]

The Council could take some comfort in the support they received from Hancock and Cushing for maintaining traditional charter government, but they realized, as had the sympathetic congressmen, that they would have to give in. Their own future was in the balance should they insist on the exclusive right to appoint militia officers. When the General Court met again and turned in mid-December to the preparation of a militia bill, the Council let it be known that it would allow the House to appoint militia officers, retaining only the right to veto the choices made

22. John Adams to James Otis (President of the Council), Philadelphia, 23 November 1775, in *Amer. Arch.*, 4th ser., 3: 1653–54; Adams to Hawley, Philadelphia, 25 November 1775, in Adams, ed., *Works*, 9: 367–68.

23. Samuel Adams to James Otis, John Adams to James Otis, Philadelphia, 23 November 1775, in *Amer. Arch.*, 4th ser., 3: 1653–54; John Adams to Joseph Hawley, 25 November 1775, in Adams, ed., *Works*, 9: 367–68.

24. Hancock and Cushing to the Council of Massachusetts, Philadelphia, 24, 29 November 1775, in *Amer. Arch.*, 4th ser., 3: 1662, 1705.

by the House.[25] The first appointments were made public on January 23, 1776, and, while some moderates reacted with disgust,[26] they conceded victory to those reformers who believed that the appointive powers of a royal governor should not be retained by proxy, and that the people themselves or their representatives must exercise those powers hereafter.

The militia controversy had dual implications: it coincided with, and even helped along, the final split in the leadership of the old Popular party while at the same time it convinced both reformers and moderates that the internal political question of who should rule in Massachusetts, and under what form of government, had not been settled with the reversion to the charter of 1691; rather, the question had simply been temporarily swept under the rug. Each of these developments needs some examination.

The split in the Popular party had been coming for some time. Both Cushing and Hancock were merchants and had shared the merchants' distrust of Sam Adams from at least the early 1770s. Hancock had the amazing chameleonlike quality of reflecting the views of whatever side he was associating with at the moment, but Cushing was moderate in every sense of the word: he opposed Independence; he had squabbled openly with Sam Adams in the Provincial Congress in opposition to military preparedness; and he dragged his heels on almost every question that drove the wedge between Britain and America deeper and deeper. Though he maintained his friendship with many of the Popular party leaders, such as Joseph Hawley, he thoroughly exasperated the close friends of Sam and John Adams. Before Bunker Hill, when he urged the reduction of the colonial force around Boston because Gage was not apt to receive many reinforcements, James Warren speaking as an Adamsite, wrote that "if he [Cushing] had been in the clouds for seven years past, I think he would have had as just ideas of our situation and necessities as he has expressed to his friend Hawley."[27] In July, when

25. James Warren to Samuel Adams, Watertown, 19 December 1775, in Ford, ed., *Warren-Adams Letters*, 2: 429.

26. *BG*, 5 February 1776. The disapproval of two moderates is expressed in letters from Joseph Palmer and David Cobb to Robert Treat Paine. Palmer wrote: "We have passed a militia bill, not altogether such as we best liked, but 'twas necessary to have one." Watertown, 31 January 1776, in Robert Treat Paine Papers, vol. 2. Cobb's comments on the militia appointments for Bristol County were in verse: "If such men are by God appointed / The Devil may be the Lord's annointed." The appointments, he felt, would put "a final stop at once to all military business here." Taunton, Bristol County, 11 February 1776, ibid.

27. Thomas Cushing to Arthur Lee, Boston, September 1773, in "Cushing Let-

Bostonian exiles met at Concord to choose representatives to the newly reconstituted General Court, Cushing was bypassed, to the great chagrin of the few moderate merchants who were there, even though his fellow delegate to the Continental Congress, Sam Adams, was elected. Cushing continued to sit in Congress, of course, for he was quite rightly considered an important figure in the revolutionary movement, but throughout the Second Congress, the Adamses complained, in the words of John's wife Abigail, that "they have to combat not only other provinces but their own—a doubly difficult task when those who ought to aid, become stumbling blocks."[28]

The militia controversy changed this. The reformist House was impressed by the reply of the Adamses to the Council and James Warren reported that their "credit and reputation" was increasing while "a certain colleague of yours has lost or I am mistaken a great part of the interest he undeservedly had." This assessment proved correct, for as soon as the militia bill was introduced in December, the House chose new delegates to Congress for the coming year, returning all of the old members but Cushing, "whose absence could no longer be dispensed with!" Elbridge Gerry, who had worked more agreeably with the Adamses in the past, was Cushing's replacement.[29]

Cushing, back in Massachusetts, however, was in a position to play politics with the best of men. Since he had been elected to the Council the previous summer, his seat was ready and waiting upon his return, and he quickly became its leader, thereby adding more strength to the moderate faction. And he maintained close ties with his friend John Hancock, who still sat in Congress. Some people would like to think that Cushing had been completely deserted by his friends, wrote Hancock, but "by no means, my good friend, let the circumstances of the election discourage you from the noble pursuit in which you are engaged, your

---

ters," *MHS Collections*, 4th ser., 4 (1858): 360; Stephen Collins to Robert Treat Paine, Philadelphia, 14 January 1775, in Robert Treat Paine Papers, vol. 2; James Warren to John Adams, Watertown, 11 June 1775, Adams Papers, reel 344.

28. John Pitts to Samuel Adams, Watertown, 20 July 1775, in Samuel Adams Papers; Abigail Adams to Mercy Warren, Braintree, 24 July 1775, in Adams Papers, reel 344. On 22 December 1775, Samuel Adams wrote to John Adams, who had left Philadelphia for Massachusetts, that "our colony has sometimes been divided on questions that appeared to me to be important. Mr. C. has no doubt a right to speak his opinion whenever he can form one." Ibid., reel 345.

29. James Warren to John Adams, Watertown, 3 December 1775, in Adams Papers, reel 345; Warren to Samuel Adams, 19 December 1775, in Ford, ed., *Warren-Adams Letters*, 2: 430.

cause is just, and I am confident your conscience will acquit you."[30]
Cushing, however, was less discouraged than bitter and eager for revenge. Thus, when the House elected three major generals for the
militia, the Council accepted two and, under Cushing's direction, vetoed
the choice of James Warren, speaker of the House and an Adams man.
"I am glad to be out of the list," wrote Warren, "but the council have
done it in a manner as ungracious and indelicate as Bernard or Hutchinson would have done."[31]

The open rupture in the Popular party extended beyond Cushing, of
course, since John Hancock sided with Cushing. Gossip as far away as
New Jersey had it that there was "an irreconcilable difference . . . between those eminent worthies, John Hancock and Samuel Adams."[32]
But the disunity increased when, in the winter of 1775–76, the Adamses
alienated the fifth member of the Congressional delegation, Robert Treat
Paine. The trouble with Paine grew out of a rather ill-conceived letter
from James Warren to John Adams that, unfortunately for them, fell
into Paine's hands. Warren noted that Paine had "gone to satisfy his
curiosity in Canada"—as indeed he had, on behalf of the Congress. But
Warren went on to say that "he may possibly do as much good there as
at Philadelphia" and that there were people in Massachusetts who
thought him ill-qualified for special assignments.[33]

Paine's discovery of the letter prompted him to write letters to several
of the Popular leaders in Massachusetts. To Joseph Palmer of John
Adams's own town of Braintree, he wrote that "at present my mind is
much agitated on the discovery of a malicious and slandering correspondence between James Warren and John Adams respecting Mr. Cushing and myself." Paine wondered why he was exposing himself to the
"vengeance" of the British administration while people who were supposed to be his friends were undermining his "importance, happiness,
and safety." With great bitterness, he informed Palmer that he was
turning down the recently offered position of justice of the Supreme
Court because the chief justice was to be John Adams. Surely, he
thought, "some imperceptible influence had regulated the appointment
of a chief justice upon political or other principles than what are usual

30. Hancock to Cushing, 17 January 1776, in "Letters of John Hancock, 1776,"
*MHS Proceedings* 60 (1927): 98.
31. Warren to Samuel Adams, Watertown, 14 February 1776, in Ford, ed.,
*Warren-Adams Letters*, 2: 435–36.
32. *New Jersey Gazette*, 14 January 1776, quoted by Wells, *Samuel Adams*, 2:
384.
33. James Warren to John Adams, Watertown, 3 December 1775, in Adams
Papers, reel 345.

in such cases." Such things greatly disturbed him and he added that "if a junto of two, three, or four men are able to combine together, settle a test of political rectitude and destroy every one who will not comply with their mode of conduct, I must confess things are like to take a turn very different from what I expected."[34] His indignation thoroughly aroused, Paine then wrote to James Warren, reminding him that "union is undoubtedly the platform of our opposition [to Great Britain]" and that "whoever directly or indirectly doth anything to break this union is so far an enemy to American liberty, whoever abuses, disparages, or discourages a fellow laborer is so far an enemy to the house." Normally, Warren would have agreed, but under the circumstances, Paine's letter seemed "a model of invective and dullness."[35]

Paine, however, quite naturally found common cause with Thomas Cushing. Cushing extended the hand of friendship in two letters in February 1776, pointing out that men "whom I need not mention" had endeavored to prevent the reelection to Congress of both Cushing and Paine."It seems we are not men to suit their turn. We are not subservient enough." In both cases, wrote Cushing, the nameless men had used "some low dirty arts" to influence "some of the new members" with the insinuation that "we were timid, cautious, irresolute, etc., and not fit to answer their purpose in the present day." Or, in so many words, Cushing and Paine had been branded as moderates of the sort that impatient western reformers already believed were slowing down the revolutionary movement. Cushing explained that he was doing everything he could to vindicate Paine's character and that "you may depend on the continuance of my friendship," a clear offer of political alliance.[36]

Aside from its influence in the breakdown of the Popular party, the militia controversy did much to strengthen the reformers' determination to control the government of Massachusetts, at both a theoretical and a practical level. In theory, it was now obvious that the charter of 1691

34. Robert Treat Paine to Joseph Palmer, Philadelphia, 1 January 1776, ibid., also see Paine's copies of his letter to Palmer and a similar one to Joseph Hawley likewise dated 1 January 1776, in Robert Treat Paine Papers, Box 1766–76.

35. Robert Treat Paine to James Warren, Philadelphia, 5 January 1776, in Adams Papers, reel 345. The copy in the Adams Papers is one prepared by Warren and sent by him to John Adams. Paine's original was drafted by him on 1 January 1776, and can be found in Robert Treat Paine Papers, Box 1766–76. Warren's comment on the letter is in his letter to Adams dated 31 January in Adams Papers, reel 345.

36. Cushing to Paine, Watertown, 13 February 1776, in Robert Treat Paine Papers, vol. 2. See also Cushing to Paine, 29 February 1776, ibid. Joseph Palmer proved to be much less sympathetic to Paine than did Cushing. Palmer to Paine, Watertown, 24 January 1776, ibid.

simply retained too many of the features of government that reformers objected to. "Our government," wrote James Warren in December 1775, "however disposed to promote virtue and the public and private happiness of the people, is not considered here as permanent. We are all in continual expectation of another change, and besides, the late conduct of the Council has weakened that confidence and reverence necessary to give a well disguised [sic] government its full operation and effects."[37] By the end of February, to the horror of most members of the Council, the minority of councilors who favored the extension of popular sovereignty proposed a petition to Congress "praying liberty to take up and exercise such form of government as may be judged most conducive to the people's good under the present embarrassed circumstances." Thomas Cushing wrote, with relief, to Robert Treat Paine, that "this motion did not obtain, a great majority being against it," but he wanted to know how Congress might react to such a suggestion,[38] undoubtedly in anticipation of a continuation of the struggle.

Moderates, of course, had their own view of what was needed in Massachusetts government and the reestablishment of all three branches of government was a necessity. The judiciary was a major problem. Since the disruption of all civil government in 1774, the courts had failed to operate—much to the distaste of creditor-merchants and their allies, who were unable to resort to the law in order to press delinquent debtors. "Shall debtors defraud and starve their creditors, and every species of dishonesty be countenanced and encouraged by a delay of justice, which is virtually a denial of it?" asked Josiah Quincy of John Adams.[39] Urged on by such newspapers as the *Essex Gazette*,[40] in September the Council, acting as governor, appointed judicial officers for the various county and provincial courts.[41] By January 1776, however, the Council had to issue a proclamation reminding the citizenry that government "in all its branches" was now under the influence and control of the people, and

37. James Warren to Samuel Adams, Watertown, 5 December 1775, in Ford, ed., *Warren-Adams Letters*, 2: 428. Joseph Palmer expressed the similar hope that Congress would "set us free, free from a charter which has been a curse to our fathers as well as us." To Paine, Watertown, 1, 11 November 1775, in Robert Treat Paine Papers, vol. 2.

38. Cushing to Paine, Watertown, 29 February 1776, Robert Treat Paine Papers, vol. 2.

39. Quincy to Adams, 25 October 1775, in Adams Papers, reel 345.

40. *Essex Gazette* (Salem), 14 September 1775. See also Cushing, *History of the Transition*, pp. 84–92.

41. *Essex Gazette* (Salem), 5, 12 October 1775; Perez Morton to Robert Treat Paine, Watertown, 28 October 1775, in Robert Treat Paine Papers, vol. 2.

therefore more free and happy than what was enjoyed by their ancestors. Furthermore, "the major part of the Council have appointed magistrates and courts of justice in every county, whose happiness is so connected with the people, that it is difficult to suppose they can abuse their trust." As it was the business of these officers to enforce the laws, concluded the proclamation, anyone failing to support or give necessary assistance to them would be considered a disturber of the peace and subject to punishment.[42]

One historian has shown previously the opposition that existed in the two westernmost counties of Massachusetts to the courts of law. Beginning in Berkshire in the fall of 1775, and moving thereafter into Hampshire, western radicals rejected the Council's judicial appointees for the several courts and demanded that the people themselves either elect directly or at least nominate the judges of the inferior courts and the justices of the peace. Under the direction of Reverend Thomas Allen of Pittsfield, radicals in Berkshire conducted a wholesale attack on the resumed charter of 1691, warning people of "the dangerous effects of nominating to office by those in power" and calling for a democratic choice of civil and military officers. The very point of the Revolution, they said, was to destroy the governor's system which, like a "secret poison" had spread into every town connecting "great multitudes" with "the corrupt designs of an abandoned administration." To transfer such power to any other body of men would be equally dangerous.[43]

But the dissatisfaction apparent in Berkshire and Hampshire was not confined to those two counties. David Cobb, of Taunton in Bristol County, reported that "there is so much uneasiness among the people . . . that I am fearful they will not effect it [the proclamation]."[44] Reformers in the House must have been perfectly aware of this uneasiness, for though they concurred in the proclamation, two days later they "resolved and ordered" that the Inferior Courts of Common Pleas throughout the colony should be closed temporarily because the fees of judicial officers needed adjusting. The resolve also forbade the entering of any civil action with any justice of the peace or the rendering of judgment in any action then pending.[45] The result of such a move was to provide immediate protection for debtor farmers while at the same time to pre-

42. *BG*, 12 February 1776.

43. Robert J. Taylor, *Western Massachusetts in the Revolution* (Providence, 1954), pp. 80–87; Taylor, ed., *Massachusetts, Colony to Commonwealth*, pp. 16–19, 22–23.

44. Cobb to Robert Treat Paine, Taunton, 11 February 1776, in Robert Treat Paine Papers, vol. 2.

45. *BG*, 26 February 1776.

vent the appointees of the Council from collecting legal fees of any kind. The House claimed, in fact, that its order was necessary because of corruption among the new officials, a charge curiously in agreement with similar ones coming out of Berkshire County. When "a new fee table" could be prepared, the courts would reopen but, as Joseph Hawley explained to Robert Treat Paine, the House seemed in no hurry to introduce a fee bill since many members believed "other matters" to be more important.[46]

The House stalled for three months. On April 6, the first of a series of resolves declared the Superior Court of Judicature for the County of Middlesex adjourned until October. On April 18 and 29, similar resolves adjourned the courts of Hampshire, Worcester, Plymouth, and Barnstable counties.[47] When, finally, the preparation of a fee bill was begun, James Warren exclaimed that it would "drive every man of interest and ability out of office."[48] Thomas Cushing lamented to Robert Treat Paine that "the fees are considerably reduced. There is no provision for any fees in the bill for the judges of the Superior Court. The lawyers do not relish the bill at all."[49] One such lawyer, William Stearns, complained to John Adams that anti-lawyer sentiment was widespread throughout the colony and that though "a large majority" of the Council "are averse to curtailing fees . . . it is thought the House will worry them out, or wait till after election, when a more pliant board are expected."[50] Since class legislation was no part of the program of the Adams group, they objected just as strenuously as did the moderates. "I dread the consequences of the leveling spirit," wrote James Warren, "encouraged and drove to such lengths as it is." John Adams (who, one might remember, was the new chief justice) replied that he was greatly concerned. Were the salaries and commissions of judges, he asked, to "lie at the mercy of Col. Thompson, Col. Bowers, and Mr. Browne of Abington," three members of the House? "This is a great constitutional point in which the lives, liberties, estates, and reputations of the people are concerned," wrote Adams, "as well as the order and firmness of government in all its branches, and the morals of the people besides."[51] But the Council, as

46. Joseph Hawley to Robert Treat Paine, Watertown, [19] February 1776, in Robert Treat Paine Papers, vol. 2.

47. *BG*, 15 April, 6 May 1776.

48. Warren to Adams, 30 March, 3 April 1776, in Ford, ed., *Warren-Adams Letters*, 1: 217–20.

49. Cushing to Paine, Watertown, 29 February 1776, in Robert Treat Paine Papers, vol. 2.

50. Stearns to Adams, Worcester, 1 May 1776, in Adams Papers, reel 346.

51. Warren to Adams, 30 March, 3 April 1776; Adams to Warren, 16 April 1776,

William Stearns had suggested, were worried out and on May 2, the new act for regulating fees passed the General Court.[52]

The Popular leaders clearly found themselves thrust upon the horns of the proverbial dilemma. In one month they had to side with the popular wish for government close to the people; in another they had to throw their support to moderate promoters of stability. They were caught in the age-old tension between liberty and authority. But it was into this milieu of social and ideological tension that the issue of Independence was injected and out of it support for a complete break with Great Britain was to come.

When Elbridge Gerry wrote from Congress to James Warren on March 26, 1776, urging the latter to "originate instructions . . . in favor of independency,"[53] the issue had already become a major concern in the public prints. *Common Sense,* which had appeared in Massachusetts in February, had started the controversy, or at least had brought it into the open.[54] "Probus," writing in the *Boston Gazette* of March 11 asked for "those (if any such there be) who wish for an accomodation with G. Britain, on terms which shall make us in the least degree dependent on her; give as is their duty, their reasons to the public, and the terms on which we may safely accept such an accomodation." A farmer, quoted in the *Boston Gazette* from the *Pennsylvania Journal,* declared that he could see no probability of Britain's offering acceptable terms to the Americans. "I consider this year," he said, "as the grand and final period of British administration in this American world."[55]

Yet there is no doubt that the opposition to Independence in Massachusetts was both sizable and influential, even among people who can in no sense be considered Tories. "Some timid minds," wrote Elbridge Gerry, "are terrified at the word Independence." If necessary to get the General Court to approve Independence, wrote Gerry to James Warren, and "if you think caution in this respect good policy, change the name."[56] Clearly, Massachusetts offers no substantiation for the persistent idea

in Ford, ed., *Warren-Adams Letters,* 1: 217–20, 226–27.

52. *Acts and Resolves,* 5: 486–95.

53. Letter reproduced in James T. Austin, *The Life of Elbridge Gerry* (Boston, 1859), p. 174.

54. The *Boston Gazette* was advertising *Common Sense* in late February 1776. Joseph Hawley, who had received a copy direct from Philadelphia, wrote on 18 February 1776, that he had read it "and that every sentiment has sunk into my well prepared heart." To Elbridge Gerry, in Austin, *Life,* p. 163.

55. *BG,* 25 March 1776, from *Pennsylvania Journal,* 18 February 1776.

56. Gerry to Warren, 26 March 1776, in Austin, *Life,* p. 174.

that, in its origin, the American Revolution represented a conscious desire on the part of Americans for complete independence from Great
Britain, and assertions that it did represent such a desire ignore what
the participants themselves said. John Adams, writing in 1821, drew
attention more carefully than subsequent historians to the ambiguity
existing in the term "independence" itself. "It is true," he wrote, "there
always existed in the colonies a desire of independence of Parliament,
in the articles of internal taxation, and internal policy; and a very general if not a universal opinion, that they were constitutionally entitled
to it, and as general a determination if possible, to maintain and defend
it—but there never existed a desire of independence of the Crown, or
of general regulations of commerce, for the equal and impartial benefit
of all parts of the empire."[57]

Adams's comments are confirmed by newspaper reports and private
letters at the time of Independence. "Americanus," in the *Essex Gazette*
reminded his readers that "there nèver was a grosser falsehood invented
by the father of lies, than that we aimed at independence, while we were
treated in any measure as brethren or even as children in our minority.
But," he continued, "if our only alternative is independence or slavery,
who can think we can hesitate a moment which to choose?"[58] "I.F. behind the curtain" sounded the same theme when he wrote that those
whom Governor Hutchinson had branded as incendiaries, far from aiming at Independence, "meant no more than to rouse the people to a sense
of their rights, and to an opposition to acts of parliament which they
thought infringed them."[59] While it is true that many of the patriot
leaders were actively working for Independence by 1774, such comments
show how necessary it was for them to deal with the still strong urge for
reconciliation, which had remained a theme of letters appearing, particularly in the eastern newspapers, throughout 1775. "An American,"
writing in the *Essex Gazette* on June 1, 1775, was typical in his hope
"that these colonies may be enabled to give freedom and happiness to
our oppressed land and nation [i.e., Great Britain], without injury to
any person, and the once happy union between British and Americans
be restored, and both forever live together as brethren."[60]

While public opinion is always difficult to assess, John Adams, at
least, was convinced that general support for Independence would not

57. See for instance Richard B. Morris, "Class Struggle and the American Revolution," *WMQ*, 3d ser., 19 (1962): 3, 4, 7, 29. Adams to George A. Otis, 9 February
1821, in *The New England Historical and Genealogical Register* 30 (1876): 329–30.
58. *Essex Gazette* (Salem), 21 March 1776.
59. Letter dated 27 March in *BG*, 8 April 1776.
60. *Essex Gazette* (Salem), 1 June 1775.

have been forthcoming in 1775. Writing on July 3, 1776, he admitted that the great change in sentiment had been effected among the people during the past six months, though he doubtless exaggerated the completeness of the change. "The hopes of reconciliation, which were fondly entertained by multitudes of honest and well-meaning, though weak and mistaken people, have been gradually and at last totally extinguished." Pamphlets, newspapers, conventions, and private conversations, thought Adams, had prepared the people in every colony to adopt Independence "as their own act" where a declaration six months before might have provoked "heats, and perhaps convulsions."[61] Thus when the Continental Congress declared in July 1775 that "we have not raised armies with ambitious designs of separating from Great Britain, and establishing independent states,"[62] it did so not only to mollify reluctant revolutionaries in Congress itself, but also to express the sincere belief of a great many moderate Americans. There were large numbers of such people in eastern Massachusetts.

To suggest, however, that pamphlets such as *Common Sense* and newspaper propaganda were the only factor in bringing the people to an acceptance of Independence is an over-simplification, as is the idea that all people saw in Independence the same thing. In Massachusetts, the split that had developed on many issues appeared again on the issue of Independence though, in the end, both of the developing political parties accepted it, whether avidly or reluctantly. For the reformers, many of whom had not become involved in the revolutionary struggle until 1774, Independence was the *sine qua non* of revolution. They knew from experience that no royal administration would allow them to appoint militia and civil officers, adjourn law courts at will, regulate fees of executive and judicial officers, establish admiralty courts with juries, or limit plural office-holding. And they believed that Independence must guarantee them these rights. In its most extreme form, the reform position was expressed by the Berkshire constitutionalists: "If the right of nominating to office is not invested in the people, we are indifferent who assumes it, whether any particular persons on this or the other side of the [w]ater."[63] In a more general way, the duality of the Revolution was expressed from the reformist point of view in an unidentified letter that appeared in the *Boston Gazette* in April 1776. "The two great ob-

61. To Abigail Adams, in Adams, ed., *Works*, 9: 419–20. See also Adams to Archibald Bullock, 1 July 1776, in *Amer. Arch.*, 4th ser., 6: 1193.
62. *Essex Gazette* (Salem), 27 July 1775.
63. Petition of Pittsfield, 26 December 1775, in Taylor, ed., *Massachusetts, Colony to Commonwealth*, pp. 17–19.

jects now in the view of every friend to this country," stated the letter, "are to ward off the tyranny and usurpation of Great Britain and to prevent a like tyranny and usurpation from springing up in our own bowels, (for human nature is the same in America as in Great Britain and must not be entrusted without a sacred inclosure)." To secure both of these objectives, "the only alternatives before us are servitude and bondage to Great Britain, or freedom and independence."[64]

Eastern moderates were just as aware of the internal aspects of the movement for Independence as the reformers were, and for this reason they held out longest for reconciliation with Great Britain. Elbridge Gerry wrote to James Warren that he believed Virginia might declare Independence itself, even before Congress had done so, "unless you send some of your cool patriots among them." Joseph Hawley believed that people in the country and in the army were ready for complete Independence by May 1776, but he said nothing about eastern merchants. As for such merchants, Isaac Smith of Salem wrote at the same time to John Adams that "if matters could be settled to our liking, [it] would be preferable [to Independence]." William Tudor said that, around his home in Cambridge, "some timid piddling souls shrink at the idea" of Independence, though he believed the majority were for it. Sam Adams wrote that he knew the "moderate prudent Whigs" of Massachusetts would be shocked that he was now openly advocating Independence, but, he added to James Warren, "you know I never overmuch admired them. Their moderation has brought us to this pass, and if they were to be regarded, they would continue the conflict a century."[65]

Men who were moderates on internal issues proved to be moderate also on Independence. When, for instance, the House of Representatives resolved to consult their constituents on the matter of Independence, the Council, under Thomas Cushing's direction, refused to concur.[66] Not to be so easily put off, the House forwarded its resolution to the *Boston Gazette*, where it was published on May 13. The resolution requested each town to call a full meeting to advise their newly elected representatives to the General Court whether, should Congress declare Independence, they would "solemnly engage, with their lives and fortunes, to support them in the measure."[67]

64. *BG*, 15 April 1776.
65. Gerry to Warren, Philadelphia, 1 May 1776, in Austin, *Life*, pp. 177–78; Hawley to Gerry, Watertown, 1 May 1776, ibid., pp. 175–76; Smith to John Adams, Salem, 22 April 1776, in Adams Papers, reel 346; Tudor to John Adams, Cambridge, 29 February 1776, ibid., reel 345; Samuel Adams to Warren, Philadelphia, 16 April 1776, in Ford, ed., *Warren-Adams Letters*, 1: 224–25.
66. [Samuel Cooper] to Samuel Adams, 13 May 1776, in Samuel Adams Papers.
67. The resolution was dated May 10, 1776.

That there was a genuine fear among coastal towns that rural extremists were bent on complete control of Massachusetts is evidenced by the events in the spring of 1776. It was no secret that reformers planned to get control of the Council at the beginning of the next session.[68] It was further apparent to the easterners that Independence could place the seal of permanence on a reformist victory. Hoping to seize the initiative, in April 1776 the Salem and Marblehead committees of correspondence issued a broadside calling for all Essex County towns to send delegates to a political convention. "As the connection between Great Britain and this continent is growing every day more and more loose and uncertain," began the broadside, "and . . . as we may soon be obliged to take up Independency for ourselves, and upon this supposition, as undoubtedly a Republic or Commonwealth will be our form of government, it therefore becomes more serious and important, that every man have equal liberty, and equal right to representation in the legislature."[69] As events were to show, the Essex County men equated an "equal right to representation" with control of the new state by moderates.

The convention that met at Ipswich on April 25 agreed wholeheartedly with the arguments of the Salem and Marblehead committees. The present method of representation, they believed, was unjust in that it allowed every town with 30 freeholders the right to one representative in the General Court, while towns many times larger could not send proportionately more. The petition they formulated, and which was presented by their agents to the General Court on May 2, claimed that 30 western towns paid less in taxes than any one town in Essex County and yet had 15 times the weight in the legislature. A majority in the House, they continued, could be obtained from the representatives of towns that paid not more than one-quarter of the public tax. Ipswich alone had property and population equal to eight western towns. The eight, they demonstrated, sent 10 members to the House while Ipswich sent only 2.[70]

The Essex County petition was received by the General Court near the end of its session. It is probable that members who lived far from Watertown had already begun to depart. Whatever the case, the petition was effective and, in one of the quickest legislative moves of the session, the General Court passed an act "for providing for a more equal representation in the General Court." No town was to lose the number of

68. William Stearns to John Adams, Worcester, 1 May 1776, in Adams Papers, reel 346; John Adams to John Lowell, 12 June 1776, Adams to John Winthrop, 23 June, and Adams to Joseph Hawley, 25 August 1776, in Adams, ed., *Works*, 9: 392–93, 410, 435.
69. *EIHC* 36 (1900): 104.
70. *Acts and Resolves*, 5: 542.

representatives it already had, but those with 220 freeholders could elect three; those with 320, four; and so on.[71] Only four days elapsed between the introduction of the petition and the enactment of the new law by the General Court. The clear victory for the east moved James Warren to write promptly to John Adams: "Being threatened to be overrun from the frontiers, the county of Essex stirred themselves and sent a petition well supported for a more equal representation."[72]

Not willing to rely solely on the new system of representation to restore control of the House to the eastern towns, the moderates carried their election campaign into the newspapers. "O.P.Q.," writing "to the electors of representatives for the colony of Massachusetts," through the columns of the only western newspaper, the *Massachusetts Spy,* appealed to traditional values by suggesting that many of the previous representatives had been weak, selfish, cursing, designing, and (of course) "pretended patriots." The solution, wrote O.P.Q., was to return the powers of government to those "who will act upon the genuine and unadulterated principles of the constitution and . . . promote the greatest happiness of the greatest number." Such men, he said, would not devote their time to personal aggrandizement. And, perhaps more important, they would "not do everything in their power to destroy the commercial part of the community, without considering that the value of our lands is enhanced in proportion to the demand, which an extensive commerce, the opulence of the merchant, and the number of mechanics necessarily occasion." Finally, his traditionalist attack on selfishness giving way completely to interest politics, he launched into an attack on "the oppressive taxation of the trading and monied interests, which obtained in the last assembly." Such measures, he said, would drive every man of trade out of the colony.[73]

"One of your Number," writing in the *Boston Gazette,* was less specific than O.P.Q. but, nevertheless, reminded the Massachusetts electorate that "every man who is a professed and sincere friend to his country is not qualified for a legislator. The truth of this position," he continued, "has been . . . made apparent in the numbers of the late General Court." In conclusion he urged the election only of "men of learning and integrity."[74]

The elections of May 1776 completely reversed the short-lived social

---

71. *House Journals,* 2 May 1776; *Acts and Resolves,* 5: 502–3; *BG,* 6 May 1776.
72. Warren to Adams, 8 May 1776, in Ford, ed., *Warren-Adams Letters,* 1: 239.
73. 18 May 1776, in Taylor, ed., *Massachusetts, Colony to Commonwealth,* pp. 29–30.
74. *BG,* 13 May 1776.

revolution that had swung control of government to the agrarian reformers. Boston's representation sprang from 4 members to 12; Salem's from 2 to 7; Ipswich's from 2 to 5; and so on. Nine of the 12 Bostonians were merchants, as were 4 of the Salemites.[75] As a matter of fact, sea captains and prominent merchants constituted a major part of the eastern delegation, while towns in Essex and Suffolk with a few in eastern Middlesex were almost the only ones to benefit from the new representation law. The eastern counties could now control a majority of the House of Representatives. (Compare columns 3 and 4 in Appendix C.)

So concerned were the Massachusetts delegates in Congress over the factionalism rampant in their home province that scarcely a letter written by them during this period failed to express their dread of "party spirit." Sam Adams wrote that he hoped "no little party animosities can ever exist much less prevail in our councils" that would obstruct so necessary a measure as the defense of Boston harbor. John Adams, thinking his compatriots might be moving toward a new constitution and the election of a governor, wrote that he dreaded the consequences of electing governors, "and would avoid every appearance of and tendency towards party and division, as the greatest evil."[76]

But such letters only showed how completely detached the old Popular party leaders were becoming from the realities of Massachusetts politics. Social or sectional struggle was not in May 1776, nor had it ever been, part of their program. For their purposes, harmony was essential; interest politics was out of the question. The ideal still found expression, of course. "Demophilus," speaking through the pages of the old Popular party organ, the *Boston Gazette*, wrote on the occasion of the new election of the provincial Council: "Choose no man because he lives in this or that particular part of the colony. Choose the best . . . whether they have had illustrious ancestors,—whether they have great estates or not."[77] But all attempts to heal the rift that had split the province in two were complete failures. The new Council, with no diplomatic skills needed from Joseph Hawley, included few westerners and was top-heavy with east coast merchants: James Bowdoin, Thomas Cushing,

75. The Boston merchants were William Cooper, William Phillips, John Pitts, John Brown, Benjamin Austin, Oliver Wendell, Nathaniel Appleton, Caleb Davis, and Samuel A. Otis. See Stephen E. Patterson, "Boston Merchants and the American Revolution" (M.A. thesis, Univ. of Wis., 1961), appendix. The Salem merchants were Jonathan Gardner, Jr., Richard Derby, George Williams, and Warwick Paltry or Palfray. See *EIHC* 66: 87, 3: 154–67, 42: 313, 66: 65.

76. Samuel Adams to James Warren, 12 May 1776; John Adams to James Warren, 12 May 1776, in Ford, ed., *Warren-Adams Letters*, 1: 244, 243.

77. *BG*, 27 May 1776.

Benjamin Austin, and William Phillips of Boston, as well as Benjamin Greenleaf, Richard Derby, and Azor Orne of Essex County. At the same time, the General Court failed to reelect to the Council the Massachusetts congressional delegates, though the honor had been extended to them the previous year. This meant that neither of the Adamses nor any of their friends, with the exception of James Bowdoin, sat on the new Council.[78]

The western reformers, who found themselves completely outmaneuvered, did not give up easily, even though their position was hopeless. On May 31, they moved "that the members from the town of Boston, and other towns, who have sent a larger number than they were heretofore impowered to elect, be discharged." But, as the *House Journals* record, "after some debate thereon, the matter was ordered to subside." Immediately a motion was made to call upon such members to "inform the house, what number of inhabitants qualified to vote for representatives, their respective towns consisted of." The motion being put to the vote, "it passed in the negative."[79]

The theory advanced here that the question of Independence was intertwined with an internal struggle in Massachusetts—that is, that many agricultural towns saw in Independence their only chance for political preeminence in Massachusetts, while moderates feared Independence in part for the same reason—is further substantiated by the pattern of response to the resolution of the General Court regarding Independence. Essex County towns, at least, seemed reluctant to vote for Independence until they were sure that maritime towns would control the new state government.

On June 7, when the House called upon its members to declare their constituents' wishes regarding Independence, it was found that "many towns" had taken no action. With the explanation that the newspaper report of the House's resolve had not reached several towns, a resolution ordered that they be informed by handbill.[80] On June 12, James Warren wrote to Elbridge Gerry that "more than one-half of them [the representatives] are instructed fully in favor of it, and not one against it." Continuing, he wrote, "it appears to me the sentiments of our colony are more united on this great question than they ever were on any other."[81]

78. Of the 30 councilors, at least 18 were from the eastern towns. As to Congressional delegates, see Brennan, *Plural Office-Holding*, p. 116. James Warren wrote to John Adams, 2 June 1776: "you will see in the list of councilors some that I did not vote for." Ford, ed., *Warren-Adams Letters*, 1: 252–53.

79. *House Journals*, 31 May 1776.

80. Ibid., 7 June 1776.

81. *Amer. Arch.*, 4th ser., 6: 829–30.

Joseph Hawley, if possible even more optimistic than Warren, wrote Gerry that "about two-thirds of the towns in the colony had met, and all instructed in the affirmative," for the most part unanimously.[82] The buoyant optimism of these old Popular party leaders, however, disregarded the sectional response to the Independence issue and, like the June 7 resolve of the General Court, equivocated as to the reason why many towns were tardy in expressing themselves.

The argument that many towns had failed to respond to the request of the General Court because the newspaper notice had not reached them was fallacious. All of the members of the Court, after all, who had voted for the resolution and then returned home between sessions could have informed their constituents what was expected of them. Both Stockbridge and Pittsfield in Berkshire County included the consideration of Independence in their meetings to choose new representatives, showing that distance was not a factor. Pittsfield was particularly energetic in its instructions, which required its representative "on no pretence whatever [to] favour a union with Great Britain, as to our becoming in any sense dependent on her hereafter." Further, he was to encourage the House "to notify the honourable Continental Congress that this whole province are waiting for the important moment which they in their great wisdom shall appoint for the declaration of Independence and a free republic."[83]

The towns of Essex County, however, were by no means so enthusiastic about Independence before the results of their representation campaign were known. Of the 16 Essex towns whose actions were recorded, only 1 of them, Rowley, voted unequivocally for Independence before the General Court met. Newbury left the matter to the wisdom of its representatives while Lynn gave a very general instruction that its representative should concur in any act of Congress. The other 13, on the other hand, took no action until after the representation controversy had been settled in their favor. Ipswich voted for Independence on June 10; Salem and Andover, June 12; Marblehead, June 17; and so on. When Warren and Hawley were writing that one-half and two-thirds of Massachusetts towns had voted for Independence, only four Essex County towns had actually done so.[84]

82. 13 June 1776, ibid., pp. 844–45.

83. Ibid., p. 649.

84. The following dates are given in almost all of the local histories for these towns: Lynn, 21 May (concur in measures of Congress); Rowley, 22 May; Newbury, 27 May (representatives may decide); Newburyport, 31 May; Ipswich, 10 June; Salem, 12 June; Andover, 12 June; Beverly, 13 June; Marblehead, 17 June;

The reluctance of Essex County towns to take the final step towards separation from Great Britain, can, of course, be explained in a number of ways. The merchants' interest in maintaining commercial ties with the empire would certainly be an important factor.[85] But at the same time, it is clear that many people saw a connection between Independence and representation in the General Court. Boston, for instance, which had been in the possession of the British until March 17 and had played little part in the east-west struggle, instructed its representatives to support any move by Congress for Independence but followed it immediately with a lengthy instruction on representation. "It is essentially necessary," the instruction said, "in order to preserve harmony among ourselves, that the constituent body be satisfied that they are fairly represented."[86] Topsfield in Essex County, a renegade farming community that had refused to participate in the Ipswich Convention, aligned itself with the western towns by following its vote for Independence with a general condemnation of the new representation act. The question of "equal or unequal representation in Court," they held, tended towards dangerous innovation. "We heartily wish that the ancient rules in the Charter, which this province has been so much contending for, might be strictly adhered to."[87] By the following October, Topsfield was much more vociferous in its objection to the new system of representation. The act, they then claimed, "was obtained only to serve the interest of particular parties under a pretence of equal representation."[88]

Thus the acceptance of Independence in Massachusetts represented only the most superficial kind of union, for different people saw it as the opportunity to do very different things. To accept the eighteenth-century New England terminology, these differences of opinion were partisan and, by the spring of 1776, the existence of two new "party" divisions was so obvious that they had to be recognized as such, even by patriot leaders like the Adamses who argued for the traditional ideal of a united and nonpartisan society. The parties, were, of course, not highly organized—there was no state or county organization, there were no party

Boxford, 17 June; Danvers, 18 June; Bradford, 20 June; Topsfield, 21 June; Gloucester, 24 June; Haverhill, 25 June; Almsbury, 1 July.

85. See, for instance, the comments of William Pynchon, 12 February 1776, in Fitch Edward Oliver, ed., *The Diary of William Pynchon of Salem* (Boston, 1890), pp. 3–4. See also Isaac Smith to John Adams, Salem, 22 April 1776, in Adams Papers, reel 346.

86. *BG*, 10 June 1776.

87. *Amer. Arch.*, 4th ser., 6: 703–4.

88. Taylor, ed., *Massachusetts, Colony to Commonwealth*, p. 42.

names, there was not as yet a conscious appeal to the voters on a party basis—but these after all are the trappings of later political parties and there is no reason why the revolutionary parties must live up to our twentieth-century expectations of what constitutes a party. To men at the time, partisanship was a refusal to view public issues in a disinterested way, with a willingness to place the good of society above the advancement of one's self or of one's group. In republican terms, partisanship was selfishness; translated into 1776 reality, it was a political expression of economic differences, and it was this economic basis of partisanship that most disturbed the Adamses and their friends. Anyone, wrote Sam Adams to Elbridge Gerry in January 1776, "who gives his suffrage for any man to fill a public office merely because he is rich" is "a very injudicious friend" to his country, "and yet you tell me there are recent instances of this in our government." It was both "dishonourable and dangerous," thought Adams, to promote a man either because he was rich or because he was poor. "I hope our country will never see the time when either riches or the want of it will be the leading considerations in the choice of public officers," he concluded.[89]

The persistence of partisanship forced patriot leaders to analyze it further. Dr. Samuel Cooper believed that merchants would never subordinate their private interests to the public good. "Merchants have no object but their own particular interest, and they must be controlled or they will ruin any state under heaven. The statesman," he warned, "must for ever keep a watchful eye on that order of men."[90] Mercy Warren was afraid that "the selfish views, the narrow motives, the passion for power and the ambitious swellings of some among ourselves will ruin all at last." She blamed "certain connections" and "the conduct and manners of many of our [own] traders" for the moral degeneracy of the times and she particularly condemned the Massachusetts Council for trying to maintain the prerogatives of the governor during the militia controversy as being contrary to "the good of the whole." "Ought not internal bickering to cease and every man consider himself as entrusted with the right[s] and liberties of a generous people when he is pushed forward into places of trust or honor," she asked.[91] John Adams agreed that there was an economic explanation for the lack of public virtue (that is, for the existence of partisanship). "The spirit of commerce," he wrote to

89. Adams to Elbridge Gerry, Philadelphia, 2 January 1776, in Austin, *Life*, pp. 125–26. See also Gerry to Samuel Adams, Watertown, 13 December 1775, ibid., pp. 122–24.
90. Cooper to John Adams, Weymouth, 26 April 1776, in Adams Papers, reel 346.
91. Mercy Warren to Abigail Adams [Plymouth], [December 1775], ibid., reel 345.

Mercy Warren, "which even insinuates itself into families, and influences holy matrimony, and thereby corrupts the morals of families as well as destroys their happiness, it is much to be feared is incompatible with that purity of heart and greatness of soul which is necessary for an happy republic." The trouble was that the spirit of commerce was "rampant" in New England. "Even the farmers and tradesmen are addicted to commerce," he wrote, showing that he condemned any economic group that allowed its economic interest to govern its political action. "While this is the case, there is great danger that a republican government would be very factious and turbulent there. Divisions in elections are much to be dreaded. Every man must seriously set himself to root out his passions, prejudices, and attachments, and to get the better of his private interest. The only reputable principle and doctrine must be that all things must give way to the public."[92] Adams thereby reduced to its quintessence the underlying assumption of his republican ideology.

But clearly the revolutionary goals of the two emerging parties did not jibe with those of the Adams group. Reformers throughout the province used their single year in power in the General Court to clarify their objectives and to begin the democratic reforms that they believed were a necessary part of revolution. They had reformed the admiralty courts, forbidden the holding of incompatible offices, reduced judicial fees, tampered with the dispensing of justice, and placed the appointment of militia officers on a popular level. The more extreme element among them—to be found chiefly in the western counties—had asked for the continuation of popular county conventions, and the setting up of registers of deeds and of probate in every town. Perfectly consistent, John Adams condemned this "rage for innovation which appears in so many wild shapes in our province"[93] just as quickly as he condemned east coast merchants. And accepting completely the traditional idea of a class society, he warned his friends to prevent alterations in the qualifications of voters, which apparently was also a demand of some reformers. Such a move, he warned, would simply lead to more "controversy and altercation" and would tend "to confound and destroy all distinctions, and prostrate all ranks to one common level."[94] Adams, in short, was out of sympathy with the democratic ambitions of Massachusetts reformers.

92. Adams to Mercy Warren [Philadelphia], 16 April 1776, in Ford, ed., *Warren-Adams Letters*, 1: 222–23.

93. Adams to John Winthrop, Philadelphia, 23 June 1776, in "Winthrop Papers," *MHS Collections*, 5th ser., 4 (1878): 310.

94. Adams to James Sullivan, 26 May 1776, in Adams, ed., *Works*, 9: 378.

But whether out of sympathy or not, old patriot leaders had to admit that increased democracy was now the goal of many of the common people. Benjamin Kent wrote to Sam Adams in May 1776 that "the people of this province . . . have not virtue enough to set up and maintain that democracy they almost universally and most evidently are now aiming at." The trouble was, Kent thought, that "most of our people have such an aversion to absolute monarchy that they are not aware of the danger of the most popular kind of government that was ever thought of."[95] In the same vein, David Cobb wrote in horror that his town had elected "old Major Godfrey and Nathaniel Leonard" as its representatives to the General Court. "Their popularity arose from their heading the mob when the courts were opposed."[96] Thus the reform position had gained widespread acceptance among the people in Massachusetts, though, as we have noted before and will see even more clearly again, democratic reform was most strongly advocated in the least commercial-cosmopolitan towns, those concentrated largely in the western counties of the new state.

The revolutionary expectations of moderates had also become clearer during the year prior to Independence. Though willing, when forced to choose, to support a complete break with Britain, moderates had expressed considerable reluctance to sever their ties with the empire, in part because many of them had an economic stake in Britain's commercial system but also because the British connection had maintained the social primacy of the monied classes in America and was the surest guarantee against an uncontrolled democracy.[97] Thus moderates—

95. Kent to Adams, Boston, 24 May 1776, in Samuel Adams Papers.

96. Cobb to Robert Treat Paine, Boston, 27 May 1776, in Robert Treat Paine Papers, vol. 2; see also James Sullivan to Gen. John Sullivan, 6 December 1775, in Thomas C. Amory, *Life of James Sullivan: with Selections from his Writings,* 2 vols. (Boston, 1859), 2: 66. Sullivan believed that the army was a seedbed of democratic thinking.

97. John Adams was one of the active proponents of Independence, of course, but he understood as well as anyone that many men feared Independence because it might allow a leveling democracy. It was in sympathy with this point of view that he wrote from Philadelphia on 25 August 1776: "A popular government is the worse curse to which human nature can be devoted, when it is thoroughly corrupted. Despotism is better." The people must learn that their choice in elections must be based on "the public good alone," not on interest, favor, or partiality, "or you will very soon make wise and honest men wish for monarchy again." Adams to Joseph Hawley, in Adams, ed., *Works,* 9: 434–35. John Rowe, merchant of Boston, was typical of the moderates who despised extremist Sons of Liberty, associated with Tories until the evacuation of Boston, incurred the resentment of the lower orders, but accepted Independence once it was a fact. Entries of 24 October 1774; 31 January, 15 March 1775; 8 April, 15 June, 18 July, 15 August 1776, "Diary

through their spokesmen in the Council—jealously guarded the prerogatives of the royal governor in the militia controversy and later refused to act with the House in calling for popular consideration of Independence. The Essex County convention in April 1776 showed that eastern moderates were determined to have as few changes as possible in the charter of 1691 and to ensure that charter government would be controlled by the traditional ruling classes. The move towards Independence added urgency to their determination.

In conclusion, it is scarcely necessary to point out that the votes of Massachusetts towns had no direct bearing on the final separation from Great Britain. Congress, in fact, moved towards Independence for reasons not closely connected with the individual colonies at all. But the Massachusetts towns could not have known this would be the case. And the knowledge, for that matter, would not have altered the fact that many people viewed Independence largely in purely provincial terms. The question of Independence had posed for them the problem as to which section, which social group or which economic interest would control the state. Though reformers were outmaneuvered by the changes in representation effected just before Independence, their democratic goals remained the same, ensuring a continuation of the conflict between the two new parties.

---

of John Rowe," *MHS Proceedings*, 2nd ser., 10 (1896): 89, 90, 99, 100–101, 102.

# 6

## Representation and the Problem of a New Constitution

BY THE time of Independence, Massachusetts politics had again assumed the partisan dimensions that had characterized the early stages of the Revolution. While the state was not, and had never been, completely polarized into two neatly defined political parties, conflict in the legislature pitted western, reform-minded representatives against easterners more interested in social stability and political caution; both groups were beginning self-consciously to identify their interests and their memberships; and the easterners, at least, had taken the first steps towards extra-legislative organization in the Ipswich Convention of April 1776. The action of Essex County moderates was to evoke an equal and opposite reaction from westerners.

The immediate political issue, of course, was representation, but in many ways this was no simple question of the distribution of representatives, but an omnibus issue comprehending all of the thus-far unanswered questions about the future of Massachusetts society. Its resolution would determine whether popular reform or caution would prevail in the legislature, and perhaps even if institutions themselves might be changed to satisfy the democratic instincts of some people, or left alone, to mitigate the apprehensions of others. In other words, representation was the greatest of constitutional questions; it was the means to an end, and its recognition as such by Massachusetts leaders indicated their growing awareness of the nature of power and the prerequisites to its enjoyment.

Naturally enough, the tendency towards partisanship conflicted with the professed republicanism of many revolutionaries, and men frequently found themselves committed ambiguously to the creation of an idealistic single-mindedness in their respective counties to meet a very real opposition from another part of the state. Some few men began to alter their notions of consensus and to argue forthrightly for the promotion of their separate interests. But for the most part, the emerging partisanship grew without ideological justification, while it settled the "commonwealth" into a new pattern of politics in which the fortunes of contending parties rose and fell, see-saw fashion, as popular moods and leadership skills favored first one side and then the other.

The redistribution of representation in May 1776 to favor the larger eastern towns made the legislative contest an unequal one in the year following Independence, and it provoked an angry response among western (and even some small eastern) farming towns. The initial response of these towns grossly oversimplified the problem: they saw the new act itself as the cause of their dilemma and failed to consider the large number of towns unwilling or unable, because of distance or expense, to send a representative to the legislature. Viewed in their oversimplified way, however, representation in the new House was inequitable. Counting only those towns in the eastern counties which elected more than one member, we find that 28 towns with 22.5 percent of the population of Massachusetts, sent 38.7 percent of the representatives. (See Table 2.) Together with the other eastern towns, they controlled a decided majority in the House of Representatives. At the same time, 20 of the 28 councilors elected by the General Court were similarly from the eastern counties.[1] Whether fair or not, the system permitted a group of eastern towns, most of them mercantile communities, to elect a controlling majority of the province's representatives.

The eastern majority, however, did not invariably function as such; it could and did tilt the balance in favor of moderate measures, but it did not self-consciously assert its control over debate nor rebut demands for change and reform. Even as late as the second session of the General Court, which met in July, the newer members of the House, while they deplored many of the schemes proposed by "innovators," were unwilling to speak out against them. As John Lowell, from coastal Newburyport, wrote, "a timidity of opposing principles that begin to be too popular, prevent many of us from opening as we ought."[2] The schemes ranging from demands for county assemblies to town probates of will represented an honest desire by many reformers to bring government closer to the people, but there was little sympathy for this from the old revolutionary leaders. John Adams wrote from Philadelphia: "I am grieved to hear, as I do from various quarters, of that rage for innovation which

1. *House Journals,* 29 May 1776.
2. To John Adams, 14 August 1776, in Adams Papers, original in MHS, microfilm copy in State Historical Society of Wisconsin, reel 346.

appears in so many wild shapes in our province. Are not these ridiculous projects prompted, excited, and encouraged by disaffected persons, in order to divide, dissipate, and distract the attention of the people, at a time when every thought should be employed and every sinew exerted for the defence of the country?" Such projects, thought Adams, tended

Table 2. Eastern Towns That Benefited from the Representation Act of 1776

| Town | Number of representatives | |
|---|---|---|
| | May 29, 1776 | July 19, 1775 |
| *Suffolk County* | | |
| Boston | 12 | 4 |
| Roxbury | 3 | 1 |
| Dorchester | 2 | 1 |
| Milton | 2 | 1 |
| Braintree | 3 | 1 |
| Weymouth | 2 | 1 |
| Hingham | 3 | 1 |
| Dedham | 2 | 1 |
| Wrentham | 3 | 1 |
| Stoughton | 2 | 1 |
| *Essex County* | | |
| Salem | 7 | 2 |
| Ipswich | 5 | 2 |
| Newbury | 5 | 1 |
| Newburyport | 5 | 2 |
| Marblehead | 5 | 2 |
| Andover | 4 | 1 |
| Haverhill | 2 | 1 |
| Gloucester | 5 | 1 |
| Almsbury | 2 | 1 |
| *Middlesex County* | | |
| Cambridge | 4 | 2 |
| Charlestown | 3 | 2 |
| *Plymouth County* | | |
| Plymouth | 2 | 1 |
| Bridgewater | 6 | 1 |
| Kingston | 2 | 1 |
| *Barnstable County* | | |
| Barnstable | 2 | 2 |
| *Bristol County* | | |
| Taunton | 2 | 2 |
| Dartmouth | 5 | 2 |
| *Cumberland County* | | |
| Falmouth | 4 | 1 |
| Total | 104 | 40 |

NOTE: Total number of representatives, 1776: 269.
SOURCE: *House Journals,* 29 May 1776, 19 July 1775.

"directly to barbarism."[3] But this was the stuff of private correspondence. Probably no one said as much in the legislature, though unquestionably many thought as Adams did. On key votes, however, the eastern group could use its legislative power to advantage and did so on each of the major issues. These issues included the problem of a new constitution, the functioning of the courts of law, the regulation of prices, and monetary policy. A new constitution, with representation as the central factor, was the ultimate issue to westerners; but the other issues had priority for easterners, and they held the upper hand.

The almost complete lack of judicial activity had troubled moderates for nearly two years. "How long must the courts of justice remain unopened, and the law of the land unexecuted?" asked Josiah Quincy of John Adams. Presenting a view that was also shared by many merchants, Quincy spoke of the social implications of suspended justice. "Shall debtors defraud and starve their creditors, and every species of dishonesty be countenanced and encouraged by a delay of justice?" he asked. "Is not the man of *substance* reduced to a level, with those who have *none*?—Have not the dishonest *many*, in every respect, but that of being honest the advantage of [i.e., over] the honest *few*?"[4]

Opposition to opening the courts was widespread. From Barnstable, James Otis, Sr., wrote in March 1776 that the town meeting refused to choose jurymen, denied that the General Court had authority to call courts into session, and argued that there was no law. Otis hoped that by postponing the Court of General Sessions and the Court of Common Pleas until June "some of our difficulties may be got over, and others subside."[5] In Philadelphia, John Adams had heard that "the justices had been interrupted by force in Taunton, Hampshire, and Berkshire."[6] In response to Adams's request for more information, John Winthrop explained that, in fact, no courts had been held in Hampshire or Berkshire and that justices of the peace had not been appointed for Hampshire. In Taunton (Bristol County), the justices had been attacked by 30 or 40 men armed with sticks and had been prevented from going into the court house. "Some suspect," wrote Winthrop, "that the true ground of the opposition, at least with many, is an unwillingness to submit to law and pay their debts." While the courts of sessions had met in Essex and Middlesex, concluded Winthrop, the General Court had thought it best

3. To John Winthrop, 23 June 1776, in "Winthrop Papers," *MHS Collections*, 5th ser., 4 (1878): 310. Adams apparently was referring to the votes of a Suffolk County town, an account of which appeared in *BG*, 27 May 1776.
4. 25 October 1775, in Adams Papers, reel 345.
5. To Benjamin Greenleaf, 18 March 1776, in *Amer. Arch.*, 4th ser., 5: 408.
6. To John Winthrop, 12 May 1776, in "Winthrop Papers," p. 302.

to adjourn the courts in most counties, "such has been the spirit raised among the people."[7]

To get the courts operating again, the moderates took the safest course possible. At the same time that they pushed through the new representation act (at the end of the spring session of the General Court in May 1776), the Council recommended that the Superior Court sit in June at Ipswich, in Essex County, the heart of mercantile strength. Many of John Adams's friends urged him, as chief justice, to return to the province to preside over the court.[8] Unable to do so, Adams nonetheless agreed with the moderates on the necessity of law enforcement. The sitting of the court, he wrote, "will contribute to give stability to the government, I hope, in all its branches."[9]

The actual sitting of the Superior Court, both at Ipswich and, subsequently, at York in Maine, was as well planned as a Boston funeral. The General Court specifically ordered that the justices not deal with cases that were "open to dispute." After being introduced in both places by the sheriffs "with some degree of pomp and respect," the justices "took up all actions standing on the book continued before, and continued them again." The technique used was to register all complaints, admit all appeals, serve notice to contending parties that a court action had been brought in, but to decide on nothing contentious.[10]

The same method was used in lesser courts. In Hampshire County, for example, the court heard no criminal cases in any of its three sessions in 1776. The extent of its efforts was to grant permission for towns to set up inoculating hospitals.[11] In eastern counties, the gradual approach appeared to work. By September 1776, Abigail Adams reported to her husband that "the people [in Braintree] seem to be pleased and gratified at seeing justice returning into its old regular channel again." And

7. 1 June 1776, ibid., pp. 306–8. For another account of the Taunton affair, see Sally Paine to Robert Treat Paine, Taunton, 4 June 1776, Robert Treat Paine Papers, MHS, vol. 2.

8. John Winthrop to John Adams, Cambridge, 1 June 1776, in "Winthrop Papers," pp. 306–8; Abigail Adams to John Adams, Braintree, 9 May 1776, in Adams Papers, reel 346; James Sullivan to John Adams, Boston, 17 May 1776, ibid.

9. To Abigail Adams, Philadelphia, 27 May 1776, in Adams Papers, reel 346.

10. A series of resolves was made by the General Court on the subject of the courts of law. BG, 24 June 1776; House Journals, 15 June 1776. Orders published in the newspapers were not so detailed in explaining the technique to be used as is the letter of Thomas Cushing to John Adams, Boston, 29 July 1776, in Adams Papers, reel 346.

11. Robert J. Taylor, Western Massachusetts in the Revolution (Providence, 1954), p. 87.

Thomas Cushing believed that Massachusetts had "got into [a] much better state. . . . The courts of justice go on. The reins of government are strengthened."[12]

The cautious reopening of the law courts was a step in the direction of stability, but the problem of a seriously inflated wartime economy was much more difficult to solve. Massachusetts, like all other states and the Continental Congress itself, had resorted to the emission of paper money to finance the war. It was a reasonable process that had been used effectively in colonial times, and one that worked essentially as a tax on the wealthy since the paper depreciated in the hands of the holders, but hurt no one through whose hands it quickly passed. Even the inflation that accompanied paper emissions had generally been bearable, but this time the practice was complicated by other factors. For one thing, to show its good faith with all Americans engaged in the defense of liberty, Massachusetts accepted the paper currency of all states plus that of the Congress. Secondly, since the first year of the war was centered in Massachusetts, much (if not most) of the new money found its way into New England. From the winter of 1775–76 onward, complaints grew in number that debtors were paying their debts in "fictitious dollars," while "persons who came from the southwards" were charged with fraudulently passing off their own depreciated currency at many times its value.[13]

Many men believed that only the Congress could solve the problem by imposing a general solution on all of the states. Moderates in Massachusetts, however, realized that they could at least put their own house in order and in June 1776 began the task. They ordered that Massachusetts paper must be accepted at face value, but switched their emphasis from new paper emissions to large-scale borrowing to meet their financial needs. From June to the end of the year, when they ended all paper emissions, they borrowed nearly twice as much as they printed in new currency.[14] Furthermore, they secured all loans with orders for

12. Abigail Adams to John Adams, Braintree, 15 September 1776, in Adams Papers, reel 346. On the success of the Superior Court at Ipswich, see David Sewall to John Adams, York, 15 July 1776, ibid. See also Thomas Cushing to Robert Treat Paine, Boston, 9 September 1776, and Abigail Greenleaf to Robert Treat Paine, Taunton, 12 September 1776, in Robert Treat Paine Papers, vol. 2.

13. Josiah Quincy to John Adams, 25 October 1775; William Tudor to John Adams, Cambridge, 28 October 1775, in Adams Papers, reel 345. See also Abigail Adams to John Adams, Braintree, December 1775, ibid.

14. For a discussion of some of these matters, see Ralph Volney Harlow, "Economic Conditions in Massachusetts during the American Revolution," *CSM Publications* 20 (1920): 163–90. In the period from June to December 1776 inclusive, Massachusetts issued £295,042. See *Acts and Resolves*, 5: 547–49, 559–61, 589–91,

future taxes which were to be collected without any further directions from the legislature (an obvious reaction to the shifting tides of Massachusetts politics). In a brilliant move to tap patriotic sentiment and exploit the machinery of the Revolution, they appointed the Committees of Correspondence to serve as agents for the sale of the new treasurers' notes. In the same vein, both privately and as a legislature, they urged the Continental Congress similarly to switch its financing from paper money to interest-bearing bonds. Congress, of course, could not afford to give up its paper emissions, but it did begin to issue bonds as well in the fall of 1776. Finally, moderates succeeded in getting an agreement from a conference of New England legislators who met in December 1776 to end paper emissions in New England and to resort to borrowing and taxation.[15]

The efforts of Massachusetts moderates were in keeping with the soundest financial thinking of the time, as they conceived it. But in proportion to the problem, their measures were mere palliatives. Hundreds of thousands of pounds in unbacked paper still circulated. "[S]ome method must be taken, as speedily as possible, to sink the bills of credit," wrote Joseph Palmer. In May 1777 another source of paper was checked when the legislature ended its recognition of other state currencies as legal tender. But by the summer of 1777, the matter had reached crisis proportions. "The state of our currency is in a wretched situation and requires the most capital attention," wrote James Warren. Taxation was probably the answer, he thought,[16] but taxation was not a popular solution.

---

606–8, 610–12. During the same period, the state borrowed £556,400, promising 5 percent interest at first, but raising it to 6 percent in October, even on the money already borrowed. Ibid., pp. 660–61.

15. The provision for future taxation may be noted in the act of 2 December 1776, in *Acts and Resolves*, 5: 604–5. The use of the Committees of Correspondence, Safety, and Inspection as loan agents was voted on 6 December 1776, ibid., p. 661. Protests to Congress began with the decision of 29 June 1776, *House Journals*, p. 52. See also Joseph Hawley to Elbridge Gerry, Watertown, 2 June 1776, 11 September 1776, in Samuel Adams Papers, New York Public Library. For a discussion of the action of Congress, see E. James Ferguson, *The Power of the Purse: A History of American Public Finance, 1776–1790* (Chapel Hill, N.C., 1961), pp. 25–36. The recommendations of the conference of committees of New England states meeting at Providence, 25 December 1776, can be found in *Acts and Resolves*, 5: 813.

16. Palmer to John Adams, Boston, 16 April 1777, in Adams Papers, reel 347; *Acts and Resolves*, 5: 639–40; Warren to John Adams, Boston, 4 September 1777, in Worthington Chauncey Ford, ed., *Warren-Adams Letters*, 2 vols. (Boston, 1917–25), 1: 365.

Paper money was the cause of economic crisis, but inflation was the result, and it was inflation that more than anything else aggravated the already existing distrust between east and west in Massachusetts and that sharpened class antagonisms to a razor sharpness. The moderate-controlled legislature struggled to cope, but it met with less success than with any other issue it faced in this year.

The mark of inflation is rising prices. In March of 1776, a number of Suffolk County towns petitioned the General Court about the "extravagant price which is demanded for English goods," while later, several Essex County towns protested that both "merchants and farmers" were overcharging. When the Council refused to discuss the problem, the General Court did nothing.[17] By May, however, James Sullivan believed "that public virtue is almost swallowed up in a desire of possessing paper currency," while Abigail Adams complained in June that the cost of living "is double what it was one year ago."[18] Acrimony between farmer and merchant, each blaming the other, grew throughout 1776 while the General Court concentrated on its attempts to control paper emissions. When it became obvious that this would not solve the problem, however, the legislature took the fatal step of fixing prices.

The Act to Prevent Monopoly and Oppression, passed in January 1777, was filled with unworkable and unenforceable provisions. Its maximum prices were quickly viewed as the going rate, and then as minimums. Generous mark-ups were allowed merchants, but they were supposed to list their cost along with their selling price to prove their good faith—a requirement almost universally ignored. And though the act placed regulations on both merchants and farmers, each thought that the other was responsible for the continuing inflationary pressure, while each sought to profit as much from it as he could.[19]

The effects of the act simply could not be foreseen. "The attempt of New England to regulate prices is extremely popular in Congress," wrote John Adams, reflecting the initial assumption that all would go well. But within two months of its adoption, farmers and merchants were at each others' throats. In Boston, where the act was broken "in open daylight," produce markets languished for want of goods. The act, wrote James Warren, "has yet produced no other consequences but bitterness and wrath between the town and country, the last of which is endeavour-

17. *Acts and Resolves*, 5: 669.

18. Sullivan to John Adams, 19 May 1776, in Thomas C. Amory, *Life of James Sullivan: with Selections from his Writings*, 2 vols. (Boston, 1859), 2: 77; Abigail Adams to John Adams, Braintree, 28 May 1777, Adams Papers, reel 347.

19. *Acts and Resolves*, 5: 583–89. For a general discussion, see Harlow, "Economic Conditions in Massachusetts," p. 174.

ing to starve the town in return for what they consider ill usage from them." "We are got into a wretched hobble," wrote Cotton Tufts, who thought the act had been carefully drawn.[20] The problem, said a Plymouth County convention, was the "extraordinary lust for gain." By May, Boston was calling for an end to the act, since its sole effect had been to drive a wedge between country and town. The new General Court, however, for reasons which will be obvious shortly, refused to rescind the act, but revised some of the price ceilings upward instead.[21]

The economic climate set the stage for the constitutional discussions that took place in this year following Independence, and it quite naturally reinforced the already divergent attitudes of Massachusetts people. To return to June 1776, westerners were determined to have a new constitution immediately; their constituents in some cases had instructed them to prepare one in the General Court, and thus the matter was one of the first raised when the legislature settled down to business. On June 4 they approved a plan to appoint a committee to prepare a new constitution, and two days later one representative from each county was named to the committee.[22] From ensuing comments, it is apparent that

20. John Adams to Abigail Adams, Baltimore, 7 February 1777, in Edmund C. Burnett, ed., *Letters of Members of the Continental Congress*, 8 vols. (Washington, 1921–36), 2: 237; James Warren to John Adams, Boston, 23 March 1777, in Ford, ed., *Warren-Adams Letters*, 1: 305–6; Cotton Tufts to John Adams, 14, 24 April 1777, in Adams Papers, reel 347. See also Samuel Adams to Mrs. Betsy Adams, Philadelphia, 19 March 1777, in Harry A. Cushing, ed., *The Writings of Samuel Adams*, 4 vols., (New York, 1904–8), 3: 364.

21. *BG*, 16 June 1777; 18 *BTR*, pp. 284–85; James Warren to John Adams, Boston, 11 June 1777, in Ford, ed., *Warren-Adams Letters*, 1: 329–30. While merchants almost universally opposed the old act and protested the creation of a new one in June 1777, farmers apparently had come to the decision that it must continue. See [Samuel Cooper] to Samuel Adams, Boston, 12 June 1777, in Samuel Adams Papers. James Warren believed that even those in favor of the act could see the impossibility of enforcing it, but that they refused to give in, such was the "Increasing Animosity between Town and Country." To Samuel Adams, Boston, 16 June 1777, in Ford, ed., *Warren-Adams Letters*, 2: 449. Many people, including some Bostonians, believed that Boston was the chief offender. Paul Revere wrote that "we are over run with sharpers, and hawkers, forestallers and monopolizers, this Town is become the very sink of the United States." To Samuel Adams, Boston, 24 August 1777, in Samuel Adams Papers. How farmers were able to continue price-fixing over the objections of merchants is indicated in the discussion below of the elections of 1777. The acts of January and June 1777 were finally repealed in September 1777 upon the recommendation of the convention of all New England states. See Harlow, "Economic Conditions in Massachusetts," pp. 174–75.

22. *House Journals*, 4, 6 June 1776.

each of the two contesting interest groups was represented, and that earlier experiences had conditioned their views.

During the previous year, when they controlled the House of Representatives, the reformers had come into conflict with the moderate Council. It was natural, perhaps, that some reformers would want constitutional revision that would exclude the upper house of the legislature. This was Joseph Palmer's wish when he wrote to John Adams in December 1775. "A representative body, equal and frequent, with their com[mittees] will do better, and more business, in like time, than 3 branches," wrote Palmer. "I freely own that I do not wish for any gov[erno]r or Council, not even if chosen by ourselves."[23] As the committee began discussion in June 1776, it became clear that Palmer's view was widely held. Francis Dana wrote that pressures existed to dispose of both governor and Council in the new constitution. "I have some fears," he said, "whether under the idea of establishing the freest possible government ours will not consist of a single assembly."[24] Abigail Adams found that, by August, there were some who wished to abolish both House and Council and return to the looser organization of a congress.[25]

Faced with this kind of opposition, the moderates were forced to move cautiously. First, the constitutional committee was limited to members of the House. Councilors, while they objected privately, apparently cooperated.[26] Second, the distribution of membership on the committee was based on counties to prevent charges of packing. Here again, such moderates as the merchant John Lowell objected, but kept their remarks private: "They would have taken better men in some instances, if they had not confined themselves to counties."[27]

While the General Court went through the motions of preparing for a new constitution, it does not appear that the moderate group was interested in actually accomplishing anything. Given the unsettled state of society and the "rage for innovation," they were content to give the semblance of activity. Their letters, however, revealed their true feelings. James Sullivan, for instance, wrote that he had "not the least idea of dissolving the old and making an entire[ly] new form of government." Such action, he thought, "would be attended with the greatest anarchy as it would leave the people for a time without any government." As to

23. Watertown, 2 December 1775, in Adams Papers, reel 345.
24. To John Adams, Boston, 28 July 1776, ibid., reel 346.
25. To John Adams, Boston, 14 August 1776, ibid.
26. Francis Dana to John Adams, Boston, 28 July 1776, ibid.
27. To John Adams, Boston, 14 August 1776, ibid.

the suggestion that Congress be consulted on the matter, Sullivan wrote that he doubted whether the internal affairs of any colony should concern Congress. "I am therefore for attending to this matter ourselves and for altering our constitution piece by piece in a manner the least alarming to our sister colonies, until we shall reduce it to true Republican principles."[28] John Lowell concurred in this opinion. "We have *now* such a constitution as will answer our present exigencies, tho it may doubtless receive great amendments, but by delay we may avail ourselves of the wisdom and in some measure of the experience of our sister states in their forms of government."[29] Francis Dana, a member of the Council, had a vested interest in retaining the old charter. He argued, too, that "the freedom of the community will be better secured by adopting our old form with few alterations."[30]

The retention of the old charter was not the cautious wish of only a conservative handful of legislators. A number of towns, almost all of them in the east, agreed that the time was not propitious for preparing a new constitution. Thus when the General Court decided in September to canvass the towns throughout the state as to whether they wanted the General Court to prepare a new constitution, about a quarter of those replying said they did not, and a significant number of these expressed their complete approval of the present arrangement. Boston took the lead in arguing that caution must be exercised; the people needed time to collect the wisest sentiments, and channels of information must be opened to the public before a "judicious, happy constitution" could be formed. Other equally moderate towns, however, were willing to allow the General Court to act provided, as Gloucester said, the Council and House had "equal voice."[31]

Western towns did not all react to the canvass in the same way either, although the desire for reformed institutions was widespread. Some towns, particularly in Hampshire and Berkshire, believed that a constitution was the basic ingredient of reform, and they therefore voted for the resolution without hesitation. A very large number of others, however, affirmed their wish for a constitution, but not one formed by the present General Court. Some, like Ashfield in Hampshire County, voted that the House without the Council should form a constitution

28. To John Adams, Watertown, 9 May 1776, ibid.
29. To John Adams, Boston, 14 August 1776, ibid.
30. To John Adams, Boston, 28 July 1776, ibid.
31. About 90 towns replied to the General Court's question; 25 of these were negative, although some wanted a constitution drawn up in another way. Almost all of the towns flatly opposed were from the eastern counties. Mass. Arch., 156: 121–91. Returns of Boston and Gloucester, ibid., pp. 160, 156.

which should then be submitted to the towns for ratification. Others insisted that a state convention be called specifically to draft a plan. One farming town declared its belief "that power always resides in the body of the people" and therefore "we apprehend it would be proper that the form of government for this state . . . originate in each town." Many of these towns, moreover, took the opportunity to state the particular reforms they expected. Several wanted a unicameral legislature. Though few expressed themselves so colorfully as Ashfield, several agreed with it "that we Do not want any Goviner but the Goviner of the univarse." Ashfield also called for payment of legislators from the public treasury, while others called for universal manhood suffrage, recall of legislators, and a register of deeds in every town. Whether they agreed or disagreed with the General Court's forming a constitution, most agricultural towns expected, with Topsfield, that no plan would be effected "until such time as the whole of the people of this colony have liberty to express their sentiments in respect to that affair as fully as they have in the case of independence."[32]

For most people in Massachusetts, the question in their minds was not whether to have a new constitution or not; it was a question of when, what kind of constitution, and formed by whom? The simple affirmative or negative replies to the General Court's question therefore are far less significant than the other comments of the towns, and of these, the single most divisive issue was the question of representation. Ever since the new act giving bigger eastern towns more representatives, this had become the central issue in constitutional discussions. Boston instructed its representatives to make an "equal representation" the prerequisite to constitutional change.[33] A Watchman, writing at the same time, argued that the late act changing the system of representation was the only guarantee against tyranny and anarchy. Prior to that act, he said, an equal representation had "only existed in theory." "The country should ever give the assembly credit for that act, which, though not perfect, may lead to one that is so."[34] But the nature of perfection was disputable. At the end of the summer, during which the legislature's constitutional committee accomplished little, Samuel Adams wrote that

32. See returns of Ashfield, Acton, Bellingham, Warwick, Topsfield, ibid., pp. 131, 188, 198, 132, 183. See also Samuel E. Morison, "The Vote of Massachusetts on Summoning a Constitutional Convention, 1776–1916," MHS Proceedings 50 (1917): 241–49.

33. BG, 10 June 1776.

34. To the People of Massachusetts-Bay, 12 June 1776, in Amer. Arch., 4th ser., 6: 830–32.

"their great difficulty seems to be to determine upon a free and adequate representative."[35]

Given the opportunity by the General Court's canvass to speak out against the new act, numerous agricultural towns pointed specifically to the representation issue as the reason why they would not grant the General Court unlimited powers to draft and enact a constitution. Attleborough in Bristol County claimed that "the present honorable House is not a fair representation of the inhabitants of this state."[36] Topsfield went even further in accusing the mercantile interest of having stolen control of the House. "We cannot but hope before the next choice of representatives, the late act of toleration for towns to send to Court such number of persons . . . will be repealed and the Court will return to or near the ancient rule of representation." The new act, claimed the inhabitants of Topsfield, "we fear was obtained only to serve the interest of particular parties under a pretense of equal representation." Topsfield, however, was willing as were several other towns, to allow the General Court to draft a constitution to be submitted to the towns for their approval.[37]

The response to the canvass, even among towns eager for a government closer to the common people, was therefore disorganized and inconsistent until later in the fall when the towns of Worcester County collectively rejected the General Court's proposal. In a manner reminiscent of the Essex County convention that had met in Ipswich in April 1776, a convention met at the Court House in Worcester on November 26. Its object was to create a unified front: in its resolutions, sent to all of the newspapers in the state, the convention frankly admitted its purpose was to reconcile the various sentiments of the inhabitants and to preserve unanimity in the county. As the decision of each town was taken respecting the resolve of the House of Representatives, the similarity of their sentiments became quickly apparent. "Oxford, dissented by reason of unequal representation . . . , Sutton, Bolton, Sturbridge, Holden, Northbridge, dissented for unequal representation." Dudley and Charlton simply "objected to the present house" while Petersham added that it was "against any Council."[38]

Such unanimity pointed to a common conclusion: "a system of government is necessary to be established in this state so soon as it may be done with safety," but the General Court could not be trusted with the

35. To John Adams, Boston, 16 September 1776, in Adams Papers, reel 346.
36. Mass. Arch., 156: 171.
37. Ibid., p. 183.
38. *Massachusetts Spy* (Worcester), 4 December 1776.

task. Because of the act of "the late General Court, making the representation of the state very unequal and unsafe, this convention is of the opinion that the present General Court is not the most suitable body to form a system of government for this state." Worcester County, they concluded, wanted a state congress elected for the sole purpose of writing a constitution, the basis of representation being that of 1775.[39]

The Worcester Convention was important in two respects. It showed, first, that a considerable number of western towns agreed that the new system of representation operated directly against their best interest. Perhaps more important, however, it showed that western agrarian towns were prepared to organize for political purposes. How much further they actually went in planning tactics for the next election is not clear. From what happened, however, one would suspect that some conscious effort was made to get rural towns at least to exercise the rights they already had.

The response of Massachusetts towns to its resolve was so variegated that the House of Representatives found itself unable to take any positive action on a new constitution. Even old revolutionary leaders were divided on what course to follow. Joseph Hawley, though a westerner, decided that the matter should wait until later.[40] James Warren wrote that he was constantly "urging the necessity of going about it" but that neither the form of a constitution nor the manner of creating one could be agreed upon. "Many are for having it done by a convention," he wrote to John Adams, "and many are for one branch only."[41] The confusion thus made delay possible, to the satisfaction of moderates, until finally the decision was made to defer the matter until after the spring elections.

At the end of March 1777, the House determined that, in the ensuing state elections, the towns should empower their representatives to sit in a convention for the purpose of writing a constitution.[42] The convention and the General Court would then be sitting simultaneously and would, in fact, be the same body. The resulting constitution would be

39. Ibid.

40. Hawley apparently saw the futility of trying to change the constitution at that time. He thought that Congress should recommend to the various states "the vast importance of supporting and conforming to the forms of civil government for the time being subsisting in the respective states whatever alteration they may hope for and have in contemplation." Such a recommendation, he thought, would "tend greatly to compose the minds of the people." To Elbridge Gerry, Watertown, 13 October 1776, in Samuel Adams Papers.

41. To John Adams, Plymouth, 22 February 1777, in Ford, ed., *Warren-Adams Letters*, 1: 296.

42. James Warren to John Adams, Boston, 3 April 1777, ibid., pp. 309–10.

submitted to the towns for their approval. With this system, the question of the distribution of representation in the convention would not become a problem. The Council, alarmed by growing sentiment for a unicameral legislature, tried to delay concurring in this plan, but the House insisted that now was the best time to act and the Council acquiesced.[43] The General Court resolved that the towns should instruct their representatives "relative to forming a constitution of government."[44]

The mercantile east approached the elections of May 1777 with an unreasonable confidence. The unwieldy nature of the House from 1776 to 1777 had frequently brought the comment that the number of representatives was too great.[45] At the same time, many of the eastern towns that had exerted themselves to send so many representatives the previous year quite probably had found the expense burdensome. The result was a marked decrease in the number of representatives chosen from the eastern counties. Suffolk dropped from 43 to 24 members, Essex from 48 to 32, and so on. Altogether, the eastern counties decreased their participation in the legislature by close to 50 percent.

When the members assembled in Boston on May 28, the moderate leadership must have been shocked. Confronting them were gigantic delegations from the western counties, clamoring for revenge. Worcester County was in the vanguard with 62 representatives—almost twice its representation of the previous year—and equal to the combined representation of Suffolk, Essex, and Barnstable counties. Hampshire jumped from 28 to 41 members, Berkshire from 11 to 20. The three western counties alone had 123 members, and even with minimal support from agricultural towns in other counties, they had a clear majority. (See column 5 in Appendix C.)

Unfortunately for the western members, they had more power than they knew how to use. At least half of them were new,[46] and, it would appear, pliable. Thomas Crafts commented that Worcester County had exerted itself to choose "men of the *greatest piety* and least *political knowledge*."[47] The first thing facing the Court was the election of a Council. With their strength, the westerners could have dominated the

43. Samuel Freeman to John Adams, Boston, 23 April 1777, in Adams Papers, reel 347.

44. 18 *BTR*, p. 283.

45. David Sewall to John Adams, York, 15 July 1776, in Adams Papers, reel 346; Joseph Hawley to General Washington, Watertown, 21 July 1776, in *Amer. Arch.*, 4th ser., 6: 1015.

46. James Warren to John Adams, Boston, 5 June 1777, in Ford, ed., *Warren-Adams Letters*, 1: 327.

47. To Gen. Benjamin Lincoln, Boston, 16 June 1777, Emmett Collection, New York Public Library, 5001.

election completely. In fact, so certain were they that defeat was immi-
nent, that James Bowdoin and several other councilors resigned their
positions.[48] Eastern moderates plus the 28 members of the Council
together apparently had less than a majority. Circumstances, however,
played into the hands of the easterners. Numerous representatives—as
many as 30 according to Samuel Cooper, most of them from Hampshire
and Berkshire—had come with instructions to form a constitution with
a unicameral legislature. Instead of waiting to press this matter in the
constitutional convention, they insisted that the Council be immediately
abandoned. When their demands got them nowhere, they refused to
vote for councilors.[49] This reduced the difference between the competing
groups to almost nothing. The election that followed dragged on for
two days. In the end, four new councilors had been chosen, all from
the rural counties.[50] Those who had resigned, however, were all reelected. Significantly, Thomas Cushing, the leader of the moderate
group in the Council, was the last man chosen.

For most of the westerners, the question of representation, and not
the election of councilors, was the pressing issue. On June 5, James
Warren wrote to John Adams informing him of the latest developments.
The "upper counties" as he called them, "are largely represented, more
than 60 already returned from the County of Worcester." The mood of
the westerners was clear. "They came high charged," said Warren, "and
yesterday moved for a repeal of the act for a more equal representation."[51] They failed, however, to carry the motion. Reminded that they
were soon to form a new constitution, some were convinced that they
should settle the representation issue as part of the constitutional discussion and then incorporate it into the document itself. This, of course,
was what was done. As James Warren explained of the westerners,
"some of them had patience to wait till a constitution was formed."[52]

Maintaining his consistent plea for unanimity, John Adams wrote to
James Warren that he hoped the General Court would "proceed in the
formation of a constitution without any hurtful divisions, or altercations.
Whatever the majority determine, I hope the minority will cheerfully

48. *House Journals*, 28 May 1777.
49. Samuel Cooper to John Adams, Boston, 29 May 1777, in Adams Papers, reel
347.
50. The new councilors were Daniel Hopkins and Josiah Stone (Middlesex
County), Oliver Prescott and Timothy Edwards (Berkshire County). See *House
Journals*, 28–29 May 1777.
51. Ford, ed., *Warren-Adams Letters*, 1: 327.
52. To John Adams, Boston, 5 June 1777, ibid.

concur in."[53] Such amiability, of course, was to prove impossible, for as Abigail Adams pointed out, "some have instructed their rep[resentative]s to form a government, others have directly forbid them."[54] The town of Boston was foremost among those opposed. As the instructions of the town's representatives read: "With respect to the General Court's forming a new constitution, you are directed by a unanimous vote of a full meeting, on no terms to consent to it, but to use your influence, and oppose it heartily, if such an attempt should be made." A constitution could be formed, they insisted, only when the people "delegate a select number for that purpose, and that alone." At that time, they suggested, they would propose, among other things, that the Council be strengthened by being made "entirely independent of the house."[55]

Without control of the House of Representatives, the moderates were powerless to prevent the General Court from beginning work immediately on a constitution. By June 15, both House and Council had agreed to begin and by the end of the month, referring to itself as a convention, the General Court had appointed a committee with members from both houses to draft the document.[56] "You must know," wrote James Warren to John Adams, "that the Council (of whom several are on the committee) are almost to a man against a new constitution, and are forced to come to it with the greatest reluctance."[57] Upon another occasion, Warren wrote, "I conceive the matter of representation will be our greatest difficulty."[58] Sectional tensions clearly would continue.

The development of a constitution is the beginning of another story. But from the political and economic course of the year following Independence, it should be clear in what atmosphere the constitutional convention began its work. The year had been one that aggravated rather than ameliorated the contention that existed between eastern and western political groups in Massachusetts, and had stimulated the formation of quasi-partisan organizations both in Essex and Worcester counties. It had been one in which economic conditions—the regulation of prices, the problem of inflation, the credit of continental and state paper money

53. Philadelphia, 11 June 1777, ibid., p. 329.
54. To John Adams, Braintree, 15 June 1777, in Adams Papers, reel 347.
55. 18 BTR, p. 284.
56. Abigail Adams to John Adams, Braintree, 15 June 1777, in Adams Papers, reel 347; James Warren to John Adams, Boston, 22 June 1777, in Ford, ed., Warren-Adams Letters, 1: 334–35.
57. Boston, 10 July 1777, in Ford, ed., Warren-Adams Letters, 1: 341.
58. To John Adams, Boston, 22 June 1777, ibid., pp. 334–35.

—had added fuel to the fire of internal discontent. Social and sectional animosities were so glaring that they could not escape the attention of old Popular party leaders. Yet the comments of such men as Samuel and John Adams reflect how completely they had become disconnected from the internal power struggle taking place. "I am greatly afflicted to find that angry disputes have arisen among my dear countrymen," wrote Samuel Adams on June 30, 1777, "at a time especially when perfect good humour should subsist and every heart and tongue and hand should unite in promoting the establishment of public liberty and securing the future safety and happiness of our country."[59]

Boston's position seemed particularly regrettable, to these men, in light of its old leadership of the Revolution. "I am very sorry to see in the papers," wrote John Adams, "the appearance of dissensions between the General Court and the Town of Boston, and to learn from private letters, that there are divisions between the eastern and western part of our commonwealth."[60] That the conflict here was social as well as sectional is underlined by the comments of James Warren, although he tried to minimize the seriousness of the split. "Some gentlemen," he said of the western members, "came down with a few prejudices against the trading interest, others with very self important notions, and when the first had examined a little, and the others had vented themselves, the cloud dispersed without much lightning, and no bad effects."[61] But if the fireworks of the first month of the new General Court had ended, the basic social and political differences between western-centered reformers and eastern-centered moderates remained as the significant fact of Massachusetts wartime history.

59. To James Warren, Philadelphia, ibid., pp. 338–39.

60. To James Warren, Philadelphia, 19 June 1777, ibid., pp. 332–33. Samuel Adams acknowledged the existence of a traditional rivalry between Boston and the country towns which he believed had been exploited by "our common enemies" (undoubtedly the Tories). He believed, however, that he and his fellow Whigs had brought about cooperation between the two through the Committees of Correspondence, and he greatly regretted that they had again become divided. See Samuel Adams to John Scollay, Philadelphia, 20 March 1777, in Cushing, ed., *Writings of Samuel Adams*, 3: 365–66.

61. To John Adams, Boston, 10 July 1777, in Ford, ed., *Warren-Adams Letters*, 1: 341.

# 7

---

# The Constitution of 1778 and Its Rejection

THE HUGE contingent of westerners who sat in the General Court in June 1777 had every reason to be confident. They would form a constitution, they thought, which would incorporate their demands for democratic reform and—by sheer weight of numbers—they would get it accepted. But they failed. In fact, three years elapsed before Massachusetts got a constitution, during which time two plans were submitted to the people for their approval. Worse still for the westerners, the legislature, which they easily dominated in June, at least in numbers, within a very short time passed some economic legislation that was completely out of keeping with the wishes of the agricultural population. How could these "radicals" collapse so completely? For one thing, of course, almost none of the westerners knew anything about politics.[1] They discovered as the year progressed that the business of politics is often one of house management and that delaying tactics and other tricks could give considerable power to easterners, regardless of the latter's numerical inferiority. Secondly, their only strength—numbers—disappeared completely when many westerners proved lax in their attendance. Still, with some surprising help from two easterners, they salvaged something of their constitutional demands and, though the final plan was not exactly as they would have written it, it was a compromise that at least gave them something.

Most historians agree with contemporary comment that the first planned Massachusetts state constitution—that of 1778—was weak, inadequate, and poorly framed. The consensus seems to be that the constitution of 1780, because accepted, was the "best" constitution and that

1. Thomas Crafts to Gen. Benjamin Lincoln, Boston, 16 June 1777, Emmett Collection, New York Public Library, 5001.

171

of 1778, because rejected, was decidely inferior. To restore a proper perspective, it must be noted that neither constitution, in its original form, was acceptable to the voters of Massachusetts. They rejected the first one outright. Since no provision was made for revision to make it acceptable, it died. The original form of the 1780 constitution was also disapproved by a majority of the voters. The convention, however, after careful examination and "revision" of the vote, managed to find a two-thirds majority for the constitution, without amendment.[2]

In neither case did the vote really reveal the divided opinion in the state as to the kind of government best calculated to achieve "the happiness of society." The comments and suggested amendments made by the various towns in each case, however, show that the state was indeed divided: that many people—particularly in the rural west—demanded a constitution considerably more democratic than the old charter of 1691, while others, particularly from eastern or "maritime" towns, resisted democratic reform, and pressed for a stable "mixed government," little different in form from the charter of William and Mary. Only the contest between the two developing political parties explains the failure of one constitution and the success of the other.

When the General Court met for its new session at the end of May 1777, the western members soon got a lesson in political management. As noted previously, they failed to take control of the Council or, as some of them wished, to destroy it. By mid-June, they discovered that the Council was very reluctant to proceed to the formation of a constitutional convention which might ultimately decide to abolish an upper house. On June 12, the House called upon its members "to know what instructions their towns have given to them relative to forming a new constitution of government."[3] The response was considered sufficient to justify the immediate formation of a convention and the Council was therefore informed of the House's wish to proceed. The Council, however, set in motion a series of delaying tactics: sending testy notes to the House, setting appointments for joint meetings and then postponing or cancelling them at the last moment, refusing to meet in the House but insisting on discussions with small House committees only and in the Council chambers.[4] Within a year of Independence, it seemed, repre-

2. The idea that the constitution of 1778 was inferior appears in almost all of the town histories. The actual votes in 1778 and in 1780 are recorded, with analysis, in Samuel Eliot Morison, "The Vote of Massachusetts on Summoning a Constitutional Convention, 1776–1916," *MHS Proceedings* 50 (1917): 241–49, and "The Struggle over the Adoption of the Constitution of Massachusetts, 1780," ibid., pp. 353–411.

3. *House Journals,* 12 June 1777.

4. Ibid., 13, 16, 17 June 1777.

sentatives of the people stood as far apart as ever Court and Country partisans had.

Finally, however, after days of petty bickering and jealous safeguarding of their privileges, the two houses met, resolved themselves into a convention, appointed Jeremiah Powell, a councilor, as chairman, and then proceeded to choose 17 committeemen to draft a constitution. Of these, 13 were representatives and 4 were councilors. Geographically, the committee was well balanced with 1 from each of the counties, and 5 members chosen at large.[5]

Since its work could not continue until a report was prepared by the committee, the convention had no reason for continuing to sit. The members went about their business as members of the General Court; they resolved themselves into convention about once a month to inquire of the progress of their committee, but they accomplished nothing until December. The committee, however, went to work at once. Only five days after its formation, James Warren, a member, reported that the committee "have met several times, and are well agreed as to the main points in the Connecticut form." Voting qualifications had been settled, he said: "freemen of 21 years of age, resident for a certain time in each town, and such as have paid public taxes." Warren personally had hoped for a property qualification, "but," he reasoned, "as it [the constitution] is to have the sanction of the people at large, I question whether that

---

5. The journal of the convention appears in Mass. Arch., 156: 269–92. The committee was elected on 17 and 18 June 1777, ibid., pp. 268–71, and the list appeared in *BG*, 23 June 1777. The committeemen were (councilors with asterisks):

| Suffolk | *Hon. Thomas Cushing | Boston |
|---|---|---|
| Essex | John Pickering | Salem |
| Middlesex | Hon. James Prescott | Groton |
| Hampshire | Hon. John Bliss | Wilbraham |
| Plymouth | George Partridge | Duxbury |
| Barnstable | *Hon. Daniel Davis | |
| Bristol | Hon. Robert Treat Paine | Taunton |
| York | Joseph Simpson | York |
| Dukes | — | |
| Nantucket | — | |
| Worcester | Seth Washburn | Leicester |
| Cumberland | *Hon. Jeremiah Powell | |
| Lincoln | *Hon. John Taylor | |
| Berkshire | John Bacon | Stockbridge |
| At Large | Hon. James Warren | Plymouth, Plymouth |
| | Azor Orne | Marblehead, Essex |
| | Noah Goodman | South Hadley, Hamp. |
| | Capt. Isaac Stone | Oakham, Worc. |
| | Col. Eleazer Brooks | Lincoln, Middle. |

would not render the whole abortive, and from that principle have conceded to it as it is." The greatest problem, thought Warren, would be the matter of representation. That question would be considered next, he said.[6]

James Warren's comments suggest that, at this stage, the committee fairly reflected the wishes of the western-dominated General Court. Warren, however, who, like the Adamses considered himself above partisanship, was extremely dubious of the capabilities of his fellow committeemen and of the committee's ultimate hope for success. "I wish you was one of us," he wrote John Adams. "This is a subject of such magnitude and extent that I feel myself very unequal to, and in want of the judgment and wisdom of those who I have the greatest confidence in and opinion of instead of the narrow sentiments, trite trifling, and sometimes ludicrous observations of those whose abilities and judgements I despise."[7] The abilities of the other members, however, were not so limited as Warren suggested. Thomas Cushing, former delegate to the Continental Congress, and probably now chief among merchant-politicians from Boston, was, as already noted, a close friend of John Hancock, whose political ambitions in Massachusetts were acceptable neither to Warren nor to his friends, the Adamses. Among the other committeemen, Robert Treat Paine had been a competent congressional delegate but was as tainted as Cushing, from Warren's perspective; Azor Orne, a prominent Essex County merchant, had been a councilor; Seth Washburn was a major in the state militia; and Eleazer Brooks from Middlesex County was a colonel. Several of the committeemen were leading politicians in agricultural towns: Noah Goodman of South Hadley in Hampshire, Seth Washburn of Leicester in Worcester, and John Bliss of Wilbraham in Hampshire were all to be heard from in later years as spokesmen of the western counties.

Warren's criticisms of his colleagues' abilities plainly had more to do with their political views than their talents, for he believed them to be limited by their economic interests and their political ambitions rather than motivated by a higher regard for the good of society as a whole. Still, he was not the only one to criticize the caliber of representatives. "A Round Head" in the *Boston Gazette* wondered if voters had chosen "the most suitable men; men of the greatest experience and knowledge . . . and the most finished statesmen."[8] William Gordon, a clergyman from Roxbury, thought the House totally inept. "Such blundering mis-

6. To John Adams, Boston, 22 June 1777, in Worthington Chauncey Ford, ed., *Warren-Adams Letters,* 2 vols. (Boston, 1917–25), 1: 334–35.
7. Ibid.
8. *BG,* 7 July 1777.

management as our General Court has been guilty of, puts me almost out of patience," he wrote to George Washington. "The fault is chargeable chiefly, if not wholly, upon the House of Representatives. Alas, for us, they are not equal to the great affairs of war, and yet are too conceited to entrust the proper powers with a suitable executive." At a time when provision should have been made for securing Fort Ticonderoga in New York, said Gordon, "that was foolishly omitted that they might attend to a new constitution."[9] Gordon apparently was oblivious to the inconsistency of his arguing for a strong executive—which would require constitutional change—and his opposition to the General Court's move for a new constitution. But the attitude was typical of the moderates, and reflected the sentiments of moderate-controlled institutions like the Council and the Boston town meeting.[10] At a time when democratic elements were actively seeking constitutional change, it was politically expedient to insist that the legislature concentrate on the problems of war.

The difficulties that the committee began to encounter during the summer of 1777 seem to have been less the fault of the newer, less-experienced westerners than of the councilors and other moderates who simply did not want a change. "You must know," wrote James Warren to John Adams, "that the Council (of whom several are on the committee) are almost to a man against a new constitution, and are forced to come to it with the greatest reluctance. Some of us are lukewarm and others consider it as a business by the bye." The committee, he added, had adjourned until a week before the General Court's next sitting. But, a month later, it had still accomplished nothing further. "I hope when we meet again, we shall get along with it, and form a tolerable one," wrote Warren, "but I tremble with diffidence every step I take."[11]

The problem of constitution-making was considerably magnified by rapidly changing economic conditions in Massachusetts. Prices soared during the summer of 1777. "We must study to make the most of our husbandry or we must starve," wrote Abigail Adams to her husband in August; "3 dollars will not purchase what one would (of any article that can be mentioned) two months ago."[12] An act passed the previous January for limiting prices, far from controlling inflation, only stirred up bitterness. Merchants and townspeople accused the farmers of with-

9. Roxbury, 17 July 1777, in "Letters of the Reverend William Gordon," *MHS Proceedings* 63 (1931): 346.

10. See votes of 22 and 26 May 1777 in 18 *BTR*, pp. 283–85.

11. Boston, 10 July, 10 August 1777, in Ford, ed., *Warren-Adams Letters*, 1: 341, 351.

12. Braintree, 12 August 1777, in Lyman H. Butterfield, ed., *Adams Family Correspondence*, 2 vols. (Cambridge, Mass., 1963), 2: 309.

holding produce while the farmers charged merchants with monopo-
lizing and raising prices of imported goods. John Adams was scandalized
at the behavior of his countrymen. "I am grieved to hear of the angry
contentions among you," he wrote to his wife. "Instead of the acrimoni-
ous altercations between town and country and between farmer and
merchant, I wish, that my dear countrymen would agree in this virtuous
resolution of depending on themselves alone."[13]

Had it not been for the massive contingent of westerners who greeted
them in the General Court, easterners might have taken immediate steps
to deal with the economic crisis which gripped the state. Bostonians, at
least, were fully aware that economic conflict only aggravated the political divergence that existed between farming and mercantile areas. At
their town meeting in May, they had instructed their representatives to
vote for the repeal of the act regulating prices, which, they said, was
"a growing source of animosity and ill will, tending to raise a difference
between town and country." The "interest and happiness" of the towns
were inseparable from that of "our brethren in the country," they continued, "and if ever the trial is made, we shall assuredly find that a
disunion and separation of such interest will be the ruin of both."[14]

But farmers could afford a certain indifference. Farm prices were high,
money plentiful, and debts contracted in the past payable in depreciated
currency. Court fees, set by an agrarian-controlled House in 1776, were
now lower still, given the availability of paper money. Agrarians were
interested in a constitution and, as William Gordon suggested, other
matters could go by the wayside.

The preoccupation of westerners with a new constitution proved to
be their undoing, however. Having appointed a committee to draft one
in June, their exertions to hold control of the General Court ended. When
the legislature met next in August, numerous westerners—many of them
probably engaged in the harvest—did not attend. The decline of western
participation was immediately noticeable in the appointment of House
committees. Committees were the workhorses of Massachusetts legislatures. All bills were reported from committees; all petitions were submitted to them. In fact, a legislative session in great part simply involved
the appointing of committees and the receiving of their reports. Debate
almost always was confined to the points raised by a report. By culling

13. Philadelphia, 8 September 1777, ibid., 2: 338–39. For effectiveness of the
price limiting acts, see Fitch Edward Oliver, ed., *The Diary of William Pynchon of
Salem* (Boston, 1890), p. 33: "The acts of the state absolutely prohibit every kind
of depreciation of the paper currency, either by word or actions; yet every trader,
huckster, marketman, and peddler, with open mouths, unitedly declare and publicly
say it is of little or no value."

14. 18 *BTR*, pp. 284–85.

the names of appointees to committees from the journals of the House, one can determine who was doing the work during any session. For the August sitting, 14 men stand out above the others in the frequency of their appointments. Each served on four or more committees. Of these, Ellis Gray of Boston proved most active. Gray and eight others from Suffolk, Essex, and Bristol counties held a total of 46 appointments. The other 5 of the top 14 committeemen came from Middlesex, Worcester, and Hampshire counties. The Middlesex men, from Cambridge and Concord, were actually within Boston's orbit. Only 2 of the foremost committeemen came from Worcester County and 1 from Hampshire. Together, these 3 held only 13 appointments, yet their counties with Berkshire in May had provided half of the representatives in the General Court.[15]

The August sitting of the General Court was short and nothing material was accomplished aside from stacking committees with easterners. By September, however, moderates had prepared an economic program that would favor the eastern towns by reorganizing the state's monetary policy, building in a stability that could not easily be disturbed by subsequent legislatures. In fact, the session of the General Court that began on September 10 approved the most significant financial legislation of the war years.

An examination of committee appointments for the first month of the session again shows clearly that the eastern section of the state did an inordinate share of the work. Twenty-one men each received 7 or more appointments in this month. Again, Ellis Gray heads the list with 18 appointments; Azor Orne of Marblehead follows closely with 15. Fifteen of the 21 were from eastern towns with three more from Middlesex towns

---

15. *House Journals*, 5 August *et seq*. The towns which each man represented are listed in *Acts and Resolves*, 20 (1918): Appendix XV, 3–6.

| Committeemen | Town, cty. | No. of appts. |
| --- | --- | --- |
| Ellis Gray | Boston, Suffolk | 9 |
| Stephen Sewell | Cambridge, Middlesex | 9 |
| Col. Moses Little | Newbury, Essex | 7 |
| Joseph Hosmer | Concord, Middlesex | 7 |
| John Pitts | Boston, Suffolk | 5 |
| David Jeffries | Boston, Suffolk | 5 |
| Israel Nicholls | Leominster, Worcester | 5 |
| Stephen Cross | Newburyport, Essex | 4 |
| Jacob Boardman | Newburyport, Essex | 4 |
| James Ingalls | Methuen, Essex | 4 |
| Caleb Davis | Boston, Suffolk | 4 |
| William Dunsmore | Lancaster, Worcester | 4 |
| Robert Breck | Northampton, Hampshire | 4 |
| Robert T. Paine | Taunton, Bristol | 4 |

close to Boston. Again from Worcester, Hampshire, and Berkshire, there were only three men. These western leaders were Amos Singletary of Sutton and George Kimball of Lunenburg, both in Worcester County, and Colonel John Bliss of Wilbraham in Hampshire. The pattern continues for the less prominent committeemen with the east dominating by two or three to one.[16]

The economic program legislated in the fall and winter of 1777–78 can be reduced to four main areas. First was the abolition of Massachusetts paper currency by a funding operation; second, the beginning

16. *House Journals,* 10 September–10 October 1777. Also, towns are listed from *Acts and Resolves,* 20: Appendix XV, 3–6.

| Committeemen | Town, cty. | No. of appts. |
|---|---|---|
| Ellis Gray | Boston, Suffolk | 18 |
| Azor Orne | Marblehead, Essex | 15 |
| George Partridge | Duxbury, Plymouth | 13 |
| Joseph Hosmer | Concord, Middlesex | 12 |
| John Pitts | Boston, Suffolk | 10 |
| Amos Singletary | Sutton, Worcester | 10 |
| John Bliss | Wilbraham, Hampshire | 10 |
| John Greenough | Wellfleet, Barnstable | 9 |
| Josiah Batcheldore | Beverly, Essex | 9 |
| Increase Sumner | Roxbury, Suffolk | 9 |
| Samuel Niles | Braintree, Suffolk | 9 |
| George Kimball | Lunenburg, Worcester | 8 |
| Stephen Sewell | Cambridge, Middlesex | 7 |
| James Ingalls | Methuen, Essex | 7 |
| Moses Little | Newbury, Essex | 7 |
| Oliver Wendell | Boston, Suffolk | 7 |
| Robert T. Paine | Taunton, Bristol | 7 |
| Eleazer Brooks | Lincoln, Middlesex | 7 |
| Joseph Simpson | York, York | 7 |
| John Pickering | Salem, Essex | 7 |
| Ebenezer Wales | Dorchester, Suffolk | 7 |

Taking the leading committeemen and the number of their appointments, the following table will suggest the relative strength of each county in performing the business of the house.

| County | No. of men | No. of appts. | County | No. of men | No. of appts. |
|---|---|---|---|---|---|
| Suffolk | 6 | 60 | Middlesex | 3 | 26 |
| Essex | 5 | 45 | Worcester | 2 | 18 |
| Plymouth | 1 | 13 | Hampshire | 1 | 10 |
| Bristol | 1 | 7 | Berkshire | — | — |
| Barnstable | 1 | 9 | Total | 6 | 54 |
| York | 1 | 7 | | | |
| Cumberland | — | — | | | |
| Lincoln | — | — | | | |
| Total | 15 | 141 | | | |

of a vigorous program of taxation to decrease the money supply; third, the repeal of price regulating acts; and fourth, the raising of the fees for all civil officers. The program was deflationary and fiscally sound, but it raised a storm of protest in the west that grew, with varying degrees of intensity, until it burst into Shays's Rebellion.

The question of calling in Massachusetts bills of credit was immediately taken under consideration by the General Court, the House sitting as a committee of the whole. Ellis Gray and Azor Orne figured almost always in the smaller committee appointments to investigate special aspects of the problem. From the committee emerged two suggestions. A considerable sum should be called in as a tax payable in state or continental paper. All other state paper should be funded, bills of credit being exchanged for treasurer's notes to bear 6 percent interest. To guarantee the redemption of the notes when they became due, from 1780 to 1782, the report proposed that a tax should be provided for those years even if the legislature at that time should fail to act. With minor revisions, the treasurer's note bill passed the House on October 8.[17]

On October 2, a committee of three was appointed to draft a tax bill. The House directed that the sum collected should be £300,000. The eastern-dominated committees reported a bill which, by October 24, was passed by both houses. Further, during the procedure of passing the tax bill, the House resolved "that the future expenses of the state in carrying on the war be supported by taxation only."[18]

Simultaneous with the effort to take a considerable proportion of paper money out of circulation, the General Court turned its attention to the acts for regulating prices passed earlier in 1777. Both acts, designed to prevent "monopoly and oppression," had failed to answer "the salutary purposes for which they were intended." As the Boston town meeting had suggested, the law generated considerable hard feeling between farmer and townsman and it was not enforceable anyway. The House pushed the repeal bill towards final reading quickly and, by October 13, it had passed both houses.[19] Within little over a month, the General Court had laid the foundations of financial policy for the next decade. Taxation would be high and deflationary. Paper money issued by the state would be funded. The state would acquire a sizable debt which it would service at 6 percent.

17. *House Journals*, 20, 23, 25, 26, 30 September, 1, 2, 8 October; *Acts and Resolves*, 5 (1886): 734–37, 740–42.

18. *House Journals*, 26 September, 2, 7, 9, 24 *October; Acts and Resolves*, 5: 742–58.

19. *House Journals*, 9, 10 October 1777; *Acts and Resolves*, 5: 733–34.

The effects of the deflationary policy were immediate. Though the time for stopping the circulation of state currency was still in the future, said James Warren, the act had already "had great effects." "I am told that all kinds of goods are falling [in price]," he added.[20] When John Adams returned from Congress in December, his travels into Essex County corroborated what Warren had said. "The fashionable conversation all along the journey," he wrote to his wife, "is that goods are fallen and falling in consequence of calling in the money."[21] For a short time, merchants felt the pinch as people began to spend less freely. "Money is growing scarce and goods of all sorts seem to be at a stand," wrote George Williams from Boston. "People begins [sic] to look on money [as] worth some things [sic] and many families won't purchase only eatables."[22]

But if merchants temporarily suffered from a decline in consumer buying, the rewards they gained from a more stable currency were immeasurably more welcome. Moreover, the people in the rural areas immediately raised the hue and cry that the funding operation was largely designed to benefit wealthy merchants to whom the state would now be obligated at 6 percent interest. All over Worcester County, and from farming communities in Hampshire, Middlesex, and some of the eastern counties, towns met and drafted petitions. Possibly some agrarians even recalled an identical protest made by the Country party in the late 1750s, when merchant supporters of the Court party were similarly financing the colony's war operations at 6 percent interest.

During November and December, the petitions of 32 towns reached the legislature. Together they had been represented in the legislature in May by 44 representatives. In some instances, their representatives, by voting for the treasury note scheme, had not reflected their wishes. Taunton, for instance, a Bristol County town that seemed to vacillate between the moderate viewpoint and democratic reform, differed with its moderate representative, Robert Treat Paine, on this issue.[23] The bulk of the protest, 17 of the 32 towns, came from Worcester County, and apparently their representatives had for the most part been absent. The

20. To Elbridge Gerry, Boston, 24 November 1777, in James T. Austin, *The Life of Elbridge Gerry* (Boston, 1859), pp. 227–28.

21. Newburyport, 13 December 1777, in Butterfield, ed., *Adams Family Correspondence*, 2: 369–70.

22. To Timothy Pickering, 29 December 1777, in "Revolutionary Letters Written to Colonel Timothy Pickering by George Williams of Salem," *EIHC*, 42 (1906): 327. Compare this letter with that of 3 November 1777, ibid., pp. 321–22, in which Williams writes, "I am grieved to think of the high price of goods."

23. The petitions are in Mass. Arch., 156.

objections of rural towns were similar. Pepperrell in Middlesex considered the paying of interest would be "attended with many and great evils to this state." By calling in such a large sum, people would be deprived of the means of paying their taxes. Far better to have called it in "a little more moderately by a tax."[24] Belcherstown in Hampshire concluded that the bill was the result of pressure from monopolizers. They were responsible for depreciating the paper and "by that means have gathered great quantities of them into their hands." "Whether these people are in Boston or in the country," they added, "we are not able to say, but we apprehend they have persuaded your honours to call in their bills which they have unrighteously gained." The motives of these monopolizers were clear, they thought. It was to make money scarce. "What little of our estates will be left at the end of the war," they protested, "must go to pay the principal and interest of said contract."[25]

On December 4, the General Court appointed five men to prepare an answer to the petitions, showing upon what basis the act had been passed. The appointees were Paine of Taunton, Phillips of Andover (Essex County), Sumner of Roxbury (Suffolk), Hosmer of Concord (Middlesex), and Pickering of Salem (Essex)—all easterners. Within a few days the General Court passed an act calculated to force the petitioners to silence. Any town which so wished could levy a tax beyond that required by the legislature. The excess, in state bills, could be turned into the treasury in return for the 6 percent treasurer's notes. The town could then apply the interest on its notes to subsequent tax assessments.[26] While it did not meet the objections of the towns to filling the pockets of "monopolizers," the act did tend to undercut their argument.

After the triumph of conservative monetary policy had demonstrated their control of the House, the easterners in January 1778 proceeded to

24. The preponderance of western protests is indicated by the following tabulation by counties. *Acts and Resolves*, 5: 816–18.

| County | No. of protests |
|---|---|
| Worcester | 17 |
| Hampshire | 2 |
| Middlesex | 4 |
| Bristol | 4 |
| Plymouth | 3 |
| Barnstable | 1 |
| Suffolk | 1 |
| Essex, etc. | 0 |
| Total | 32 |

25. Ibid., p. 817.
26. Ibid., pp. 817, 760.

undo the work of an earlier, reformer-controlled House by revising the fees of civil officers. It is true that inflation had made most fees "inadequate to the services whereto they are annexed," as the act of January 24, 1778, stated. But court fees were a subject upon which westerners, and farmers generally—particularly debtors—could wax eloquent. In some cases the revisions upward were slight and reasonable. In others, such as the justice of the peace's fee for issuing a writ of attachment, the cost went from 3d. to 2s., 6d.—an advance of 1000 percent. For entering any court action, the justice of the peace would receive 2s., almost a three-fold advance over the old fee.[27] So while they fixed financial policy for the next decade, the easterners at the same time provided the basis of a grievance that was to continue through the 1780s as town after town, particularly in the west, attacked the high cost of court actions.

This General Court, in which eastern moderates now flourished, was the one which, in its capacity as a convention, accepted from committee a final draft of a new constitution. Undoubtedly, the prospects for moderates looked considerably better in late 1777 than they had in June of that year. By November, a Boston merchant was writing that "there is great expectation of a new form of government in our state."[28] His tone of approval contrasted sharply with the unanimous opposition in Boston the previous spring to the creation of a constitution. But the members of the committee appointed to draw up a plan differed sharply as to the kind of government wanted. Easterners wanted a strong executive, a property qualification for voting, a bicameral legislature, and a separation of legislative, executive, and judicial power. Above all, they wanted what they called "an equal representation."[29] Though not agreed, westerners voiced demands for a unicameral legislature, no governor or a very weak executive, and no property qualification for voting. As their petitions before and after indicated, western and other farming towns tended to seek a government closely dependent on the people and responsive to their wishes.[30] Since some of their work had been done in

27. Ibid., pp. 761–70, Chapter 17. Fees are compared with those of Chapter 23, 1775–76, ibid., pp. 486–95.

28. Samuel A. Otis to Elbridge Gerry, Boston, 22 November 1777, in Austin, *Life*, p. 266.

29. 18 *BTR*, pp. 283–85; Francis Dana to John Adams, Boston, 28 July 1776, Adams Papers, original in MHS, microfilm copy in State Historical Society of Wisconsin, reel 346; *BG*, 10 June 1776; *A Watchman*, 12 June 1776, in *Amer. Arch.*, 4th ser., 6: 830–32.

30. Joseph Palmer to John Adams, 2 December 1775, in Adams Papers, reel 345;

June 1777, when western spirits were highest, the tenor of early committee decisions tended to reflect the wishes of the western-dominated convention. By December, however, when the committee finally reported, the convention membership, like representation in the House, was more eastern than western.

On December 11, the committee reported a draft constitution to the convention, which immediately ordered it printed to allow every member a copy. On the very same day, a campaign begain in the Boston newspapers to push moderate constitutional views. "The Observer" began a series of letters in the *Independent Chronicle,* all of which tended to use arguments that had been heard in Boston for some time. Legislators, he said, should be chosen from those who are men of learning and who have no narrow views. Later he was to insist on a strong executive. "A Bay-Man" urged caution: Massachusetts should wait until the Articles of Confederation have been examined. A constitution formed in agreement with the principle of the Articles, he suggested, would "have the greater weight with the public." Most significant was the writer's earnest wish that the people of Massachusetts should have a constitution which would attract the united support of all the people "without endangering our dividing into a multitude of contending parties."[31]

Confronted by a very real division in interest and subsequent constitutional thinking among the people of Massachusetts, the eastern moderates found it doubly necessary to stress the idea of union. Far from dividing America, "the great Author of Reform has wonderfully united its inhabitants in the most resolute defence of their common rights," wrote "Eleutheros" in the *Boston Gazette,* thus falling back on the traditional ideal of the unified society. "Nothing is more to be wished," he continued, "than that such a form of government may be hit on for the whole, as may effectually secure freedom and justice to every member . . . and absorb all party names and separate interest into one great commonwealth, having coherence and stability within itself."[32] It might also have occurred to this writer that a constitution which would serve no "separate interest" and "absorb all party names" might be acceptable to almost no one. His comments, however, did underline the basic consti-

---

Francis Dana to John Adams, Boston, 28 July 1776, ibid., reel 346; Robert J. Taylor, ed., *Massachusetts, Colony to Commonwealth: Documents on the Formation of Its Constitution, 1775–1780* (Chapel Hill, N.C., 1961), p. 43; vote of Bellingham, 17 September 1776, Mass. Arch., 156: 198.

31. *Independent Chronicle,* 11 December 1777, 15 January 1778.

32. *BG,* 22 December 1777.

tutional conflict: he acknowledged the existence of separate interests and of the parties that represented them; his choice of words demonstrated the importance of the reform spirit implicit in many of the demands for constitutional change; and his recourse to the old rhetoric of the Revolution—stressing the "union" of the people "in the most resolute defence of their common rights"—plainly sought to create the semblance of unity where diversity was the more apparent.

It was not the intention of easterners to adopt a constitution quickly and present it as a fait accompli to the still under-represented western counties. Rather, they directed that newspapers throughout the state should warn all representatives that the draft would be taken under consideration in January.[33] Even then, easterners still outnumbered westerners in the convention.

The convention began consideration of the draft on January 15, 1778, agreeing first to discuss and pass each of the 36 articles paragraph by paragraph.[34] After several days of debate, during which the greater part of the plan passed, it became clear that the power of the governor and representation in the lower house were the chief causes of friction. The draft proposed that only towns with 100 voters should have the right to send their own representative, although towns with fewer could join with one another to make up the required number of voters. Each additional 250 voters allowed a town another representative.[35] Both east and west objected. Some westerners wanted all towns equally represented, regardless of size. Large eastern towns, on the other hand, wanted a proportionately greater representation. A special committee which reported on February 3 changed only slightly the plan in the draft. A town still needed 100 voters to send its own representative, but a town of 300, instead of 350, could send two. Additional members would be allowed towns with large populations, although the ratio of members to voters steadily decreased.[36] The new plan favored towns with between 100 and 1000 voters and discriminated, more so than the first plan, against any very large town—in this case, against Boston. The new plan did nothing to placate the westerners, however, and they immediately moved that "every incorporated town within the state have a right to

33. Mass. Arch., 156: 276; *BG*, 22 December 1777.

34. Mass. Arch., 156: 227.

35. Articles 24 and 25 as they appear in the printed report, ibid., p. 207.

36. The committee was appointed on January 31 after five days of debate. The members were Jeremiah Powell, John Greenough, Brig. Danielson, Capt. Stone of Cobham, Noah Goodman, John Pickering, Mr. Phillips, Col. Grout, Mr. Spooner. Ibid., pp. 282–84.

send a representative." Their efforts, however, were futile. The motion failed and the convention adopted the committee's report.[37]

Up to this point in the convention, it does not appear that anyone actively sought a compromise that would reduce the bitterness between east and west. Within three weeks, however, two men—one a councilor, the other a member of the House—emerged as compromisers. They were two easterners: Thomas Cushing of Boston and John Pickering of Salem.

The compromise began inauspiciously. On February 24, it was moved that each town should constitutionally be required to pay the expenses of its own representatives. Westerners, particularly, had objected to this in the past, since the expenses of their members were necessarily greater than those of easterners. The convention, however, rejected the motion. The proposal, contrary to most, represented the introduction of something completely new into the constitution. Immediately, Cushing and Pickering advanced another proposal equally new. The governor, they suggested, should be deprived of veto power.[38] Such a proposal was a drastic switch from the general position of moderates. But westerners who had always wanted a weak executive quickly concurred. The new article passed. In this way, Cushing and Pickering established themselves as compromisers and westerners began to become more confident. On February 26, the agrarians again moved that every incorporated town be allowed a representative. Also, they added, a town should have 500 voters to have two representatives and multiples of 500 voters for each additional member. Though the motion failed, the vote was close, possibly indicating that western participation in the convention was increasing.[39]

The next day, the compromise was effected. The latest demands of both east and west were incorporated into a single motion—each incorporated town could send a representative but each town must pay its representative's expenses. Westerners had won their key point while easterners knew, from past experience, that the necessity of footing the bill would prevent many small farming communities from sending a representative. The compromise complete, the convention passed the constitution *in toto* the next day and then directed their president, clerk, and one other person to rearrange it and have it printed.[40]

37. Ibid., p. 284.
38. Ibid., p. 289.
39. Ibid., pp. 290–91. A vote of 98–92 is noted in the journal. Votes, however, were not recorded regularly and, when they were included, the system of recording varied.
40. February 27, 1778. The vote on the compromise is recorded as 66–93. Because of the confusing system of recording the votes, this may be 66 out of 93

There were doubtless a number of factors that made compromise possible. Westerners were growing in numbers in the convention and hence becoming more powerful. Easterners may well have sensed that the constitution would never be acceptable to two-thirds of the towns and hence did not really care to remain adamant. But despite these factors, the actions of Thomas Cushing and John Pickering are significant. Why did they become compromisers? Why did they work so hard to push through a constitution that, within two months, was to arouse thoroughly the opposition of their hometowns, Boston and Salem?

The answer lies outside the convention. First of all, Thomas Cushing and John Pickering were among the closest political allies of John Hancock. Hancock, as almost any politically knowledgeable person in Massachusetts knew, desperately wanted to become governor. As soon as the towns had decided, in the spring of 1777, to allow their representatives to write a constitution, Hancock had hurried back to Massachusetts from Congress. "Mrs. H[ancock] was not willing to go till May," John Adams had written, "but Mr. H[ancock] was determined upon April. Perhaps the choice of a governor may come on in May. What aspiring little creatures we are! How subtle, sagacious, and judicious this passion is! How clearly it sees its object, how constantly it pursues it, and what wise plans it devises for obtaining it."[41]

Hancock, of course, had misjudged if he had thought a governor would be chosen in May 1777. But when he again returned home in November, it was with a considerably more accurate expectation that a constitution would soon be prepared and an election called. His welcome in Massachusetts was lavish. Immediately, he plunged into civic affairs and was elected moderator of the town meeting. In fact his activity suggested that he wished nothing so much as to impress his countrymen with both his suitability and his availability for political office. In December, he donated 150 cords of wood to the town poor.[42] In January, as William Gordon wrote to George Washington, Hancock was spreading the rumor that Washington would soon retire.[43] By implication,

rather than 66 to 93. The final vote, on February 28, by which the whole plan was accepted, reads 39–53. However, "out of" has been inserted over the dash, again confusing the figures. Ibid., pp. 291–92.

41. 17 February 1777, in Lyman H. Butterfield, ed., *Diary and Autobiography of John Adams,* 4 vols. (Cambridge, Mass., 1961), 2: 259–60. See also Adams to James Warren, Philadelphia, 7 July 1777, in Ford, ed., *Warren-Adams Letters,* 1: 340.

42. John Hancock to Robert Morris, 12 January 1778, cited in Herbert S. Allan, *John Hancock: Patriot in Purple* (New York, 1948), p. 274; 18 BTR, pp. 293, 294.

43. Roxbury, 12 January 1778, in "Letters of William Gordon," pp. 371-72.

Hancock was inferring that he was next in line to be commander-in-chief. And, in February, just before the compromise brought a close to the constitutional debate, Hancock placed an advertisement in the Boston papers. He requested all his debtors to pay him as soon as possible, but, he noted at the bottom, he would actually prefer the plentiful continental or state paper over hard money in payment of the debts.[44] The magnanimity of his gesture was lost on no one.

With Hancock working as hard as he was to impress people with his candidacy, it is inconceivable that he would not also seek to influence the convention, particularly if it appeared that that body might fail to produce a constitution. If a compromise was needed, who were better able to produce it than Hancock's own henchmen, Cushing and Pickering? William Gordon, for one, was firmly convinced that the constitution had been designed so that Hancock could become governor. After lambasting the plan in the newspapers, Gordon wrote to Horatio Gates explaining his antipathy. "Some may not get to be governors so soon as they expected, nor be suffered to go on governing so long as they ardently desired, and therefore be full of wrath." But unless these nameless persons are held in check, said Gordon, "they will leap the bounds of the peoples' rights." Leaving no doubt that it was Hancock to whom he referred, he concluded: "I can observe that popular men are ambitious men, and tho' called the sons of liberty can act inconsistently, for themselves and families."[45]

Hancock and Cushing, two of Boston's foremost sons of liberty, certainly seemed to be acting inconsistently, by siding with westerners and effecting compromise. But it was precisely such inconsistency upon which they were to thrive politically. From this point on, Hancock, Cushing, and Pickering had allies from the west—allies who could help to make Pickering speaker of the House in the very next session, and, two years later, Hancock and Cushing governor and lieutenant-governor. And for the first time, in 1778, his contemporaries began to refer to a "party" or faction of which Hancock was the acknowledged leader.[46]

44. *Independent Chronicle,* 5 February 1778.

45. Roxbury, 28 April 1778, in "Letters of William Gordon," p. 401. After it became obvious the constitution would not be accepted, Gordon wrote an enigmatic letter to George Washington in which he ridiculed the constitution. He may well have been referring to the scheme to make Hancock governor when he concluded thus: "The scheme of a change being laid before the public ere it was ripened, tended to prevent it, and the voice of the people was so against it, that no one would dare to own that there was any such design—it was denied by some that I am morally certain were seeking it." 15 April 1778, ibid., p. 397.

46. John Pickering, the elder brother of Col. Timothy Pickering, was also Register

The Hancock faction, of course, did not change the basic economic and political cleavage between east and west. It existed, rather, in spite of that cleavage, its strength lying in the popularity of its leader and its ability to please the right people at the right time. But if a mugwump faction could exist in Massachusetts, a mugwump constitution could not.

The constitution as accepted on February 28 epitomized neither the eastern nor western concepts of government. As a compromise, it was probably the most acceptable constitution westerners could hope to get. Their concept of representation had triumphed to the extent that every town, regardless of the number of voters, could send a representative. There was to be a bicameral legislature as easterners had wished, but, contrary to their hopes for a strong executive, the governor had very limited powers. He possessed no veto and only such powers of disapproving legislation as any single member of the senate, of which he was president. The governor would have the power of appointment except for salaried offices, which would be dispensed by the General Court. Voting qualifications were again a compromise: a property qualification was required of voters for senators, governor, and lieutenant-governor. But voting for representatives was open to all white, adult males. Representation in the 28-man senate was distributed according to population among five districts. Voting for senators was to be preceded by a primary in which all the voters would be allowed to choose two candidates for each senatorial seat. The governor and lieutenant-governor would need a simple majority to win. If no candidate should receive that majority, the General Court, by joint ballot, would choose from the top three. Civil appointments were grouped into three categories. Judges and justices of the peace would be appointed during good behavior by the governor. The secretary, treasurer, and commissary general would be appointed annually by the General Court. The attorney general, sheriffs, registers of probate, notaries, and naval officers would be appointed by the governor during pleasure. Finally, the constitution guaranteed freedom of religious profession and worship for all Protestants.[47]

---

of Deeds for Essex County from 1777 to 1806. Octavius Pickering, *The Life of Timothy Pickering*, 4 vols. (Boston, 1867–73), 1: 139. Re Hancock "party," see James Warren to John Adams, Boston, 7 June 1778, and Warren to Samuel Adams, 31 May 1778, in Ford, ed., *Warren-Adams Letters*, 2: 13–14, 19–21.

47. *Journal of the Convention for Framing a Constitution of Government for the State of Massachusetts Bay . . . , 1779–1780* (Boston, 1832), pp. 255–64. Appendix V contains the constitution of 1778.

The form of ratification of the constitution practically predetermined its failure. On March 4, the General Court resolved that printed copies of the plan be sent to all towns where, at meetings of all adult males, it would be considered and approved or disapproved. No provision was made for suggesting amendments. The voters must accept it in its entirety or not at all. The selectmen were to return the numbers voting for and against. In June, should the General Court find two-thirds of the voters for the constitution, it would be established.[48]

Like most compromises, the constitution of 1778 satisfied almost no one. To reformers who had not followed its tortuous path through the convention, the form proposed a government that was too powerful. To the easterners, it was far too weak. For those who wished to eradicate the evils of the colonial government, the constitution seemed only to perpetuate them. One writer, with more objectivity than most, asked his readers to "look back and survey" the colonial form of government. Under it, he said, the people had "seen with amazement, a numerous and powerful party, formed under the direction of a governor, born and educated among us, laboring and exerting every nerve to subjugate this country to the most abject slavery, to a foreign power." How could a man create such a party? "He did it chiefly by exerting the powers vested in him by the constitution. For where the power is lodged, of disposing of posts of profit and honour, there will be the power of forming a numerous party, who may with less pangs of conscience be persuaded to introduce native, than foreign tyranny." The new constitution, he suggested, must not become the instrument of a party.[49]

To suggest that the ensuing debate over the constitution pitted democratic against undemocratic arguments would be silly. On the matter of representation, for instance, neither side (at this point, at least) was ready to suggest a strict division of the state into representative districts according to population. Westerners wanted a representative for every town—a method which gave small towns an inequitable weight in gov-

---

48. *Acts and Resolves*, 20: Appendix XV, 315. The constitution appeared in the *Independent Chronicle*, 19 March 1778.

49. "Occolampadius," *Independent Chronicle*, 26 March 1778. The constitution reached the people at a time when easterners were disgusted with the high prices farmers were then charging. "Tradesmen and salarymen grumble at the countrymen's extortion," wrote William Pynchon of Salem, in Fitch, ed., *Diary*, p. 52. William Gordon found the same feeling in Boston. "The country made such a prey of them before, have plundered them so since by their exorbitant prices, and have so reduced them, that they would venture themselves upon the mercy of GB, I imagine sooner than stir." To Horatio Gates, 17 March 1778, "Letters of William Gordon," p. 394.

ernment (in theory at least) and which, of course, favored the west. Easterners would give small towns no representation whatever. The conflict, on the surface, was a power struggle between regional groups. But, although the westerners were not perfectly consistent idealists—in that they argued for a system of representation that was not, strictly speaking, democratic—their intention was still democratic in a practical sense. For they knew from experience that rural areas had great difficulty keeping a representative in the legislature throughout its several sessions each year, and only if the system of representation favored them could they hope to maintain a roughly equal balance with the larger eastern centers.

In the west, the debate over the constitution was confined almost solely to town meetings and private conversation. In the east, however, it spilled over into the newspapers and into specially called conventions. William Gordon, a Congregational minister in Roxbury and chaplain to the General Court, was the chief newspaper critic. Many of his objections were to be reiterated by town meetings throughout the state. The lack of a bill of rights, the system for amending the constitution, restrictions against ministers serving as representatives, the prohibition of Negro voting, and the excessive powers of appointment allowed the governor were his chief objections. For his criticisms, the General Court summarily dismissed Gordon as their chaplain (something with which Hancock's friends doubtless had a lot to do, since Gordon was also an ardent critic of Hancock). Gordon, however, thought his efforts worth it. "By the liberty I have taken in lashing the General Court and late convention for the maltransactions they give into," he wrote to Horatio Gates, "I have incurred the resentment of many of their High Mightinesses, but care not for that and console myself in the apprehension that I have contributed and shall still further contribute towards preventing the stealing in upon the Bay people a most, or at least a very, imperfect constitution."[50]

Essex County, as in 1776, took the lead in collective opposition to the constitution. On March 27, the town of Newburyport voted that the new constitution was "not founded on the true principles of government," the chief objection being the "unequal and unjust" system of representation. Secondly, the town voted to call a county convention to consider the constitution. Theophilus Parsons, Tristram Dalton, Jonathan Greenleaf, Jonathan Jackson, and Stephen Cross—two lawyers and three merchants—were chosen delegates.[51] Essex County towns, however, as they

50. *Independent Chronicle*, 2, 9, 16, 30 April. Gordon to Horatio Gates, Roxbury, 28 April 1778, "Letters of William Gordon," p. 401.

51. Theophilus Parsons, *Memoir of Theophilus Parsons* (Boston, 1859), p. 49.

had shown before, were not united in sentiment on such things as representation, and farming communities resented the pressure exerted on them by the commercial towns to add weight to the moderate position. Rowley on April 7 considered the recommendations of Newburyport and voted against submitting the constitution to the proposed convention. Altogether, nine Essex towns refused to participate.[52]

The Essex Convention met in Ipswich from April 29 to May 12, 1778, and it produced the famous "Essex Result," conceived primarily as an attack on the proposed constitution, but, more important, the first systematic statement of the eastern moderate position. The membership of the convention was largely made up of merchants, ship captains, or lawyers whose business in that county was largely with the commercial community. The "Result," attributed to the pen of Theophilus Parsons, a young lawyer, was drawn up from 18 points voted on by the delegates. It made no pretense that Massachusetts society was united and homogeneous. It was a society of classes—of farmers, merchants, tradesmen, and laborers. Among the "gentlemen of education, fortune, and leisure" were to be found the "largest number of men, possessed of wisdom, learning, and firmness and consistency of character." From the bulk of the population, on the other hand, was to be found the "greatest share of political honesty, probity, and a regard to the interest of the whole." The legislative body should therefore embody both elements of society: the "aristocracy" and the "democracy."[53]

So that the government would not become the tool of a single party, the "Result" argued for a separation of the legislative, executive, and judicial powers, each to be independent of the other. Both property and population ought to be represented in government and all persons of "discretion" should be eligible to vote. The principle of representation should be to reproduce in the legislature a miniature of the whole population. Therefore "equal interest among the people, should have equal interest among the body of representatives." But, added the writer, the legislative body must not be too large and unwieldy. If it were, parties would be inevitable and the "members would list under the banners of their respective leaders . . . and the result would tend only to promote the ambition or interest of a particular party." The statement sounded like an objection to recent Massachusetts legislatures, which easterners had often found large and unwieldy. The tendency to split

52. Thomas Gage, *The History of Rowley* (Boston, 1840), p. 260. The nine towns were Rowley, Haverhill, Newbury, Marblehead, Andover, Beverly, Almsbury, Bradford, and Middleton. Parsons, *Memoir of Theophilus Parsons*, pp. 49–50. See also George Wingate Chase, *The History of Haverhill* (Haverhill, Mass, 1861), p. 406.

53. Parsons, *Memoir of Theophilus Parsons*, p. 370.

into parties, concluded the writer dogmatically, "has always been in some degree, the course and event of debates instituted and managed by a large multitude."[54]

The system of representation proposed by the constitution was calculated to produce a most defective legislature, said the author of the "Result." It would be too large and unwieldy, he argued, and would not equally represent interests. A fraction of the population could make laws governing the entire population and property of the state. The method of selecting senators would inevitably throw the final choice of the upper house into the house of representatives, thereby destroying the senate's independence. And the method of electing a governor was "open to and will introduce bribery and corruption, and also originate parties and factions in the state."[55]

The power of the house of representatives was perhaps the greatest objection of the "Result" to the constitution, next to the system of representation. It saw the house unduly influencing the senate and the governor. It objected to the article allowing the speaker of the house to be one of the three men, the majority of whom could grant pardons. Here again the "Result" underlined the undesirability of partisanship. The speaker, said the "Result," "would not probably be disposed to offend any leading party in the house, by consenting to, or denying a pardon." It would be impossible to impeach a speaker guilty of improper exercise of his pardoning power "as he is commonly a favorite of a considerable party in the house" and "his party will support him."[56]

The "Essex Result" was inconsistent and contradictory, but this may be its essential significance. Many parts of the constitution were objectionable because they would "promote" or "originate" parties. Others were equally undesirable because they would favor an already existing party which, apparently, would be inevitable in any legislature. Society was pluralistic and the constitution must incorporate its diversity, but harmony and unanimity were still powerful ideals. The "Result," clearly, stood astride the barrier between the traditional and the modern, with one foot still firmly planted in the town meeting society, the other placed lightly in the accommodative order of liberalism. But the weight of moderate thinking was shifting.

An undiscerning reading of the objections of Massachusetts towns to the constitution would give the appearance that, in the main, they objected to the same things. Dunstable in Middlesex County, for instance,

54. Ibid., pp. 373–77.
55. Ibid., pp. 384–86.
56. Ibid., pp. 386–88.

objected "because there is not an equal representation,"[57] an objection which, though from a farming community, differed superficially in no respect from the objection of the Essex towns. But what each group meant by an equal representation was something else again. For maritime towns, the proposed system of representation threatened their influence in government. As the town of Plymouth concluded, the sixth article of the constitution prescribed an inequality of representation— "an inequality which may operate to the disadvantage of this town, bordering on the sea coast, whenever any commercial question shall be agitated in the General Assembly."[58] For the agricultural towns, on the other hand, even the concession of allowing larger maritime towns more than one representative was too much. Samuel Cooper probably stated the issue as succinctly as anyone. The constitution would perhaps be rejected by many towns, he said, "particularly because in the opinion of the maritime towns, representation is too unequal, while in the opinion of others it is too nearly equal."[59]

Farming communities could find a lot besides representation to protest. Westminster in Worcester County voiced the radical demand for government close to the people. The nineteenth article, providing for the appointment of civil officers, it found particularly objectionable, "because it deprives the people at large of appointing their own rulers and officers and places the power where it may no doubt be greatly abused." "The oftener power returns into the hands of the people the better," said its protest. The whole point of the Revolution, it said, was to allow the people to choose their own officers. "Why," it asked, "do we waste our blood and treasure to obtain that which, when obtained, we are not fit to enjoy . . . [I]f but a selected few only are fit to appoint our rulers, why were we uneasy under George . . . [?]" Dunstable chimed in that the constitution "invests the governor with too unlimited a power."[60]

Carrying the democratic argument to its logical conclusions, a number of western towns demanded the end of all property qualifications either for voting or for officeholding. "Money ought not to be made a necessary qualification of a senator or representative, which countenances avarice

57. Elias Nason, A History of the Town of Dunstable (Boston, 1877), p. 130.

58. Records of the Town of Plymouth, 3 vols. (Plymouth, Mass., 1899–1903), 3: 345–46.

59. To Benjamin Franklin, 1 June 1778, in Sparks Papers, 16: 252–53, quoted in Harry A. Cushing, History of the Transition from Provincial to Commonwealth Government in Massachusetts (New York, 1896), p. 219.

60. William Sweetzer Heywood, History of Westminister (Lowell, Mass., 1893), p. 185; Nason, Dunstable, p. 130.

and rejects merit," protested the town of Lenox. A property qualification for voters, it went on, in effect "declares honest poverty a crime." A number of towns agreed with Upton that payment of representatives by the legislature was a necessity, and only if the legislature were "universally and equally elected" with a "just support from the public chest" would the "waxing and waning" of members in the legislature be prevented. Speaking directly to the problems experienced by westerners in the previous year, Upton declared that its proposals alone could remove the "heart burnings and jealousies from one part of the state against the other, which are become so dangerous and hurtful at this time."

It was principally the western towns, also, which took up the cause of the Negro slave and demanded that the principles of the Declaration of Independence be carried to their logical conclusion. Hardwick declared that slavery is "very contrary to the law of God and liberty," while Sutton in Worcester County argued that the denial of civil rights to Negroes simply added "to the already accumulated load of guilt lying on the land in supporting the slave trade." The constitution must be condemned for under it, even if the Negroes in the state, "or any of their posterity obtain their freedom and a handsome estate, yet they must [be] excluded the privileges of men."[61]

Though their reasons differed, eastern towns joined with western towns in condemning the proposed constitution, and in doing so they effectively prevented its establishment. Very few people actually voted on the issue, but the defeat was overwhelming.[62] Since they had not wanted a new constitution anyway, however, eastern moderates could claim a double victory. Nowhere was this more apparent than in Boston, where 968 people voted unanimously against it and appointed a committee of six (five of them merchants) to draw up objections. Boston had been right the previous year, the committee said, in believing the General Court "improper for this business." Representation under the new form was chaotic. It should "be conformable to some rule, either property or numbers, or both; but in the present no regard is had to either." But these were details; the real point was "that a time of war is not the time to form constitutions." Rather, "we look upon [the old constitution of 1691 as] equal to the exigencies of the times, and hold ourselves bound to support it with our lives and fortunes." Perhaps even

---

61. Mass. Arch., 156: 375–81, 389, 366, 344, 343–44; 329–30, 347–58.

62. The *Continental Journal* (Boston) reported the vote for the state as "Yeas 2083, Nays 9972," 8 October 1778. See also the votes of individual towns in Mass. Arch., 156: 304–428; 160: 1–31. Robert J. Taylor calculated the vote at 10,716 against the constitution to 2,093 for. Robert J. Taylor, *Western Massachusetts in the Revolution* (Providence, 1954), p. 88.

more to the point was their closing remark. In a "day of tranquility," Massachusetts might adopt such a constitution "as shall please all good men, and save us from the dissensions which we find attending the present time."[63]

James Warren, who had approved the constitution as being the best that could be obtained at the time, was bitter in his denunciation of the part played by "maritime towns" in preventing the adoption of the constitution. Writing to John Adams, he charged that "the town of Boston . . . and the County of Essex have had a great share and influence in this determination, for you must know it has become very popular to find fault with the doings of the General Court or convention, by those who can't mend them, and a little clamour, much more a great one, may easily damn any measure, good or bad." As for Warren, his self-styled maritime town of Plymouth decided to dispense with his services for the coming year. This he attributed to the "Tories and the influence from Boston," the latter, he imagined, being directed by his inveterate enemy, John Hancock.[64]

The failure of westerners to get an acceptable constitution again emphasized the weakness of reform forces in Massachusetts. They were capable of periodic but not sustained bursts of political enthusiasm, a matter not wholly their fault. It cost money to maintain control of the House of Representatives—money which small towns did not have. And the obvious might be added: it cost small western towns considerably more to send a representative than it did the towns close to Boston. Naturally, numerous small towns were eager to have the General Court assume the cost of attendance for all representatives. The fact that it did not was in large part responsible for the moderate triumph in a year reformers had hoped with be theirs.

The emergence of the Hancock faction in 1778 should not be allowed to blur the division between eastern and western Massachusetts. The Hancockites, after all, appealed to no set of principles nor to any particular interest. As later, they seemed now only to be pushing for control of the executive, not the legislature, and the vehicle of their advance was popularity. By compromise and inconsistency, they sought to win friends and influence people. But though they had played a part in getting a constitution before the voters, they could not alter by a jot the reaction of the people to it. Once it became obvious that the constitution was a hot potato, the Hancockites had nothing more to do with it.

---

63. 26 *BTR*, pp. 22–24. The committeemen were John Winthrop, Joseph Barrell, Perez Morton, Ezekiel Price, Nathaniel Appleton.

64. Boston, 7 June 1778, in Ford, ed., *Warren-Adams Letters*, 2: 19–21.

The year 1778, far from blurring the east-west split in the state, rather seemed to confirm it as the basic political cleavage in revolutionary Massachusetts. Documents of the time are replete with reference to conflict between merchants and farmers, maritime towns and country towns, the eastern and western sections of the state. Each "party" had also been forced to grapple with political theory—to define its concept of the role of government. The best exposition of the maritime position was the "Essex Result." The resolutions of town meetings upon consideration of the constitution were no less significant. From those of the western towns, we learn that democracy was an important issue. Though they were willing to use undemocratic means to achieve their goal, westerners still demanded a government strictly limited by the constitution and closely dependent on the people. The Revolution, they thought and said, had been wrought to put government into the hands of the people. And the Revolution, they seemed to imply, must go on until such democratic changes had been effected.

# 8

## Eastern Politicians and Western Constitutionalists, 1778-1779

THE POLITICS of modern states usually has two levels of development —a leadership level and a popular level; and while one would expect there to be a connection between the two, it has not always been a simple nor necessarily a very secure one. This was true of revolutionary Massachusetts. At the popular level, the state was split into two broad groups, expressive of the divergent interests and values of the people and partisan in their behavior. At the leadership level, there were two principal factions, the Adams men and the Hancockites, whose conflict sprang from differences of personality, of principle, and of tactics. How a divided leadership attempted to relate to the popular level of politics must now concern us.

The contest between factions of the old Popular party leadership which had developed in the early 1770s and continued unabated through the crisis of Independence was, by 1778, a very unequal competition. The "brace of Adamses" were almost constantly absent from the state, serving in Congress or in Europe; their friend Elbridge Gerry was similarly a frequent congressional delegate; while James Warren of Plymouth, husband of the volatile Mercy Otis, was altogether too diffident to exert much influence either in the legislature or outside. Hancock on the other hand, had allies in the Council and the House, stature as one-time president of the Continental Congress, and a popularity that almost equalled the flamboyance of his political style. He had, furthermore, the money to return frequently from Congress to keep his political fences mended as well as solid anti-Adams credentials that enhanced his image in the eyes of Boston merchants, now back in control of local government. His great ambition was to become governor and this he accomplished, not by attaching himself to one of the two emerging parties, but by aiming for the widest possible support, and by not committing himself wholly to either group.

Hancock's tactics were practical and *ad hominem*. After it had become clear that the constitution of 1778 had been defeated, he went to work to build support for another try at it, and he sought his support among the commercial elite of Boston who had solidly opposed all earlier moves for a constitution. To gain their confidence, he directed a campaign against the Adams men, spreading gossip about a "conspiracy" against Washington in which Sam Adams was supposedly involved, publicly reprimanding Adams in the town meeting,[1] and then, according to James Warren, influencing the voters of Plymouth to reject Warren in the election for representatives. The "influence from Boston" was decisive in his defeat, thought Warren, and it continued to prevent the legislature's election of him to the Council. "The complexion of the House," he explained, "consisting of members (the most influential of them) whose politics are very different from mine, and who are of the moderate class which you know I never belonged to, may account for my not being elected." But the chief reason for his humiliation, he was sure, was his friendship with Adams, which "has rendered me obnoxious to a certain great man [Hancock] and his numerous party," whose "policy therefore has been to get me out of sight and prevent my being an obstacle to his glory and ambition."[2]

Warren's description of the leading members of the General Court as "of the moderate class" is significant, for he referred to that same group of men whom Sam Adams had earlier called "moderate prudent Whigs."[3] These were the men who had opposed nonimportation, had flirted with Hutchinson in the early 1770s, and had temporized on Independence. "I can't bear the influence of men who were so hid in holes and corners a few years ago that it was difficult to find them; and when found dared not tell you which side they belonged to," wrote Warren bitterly, convinced that the Revolution was slipping out of the hands of true republicans. "These men," he wrote, drawing a parallel with the early 1770s, "must have an idol. They most of them worshipped Hutchinson; they all now worship another who, if he has not H[utchinson]'s abilities, certainly equals him in ambition and exceeds him in vanity."[4]

The bitterness aside, Warren was right: Hancock was building an

1. Adams to James Warren, Yorktown, 25 May 1778, in Worthington Chauncey Ford, ed., *Warren-Adams Letters*, 2 vols. (Boston, 1917–25), 2: 12–13.

2. Boston, 7 June 1778, ibid., pp. 19–21; see also Warren to Samuel Adams, Boston, 26 June 1778, ibid., pp. 24–25.

3. Adams to James Warren, Philadelphia, 16 April 1776, ibid., 1: 224–25.

4. Warren to Samuel Adams, Boston, 18 August 1778, ibid., 2: 42.

alliance among eastern moderates. But what was clear to Warren was not obvious to westerners, and of course this is the way Hancock wanted to keep things. To the farmer of Massachusetts, Hancock must appear the disinterested leader, a hero. Hancock worked at developing this image. As soon as the elections were over, he set out for Congress, making his departure with the "pomp and retinue of an Eastern Prince."[5] After his departure, his now-famous advertisement, calling on his debtors to pay him in paper currency, appeared again in the Boston papers, although by this time his purposes were becoming obvious, at least to some. "Does Mr. H[ancock] in fact mean to give his debtors the difference," pondered William Pynchon of Salem, "or to induce his own creditors to take of him their dues at that rate because he takes his dues at that rate; or to become popular, and obtain votes at the choice of governor next May?"[6]

Within six weeks, Hancock was back in Boston (much to the chagrin of the Adams men)[7], where he donned the uniform of an army general, swung himself atop a horse, and rode off to Rhode Island to join the French in their campaign against the red coats. Wisely, the Boston general made a hasty withdrawal when the French decided to pull out their fleet for repairs, and when the expedition turned into a retreat he wrote urgently to the president of the Massachusetts Council "that my name may not be annexed to these particulars in the paper." Back in Boston, he reportedly joined in the general condemnation of the French for their failure, but willingly accepted the popular applause for his own efforts. James Warren took cynical delight in ridiculing Hancock, but again was at least partly right when he wrote that Hancock "went on the R. Island expedition and there stayed just long enough to gain among the multitude the popular eclat, and then left it so soon as to make the more discerning laugh."[8]

The discerning Adams men may have laughed, but the fact is they were coming off very poorly in their undeclared war with Hancock and his "moderate" friends. In Boston, the story was widely circulated that Adams was the "patron" of a common knave who had recently been

5. Warren to John Adams, Boston, 7 June 1778, ibid., pp. 19–20.

6. 25 June 1778, in Fitch Edward Oliver, ed., *The Diary of William Pynchon of Salem* (Boston, 1890), pp. 54–55.

7. [Samuel Philips Savage] to Samuel Adams, Boston, 29 July 1778, in Samuel Adams Papers, New York Public Library.

8. Hancock to Jeremiah Powell, 22 August 1778, quoted by Herbert S. Allan, *John Hancock: Patriot in Purple* (New York, 1948), pp. 284–85; James Warren to Samuel Adams, Boston, 2 September 1778, in Ford, ed., *Warren-Adams Letters*, 2: 46; Warren to John Adams, Boston, 7 October 1778, ibid., pp. 52–53.

court martialed from the army. "You can hardly conceive with how much pleasure this, and indeed every other story to your disadvantage is received and propagated here by a party who are determined at all events to ruin your interest," reported Adams's faithful friend Warren.[9] By October, the campaign against Adams was reaching its peak when the legislature made the unusual decision to choose its Congressional delegates for the following year. "This early assignment," wrote Warren, "was the policy of some men to strike at some of the present delegates with more certain success, and particularly at Mr. Adams. If the great man [Hancock] fails he will be mortified indeed."[10]

Sam Adams, annoyed but stoical, was not prepared to fight back as he had in 1768 and 1771. "I am in no pain about such an event [being recalled]," he wrote to his wife, "for I know there are many who can serve their country here with greater capacity, though none with more honesty. The sooner, therefore, another is elected in my room the better. I shall the sooner retire to the sweet enjoyment of domestic life."[11] But Adams was not turned out to pasture. The Hancockites found that they could malign Adams but they could not get him dismissed from a position that was hard to fill with good men. The General Court reelected Adams to another year in Congress, bringing the Hancock campaign to a halt short of its goal.

All, clearly, was not smooth sailing for the ambitious Hancock. The position of a fence-straddler, after all, was difficult indeed in a state so sharply divided between agricultural and commercial interests, between avowed reformers on the one hand and "moderates" (sometimes tinged with Toryism) on the other. In fact, Hancock was presented with conflict in Boston itself. When he arrived back from Congress in July 1778, he found that a number of irate townspeople had drawn up a vigorous petition "for a meeting to prevent the return of the Tories."[12] Now, this kind of action from Boston did not fit in with Hancock's plans, for he counted on the support of well-to-do merchants and other moderates whose sympathies were entirely with other members of their class— whether Tory or not. In fact, the return of some Tories would do much

9. To Sam Adams, Boston, 18 August 1778, in Ford, ed., *Warren-Adams Letters,* 2: 42.

10. To John Adams, Boston, 7 October 1778, ibid., pp. 52–53.

11. Philadelphia, 20 October 1778, quoted in William V. Wells, *The Life and Public Services of Samuel Adams,* 3 vols. (Boston, 1866), 3: 54–55; see also Adams to [John Bradford], Philadelphia, 21 September 1778, in Edmund C. Burnett, ed., *Letters of Members of the Continental Congress,* 8 vols. (Washington, 1921–36), 3: 420.

12. [Samuel Philips Savage] to Samuel Adams, Boston, 29 July 1778, in Samuel Adams Papers.

to bolster the strength of Boston's upper class. With the skill gained from many years of practice, the Boston town leaders therefore saw to it that the "republican" petition came to nothing. By the fall session of the legislature, moreover, Boston's representatives were to be found voting for a motion to allow the return of former treasurer Harrison Gray, a Dr. Gardner, and James Anderson, all of whom had been named in the proscription act earlier in 1778.[13]

To the Adams men, the proposed relaxation of laws against America's enemies would be disastrous. "You would be surprised at the state of the political system here," wrote Warren to Adams, "at the little and the great arts that are practised to pull down the fabric of the last twelve years, and at the prime conductors. The design seems to be to lay it in ruins and under them to bury the fabricators." Warren, in so many words, was accusing Hancock and his Boston allies of counter-revolutionary activity. He condemned the Boston members for supporting the motion on behalf of the Tories, but he added, "in justice to the House I must also tell you it [the motion] did not obtain at that time." In fact, urged on by strong "republicans" and by the need to strengthen the state's financial condition, the General Court was simultaneously considering a bill to confiscate the estates of Tories. With the House so closely balanced between contending factions, however, the confiscation bill received rough handling. "[I]t labours very hard," wrote Warren, "and if it passes at all will not be very comprehensive."[14]

What could Hancock do with a ticklish situation like this? "Some people of influence are against the principle and consequently every part of it [i.e., the act]," wrote Warren with obvious reference to the eastern moderates whom he despised. The republican view had strong support in the rural areas, however. Warren's prediction was that the Hancockites "having no principle themselves but their own ambition and popular applause, will contend with violence for the principle [of confiscation] and then reduce it to nothing by the small number [of names] to be inserted. The first is to please the Whigs," he concluded with cynical exaggeration, "the last the Tories." As the bill progressed, the moderate easterners must have been the more pleased. By October 7, the bill had received two readings, but, reported Warren, "I am told

13. James Warren to Samuel Adams, 30 September 1778, in Ford, ed., *Warren-Adams Letters*, 2: 47–48.

14. Ibid. William Gordon was another who feared the growth of counter-revolutionary sentiment. On March 11, 1778, he wrote to Elbridge Gerry: "What will you say when I tell you that yesterday I was informed from good authority that one of our council lamented that unhappy event the *declaration of Independency?* Are men of that cast fit for the helm?" Elbridge Gerry Papers, MHS, Box 1772–1882.

there is no probability of its succeeding on the third; so far from it that some members of the B[oston] seat have without reserve expressed their sentiments that they [the Tories] should be suffered to return. *Tempora Mutantur*."[15]

Times were changing indeed when his own countrymen could consider allowing Tories like Gray and Gardner to return, said Sam Adams. And to the news that confiscation "labours very hard," Adams was aghast. "Shall those traitors who first conspired to ruin our liberties; those who basely forsook their country in her distress, and sought protection from the enemy, when they thought them in the plenitude of power, who have been ever since stimulating and doing all in their power to aid and comfort them, while they have been doing their utmost to enslave and ruin us,—shall these wretches have their estates reserved for them and restored at the conclusion of this glorious struggle, in which some of the richest blood of America has been spilled, for the sake of a few who may have money in England, and for this reason have maintained a dastardly and criminal neutrality?" Adams hoped that his countrymen would answer no, rejecting the efforts being made on behalf of Tories.[16]

To Adams and his friends, the Revolution was in danger of falling into the hands of counter-revolutionaries. Merchants tinged with Toryism were taking control, and Hancock was cooperating with them. "I am of your opinion respecting Tory and commercial plans," wrote Samuel Cooper to Adams, "and wish all honest men would watch and guard against them. We have not enough vigilance in this state in this and other matters, and some in power, whom you know, and were always either designing or indecisive, do not discover sufficient zeal for what I take to be the root of our cause."[17]

But for all of their fears, Adams and his followers failed to grasp hold of the situation and save the Revolution from reaction, and their failure to do so reflected the limitations of their republican ideology. In their attack on the colonial establishment, in their struggle for Independence, and in their fervid activism, they appeared "radical." But their goal was social cohesion, not social conflict, and it was thus impossible for them to provide leadership for those who sought to democratize Massachusetts society at the expense of the commercial classes. Republicanism was not synonymous with democracy and, in fact, many republican leaders saw

15. Warren to Samuel Adams, 30 September 1778, in Ford, ed., *Warren-Adams Letters*, 2: 47–48; Warren to John Adams, Boston, 7 October 1778, ibid., pp. 51–52.
16. To James Warren, Philadelphia, October 1778, quoted in Wells, *Life of Samuel Adams*, 3: 49–50.
17. Boston, 19 January 1779, Samuel Adams Papers.

the democratic urge as an expression of partisan behavior, to be condemned equally with the partisan behavior of the Tory-tinged commercial elements. Samuel Adams therefore had no more to offer the rural
masses than he had the Boston crowd. The western reformers thus failed
to find themselves a leader among the old revolutionaries. Instead,
dazzled by the man who was alternately president of Congress, general
in the American army, philanthropist, and politician, they turned to the
enigmatic Hancock, whose intricate political maneuverings and alliances
they never suspected.

Despite its lack of leadership, however, the group that was variously
described as agrarian, democratic, "dangerous innovators," and "the
forces of disorder," was increasingly becoming recognizable as a single
political force. And for proof of this assertion, we have simply to look at
events in backcountry Massachusetts in this year following the rejection
of the 1778 constitution. In fact, the complete reports from the various
towns on the matter of the constitution had not all been received when
it became obvious to the General Court that uneasiness was spreading
throughout the farming areas. For into their discussions of the constitution, farmers were interjecting their condemnation of the new fee bill
which would, they believed, make litigation prohibitively expensive.[18]
The General Court knew from past experience what it would have to do.
It quickly passed resolves on May 29 and June 3, 1778, adjourning the
courts of General Sessions of the Peace and Inferior Courts of Common
Pleas in such previously troublesome spots as Taunton (Bristol County)
and Worcester. In both cases, of course, the reason offered for the
adjournments was that "there is not much business likely to come before"
the courts.[19]

The General Court, however, was simply avoiding the issue. Rural
uneasiness could not be adjourned, as was all too obvious when all the
reports of the backcountry towns on the constitution were received and
examined. Reform-minded towns did not all make the same objections
to the constitution, as noted in the last chapter, but they were ideologically united in their demands for government close to the people and for
a decrease in the power of old ruling groups. In this respect, the abortive
constitution of 1778 played a definite role in the development of political
parties in revolutionary Massachusetts. Even though it was defeated,
the discussion that it generated made people, particularly those in the
backcountry, articulate their feelings about government and society,

18. See, for instance, the returns of Charlemont, Belcherstown, New Salem, and
Blanford, in Mass. Arch., 156: 332, 334–35, 366, 414.
19. *Acts and Resolves*, 20: Appendix XV, 423, 426.

and once they had done so, and committed their thoughts to paper, they provided themselves with much clearer bonds of association than they had previously enjoyed.

These strengthened bonds were obvious among the towns of Berkshire County. While there was political division in some towns, (for the most part, as we shall see, between the upper and lower classes), and dogged opposition to the direction the state was taking, the concept of political equality had been put into force at the local level, with the result that the voice of Berkshire was decidedly reformist and democratic. Berkshire wanted a constitution formed by the people and incorporating the principles of the Revolution as they understood them, and to make known their demands they busied themselves during the month of August in electing delegates to a convention which met in Pittsfield on August 26, 1778.[20] The convention claimed to represent four-fifths of the inhabitants of the county, all of whom, stated its petition to the General Court, opposed the operation of courts of law in the county so long as the state remained without a constitution. The delegates stressed the fact that Berkshire had vigorously supported the American cause from the time of the Stamp Act and that, in so doing, had "manifested a constant and uniform abhorrence and detestation (not only in sentiment but in overt actions) of all the unconstitutional measures taken by the British parliament to tax, depauperate and subjugate these now United and Independent States of America." But having fought for their constitutional rights, the men of Berkshire were now unwilling that they should be subject to courts of law that had no constitutional foundation. "It is true we were the first county that put a stop to courts, and were soon followed by many others, nay in effect by the whole state," read their petition. "And we are not certain but that it might have been as well (if not better) had they continued so, rather than to have law dealt out piece meal as it is this day, without any foundation to support it." Vowing to keep the courts closed, and adding a threat of secession should their demands not be heeded, the Berkshire men concluded by asking the General Court to call a convention representative of all the towns in the state for the purpose of forming a new constitution.[21]

There were many in Massachusetts who agreed with the petition of Berkshire County, as both the replies to the constitution of 1778 and subsequent actions of towns elsewhere would suggest. There were also, of course, those who condemned the Berkshire petition as tending

20. *Records of the Town of Lee* (Lee, Mass., 1900), p. 12.
21. "A Berkshire Petition to the General Court, Pittsfield, Aug. 26, 1778," in *Acts and Resolves*, 5: 1028–29.

towards factionalism, destroying from within the union that was so necessary to success in the war with Great Britain. One such condemnation came (surprisingly, in light of its past conduct), from the Committee of Correspondence of the town of Worcester. "The idea of committees forming county conventions, and these county conventions advising state conventions to act in opposition to, or in conformity with the General Court, the supreme authority of the state, seems to us at present," wrote the Worcester committee, "to involve it in the greatest absurdity and to be entirely inconsistent with the best and most established maxims of government." The committee, reflecting the republican concept of a unified and cohesive society, called upon the Berkshire men to allow the reopening of the courts of law. "We wish not to inflame and excite passions but to promote and cement union and harmony among us, which at present we conceive necessary to save the states from ruin."[22]

In the General Court, the Berkshire petition received similar disapproval. In fact, probably urged on by other warnings and reports from Berkshire's aristocracy, the decision was made to send a committee west to meet with a convention of the Berkshire towns and to report on their grievances.[23] To men like the aristocratic Theodore Sedgwick of Sheffield, the committee was a godsend. The forces of order (as Sedgwick's friends considered themselves) thereupon determined to make a stand, and they attended the second convention, which met in Pittsfield in November, hoping to bring moderation to its proceedings.

At this convention, wrote Sedgwick, the committee of the General Court "laboured with great coolness, temper, patience, and candor" and its report, he was certain, would give the legislature "a general idea of the state of party among us." What kind of party was this? Sedgwick wanted to make certain that his friends in the east thoroughly understood its political and social ideas: "Your knowledge of the human heart, the ebullitions of the passions, when unrestrained, the fondness for Independence, the malice against those of different opinions, the envy against those any way distinguished from the comm[on]alty, which are only smothered by vigorous government and which are apparent upon every return to a state of political equality—your knowledge, I say, of these matters will enable you to form some idea of the dangers to which

22. William Williams Collection, Berkshire Athenaeum, 376–79, in Robert J. Taylor, ed., *Massachusetts, Colony to Commonwealth: Documents on the Formation of Its Constitution, 1775–1780* (Chapel Hill, N.C., 1961), pp. 95–97.

23. Robert J. Taylor, *Western Massachusetts in the Revolution* (Providence, 1954), p. 93.

the friends of order are exposed in this county."[24] Sedgwick could not have better expressed the issues involved. Massachusetts had a choice between "vigorous government" supported by the "friends of order," and a "state of political equality," promoted by a "party" passionately fond of Independence.

For a while, Sedgwick's friends of order gained the upper hand. At the convention, they and the commissioners from the General Court made their presence felt and, as Sedgwick reported, "the party who have so long given us disturbance by opposing the re-establishment of order were obliged for very shame to submit to the weight of superior arguments."[25] The address of the convention thus turned out to be a curious mixture of constitutional demands and moderation. Its basic argument was for democracy, but "liberally" defined to acknowledge the desirability of majority rather than consensual rule. "In free states the people are to be considered as the fountain of power," it stated. Among the inalienable rights of the people, it went on, was that of being "governed by the majority in the institution or formation of government." To allow government by the minority "is not only contrary to the common apprehensions of mankind in general, but it contradicts the common law of justice and benevolence." From this assertion of Lockean principle, the address then went on to suggest that the formation of a constitution by the General Court would be impossible since it was not elected to do so and thus would not represent the will of the majority. But then, the address began to soften. Despite the fact that there was no constitution in Massachusetts, the Council and House of Representatives could not be considered tyrants. In fact, state congresses and the General Court had performed useful services to the state in authorizing taxes and raising an army. Furthermore, Berkshire's opposition to the operation of the courts had never been meant as an affront to organized government, but had been designed to bring the state more quickly to the determination of a new constitution. And finally, capitulating completely, the address concluded that, if the people of Berkshire would agree, "we are willing to forego our own opinions and . . . submit to the establishment of the executive courts in this county."[26]

The victory of the forces of order was thus great, but Theodore Sedgwick might also have mentioned the fact that the representatives of only 7 towns saw fit to sign the address of the November convention, whereas 18 towns had been represented in the petition of August. Never-

24. Sedgwick to James Sullivan, Sheffield, 10 January 1779, in Theodore Sedgwick Papers, MHS, vol. A, no. 29.
25. Ibid.
26. Acts and Resolves, 5: 1030–32.

theless, he could report that "the public aspect was placid and I really thought opposition at an end." But the political calm was too good to be true, for by January, the "party," "always attentive," had got themselves a new issue and in no time the county was "thrown back into our former state of anarchial confusion."

The issue arose when several men from the town of Hancock in Berkshire County, arrested while carrying arms, were accused of treason, and were taken to Springfield to be tried before the Superior Court. Before a verdict was returned, the General Court in Boston ordered its own commissioners and the Hancock selectmen to seize the property of the defendants in case the court should order it confiscated. The over-zealous selectmen, however, seized about £2,000 worth of property, "some part of it the property of those persons [i.e., the accused] but much the greater part belonging to those whom they were disposed to call Tories." Shortly, however, the defendants were acquitted of the charges laid against them and they returned home only to discover that the townspeople of Hancock were unwilling to allow the restoration of their property. Indeed, those whom Theodore Sedgwick called the forces of disorder "declared that no regard ought to be paid to the decision of a court who would acquit persons taken in arms against their country." Such talk, of course, only hardened the feelings that already existed against the courts of law. Enraged, the townsmen of Hancock "met in town meeting and appointed a mob captain, a man destitute of every valuable qualification," in Theodore Sedgwick's judgment, "and recommended only by a blind and outrageous zeal against courts, law, and order. Under his command the most cruel and inhuman punishments even without the formality of a mob trial, were inflicted, not on those only who had been acquitted, but [on] those whose property they surreptitiously detained."

In no time, the disturbances in Hancock spread elsewhere in the county, the forces of disorder declaring that they would never submit to be governed by those then in control in Massachusetts government. But further than this, they turned on old members of the Berkshire aristocracy. "They said they now had full evidence of what they always suspected, that all the great men were Tories. They protected Tories. They endeavoured to oppress Whigs etc. etc." A mob, wrote Sedgwick, had even been raised in his neighborhood to question him on the subject. Sedgwick's answer was a plea to the General Court to send another committee west to settle grievances. But meanwhile, he said, the "cry of Tory" gives an advantage to the forces of disorder.[27]

27. Sedgwick to James Sullivan, 10 January 1779, and Sedgwick to the Hon. N. and B., 10 January 1779, in Sedgwick Papers, vol. A, nos. 29, 30.

The cry of Tory worked, like similar political slurs today, as a tool of the reformist party in Berkshire County. With it they could rally the people to renew their demands for a constitution and for reform. But the cry of Tory was more than a mere political trick. It worked because it rang true to the generality of Berkshire's population. It worked because Berkshire men honestly believed the American Revolution to be a movement to take power out of the hands of "great men" and to replace it with government founded upon constitutional principles approved by the people. Such a demand for political and social change was the very essence of the Revolution to Berkshire men, and they believed that the opposition to such change by men like Theodore Sedgwick entitled them to the name of Tory just as surely as if they had fled behind British lines in 1775. The cry of Tory and the incident that generated it in Berkshire were, after all, the epitome of internal revolution in Massachusetts. Opposition to Great Britain and opposition to old forms of government were one and the same to reformers. It seemed natural, therefore, to brand as Tory the men who controlled the General Court (and who, from all appearance, were resisting reforms or constitutional change) as well as the local aristocrats (who appeared in league with antireformers). And in doing so, the men of Berkshire drew even more sharply the lines of partisanship that separated them from Theodore Sedgwick and his eastern friends.

On the other hand, the cry of Tory brought westerners and the old republican Adams men closer together, at least in sentiment. Together, they opposed what they believed to be counter-revolution exemplified by such things as the failure in the fall of 1778 of the act confiscating Tory estates. The failure of confiscation followed by the torrent of anti-Tory sentiment in the backcountry automatically made the treatment of Tories a partisan issue, and confiscation a symbol of the struggle between reform and reaction. By the spring of 1779, the issue was squarely joined when western representatives, free to travel now that the winter snows had disappeared, swarmed into the General Court demanding that confiscation be reconsidered. It was. Moderates, Tory sympathizers, or whatever name they were given, realized that this time their political opposites meant business and on April 30, confiscation, which had "laboured hard" in the fall of 1778, became a fact.

Confiscation was accomplished in two acts,[28] which together stripped Tories or loyalists of their rights as citizens of Massachusetts and allowed the state to seize all of their personal property and real estate. The first of these acts, the conspiracy act, was directed against 29 "notorious conspirators" therein named, including Francis Bernard and Thomas

28. *Acts and Resolves*, 5: 966–67, 968.

Hutchinson, as well as 19 Mandamus Councilors, the commissioners of customs, and other royal appointees. These men lost "their property, rights, and liberties" and were henceforth to "be considered as aliens." All property both real and personal accrued to the state except in cases where such property had legally changed hands before April 19, 1775. The act did, however, provide for families left behind.

The second and more general act confiscated "the estates of certain persons commonly called absentees." It declared that every government has the right to command the personal services of its members in time of invasion and that those who deprive the state of these services forfeit their rights, liberties, and property. The act would apply to all who had "levied war" against the United States, adhered to the king, given "aid or comfort to adherents of the king," or who, since April 19, 1775, had "withdrawn without the permission of the legislature or executive authority" into lands or vessels under the protection of or belonging to Great Britain. But the act also specifically included those who had fled to Boston before April 1775 to receive the protection of General Gage and his troops. Exempt, however, was anyone who had returned to the United States and been received as a subject, taking an oath of allegiance if necessary. The act provided for the mode of trial under which the confiscation would be undertaken, although the state was almost guaranteed success since the absentee was to be advised of the action against him by a notice posted on his abandoned estate.[29]

Moderates condemned the confiscation act without reservation as a harsh and vindictive measure. "To confiscate the estates of all such absentees without distinction or exception," wrote William Gordon, "I must deem, till I have more light, cruel—cruel, superlative cruel." The preamble, thought Gordon, was absurd in suggesting that Americans must have chosen sides as of April 19, 1775. "Now the king did not declare the people of the United States out of his protection nor levy war against them, till long after" that date. "It might have sufficed to have confiscated where absentees had been in arms, or had subscribed towards raising wherewithal to subdue us, or had withdrawn after the Declaration of Independence. But the state wants money; and individuals who have made a great deal of paper money during the war want to buy estates, and turn their nominal riches into real, ere they expire in their possession."[30]

29. A resolution of December 1780 did away with the practice of advising the absentee by a notice posted on his estate. See Andrew McFarland Davis, *The Confiscation of John Chandler's Estate* (Boston, 1903), p. 48.

30. To John Adams, Jamaica Plain, 8 May 1779, in "Letters of the Reverend William Gordon," *MHS Proceedings* 63 (1931): 410.

Gordon's charge that the holders of paper money had pushed through the confiscation act needs some examination. For he was repeating a prejudice that had grown up among easterners against farmers in the interior over the previous year and which serves, again, to demonstrate the split that existed geographically and socially (as well as politically) in the state. While farmers and merchants had blamed one another for their economic problems from 1776 on, by 1779 it was quite apparent that the farmers had the advantage. Temporarily, at least, the seacoast area had plunged into a state of depression while farmers profited greatly from the sale of supplies to state, continental, and French troops and from the inflated wartime prices of farm produce.[31] By May of 1778, merchants were really feeling the economic pinch. "On the whole privateering turns out but poorly and our merchant men mostly taken," wrote one Essex County merchant, "and trade is almost over with us as we have nothing to send in our vessels but lumber. I wish it was entirely over."[32] James Warren, though not sympathetic towards merchants, had to agree that "the countrymen have so long had the advantage of high prices that they don't feel the want of money so much as the merchants and the tradesmen."[33] The economic revolution was even more complete than this, thought a Bostonian, Joseph Henshaw. "Property has shifted hands," he wrote, "the poor have become rich, and the rich have become poor. We have now got to the period when those who heretofore lived comfortably and in affluence cannot be supplied by the income with necessaries for their subsistence."[34] A principal reason for the economic distress of the east, said Henshaw and many others, was "the state of our paper currency," and he blamed the farmers (who he believed were the principal holders of paper money) for its shortcomings.

The economic revolution was temporary, of course, and its completeness was exaggerated. But in any event, it was natural for easterners to add this economic grievance to the political differences that already existed between coastal and farming regions, and to condemn the farmers for both. William Pynchon of Salem made just such a connection. "The drummers and trumpeters of faction have for a long time drowned the

31. James Warren to John Adams, Boston, 7 June 1778, in Ford, ed., *Warren-Adams Letters*, 2: 19.

32. George Williams to Timothy Pickering, Boston, 4 May 1778, in "Revolutionary Letters Written to Colonel Timothy Pickering by George Williams of Salem," *EIHC* 43 (1907): 11.

33. Warren to John Adams, Boston, 7 June 1778, in Ford, ed., *Warren-Adams Letters*, 2: 19.

34. To Samuel Adams, Leicester, 20 October 1778, in Samuel Adams Papers.

voice of truth and reason," he wrote in September 1778. "Their pay is in paper and promises, and if the credit of these continue declining it is likely that a cart-load of them may, 12 months hence, purchase a bushel of turnips, if not more."[35]

The paper in question was, of course, Continental money, for moderates had taken care of Massachusetts money in 1777. But when Congress, in January of 1779, cancelled early issues of Continental paper as legal tender, and ordered the states to call it in as a tax, the remedy soon seemed worse than the disease.[36] As George Williams of Essex County reported, it simply destroyed faith in all paper money and resulted in the farmers asking even more for their produce. "If something don't put a stop to the farmers' extortion," he wrote, "I believe the poor of the sea ports [among whom he included the merchants] in case of the enemy's appearing, they would not turn out." Congress, thought Williams, should simply have ordered an immense tax instead of declaring early emissions of paper void as legal tender. "If Congress should strike dead one more emission I believe no faith for money any longer this way."[37]

Williams's letter, we might note, was written in March 1779, and, of course, within a few short weeks, the confiscation bill had been enacted by the General Court, preparing the way for the sale of estates to be paid for, presumably, in any legal tender money which would include all but the earliest Continental bills. William Gordon's charge that the confiscation act was the work of paper money holders therefore assumes some significance. For it is clear that he felt confiscation to be the work of farmers from the interior, the same men whom William Pynchon chose to call the "drummers and trumpeters of faction." We do not have to accept Gordon's assessment of the motives of those responsible for confiscation, of course, since we know that anti-Toryism and the strong feelings that had been expressed in Berkshire undoubtedly played their part. But what is important is that in the minds of Massachusetts men,

35. 28 September 1778, in Oliver, ed., *Diary of William Pynchon*, p. 57.

36. Richard Henry Lee to Thomas Jefferson, Philadelphia, 5 October 1778, in Burnett, ed., *Letters of Members of the Continental Congress*, 3: 438; John Fell, "Diary," 21, 22 December 1778, ibid., p. 545; James Duane to George Clinton, Philadelphia, 3 January 1779, ibid., 4: 2–3.

37. Williams to Timothy Pickering, Boston, 15 March 1779, in Pickering Papers, MHS, 17: 247; see also Williams to Pickering, Boston, 19 January 1779, in "Revolutionary Letters to Pickering," p. 201; Williams to Pickering, Salem, 28 February 1779, ibid., pp. 202–3; John Winthrop to Samuel Adams, Cambridge, 5 February 1779, in Samuel Adams Papers; James Warren to Samuel Adams, Boston, 12 February 1779, in Ford, ed., *Warren Adams Letters*, 2: 87–88.

all issues were becoming interrelated, and the divisions in their society seemed increasingly to represent opposite viewpoints collectively on all issues, rather than separately on each issue. Parties, in other words, were transcending issues, and were achieving a certain stability and consistency of view, whatever the issue.

Overriding the questions of law courts, confiscation, and paper money, however, was the question of a constitution, and that, said westerners, was a matter that could not be delayed further. The General Court, knowing that something had to be done, therefore resolved on February 20, 1779, that the people of Massachusetts make known their wishes with respect to a constitution. Two questions were to be posed in each town meeting: did the people want a new constitution, and should it be formed by a state convention?[38]

The General Court acted none too soon, for as word of its resolves drifted back into the western parts of the state, westerners were already considering the legality of the present government of the commonwealth. In Stockbridge, where the forces of order and the forces of disorder were struggling to win over the town meeting to their separate points of view, the town finally voted to consider themselves "bound by the doings of the General Court of this State." In Hampshire County, a number of towns met in Chesterfield on March 30, and expressed their fear "that there is designing men in this state that intends by delaying the forming a bill of rights and a free constitution to lull people to sleep, or fatigue them in other ways so as to obtain a constitution to their own minds, calculated to answer their own ends and wicked purposes." If such men get their way, "the people will lose the benefit of their Independence, and may further be said to have changed masters than measures." To guard against these designing men, and to mollify the "general uneasiness in the people in the western part of this state with regard to the execution of the law derived from the old constitution," the convention proposed that a full meeting of the towns of the county be held in Northampton on April 20. The Northampton meeting gathered as planned, and it, too, called upon the General Court to "appoint a state convention" whose work, however, must be submitted to the several towns "for their approbation, disapprobation, or amendment."[39]

Western Massachusetts men overwhelmingly favored the calling of a

38. *Acts and Resolves,* 20: Appendix XV, 626.
39. See votes of the town of Stockbridge in Taylor, ed., *Massachusetts, Colony to Commonwealth,* pp. 106–8. "Resolutions of a Hampshire Convention, March 30, 1779" and "Petition of Hampshire Towns, April 20, 1779," ibid., pp. 109–10.

constitutional convention, and they also believed that democratic ideas must be incorporated into that constitution and that the influence of "designing men" must be kept to a minimum. General Court elections in the spring of 1779 were therefore crucial, and there was possibly more partisanship shown than in any previous elections. As Theodore Sedgwick reported from Berkshire County, "I believe not a single person will be elected as a representative but those who have used all their influence to perpetuate our distractions." The elections in his own Sheffield were along strict party lines with Col. Ashley, Jr., and Daniel Raymond emerging the victors. "The former has for a year or two pretended to be for re-establishing order, but he evidently has acted with deceit either to them or us. And what determines his character is that every friend to order voted against him, and every friend to disorder for him." The second member elected, Raymond, moreover, "is the soul and life of the party. This fellow, although not possessed of a very metaphysical head has as much cunning as any man—in the year 73 or 74, he was convicted of common banditry." In response to their overwhelming defeat in town meetings, therefore, Theodore Sedgwick and his friends had to resort to the kind of partisan organization that they so condemned in the forces of disorder, by calling a convention of their own. "The friends of order in several towns have chosen delegates to convene at Stockbridge tomorrow," wrote Sedgwick, who had himself been chosen a delegate. "What will be the result I know not. Unless we are protected, every measure will be attended with danger. Something decisive must be done or we shall be reduced to the dilemma of leaving the county or making the best terms we can."[40]

Sedgwick and his friends were obviously in a hopeless minority in western Massachusetts. But antireformist sentiment was strongest in the east, after all, and it is here that one might expect to find the greatest opposition to the calling of a constitutional convention. The returns of eastern towns to the General Court do, in fact, in large measure fit into the pattern of an east-west split. Essex County, the home of the Essex Result, was naturally enough overwhelmingly opposed to any move to create a new constitution. Essex towns were supported by coastal Barnstable County and the Maine counties along with the votes of individual towns in Bristol, Plymouth, Suffolk, and Middlesex counties. But the great exception to eastern opposition to a constitutional convention came from Boston and many of the towns close to it. Boston voted unanimously

40. Sedgwick to James Sullivan, Sheffield, 16 May 1779, in Sedgwick Papers, vol. A, no. 36.

for a convention.[41] And the reason, clearly enough, was John Hancock.

Hancock had played his cards brilliantly during the past year. He had stayed home from Congress, cultivating friendships among Boston's merchant society, directing the manipulations of his supporters in the legislature, and taking potshots at Sam Adams. In doing so, Hancock laid himself open to the charge that he was part of "tory and commercial plans," but he profited immeasurably more by winning moderate merchants over to the idea of a new constitution—an essential thing, after all, if Hancock were to become governor. How he did so one can only guess, but by 1779 it must have been obvious that a new constitution could not be delayed much longer if Massachusetts were to return to that much desired state of domestic tranquility. And also, it must have been clear that a new constitution would not be a drawback provided it were safe and moderate and incorporated the social and political ideas of easterners. On May 10, therefore, when the Boston town meeting gathered to consider the questions submitted to them by the General Court, General John Hancock took the chair and the voters agreed 351–0 that there should be a new constitution. They then accepted a report (prepared by a committee of five merchants) calling for a constitutional convention with one proviso (the point, one might note, that had troubled eastern commercial towns for years): "that the convention be so formed as to contain an equal representation of the several parts of the state." With Boston's votes (plus those influenced by Boston) added to the votes of westerners, the proponents of a constitutional convention topped the opponents by a two to one margin.[42]

41. The votes on the resolution of 19 and 20 February 1779, re calling a convention, are recorded in Mass. Arch., 160: 32–123. The number of towns in each county voting for or against the resolution, beginning with the western counties and moving eastward, are:

| County | No. of towns for | No. against |
|---|---|---|
| Berkshire | 12 | 0 |
| Hampshire | 22 | 0 |
| Worcester | 29 | 4 |
| Middlesex | 13 | 8 |
| Bristol | 3 | 2 |
| Suffolk | 9 | 3 |
| Plymouth | 4 | 3 |
| Barnstable | 2 | 2 |
| Essex | 3 | 9 |
| York | 0 | 4 |
| Cumberland | 0 | 3 |

For a complete tally of the popular vote, see Samuel Eliot Morison, "The Vote of Massachusetts on Summoning a Constitutional Convention, 1776–1916," *MHS Proceedings* 50 (1917): 248.

42. 26 *BTR*, p. 63. The committeemen were John Lowell, Perez Morton, Joseph

All did not go exactly as Hancock wished, however. For while he was elected to the General Court (and there was chosen speaker), also elected was his old foe, Sam Adams, who had returned from Congress to end the sniping to which he had been subjected.[43] Secondly, Hancock's henchman, Thomas Cushing, never a very popular figure, had great difficulty getting reelected to the Council, although after two or three ballots he "squeezed in by a majority of one." But more damaging to Hancock were the repercussions of his election as speaker, for in this he failed to take into account the feelings of some of his own supporters, particularly John Pickering, the previous speaker. As William Gordon explained, "the late Speaker Mr. Pickering's friends were so disgusted at Mr. P being *unexpectedly*, I apprehend, opposed, that all the political plans of the H[ancock] party were deranged, and they have lost ground or I am mistaken." Still, Hancock managed to get the newspapers to cover up his problems. "The papers told us that Mr. Hancock was chosen speaker unanimously," wrote Gordon, "than which nothing was more false, for there were fifty-three votes against him."[44] The cover-up, of course, only worked outside the General Court, for, as often as Hancock's friends heaped new honors upon him (as they did by electing him a "sinecure delegate of Congress"), his enemies reduced him to ridicule. The result, according to Gordon, was that "the H[ancock] party weaken apace. The head had a severe basting in the house by two able speakers for not going [to Congress], nor declining; and one of his friends had no other way of getting him off but by desiring that the matter in hand might be waived."[45]

Factional squabbles among the old leadership, however, did not alter the determination of either farmers or merchants to gain the upper hand. Moderates pushed for a tax to clear up more of the Continental paper,[46] while outside the legislature the merchants moved to take action of their own against rising prices of farm produce. Throughout the week of June 15 to 19 (during which the General Court voted to call a constitutional convention) Boston merchants met daily to discuss their problems.[47] Other trading towns followed suit with the general conclusion that prices

Barrell, Ellis Gray, and Samuel Barrett.

43. Ibid., pp. 61–62. For Adams's plan to retire as Congressional delegate see his letter to Jeremiah Powell, Philadelphia, 1 December 1778, quoted in Wells, *Life of Samuel Adams*, 3: 58.

44. Gordon to Horatio Gates, Jamaica Plain, 3 June 1779, in "Letters of William Gordon," p. 412.

45. Gordon to Horatio Gates, Jamaica Plain, 8 June 1779, ibid., p. 413.

46. James Warren to John Adams, Boston, 13 June 1779, in Ford, ed., *Warren-Adams Letters*, 2: 104–5.

47. "Diary of John Rowe," *MHS Proceedings*, 2nd ser., 10 (1896): 108.

of all goods traded in the towns must be regulated locally and a price ceiling fixed for each commodity. When farm prices still remained high, merchants like George Williams of Salem angrily denounced the farmers who refused to "consider the suffering sea ports. I believe in general they have no feeling for us, but want all our money, goods, houses, and then ourselves to be their servants, as it was in Joseph's time, but hope they will be disappointed."[48]

Throughout the summer of 1779, while Massachusetts politicians prepared for a constitutional convention, merchants closed ranks, at least on economic matters. After organizing local "Associations of Merchants," they sent delegates representing most of the trading towns in Massachusetts to a convention in Concord. "I have some expectations from these measures," wrote James Warren, who was as disturbed as anyone about "the deplorable state of our currency." But as suspicious as ever of merchants, Warren wondered whether their action sprang "from fear, or a resolute fortitude, from self interest, or genuine patriotism."[49] Whatever their motives, the merchants coordinated the regulation of prices in eastern Massachusetts. Such regulation enjoyed only limited success, however, for, as it turned out, few farmers chose to send their goods east to regulated markets when they could make much greater profits by trading with other states.[50] Farmers and merchants were thus still at loggerheads when the constitutional convention met in September.

Thus it was that four distinct political forces converged on the Massachusetts constitutional convention that met in Cambridge on September 1, 1779—two of the forces divisive, two of them cohesive. The divisive forces, of course, were the two developing political parties, neither of them highly organized nor with clear-cut leadership, but both of them representative of the social, economic, geographic, and ideological disunion in Massachusetts society. The cohesive forces were the Hancockites and the Adams men. Some of the Hancockites, including Hancock himself, were probably motivated by no other principle than to make Hancock governor, while others in this group were of the "moderate" party who hoped to use Hancock's popularity to accomplish their own purposes. The Adams men, on the other hand, considered themselves

48. Williams to Timothy Pickering, Salem, 3 July 1779, in "Revolutionary Letters to Pickering," pp. 313–14.

49. Warren to John Adams, Plymouth, 29 July 1779, in Ford, ed., *Warren-Adams Letters*, 2: 112; see also "Diary of John Rowe," p. 108.

50. George Williams to Timothy Pickering, Salem, 15 August 1779, in "Revolutionary Letters to Pickering," p. 313; also see Rev. Manasseh Cutler to Rev. Enos Hitchcock, Ipswich, 20 September 1779, in *EIHC* 76 (1940): 375.

above the parties and as readily condemned the "prejudices" of the farmers[51] as they questioned the "patriotism" of the merchants. Their hope was to overcome "the spirit of party" which had "entered into all our departments."

As it turned out, the weakest of these forces both in numbers and organization, the Adams group, proved to have remarkable influence. Their strength lay in their skill with the pen, their mastery of political theory, and in their stolid self-righteousness. As Mercy Warren wrote a few weeks before the convention, "the old Republicans (a solitary few) with decent solemnity and confidence still persevere, their hands unstained by bribes, though poverty stares them in the face, their hearts unshaken by the levity, the luxury, the caprice or whim, the folly or ingratitude of the times."[52] When she heard subsequently that John Adams, who had been serving Congress in France for more than a year, would shortly return to Massachusetts, she was convinced that his return would "give a new turn to the state of parties, and eventually be productive of happy consequences."[53] Her faith in the power of rhetoric and theory was shared by Adams himself. "We shall find, by and by, that those who corrupt our simplicity, will be restrained,"[54] he wrote as Braintree's delegate to the convention. Such optimism seemed strangely out of place in the deeply divided Massachusetts of 1779. But these self-styled republicans were determined that corporate values be revived in their society, and the constitution they strove so greatly to shape was to be a monument to their efforts.

51. James Warren to John Adams, Boston, 10 July 1777, in Ford, ed., *Warren-Adams Letters,* 1: 341.
52. Mercy Warren to John Adams, Plymouth, 29 July 1779, ibid., 2: 114.
53. Mercy Warren to Abigal Adams, Eleriver, 6 August 1779, ibid., p. 116.
54. Adams to Mercy Warren [Cambridge?], [September 1779], ibid., p. 120. Samuel Adams expressed principles similar to those of the Warrens and John Adams in numerous letters, among which was his letter to James Warren from Philadelphia, 9 November 1778, ibid., p. 66.

# 9

---

# Antipartisan Theory and Partisan Reality in the Constitution of 1780

AFTER A four-year struggle, a convention separate and independent of the General Court met in Cambridge on September 1, 1779, for the sole purpose of forming a new constitution for the state of Massachusetts. Each town had the right to elect as many delegates as it could choose representatives to the General Court, and most exercised their right. A total of 313 delegates presented their credentials, 143 of whom (close to a majority) came from the three western counties of Berkshire, Hampshire, and Worcester, the leaders in the demand for a new form of government.[1] The westerners, however, mustered their numbers at the wrong time to have much influence, for the convention met in four sessions before dissolving on June 16, 1780, and at the key third session (which met during the coldest part of the winter), the westerners were outnumbered several times over. When their numbers revived in June, the constitution had already been submitted to the towns and vote-counting was the only task remaining.[2]

In its first session, the convention chose James Bowdoin as its president, a choice that gave the Adams group an initial boost since Bowdoin

---

1. Middlesex County had 47 delegates and in a real sense held the balance of power. If we may judge from the outcome of the vote on the constitution of 1780, Middlesex sided with the easterners rather than with the westerners, as at least some towns had done in the past. As we have noted before, the counties did not vote as units, and certain eastern towns voted with western reformers, and vice versa. It is therefore difficult to determine which side had the numerical superiority. An educated guess would be that they were roughly equal.

2. The first session met from 1–7 September 1779; the second, from 28 October–12 November 1779; the third, from 27 January–2 March 1780; and the fourth, from 7–16 June 1780. See *Journal of Convention*.

was, and had long been, a close friend of both Adamses. After several speeches, in one of which John Adams distinguished himself by arguing vigorously for a three-branch legislature, the members determined to appoint a committee of 31 to draft a constitution. To ensure fair representation of every part of the state, 27 of the 31 committeemen were chosen on a county basis—3 each to come from Suffolk, Essex, Middlesex, Worcester, and Hampshire; 2 each from Bristol, York, Plymouth, and Berkshire; and 1 each from the others—and the remaining four members were chosen at large. Since each county could elect its own committeemen, there was no danger that one party or group would dominate the elections. Thus Essex County elected staunch upholders of the eastern moderate position, headed by Theophilus Parsons, of Essex Result fame, while Hampshire County elected reformers headed by the lesser known, but very consistent democrat, Noah Goodman. From Suffolk County came James Bowdoin and John Adams balanced against an important leader of moderate merchants, John Lowell. When the vote came for committeemen at large, Samuel Adams was elected along with the former Hancock ally, John Pickering. By the end of the first week, the committee was ready to go to work, and, until it could report, the convention adjourned.[3]

It has been commonly accepted that John Adams wrote the Massachusetts constitution as it finally emerged in June 1780. But although Adams's contribution was large, one should note that he himself admitted that he had to struggle vigorously to get some of his ideas accepted by the committee, that in the final report of the committee some points were not expressed as he would have expressed them,[4] and, finally, that the convention made several important changes in the committee's report. In other words, Adams was not the sole architect of the constitution; he was never given a carte blanche to write the kind of constitution he wanted. But since much of the committee's report was written by Adams, and the finished constitution contains his rhetoric on almost every page, it is important that we understand his constitutional ideas—ideas that he expressed before 1779, during that year, and also later in defense of the constitution to which he contributed so much.

Basic to John Adams's beliefs was the corporate ideal of social co-

3. Ibid., pp. 24–25; 28–29; John Pickering to Timothy Pickering, Salem, 20 September 1778, in Pickering Papers, MHS, 17: 291; John Adams to Elbridge Gerry, Braintree, 4 November 1779, in Charles Francis Adams, ed., *The Works of John Adams*, 10 vols. (Boston, 1850–56), 9: 506 and n.

4. John Adams to Benjamin Rush, Braintree, 4 November 1779, in Adams, ed., *Works*, 9: 507.

hesiveness and political unity and an axiomatic opposition to partisanship or division. Adams's goal before and during the struggle with Great Britain had been, as he noted in his "Novanglus" letters, to unite the people of America and to keep them united.[5] Throughout the Revolution, he had denounced the "tendency towards party and division, as the greatest evil," and was deeply disappointed by news from Massachusetts "that there are divisions between the eastern and western parts of our Commonwealth." He knew by 1779, however, that the new constitution could not ignore the existence of these divisions, and while he doubted that they could be eliminated, he hoped that they could be constitutionally harnessed.[6] As he wrote later in his *Defence of the Constitutions* (1787), "All nations, under all governments, must have parties; the great secret is to control them." And, thought Adams, there are but two ways of providing this control, "either by a monarchy and standing army, or by a balance in the constitution."[7]

Adams's concept of a balance in the constitution tells us much about his view of Massachusetts society, for, perhaps influenced by his experience in Congress, perhaps by the persistence of division in Massachusetts, he was beginning to move to the view held by the Tories and many merchants that "the people" are not a unit, but are an amalgam of differing interests and ranks, separated by variations of wealth and ability which irrepressibly motivate them. "In this society of Massachusettensians, then, there is, it is true, a moral and political equality of rights and duties among all individuals, and as yet no appearance of artificial inequalities of condition, such as hereditary dignities, titles, magistracies, or legal distinctions," he wrote in his *Defence of the Constitutions*. "There are, nevertheless, inequalities of great moment in the consideration of a legislator, because they have a natural and inevitable influence in society." Adams went on to point out that in Massachusetts society there were inequalities of wealth, birth, merit, talents, virtues, services, reputation, and fame which had set some men apart from the rest of society as a "natural aristocracy." The existence of such an aristocracy, said Adams, must "be considered in the institution of a government" for if it is excluded "it is always the most dangerous, nay, it may

5. "Novanglus," [No. 3] in John Adams and [Daniel Leonard], *Novanglus and Massachusettensis* (Boston, 1819), p. 28.

6. Adams to James Warren, Philadelphia, 12 May 1776, 11 June, 19 June 1777, in Worthington Chauncey Ford, ed., *Warren-Adams Letters*, 2 vols. (Boston, 1917–25), 1: 243, 329, 332–33; Adams to Jonathan Jackson, Amsterdam, 2 October 1780, in Adams, ed., *Works*, 9: 510–11.

7. John Adams, *Defence of the Constitutions*, in Adams, ed., *Works*, 4: 587–88.

be added, it never fails to be the destruction of the commonwealth."[8]

Adams's conclusion was very similar to that of Theophilus Parsons: both the mass of the people and the aristocracy must be represented as the two great "interests" in society. Government, as he had earlier suggested, "should be in miniature an exact portrait of the people at large. It should think, feel, reason, and act like them. That it may be the interest of the assembly to do strict justice at all times, it should be an equal representation, or in other words, equal interests among the people should have equal interests in it."[9] By giving each of the separate interests a place in government, therefore, and by balancing them against one another, Adams believed that a just and stable government could be achieved.

But how could such a delicate balance be accomplished? It would not do, thought Adams, to place these different interest groups in a unicameral legislature. Conflict would be the result, and each group would attempt to gain control by destroying the power of the other. Each group must therefore be guaranteed control of a separate house of the legislature, and each must be made independent of the other by having the right to veto any bill. The lower house should be elected by the people since it was to represent them. The lower house, as he proposed in 1775 at least, should then elect from among themselves or their constituents an upper house or council. Both houses together would choose a governor, who would also be part of the legislature, possibly as president of the council, and who must have equal power with the other two branches by possessing veto powers. He would serve as a disinterested mediator, using his veto powers to preserve the public interest. The governor must also have the power to appoint judges with the consent of his council and should command the military forces.[10] Such, in essence, was John Adams's plan for a three-part, balanced legislature. His concept of balanced government, we should note, was not in the Montesquieu tradition—to achieve a balance among the legislative, executive, and judicial functions of government. It was rather designed to achieve balance in the legislative branch alone between the principal social and economic interest groups in his own society.

Adams called his form of government a mixed government or republic. It was not monarchy, aristocracy, or democracy but contained the best

8. Ibid., pp. 392–93, 397.
9. John Adams, *Thoughts on Government* (1775), ibid., p. 195.
10. Ibid., pp. 195–96; John Adams to Elbridge Gerry, Braintree, 4 November 1779, ibid., 9: 506.

features of each: the governor was a kind of monarch, the council represented the aristocracy, and the assembly represented the people or the
democracy. By mixing the three elements, Adams thought that all of
society would be satisfied and, since each would be independent of the
others, a balance would be struck that would prevent unnecessary conflicts among them. Such a government would promote harmony and
would control, if not prevent, partisanship.[11]

But was Adams not being partisan himself in making some of the
proposals he did? After all, the legislative structure he proposed was
really little different from what Massachusetts had had under its royal
charter of 1691, with the exception that the governor would now be
elected, and it conformed closely with the wishes of easterners, such as
Theophilus Parsons. Adams certainly knew, too, that a considerable body
of opinion in western Massachusetts had demanded reforms that included a unicameral legislature without governor or council, or at least a legislature dominated by the lower house. He knew that these same reformers had carried on a dispute with the Council in 1776, claiming the right
of the lower house to appoint militia officers (a power Adams now proposed to give to the governor). And he knew that reform sentiment expressed in various western communities demanded popular election of
judges and many government officials. Was Adams therefore siding with
eastern moderates in proposing the kind of government that they
wanted?

The fact is that Adams did not consider he was siding with either
group. He admitted in 1787 that there was then in Massachusetts and
had been "from the beginning of the revolution" a party intent upon
"deposing the governor and senate as useless and expensive branches of
the constitution."[12] But confronted with the reality of the power structure in Massachusetts society, Adams believed that in a unicameral
legislature moderates and reformers would simply tear one another's
eyes out. "I have considered this question in every light in which
my understanding is capable of placing it," he wrote to Elbridge Gerry
in November 1779, "and my opinion is decided in favor of three
branches. . . . I am persuaded we never shall have any stability, dignity,
decision, or liberty without it. We have so many men of wealth, of
ambitious spirits, of intrigue, of luxury and corruption, that incessant
factions will disturb our peace without it, and, indeed, there is too much

11. Adams, *Thoughts on Government*, ibid., 4: 195–96; *Defence of the Constitutions*, ibid., p. 309.
12. Adams, *Defence of the Constitutions*, ibid., pp. 299–300.

reason to fear, with it."[13] In Adams's eyes, he was protecting westerners, not taking sides against them.

Adams was satisfied that the committee agreed with him in principle on the necessity of a three-branch legislature and, as he wrote in November, "the committee have reported as much, though awkwardly expressed." What Adams considered awkward, obviously, was the fact that the committee reported that "the department of legislature shall be formed by two branches, a Senate and House of Representatives." The governor, whom Adams considered also a member of the legislature by virtue of his veto power, was not expressly mentioned as a member of the legislature, possibly to prevent the objections of those who had already gone on record as opposing a powerful governor. But the governor could veto legislation.[14]

The Senate, designed to represent property, was considered the "first branch of the legislature," and was to be made up of 40 men, a proportionate number of whom were to be chosen from each county on the basis of its share of public taxes. Thus Suffolk and Essex counties could each elect 6 senators, Middlesex and Worcester each 5, and the others 4 or fewer apiece. From the 40 men elected senators, however, the Senate and House of Representatives were together to choose 9 who would serve as governor's councilors. As such, they would no longer be members of the Senate, and their seats there would remain vacant. But elected councilors could refuse the honor, if they chose, whereupon House and Senate could go outside the General Court to find suitable replacements. The House and Senate had other electoral duties in that they could jointly elect senators for any district that failed to choose its full number by majority vote, and they could also jointly choose a governor or lieutenant governor should a candidate fail to get a majority. In such cases, the House would select two of the leading candidates, and the Senate would choose between them.[15]

Having committed itself in principle, if not in detail, to Adams's plan for the legislature, the committee had to determine the qualifications of governor, lieutenant-governor, senators, representatives, and of the electors themselves. It concluded that voters would qualify if they owned an estate of the value of £60, while representatives must have freehold

13. Adams to Gerry, Braintree, 4 November 1779, ibid., 9: 506.
14. Ibid., p. 506; "The Report of a Constitution or Form of Government for the Commonwealth of Massachusetts," ibid., 4: 219–67, 231, 245–51; John Adams to Benjamin Rush, Braintree, 4 November 1779, ibid., 9: 507.
15. "Report of a Constitution," ibid., 4: 234–39, 252–54, 246.

property of £100 value or other taxable property valued at £200; senators must have a £300 freehold or £600 in personal property; and the governor must own a £1000 freehold.[16] At face value at least, the property qualification for voters was an advance over the old level, although, in such times of fluctuating values, it may not have represented a real change.

The property qualifications of those elected, however, were an innovation that seemed to indicate the influence of eastern moderates. Adams himself approved of property qualifications for voters, believing that they should have a "stake in society," but he may well have disapproved the changes made as possible sources of future trouble. For, as he wrote to James Sullivan in 1776, "Depend upon it, Sir, it is dangerous to open so fruitful a source of controversy and altercation as would be opened in attempting to alter the qualifications of voters; there will be no end of it." Still, he also believed that the removal of property qualifications would "confound and destroy all distinctions, and prostrate all ranks to one common level,"[17] a rather clear indication that property qualifications were considered a means of maintaining class distinction in the suffrage process.

Despite his realistic recognition of classes and interests and his concept of a balanced legislature, however, Adams still spoke the language of corporatism and still, perhaps influenced by Samuel Adams, sought to improve men's behavior. The "republican" government he sought must be a government "of laws and not of men," a government with "an impartial and exact execution of the laws." To achieve this impartiality or disinterestedness, Adams was as convinced as he had ever been that men must subdue their private interests and that "all things must give way to the public."[18] And thus the goal of moral rejuvenation which had so influenced Adams and his republican friends from the first of the Revolution found its way into the constitution of 1780.

The essence of Adams's plan appeared in the Third Article of the Bill of Rights, destined to become the most controversial section of the constitution. "The happiness of a people," it said, "and the good order and preservation of civil government, essentially depend upon piety, religion and morality," which can only be "generally diffused through the community" by public worship and public instruction. The legislature there-

16. Ibid., pp. 241–43, 235, 238, 245.
17. Adams to Sullivan, 26 May 1776, ibid., 9: 378.
18. Ibid., 4: 194, 404; Adams to Joseph Hawley, Philadelphia, 25 August 1776, ibid., 9: 434–35; Adams to Mercy Warren, Philadelphia, 16 April 1776, in Ford, ed., *Warren-Adams Letters*, 1: 222–23.

fore must have the power to direct the towns of the state to provide funds for a "suitable support for the public worship of God, and of the teachers of religion and morals."[19]

Adams, of course, immediately laid himself open to the charge that he was illiberal, and many people in the state charged, as we shall see, that the article was an infringement upon their freedom of worship. Adams certainly did not have such an intention, but he undoubtedly erred in thinking that his fellow citizens would be as willing as he to allow state interference in the maintenance of churches. Adams was not a particularly religious man himself and his purpose in writing Article III was less religious than it was ethical. "Good morals," he wrote, are "necessary to the preservation of civil society." And it was obvious to him that the church must be encouraged to assist in the moral reform he thought so necessary.

But Adams's plan was not complete until he had written the fifth chapter of the constitution. For here, under the title "The Encouragement of Literature," he wrote that "wisdom and knowledge, as well as virtue, diffused generally among the body of the people, [are] necessary for the preservation of their rights and liberties." For this reason, the state was obligated "to cherish the interests of literature and the sciences, and all seminaries of them." The state, he wrote, had responsibilities to Harvard College, to public schools and grammar schools in the towns, and to both private and public institutions for the promotion of agriculture, arts, sciences, commerce, trades, manufactures, and natural history. Government must interest itself in such things because it is government's responsibility to inculcate "the principles of humanity and general benevolence, public and private charity, honesty and punctuality in their dealings, sincerity, good humor, and all social affections and generous sentiments among the people."[20]

Thus the draft constitution, though it contained details contrary to Adams's own ideas, embodied in its general outline and in its rhetoric the political philosophy of John Adams. It provided for a government in which partisanship and division would be controlled and their opposites, virtue or disinterestedness, would be encouraged. It expressed the corporate ideal of a united and cohesive society in which class or social

19. Adams's draft and the article in revised form appear in "Report of a Constitution," in Adams, ed., *Works*, 4: 221–22. The final form as it appears in Mass. Arch., 276: 30, is printed in Robert J. Taylor, ed., *Massachusetts, Colony to Commonwealth: Documents on the Formation of Its Constitution, 1775–1780* (Chapel Hill, N.C., 1961), pp. 127–46.

20. Taylor, ed., *Massachusetts, Colony to Commonwealth*, pp. 142–43.

rank was a foregone conclusion but social conflict anathema. And it stressed, just as John Winthrop had done 130 years before, the integrated nature of society and government—that government had responsibilities outside the political field in maintaining religious, educational, and social institutions just as these institutions, in turn, had the responsibility of instructing the people in that virtue which was the basis of government. Every aspect of Adams's draft, whether the rhetoric or the form of government itself, sought to deal with a society that was divided along social and economic lines into two developing political parties, and thus it was far more than a plan derived from political theory. It was a response to reality itself.

When the full convention met again on October 28 to consider the draft, the reality of division imposed itself on debate. As Caleb Strong of Northampton recalled much later, the first item to capture the attention of the delegates was the Third Article of the Bill of Rights, which provided state support for religious instruction. "Part of the members thought it highly important to authorize future members of the legislature to require the separate towns to support ministers, and the people to attend their public services," wrote Strong, "while others strenuously contended that no such authority should be given." The debate continued for several days "with much zeal" when the delegates decided to refer the matter to a committee of seven, John Adams among them, "to reconcile, if possible, the opposing parties."

There is no reason to suspect that the division in the convention on this issue followed what he have earlier described as partisan lines nor should there have been any reason for such a split. The issue for many was a matter of conscience or of liberty. The committee of seven, as a matter of fact, split just as the convention had, but four of them, including Adams, agreed that the article must remain. With some deft changes in the wording of the article, probably performed by Adams himself, the committee reported its conclusions. Adams may well have read the report to the convention, adding his regular plea for unanimity. In any event, "there was little or no debate, and it was adopted by an almost unanimous vote."[21]

But John Adams did not fare so well in another matter that was close to his heart. He had never been satisfied with the wording of the draft constitution with respect to the governor, whom he considered a member

<hr>

21. *Journal of Convention*, 28 October 1779; Caleb Strong to Samuel Adams Wells, Northampton, 31 May 1819, in William V. Wells, *The Life and Public Services of Samuel Adams*, 3 vols. (Boston, 1866), 3: 87–88.

of the legislature. As he wrote to Benjamin Rush, "if the committee had boldly made the legislature consist of three branches, I should have been better pleased."[22] Of great importance, he believed, was the necessity of the governor's having a veto. "The executive," he wrote to Elbridge Gerry, "ought to be the reservoir of wisdom as the legislature is of liberty. Without this weapon of defence [i.e., veto power] he will be run down like a hare before hounds."[23] A motion of November 9 was thus clearly made by Adams or his friends, calling for a change in the second chapter of the draft to read, "The department of legislation shall be formed by three branches, a Governor, Senate, and House of Representatives, each of whom shall have a negative on the other."[24]

The motion set off a debate that lasted most of the day, during which reformers' prejudices against governors were strongly voiced. In the end, it became clear that a governor equal in power to the two houses of the legislature would simply not be acceptable to a large segment of the Massachusetts population. Rather than create a stumbling block upon which the whole constitution might fail, the convention therefore determined that the powers of legislation would be vested in the House and Senate only. The governor would be given the right to make objections to any bill and to return the bill with his comments to the house in which the bill originated. But, if the measure were repassed by both houses with a two-thirds majority in each, it would automatically become law. Furthermore, so that constituents would know how their representatives voted on such contentious issues, the names of the persons voting for or against the bill were to be recorded.[25] Thus, though the governor was not left powerless, he was not given absolute veto powers in the Massachusetts constitution—a point that John Adams long afterwards considered the greatest weakness in the document.

This first debating session of the convention (and the last session attended by John Adams) ended on November 12 after determining upon several parts of the draft constitution and compromising on the matter of governor's powers in order to satisfy the demands of some reformers. Reformers were defeated, however, in trying to get the appointment of Supreme Court judges for fixed terms as opposed to their having tenure during good behavior,[26] proving that all issues were not

22. Adams to Benjamin Rush, Braintree, 4 November 1779, in Adams, ed., *Works,* 9: 507.

23. Adams to Gerry, Braintree, 4 November 1779, ibid., p. 506.

24. *Journal of Convention,* p. 44.

25. Adams, ed., *Works,* 4: 231–32 and n.

26. *Journal of Convention,* p. 42.

to be resolved through compromise. And several other issues, which in the past had proved serious matters of disagreement between eastern and western members in the General Court, were put off to be discussed at the winter session of the convention.

The winter of 1779–80 did not cooperate with constitution-makers. When the seventh day of January arrived, the date when the session was to begin, only a few hardy delegates, most of whom lived relatively close to Cambridge, straggled into the meeting house, while many more delegates sat at home, watching their woods fill up with snow. On January 10, the *Boston Gazette* advised delegates that the convention had been adjourned a week "on account of the difficulty of travelling," and it urged members to take notice and to attend as soon as possible.[27] By January 27, when the convention determined it must begin business, only 47 towns were listed in the journals as represented. Of these, the largest group came from Middlesex County—or, to be more precise, from eastern Middlesex, close to Cambridge (an area which had generally sided with eastern moderates). From Worcester County, whose delegation of 65 had been the largest at the convention's opening, there were now only 4 delegates, while Worcester, Hampshire, and Berkshire together had a total of only 10.

In fairness, however, the convention determined to take up only minor matters at first and to place a notice in the newspapers advising delegates that business had resumed. "The most important articles," read part of the notice, "such as representation;—the several departments of government, with their respective powers and checks;—the mode of appointing militia and other officials;—and other matters of great weight, have not, as yet, been taken up, from the expectation of a more general attendance."[28]

The most important articles, by the rump convention's own admission, were the very issues upon which the developing political parties in the state had divided since 1775. The matter of representation, which had plagued previous General Courts and the earlier constitutional convention, still must be settled; who would appoint militia officers (the question that had caused such dispute in 1775–76) still awaited an answer; and finally, the distribution of power in the legislature (the subject of numerous protests and addresses since 1775) must be determined once and for all. The rump convention plodded about in fields of lesser importance, however, stalling until more members appeared, until finally on

27. *BG*, 10 January 1780.
28. *Journal of Convention*, pp. 55–57, 63–64.

February 9, under pressure to get on to such important subjects as representation, it determined to debate and vote upon each article until the constitution was completed.[29]

With western reformers still greatly outnumbered, amendments that would have brought government closer to the people were squashed one by one. On February 11, it was moved that the electorate should itself choose councilors if the Senate failed to elect nine from amongst themselves. But the amendment was defeated 36–30. Then it was moved that councilors be chosen from the Senate and the House and that vacancies thus created in those two bodies be filled by new elections in the appropriate towns. But again the motion was defeated. The next day the convention overrode the wishes of many western reformers by giving to the governor in council the right to appoint all judges, justices of the peace, the attorney general, solicitor general, and sheriffs. Those who favored direct election of officials won out only in the case of coroners, and then it was determined that the appointment of both sheriffs and coroners should be reconsidered (the convention later agreed that both should be appointed by the governor).[30] Democratic innovations, in short, got nowhere.

By February 16, the convention was ready to discuss the subject of representation in the House of Representatives.[31] Representation, as we have noted in earlier chapters, was probably the most contentious political issue in Massachusetts from 1775 on. Upon it hinged the question as to which social group and which geographical area would control the House of Representatives. It had brought about the defeat of the 1778 constitution because, as Samuel Cooper assessed the matter, "in the opinion of the maritime towns, representation is too unequal, while in the opinion of others it is too nearly equal."[32] And when John Adams and the other members of the constitutional committee met to begin their draft in September 1779 one of their number, John Pickering, not unexpectedly reported that "the point most difficult to settle is the matter of representation."[33]

Four years of debate on the matter of representation had added greatly to its complexity. Many easterners, for example, argued for a system that

29. Ibid., pp. 74, 77, 94.

30. Ibid., pp. 99, 104, 130.

31. Ibid., pp. 117–18.

32. Samuel Cooper to Benjamin Franklin, 1 June 1778, in Sparks Papers, 16: 252–53, quoted by Harry A. Cushing, *History of the Transition from Provincial to Commonwealth Government in Massachusetts* (New York, 1896), p. 219.

33. John Pickering to Timothy Pickering, Salem, 20 September 1779, in Pickering Papers, 17: 291.

would provide, theoretically, for proportional representation. But in Boston, proportional representation meant representation according to population, while in Essex County, as the Essex Result illustrates, it meant representation according to property valuations as well as numbers.

Westerners, on the other hand, were less interested in the theory than in the practice of representation. Their consistently held principle, whether they were debating with the British or with their fellow citizens, was that every man has the right to be represented in the body that governs him. They remembered well that Thomas Hutchinson's legislative allies had limited western representation by creating districts on the frontier (with no right to representation) rather than incorporating new towns (which would automatically have such a right). And they had spoken out against such a practice as "against common right, and in derogation of the rights granted to the inhabitants of this colony by the charter,"[34] when, in 1775, they passed the act giving as few as 30 qualified voters the right to send a representative to the General Court.

But, by 1778, many westerners knew that it was not enough to have the "right" to representation if in actual fact it was too expensive to send and keep a representative in Boston for four or five months of the year. As their protests show, the only way a fair representation could be maintained would be for the General Court to assume travel and living expenses of members. It was therefore natural for westerners to resist moves to give increased representation to larger towns since, in practice, this would guarantee eastern domination of the General Court for the greater part of the year.

All of these problems weighed on the minds of committeemen, and they had done their best, through compromise and concessions on both sides, to overcome them. They determined that every town of 150 rateable polls should have the right to send a representative, while towns of fewer than 150 polls could join together to make up the required number. Thus they guaranteed that everyone would be represented. To answer the demand for proportional representation, they provided that every additional 225 rateable polls in a town would entitle it to an additional representative. And finally, in answer to the demands of westerners for financial assistance to representatives, the committee compromised and provided that the General Court would pay traveling expenses but not living expenses.[35]

The compromises were more acceptable to easterners (with the ex-

34. *Acts and Resolves*, 5: 419–20.
35. "Report of a Constitution," in Adams, ed., *Works*, 4: 239–40, 241n.

ception of die-hards like Theophilus Parsons) than to westerners. For, as later comments on the constitution show, there were still many in the western towns who would not concede that towns like Boston should have what seemed an almost unlimited number of representatives (with virtually no living expenses to pay) while western towns must struggle to keep a man in Boston and, almost inevitably, fail to keep him there for all sessions. Such feelings, however, were not fully represented when the rump convention took up the matter on February 16, for the simple reason that only 67 delegates were present. Nevertheless, the 67 went into committee of the whole, chose an easterner, William Cushing, to chair them, and for three days argued their respective positions on the representation issue.[36]

During this debate, two arguments in particular attracted the attention of the delegates and resulted in important changes in the draft constitution. So that towns with fewer than 150 rateable polls would not have to join with other towns to make up the required number of polls to qualify for representation, someone suggested that all towns presently incorporated should continue to have the right to send a representative but that in future no town should be incorporated unless it had 150 rateable polls. Such a change, it might be noted, would essentially restore things as they had been in Hutchinson's time, for new frontier communities would again be denied the right to incorporation and representation until they had a population of about five or six hundred (of whom 150 would be rateable polls). The Maine counties plus Berkshire and Hampshire would stand to lose the most from a provision of this sort. Still, the change was carried and became part of the new constitution.

Then, to the argument that some eligible towns would not send or at least could not keep representatives in the General Court, the delegates responded, not by providing for payment of expenses, but by authorizing the House of Representatives to impose fines upon "such towns as shall neglect to choose and return members to the same." In other words, a town was going to have to pay whether it sent its representative or not. Such were the "improvements" of the rump convention. When westerners protested that some provision must be made for the representation of "unincorporated plantations," a committee was appointed to consider the matter. But its report, delivered on February 23, was rejected by the convention, and its recommendations were not even recorded in the journals.[37] The convention did not consider the question again.

Two important matters remained for the convention's consideration,

36. *Journal of Convention*, pp. 117–18, 122.
37. Ibid., pp. 122–23, 133–34.

and they were linked together. The first was the power of the governor and the second the appointment of militia officers. There were still some persistent delegates who, like John Adams, wanted the governor to have the right to an absolute veto. On February 21, they attempted to get reconsideration of this point by softening their demands to read that the governor "shall have a negative upon all laws" but with the "advice and consent of the council." The proposal at least got the issue before the convention, and debate followed for two days. But by this time the issue was getting mixed up with another, the governor's military powers. For on February 23, it was moved "That the governor . . . have a negative upon all the laws, except those which shall be made and passed for the military defence of the State."[38]

The conjunction of these two points was a natural one for they were, in effect, the opposite sides of the same coin. The governor, as many comments and protests from reformers had indicated from 1775 on, was a symbol of the old kind of government, a position that must be done away with in any new constitution, or at least considerably weakened. Military affairs, on the other hand, had become a symbol of the popular exercise of power, for in people's armies the people themselves must have a strong voice in choosing officers and in determining military policies. Such had been the essence of the militia controversy of 1775–76, when reformers had demanded popular participation in all militia appointments, insisting that no Council, let alone a governor, could enjoy exclusive rights in the choosing of officers. Now the two issues were joined.

Well aware of past conflicts, however, the delegates rejected the attempt to give a veto to the governor, even when so modified, and the governor's power thus remained as in the draft—he could revise any law and send it back to the General Court with his comments, but a two-thirds vote in each house could override any of the governor's objections. The militia controversy, moreover, was left very much as it had been settled in 1776. Militiamen over 21 could choose their captains and subalterns, and they in turn their brigadiers. The House and Senate acting together would appoint major-generals. The governor's participation was limited to the issuing of commissions, although he could fill any position if the proper electors of officers failed to exercise their rights.[39]

But why, one might ask, did easterners not insist on the governor's veto and the appointment of militia officers when they were clearly

38. Ibid., pp. 126, 132.
39. Massachusetts Constitution of 1780, in Taylor, ed., *Massachusetts, Colony to Commonwealth*, pp. 138–39.

carrying all before them? Does this not indicate that there was no partisanship in the formation of the constitution? Actually, the concessions indicate just the opposite. For the concessions were made on points that had been well debated among the people of the state ever since 1775. Easterners knew that they would have to go at least this far in satisfying the demands for reform if the constitution were to gain acceptance among the voters. The concessions do not indicate that easterners had been won over to the need for democratic reform, but simply that they were astute enough to see what was politically necessary. Only die-hard easterners like Theophilus Parsons rigidly stuck to their principles and refused to support the concessions. Parsons, even after the constitution had been adopted, bitterly condemned "those articles which were calculated as it was thought to please the people—viz, the governor's negative—militia—etc."[40]

The convention made one last safeguard to prevent the rejection of the constitution. It provided that the document would be binding only for 15 years, and that in the year 1795, a new convention would be called to consider any revisions thought necessary. Such a "saving clause," thought William Gordon, "will probably prevent the rejection of the form."[41] The convention thereupon concluded its business on March 2, providing as it did so that the constitution would now be submitted to the towns for their approval or disapproval. The convention, so the motion for adjournment noted, would reconvene in Boston on June 1, at which time the returns of the towns would be examined, and if two-thirds of the people voting had signified their approval, the constitution would be established.[42]

Along with printed copies of the constitution which were sent to every town in the state went copies of "An Address" prepared by the convention, calling for unity in accepting the constitution. It particularly concentrated on those issues raised by reformers over the previous few years, clearly indicating that it was the westerners to whom the constitution must now be "sold." It argued that both property and the people must be represented separately in government, that "an exact representation would be unpracticable," that governors would be properly

40. Theophilus Parsons to Francis Dana, 3 August 1780, in Dana Papers, MHS, reproduced by Taylor, ibid., p. 159.

41. Chapter VI, Article X, Massachusetts Constitution of 1780, ibid., pp. 145–46; William Gordon to John Adams and Francis Dana, Jamaica Plain, 8–11 March 1780, in "Letters of the Reverend William Gordon," *MHS Proceedings* 63 (1931): 430–31.

42. *Journal of Convention*, pp. 168–69.

checked by their councils and by their popular election, and that the "dignity" of judges required that they hold their appointments during good behavior rather than for a fixed period. Replying to demands for more judges of probate in each county, the "Address" concluded that "altering the courts of justice" was "a mere matter of legislation" and should be left to a future legislature to settle.[43] In fine, the "Address" was a masterpiece of moderate propaganda, but it was not sufficient to win over the bulk of the people in the three western counties nor to obscure their demands for constitutional change that would bring government closer to the people.

The people of Massachusetts were given the chance to examine the constitution, of course, a few weeks after the convention adjourned in March, but their examination must have been conducted with great difficulty. For the convention, from all appearance, sent only one printed copy of the constitution to each town; copies did not arrive in the towns until the end of April or even the first of May; and then the towns had to examine, meet, and discuss—all within a very short space of time—in order to submit their votes to the reassembled convention by June 7. Bellingham in Suffolk County was fortunate enough to get its copy early and began discussion on April 24. They continued their meetings until June 5, enabling them to subject the document to fairly thorough criticism. But by far the greater number of towns in the state devoted two weeks or less to consideration of the constitution, while some dealt with it in a single meeting.[44]

For this reason, there could not possibly have been a thorough examination of the constitution, towns could not have compared notes with other towns, nor could concerted efforts have been made to bring about particular amendments. Time and the short supply of copies simply did not permit any considerable number of even the most interested among the electorate to read and consider the convention's address, the 30 articles in the Bill of Rights, and the six chapters of the constitution. Opponents of the constitution as it stood were almost bound to dissipate their energies in a haphazard attack on scattered parts of the document. What is surprising is that there was as much congruity as there was.

Of the 290 towns making a return on the constitution,[45] only 42 voted to accept it without amendment, while many of these 42 would have preferred one or more minor changes.[46] Of the 290 returns, at least 207

43. Taylor, ed., *Massachusetts, Colony to Commonwealth*, pp. 123–27, from Mass. Arch., 276: 9.

44. Mass. Arch., 277: 60; 276, 277 passim.

45. Ibid., 277: 124.

46. Ibid., p. 123.

are still extant and they fall, with few exceptions, into two categories: those that rejected the very fundamentals of the constitution and proposed basic changes in the structure of government or the division of power within it, and those that for the most part accepted the constitution, urging, if anything, only the need for greater safeguards of individual rights or a less popular allocation of power. The basic cleavage between the two categories is ideological, for those towns demanding basic structural changes wanted a government that was essentially more democratic, one that would allow greater participation by the people themselves and would ensure the predominance of the popular majority. The second group, on the other hand, accepted the constitution as presented, although some would have wished even fewer concessions to reformist demands. Most of the available returns fit into one or the other of these ideological molds without forcing, while 20 suffered from some ideological conflict and thus defy categorizing. Of those that consistently argued one position, 101 returns are ideologically democratic while 86 are conservative.[47]

But the vote on the constitution produced more than an ideological split among the electorate, it produced a geographical split as well. For of the 101 towns that demanded a more democratic form of government, 78 were in Berkshire, Hampshire, and Worcester. From these three west-

---

47. See Appendix B. This analysis is based on the 184 returns in Mass. Arch., 276, 277, together with 23 others in Samuel E. Morison's file entitled "Returns of Towns in Massachusetts on the Constitution of 1780," in MHS. These and a handful of other returns derived from local sources may be found in published form in Oscar and Mary Handlin, eds., *The Popular Sources of Political Authority: Documents on the Massachusetts Constitution of 1780* (Cambridge, Mass., 1966), pp. 475–930, which appeared after my initial research. The Handlin volume is a curious piece of scholarship. Its arrangement of the returns of the towns on the constitution of 1780 simply follows that found in the Massachusetts Archives, thereby obscuring the geographical, economic, and ideological patterns to be found in them. The Handlins claim, in fact, that "no clear-cut statistical conclusion was possible from an examination of the returns" (p. 475), which is true only in the sense that no detailed, numerical votes are available. The authors acknowledge that on some matters the people of Massachusetts "were divided in interests and attitudes" (p. 26), and that "such diversity was to be expected in view of the diversity of communities in the state" (p. 51). But they believe, over-all, that the documents they present confirm their own consensus view of the Revolution: that "running through the replies, whether from the coastal cities or the rural towns of the interior, was a continuing concern and intimate involvement with the momentous political issues of the Revolution" (p. 51). This attempt to gloss over the serious differences dividing the Massachusetts people simply ignores what the documents themselves say and seeks a superficial consensus in the lowest common denominator of Whig political theory and "concern" with "momentous political issues."

ern counties, as a matter of fact, only 20 towns voted for the constitution or requested nonstructural amendments. The western counties also got strong support in Bristol County, where eight towns demanded democratic changes while only four adopted the conservative position. Strongest support for the constitution, on the other hand, came from Middlesex, Suffolk, Essex, Barnstable, and the Maine counties, where 57 towns adopted the constitution or requested conservative amendments, while only 15 demanded democratic changes. Plymouth County, with both democratic and conservative neighbors, narrowly favored the constitution, six to five.[48] The returns of the towns on the constitution thus confirm the fact that Massachusetts was indeed split ideologically and geographically into two groups and that the "division between the eastern and western parts of the state" that had so concerned John Adams in 1776 was still very much in evidence.

But, to be more specific, what did the democratic opponents of the constitution find so objectionable? Fifty-four towns in the state, 46 of which were towns in Berkshire, Hampshire, Worcester, and Bristol counties, demanded that the governor's powers be decreased.[49] The most common objection was to the appointive powers of the governor, many towns demanding popular elections of judicial officers and county officials, or at least the popular nomination of candidates for these positions. Windsor was typical of those towns that remembered how royal

48. The vote by county is as follows. Counties in which a majority of the towns adopted the "democratic" position are listed first, followed by those in which the majority voted conservatively. The third column is for towns that could not be placed in one category or the other.

| County | Democratic | Conservative | No clear bias |
|--------|-----------|--------------|---------------|
| Berkshire | 13 | 3 | 1 |
| Hampshire | 31 | 3 | 5 |
| Worcester | 29 | 13 | 1 |
| Bristol | 8 | 4 | 0 |
| Plymouth | 5 | 6 | 1 |
| Middlesex | 6 | 23 | 8 |
| Suffolk | 7 | 10 | 3 |
| Lincoln | 0 | 5 | 0 |
| York | 1 | 6 | 0 |
| Barnstable | 1 | 4 | 1 |
| Essex | 0 | 7 | 0 |
| Cumberland | 0 | 2 | 0 |
| Total | 101 | 86 | 20 |

49. If the towns which wanted no governor whatever are added, the total number of towns would be 60. See Appendix B, table 2.

governors had used their patronage powers to build themselves political machines. "If we should be so unhappy as to make choice of a governor who is badly disposed," read the Windsor return, "he may (by having the power) secure to himself his future election and many other points by disposing of commissions to his favorites."[50] The town of Middleborough believed that the popular election of civil officers was as valid as the militia's choosing its captains and subalterns, and it feared that the failure to fill public offices by popular vote "will have a tendency to fill the state with the most corrupt, vicious, and sordid set of officers; therefore productive in its consequences of the greatest evil."[51] An underlying worry in several towns was that "it is not safe to put any more authority into one man's hands than what is of absolute necessity." The town of Oakham saw in the governor's veto power particularly "a direct tendency to introduce complete monarchy."[52] Six of the towns making returns demanded that there be no governor whatever.

Forty-three towns found fault with the Senate, some thinking it too large, others too powerful, while ten towns objected altogether to a second house in the legislature (see Appendix B, table 2). Rehoboth, for instance, rejected the governor, lieutenant-governor, and Senate because "our safety and happiness essentially consists in being governed by one house of representatives which shall be styled the Great and General Court of the Commonwealth of Massachusetts to be elected annually, whose rules and regulations shall be similar to that of the honourable Continental Congress."[53] The town of Buxton claimed that "long experience has been our schoolmaster" in the matter of a second house, and "that the inconveniency arising in negatives and long debates is more injurious to the good people of this state than errors which may be committed without such separate branches."[54] Other towns, such as Colrain, disliked the idea that the Senate should represent property and called upon the convention to remove the property qualifications for senators since "we consider money not a qualification in this matter."[55] Oakham believed that the Senate should not have the power to veto legislation from the House and that the House should be able to pass any measure independently with a two-thirds vote.[56]

Naturally enough, the distribution of representation in the House was

50. Mass. Arch., 276: 26.
51. Ibid., 277: 38.
52. Ibid., 276: 26; 277: 102.
53. Ibid., 276: 35.
54. Ibid., 277: 54.
55. Ibid., 276: 45.
56. Ibid., 277: 102.

a sore point with many towns. Forty-five towns adopted the position we have previously identified with the western agricultural areas (see Appendix B, table 2). The reality rather than the theory of representation was what interested the people of Springfield, in Hampshire County. They feared "that many of the more distant towns will generally omit the full exercise of these rights, and that those at or near the center of government will exercise them in their full extent," with the result that "the latter will have more than an equal proportion of influence in the conduct of public affairs in general." The problem was magnified, said Springfield (to which a great many towns agreed), by the fact that only 60 members of the House would constitute a quorum. It was therefore very possible "that in some future times, less virtuous than the present" the towns close to the center of government might "avail themselves of these advantages of situation and numbers, by an easy, speed[y] and unexpected collection, to determine interesting and favorite matters not altogether to the general satisfaction or benefit of the state." Springfield's solution was that every town, even the largest, should have its representation fixed in the constitution at a "certain moderate number."[57]

There were some towns, such as Ward in Worcester County, that felt that the interests of each town were unique and that a single representative could therefore represent the town's interest as well as several. Representation should therefore be based on towns without reference to size. The town of Lincoln in Maine not only agreed but warned that some town might in the future grow so large as to be able to "completely tyrranize over all the rest."[58]

The town of Williamsburg was one of 13 towns that insisted upon legislative payment of representatives' expenses as the only means of ensuring a fair system of representation. "Every member could attend seasonably and tarry till the business of the session be finished and they cannot otherwise." The old system, on the other hand, allowed "those members that live near the seat of government to pass acts greatly detrimental to the more distant parts of the state, which we have experienced often to have been the case." Belcherstown cleverly appealed to the corporate ideals that had been the basis of much of what John Adams had contributed to the constitution. The payment of expenses, it said, would influence representatives to "divest themselves of party and prejudice and seek to pursue the grand interest of the whole."[59] Petersham agreed that payment of expenses would prevent partiality, while Sutton

57. Ibid., 276: 66.
58. Ibid., 277: 116, 17.
59. See Appendix B, table 2; Mass. Arch., 276: 73.

in Worcester County carried the argument to its logical (from a demo-cratic point of view) conclusion by demanding that the state be divided into representative districts based on population and that all travel and living expenses of representatives be paid by the General Court.[60]

There was, it must be admitted, considerable misunderstanding of the representation issue among small, western agricultural towns. Many of them did not argue for a system that would be any fairer than the one they protested against. But they did believe (and this, after all, is what is important) that the system as they had known it in the past simply did not work to their advantage. They believed, and some of them stated so forthrightly, that coastal or mercantile towns were being given an unequal and unfair advantage. The town of Greenwich rejected the representation article completely "because the landage [sic] interest have not a proper weight in scale."[61] Washington followed suit because "each town has an undeniable right of equal representation in the General Assembly. And whereas there is a large number of delegates from the mercantile towns and but small numbers from the inland towns we have laid in our objection."[62] Oakham protested that depriving frontier towns of a representative until they had 150 rateable polls was unjust. It therefore proposed that every town in the state have the right to send one representative, and no town more than one, "except large sea ports (viz) Boston [which should have] 5 or 6, and other large sea ports in pro-portion." Such a system, it concluded, would have a great tendency to remove "jealousy" between the seacoast and the country.[63]

While many of the proposed changes in the system of representation do not superficially appear very democratic, then, the proponents of the changes certainly had democratic intentions. They knew (as a twentieth-century historian has admirably demonstrated)[64] that the majority of the people in Massachusetts lived on farms, not in coastal towns, but they knew too that their inland location posed particular problems that could be overcome only by the legislature's assuming the expenses of representatives or by a readjustment of the system of representation.

As odious to many towns as the system of representation was the con-tinuance in the new constitution of property qualifications for voting. Forty-two towns expressed their complete disapproval of property

60. Ibid., 277: 104, 112.
61. Ibid., 276: 51.
62. Ibid., p. 23.
63. Ibid., 277: 102.
64. Robert E. Brown, *Middle-Class Democracy and the Revolution in Massa-chusetts, 1691–1780* (Ithaca, N. Y., 1955).

qualifications or requested that such qualifications be lowered (see Appendix B, table 2). Many, like Stoughton, argued in the language of the debate with Great Britain, that "taxation and representation are reciprocal and inseparably connected." The right to vote, said the Stoughton return, "is not only a civil but it is a natural right, which ought to be considered as a principal cornerstone in the foundation for the frame of government to stand on."[65] Belcherstown argued that to deprive men who are free and 21 of the right to vote is to deny them "that liberty and freedom which we are at this day contending for." Colrain added that a voter should be qualified if he is 21 and "a friend to the independence of said state and of sober life and conversation certified by the selectmen." Richmond agreed that it was enough for voters to obtain certificates from the selectmen stating that they were good members of society.[66]

But how many men would be prevented from voting under the constitution? Perhaps this question is less important than how many did the people think would be disfranchised? The answer to this question was varied, understandably, since those who expressed an opinion spoke of circumstances in their own towns while property ownership was not equally prevalent in all parts of the state. Northampton in Hampshire County, for instance, argued that all taxpayers should vote, but it clearly indicated that it was speaking on behalf of a landless minority of the population. A property qualification, said Northampton, is "repugnant" to the first article of the Bill of Rights "unless it be true that a majority of any state have a right without any forfeiture of the minority to deprive them of what the said first article declares are the natural, essential, and unalienable rights of all men."[67]

But the eastern town of Mansfield, in Bristol County, was equally opposed to a property qualification because of the large number of persons it would disfranchise. "How many sensible, honest, and naturally industrious men, by numberless misfortunes, never acquire and possess property of the value of sixty pounds?" asked the Mansfield return. "And how many thousands of good honest men, and good members of society who are, at this day, possessed of a comfortable interest which before the public debts of the commonwealth are discharged, will not be possessed of a sufficiency to qualify them to vote for representatives, if this article takes place as it now stands?"[68] The town of Tyringham agreed:

65. Mass. Arch., 277: 76.
66. Ibid., 276: 40, 45, 19.
67. Ibid., p. 58.
68. Ibid., p. 33.

"We are very sensible that a very large number of the good inhabitants of this state that pay a very considerable part of the taxes of the same are by the frame of the constitution debarred of the privilege of freemen."[69]

Such scattered replies do not, of course, allow wider generalizations, but it is at least clear that a considerable body of opinion opposed connecting a man's voting rights with the ownership of property and that many people in Massachusetts considered the American Revolution a struggle for (among other things) a more democratic suffrage.

Linked with the protests against property qualifications for voting were the demands of 20 towns that property ownership not be a requirement for serving in a governmental office (see Appendix B, table 2). Lee wrote that "we think it right for the electors to elect whom they will," while Richmond objected because it foresaw that the property holdings of members of government could be lost by fire, thereby preventing them from serving. Wilbraham, however, returned the most cleverly worded protest, simply adopting the rhetoric of the constitution itself and appealing to the old values. Property qualifications were objectionable, said the return, because "social virtue and knowledge is the best and only necessary qualification of the legislator. Secondly, because that a selfish view of private interest is a disqualification of the person before us. But all qualifications of private interest are of this kind, and therefore ought not to be made a qualification for the legislator, for so far as he is governed by those selfish views, so far he is disqualified for a seat in legislation."[70]

To the protests of the 20 towns opposed to such qualifications must also be added the many more that specifically wanted the legislature forbidden to raise the qualifications in the future. Taunton was typical of the towns that thought such a power might be "exercised to the great injury of the subject." Richmond was one of a number of towns that would not even go so far as to allow the legislature the right to judge the qualifications of its own members, for such a power would be "dangerous to the liberties of the poorer class of people and [is] thereby inadmissible."[71] But, on the whole, it is clear that more people objected to property qualifications for voters than objected to similar qualifications for officeholders.

The remaining democratic objections to the constitution can be summarized briefly. Twenty-eight towns insisted that there should be a register of deeds and a court of probate in every town (or at least in

69. Ibid., p. 22.
70. Ibid., pp. 14, 19, 72.
71. Ibid., pp. 38, 19.

every three or four) to make these legal processes cheaper. Some towns suggested that the town selectmen be empowered to act in either or both of these capacities. Twenty-four towns still found the system of electing militia officers undemocratic (even though the convention had obviously made significant concessions here). The chief demand was that militiamen should have the right to participate in militia elections at the age of 16 rather than 21, a clear indicator of the youthfulness of many companies. Eighteen towns also protested that judges should hold office during a fixed period of time and not during good behavior (see Appendix B, table 2).

Beyond these objections, there were some fairly individualistic attempts to safeguard the rights of the people. Petersham argued that, if a redress of grievances could not be had from the legislature, the people should constitutionally have recourse to conventions for that purpose, while Bellingham believed that the Bill of Rights ought to provide for regular county assemblies, "to be chosen by the inhabitants of each town within the same county, said assemblies or conventions to have powers of adjournment." The people of Newton requested that provision be made for referendums in case any act of the General Court "shall be adjudged by the people to be oppressive or contrary to their freedom or privileges."[72] A good many other towns requested that plural officeholding be prohibited, or at least, as Windsor suggested, that no more than two positions of profit should be allowed state officers.[73] Such requests, to be sure, reflected a certain popular distrust of government, but, more important, they showed that many people in Massachusetts wanted a government that would be responsive to popular demands.

Such were the demands for a more democratic constitution. There were few towns, of course, that expressed all of these objections, although such towns as Athol, Douglass, Mendon, and Southborough in Worcester County; Richmond and Tyringham in Berkshire; and Pelham, West Springfield, and Wilbraham in Hampshire made practically all of the major objections we have considered democratic (see Appendix B). It is not important that all towns did not unite in their condemnation of the very same articles of the constitution, for we have already noted the considerable obstacles preventing this. What is important is that over 100 towns, representing almost half of the returns still available, rejected the constitution and would approve only with changes that would make the form more democratic.

In contrast, at least 86 towns did not request major changes in the

72. Ibid., 277: 104, 60, 22.
73. Ibid., 276: 26.

constitution that would make it more democratic (see Appendix B). They have been considered conservative here in the sense that, so far as their returns reveal, they were content to continue the old social, geographical, and political balance in Massachusetts government, or, as in a few cases, they wanted changes that would make government even less democratic. Some of those that wanted "conservative" changes proposed higher property qualifications for voters or for those elected, while others thought congressional delegates should have qualifications equal to senator or governor. The town of Wells in Maine argued that the governor must have a veto power as a check on the popular branch of the legislature. "We cannot but think it would be extremely dangerous and impolitic to trust an uncontrollable power of legislation in the hands of those who are only the representatives of particular and smaller districts of the commonwealth."[74]

Some of the towns whose returns appear conservative may, of course, not have been so at all, since the skillful appeal for unanimity in the convention's address must surely have had some influence. The town of Pittsfield in Berkshire, for instance, a leader in the demand for a constitution and for reform, accepted the new form without amendment for no explained reason.[75]

The bulk of conservative returns, however, came, as we have already noted, from the eastern part of the state, and many of these took their cues from Boston. Boston's attention was turned towards personal liberties. It requested changes in the article guaranteeing freedom of the press to protect private citizens from slander or abuse; it asked that the governor be forbidden to suspend *habeas corpus* for more than six months; and it requested that, in case of emergency, the governor have the power to move the militia out of the state if the General Court were in recess.[76] Many eastern towns simply reworded Boston's return. In most cases, as in Boston's, the "conservative" towns were unwilling that their requests for amendments should defeat the constitution and their delegates were instructed to vote for it whether the amendments could be obtained or not.

Finally, three important objections to the constitution were voiced by towns regardless of their location or political ideology. Eighty-six towns rejected the Third Article of the Bill of Rights as unnecessary govern-

74. Ibid., 277: 56.
75. Ibid., 276: 18. The town did, however, note that it wanted the constitution to go into effect as quickly as possible since "the reins of government are so relaxed and this country in particular so long deprived of all law."
76. Ibid., 277: 61; 26 *BTR*, pp. 126–35.

mental interference in the religious rights of the people. The protest, however, did not necessarily reflect a freer attitude among the Massachusetts citizenry towards religious toleration, for the second major objection was to the clause requiring the governor to be a Christian. Seventy-eight towns asked that the governor be not only a Christian but also a Protestant. Many of these towns went further and demanded a constitutional guarantee that all state officers be Protestants. And, lastly, 73 towns, eager that weaknesses in the constitution be detected early and corrected, rejected the amending process and requested that a convention meet before 1795 (as provided in the constitution) for the purpose of making any revisions necessary.[77] All three of these objections, we might note, were made by well over one-third of the towns whose returns are available, while the popular vote on the Third Article of the Bill of Rights failed to reach the necessary two-thirds majority by about 600 votes.[78] Such were the problems facing the constitutional convention as it reconvened for its final session on June 7.

It met, quite fittingly, in Boston. And, after it accepted the credentials of a few new delegates, it immediately appointed a committee of 12 to "revise and arrange" the returns of the towns. The first 4 men appointed to the committee, perhaps significantly, were from Boston, while only 2 of the 12 came from counties west of Middlesex.[79] The committee revealed its predilections towards the constitution the very next day, when it announced in a preliminary report that it had examined the returns of 76 towns, that 5,776 persons had voted in these towns, and that of these 4,564 had voted to accept the constitution as it was, or would accept it whether amendments could be obtained or not, or would accept it if two-thirds of the people agreed.[80] It appeared, at least on the surface, as if the constitution were headed for overwhelming acceptance. But beneath the surface, it must have been obvious to any delegate that the committee had erred in counting as "for" the constitution those towns whose voters would accept only if the constitution received the necessary two-thirds majority. The committee's action, however, was indicative of what was to follow.

To hasten the process of counting the votes, the convention decided on June 8 to add 12 more members to the "revising and arranging" com-

---

77. See Appendix B; "A Freeholder," *BG*, 22 May 1780.
78. Samuel E. Morison, "The Struggle over the Adoption of the Constitution of Massachusetts, 1780," *MHS Proceedings* 50 (1917): 353–411.
79. *Journal of Convention*, pp. 170–71.
80. Ibid., p. 172.

mittee. Again, only 2 of the 12 new members came from counties west of Middlesex. When a motion immediately followed that the committee consult with the delegates of any town whose vote was obscure "or dubiously expressed," it "passed in the negative."[81] In short, the convention turned over to its committee the right to be the final judge of the votes on the constitution. Since the committee was enlarged only once more (on June 12, by six members)[82] and at least two-thirds of the new members were from eastern towns, the final decision on the constitution was left essentially to easterners. How this came about is not clear, unless, perhaps, western members had still not arrived in Boston in numbers. Or perhaps they simply considered the counting of votes a mechanical process that could be honestly performed by any delegate.

But the counting of votes was neither mechanically nor honestly conducted, for the committee fixed upon a method of counting that would almost inevitably result in the acceptance of the constitution. It decided that it would tabulate the votes for and against every article of the constitution.[83] Since many towns did not vote on all articles, the highest number present at the town meeting was taken and recorded as "for" each article. If a town's vote on the constitution as a whole was, say, 64–4, then this was the vote recorded for and against each article.

Many of the towns, of course, stated that they rejected the constitution as a whole unless their proposed amendments were made. In tabulating, however, only the votes against specific articles to be amended appeared as negative. All the rest were positive. Therefore, a town that voted absolutely against the constitution as it then stood would still be recorded as for those articles it did not specifically find fault with. For example, the town of Northbridge in Worcester County, voted 0–38 to reject the constitution as proposed by the convention. But it is recorded as for every article except those it specifically rejected. Furthermore, some towns voted to reject certain articles, but failed to take a recorded vote. Northbridge, for instance, rejected article 30 of the Bill of Rights. But since it gave no numerical vote, none was listed by the tabulators at all.[84] Thus by making up positive votes where there were none and by neglecting negative votes where actual numbers were not available, the committee was able to find the two-thirds majority for the constitution.

81. Ibid., p. 173.
82. Ibid., p. 177.
83. Ibid., pp. 176-77.
84. The recorded tabulation of the returns of Worcester County is a good example of the methods described here. Mass. Arch., 277: 121–22. Northbridge: ibid., p. 101.

Even with the juggling of votes, however, the committee was still left with the problem of the Third Article of the Bill of Rights which, as we have already noted, was rejected by 600 votes beyond the two-thirds majority. In this case, the committeemen conveniently forgot to tally a good many of the negative votes, and then they went to the convention as a whole for a decision. On June 14, the committee reported its findings and a motion was put that the convention determine whether Article Three "has, or has not, been accepted by two-thirds of the persons voting thereupon." By simple voice vote, the convention determined that the article in question had indeed been accepted. On June 15, the convention went through the entire constitution, article by article, voting as it did so on the question "Is it your opinion that the people have accepted of this article?" A motion to have the members' votes recorded was decidedly negatived, and, with the final vote that the new constitution had been accepted by the people of the state of Massachusetts-Bay, the convention dissolved itself.[85]

"Our new constitution is established, and is to operate on the last Wednesday in October," wrote James Warren to John Adams, who was now back in Congress and about to embark as American envoy to the Netherlands. "The election of governor, lieut. governor, and Senate is to be made the beginning of September. Mr. B[owdoin] has again come into public life that he may with the greater advantage stand as a candidate, in competition with H[ancock] for the highest honor and rank in this state. Who will carry the election is very uncertain." Warren, however, was fairly certain that the governor's election would produce the split both he and his friend Adams had long feared. "The upper counties will be for H[ancock]," he wrote, "the interest of the other will lay in the lower ones." If Hancock were elected, he concluded, Thomas Cushing, Hancock's firmest ally, would be a logical lieutenant-governor.[86]

But Warren was wrong in thinking that the governor's election would result in an east-west split. Though Hancock had alienated some easterners by failing to settle his accounts as treasurer of Harvard College, his popularity remained undiminished in both east and west. Hancock swept the town of Boston and the great majority of towns in all counties. "His popularity is greater than ever," wrote Warren, who concluded that Bowdoin had not stood a chance. And when Bowdoin refused to accept the post of lieutenant-governor, the new General Court, which convened

85. *Journal of Convention*, pp. 179, 180.
86. Warren to Adams, Boston, 11 July 1780, in Ford, ed., *Warren-Adams Letters*, 2: 135.

on October 25, chose Thomas Cushing to fill the position thereby completing the Hancock sweep.[87]

Thus the constitutional struggle came to an end in 1780. And three of the four forces involved in the struggle had achieved a measure of success. John Adams and his friends had succeeded in placing in the constitution ideas that they thought would promote unity and control the partisanship and division that had developed in the state. John Hancock in his own way, had brought about a degree of unity in attracting what we might term bipartisan support for a constitution and for himself as governor. And easterners, though they resorted to dubious methods to do so, succeeded in preventing the democratic reforms that they seemed to dread, though, to be sure, they did make minor concessions to popular demands in the drafting of the constitution.

Those who suffered defeat, of course, were the western reformers. In over 100 towns, their thinking had predominated among the voters on the constitution, yet their demands for reform and for government closer to the people had gone unheeded. They failed, as they had failed before, because they lacked the cohesion that only a well-developed state-wide organization, or at least county-wide organizations, could have provided. But they were, after all, a party in the process of development, not a well-oiled, modern political machine. Their failures and disappointments in the 1770s taught some westerners that men of like sentiments must unite to achieve their ends, and, by the 1780s, they became even more partisan in their behavior. Continuing frustrations convinced others, however, that the political process responds only to violence. Samuel Ely and Daniel Shays became their leaders, and rebellion the logical result of their dashed hopes.

87. William Gordon to John Adams, Jamaica Plain, 22 July 1780, in " Letters of William Gordon," pp. 436–37; James Warren to Samuel Adams, Boston, 17 September 1780, in Ford, ed., *Warren-Adams Letters*, 2: 138–39.

# 10

# Conclusion

THE ADOPTION of the constitution of 1780 provides a logical conclusion to this analysis of Massachusetts politics since it brought into focus the complex variety of social, economic, and intellectual forces that both shaped and grew out of the Revolution. By this time a number of significant changes had taken place both in political attitudes and practice—changes that one can directly attribute to the "hothouse" atmosphere of the Revolution.

Most noticeable, if not most important, was the polarization of Massachusetts society along geographic and economic lines, particularly after royal government was ended in 1774. Where the parties of the early Revolution had been able to draw support from relatively scattered areas of the province, political groups after 1774 tended to be concentrated regionally either in the eastern and Maine counties or in the three western counties of Berkshire, Hampshire, and Worcester. Seventy-three percent of the "democratic" objections to the constitution of 1780 came from the three western counties, while 77 percent of the towns accepting it came from eastern and Maine counties, figures which show that the polarization was not complete but that geography was nonetheless a significant determinant of political behavior.

The polarization of society along regional lines was accentuated by the emergence of county blocs, the result of a widespread use of county conventions for purposes of revolutionary political action. Only Suffolk and Plymouth counties were closely divided between the two positions on the 1780 constitution while Hampshire, Essex, and the Maine counties were nearly unanimous in their support of one side or the other. In the other counties, at least two-thirds of the towns favored one side over the other,[1] which seems to indicate that politics was increasingly transcend-

1. See Appendix B, table 1. Bristol County, with its 8–4 support for democratic

248

ing town boundaries and that, for most people, the new consensus was to be found at the county level.

The new state was as seriously divided economically as it was geographically. In the prerevolutionary period, as Chapter 2 indicated, the opposing parties were drawn largely from the large- and medium-size towns as measured on a commercial-cosmopolitan scale. That is, they were both economically diversified to a greater or lesser extent and often faced similar problems. Certainly their conflict could not have been described as a farmer/merchant conflict, despite occasional overtones of that sort. By 1780, however, such a polarization was much more clearly in evidence. Seventy-three percent of the most commercial-cosmopolitan towns in the state supported the new constitution while 74 percent of the least commercial-cosmopolitan towns (that is, the small agricultural communities) demanded democratic reforms. Caught in the middle were the partly commercial, partly agricultural towns that had formed the basis of early revolutionary opposition. They were divided almost equally on the constitution, slightly favoring the reformist position,[2] and thus as a group were no longer a key force in the new political order. Their opposition role had, in effect, been assumed by a group of small agricultural towns that had for the most part played no role whatever in prerevolutionary politics.

The emergence of these new towns was certainly one of the most significant consequences of the Revolution in Massachusetts. Of the towns replying on the 1780 constitution, 101 of the 207 whose returns are still available were towns that had played no significant, active role in provincial politics.[3] Some of them, of course, were towns that had only recently been created. But most of them had been awakened by the Revolution itself to a new sense of the importance of the common man in government, and to an unprecedented understanding of the power of numbers and the value of political organization. Sixty-six percent of the new towns joined in the demands for democratic reform, while 34 percent adopted the conservative position. Most of the politically new towns, it should be noted, were scattered along the western and Maine frontiers.

Of these three determinants of partisan behavior—geography, com-

---

revisions of the constitution, clearly should be ranked with the reformist party. Middlesex County, which had provided support for reformers in the mid 1770s was by 1780 overwhelmingly conservative (23–6).

2. See Appendix B, table 1; Van Beck Hall, *Politics Without Parties: Massachusetts, 1780–1791* (Pittsburgh, 1972), pp. 10, 86–89.

3. Compare Appendix B, table 1 with Appendix A, table 1.

mercial-cosmopolitan level, and newness—the geographical seems to have been the most significant in the period from 1774 to 1780. An overwhelming 82 percent of new western towns made democratic comments on the constitution, but 61 percent of the new eastern and Maine towns made conservative returns just like most of their eastern neighbors.[4] Thus, the designation of the two political groups as the "eastern" and "western" parties appears most apt, provided one sees them as general rather than precise terms. In dealing with any of these determinants, one is confronted with significant deviations which must be acknowledged but without obscuring the major trends and patterns that had developed in political behavior.

Among the towns that had played active political roles in the late provincial period, there was no correlation whatever between their provincial partisanship and their response to the 1780 constitution. Both Court and Country party towns tended to favor the "conservative" over the "democratic" position, although not overwhelmingly. Their "conservative" bias is easily explained. For Court party towns that had experienced little revolutionary change the new constitution provided a form of government as close as they might expect to the old provincial charter, while for Country towns of the "republican frontier," the rhetoric gave promise of a social reformation without class upheaval or conflict in which the public welfare would prevail. In both cases, the most commercial and cosmopolitan towns tended to approve the constitution while the least commercial and cosmopolitan demanded changes,[5] but again the deviations from the norm were significant.

Eight Court party towns, for example, which ranked among the commercial-cosmopolitan centers of the state, provided leadership for the democratic reformers. These were towns, such as Worcester, which had

---

4. The question of the relative importance of determinants is really a nonissue since both commercial-cosmopolitan level and newness were largely geographically determined. That is, most small agricultural, as well as politically new, towns were concentrated in the west or in Maine. Van Beck Hall chooses to emphasize commercial-cosmopolitan variants while acknowledging the significance of the geographical. See *Politics Without Parties*, pp. 9–12.

5. Response of old Court and Country party towns on the Constitution of 1780:

| Old party | New alignment | Commercial-cosmopolitan level[a] | | |
|---|---|---|---|---|
| | | A | B | C |
| Court | 17 Democratic | 8 | 4 | 5 |
| | 22 Conservative | 14 | 8 | 0 |
| Country | 16 Democratic | 2 | 12 | 2 |
| | 25 Conservative | 4 | 9 | 2 |

[a]Hall, *Politics Without Parties*, p. 10.

felt the full impact of internal revolution. Even as the Revolution progressed, many of these towns had shunned republican rhetoric and continued to support the Court party until, as in Worcester's case, royal government collapsed in 1774. Then, in a few short weeks, the people toppled their local elites and assumed power themselves.[6] Even as they did so, their political behavior mocked that of their earlier leaders: they seemed as self-consciously "popular" as their former leaders had been self-consciously elitist, and they continued to reject the republican notion—occasional lip-service to the contrary—that all classes must be reintegrated in a new classless consensus. In other words, the behavior of popular forces in at least some of the leading towns in revolutionary Massachusetts confirmed their modernist orientation, their willingness to accept a fragmented, diversified, pluralized society and a politics that stressed competition among self-conscious interests or classes rather than an elusive consensus. To them, republican rhetoric took second place to the hard realities of the moment.

In this list of significant consequences, perhaps that point ranks first: the American Revolution in Massachusetts had accelerated the processes of change that one associates with modernization while bringing at least some men to a closer acceptance of a competitive political order that would match their diversified society. Such men were to be found both among the democratic reformers and among the conservative-minded local elites.

To take examples, Joseph Hawley of Hampshire County stands out among a generally anonymous lot as a spokesman for popular reform. He was the only early leader of the Popular party to side openly with reformers in rejecting the undemocratic features of the 1780 constitution. "The hands of the people without doors laid the foundation of this revolution," he wrote, giving a distinct class definition to the term "people"; "their hands ought also to finish it." In a lengthy letter to the constitutional convention, he protested that the constitution should have been based on the two basic principles of the first article of the Bill of Rights, that "all men are born free and equal" and that men have "certain natural, essential, and unalienable rights." But the rest of the constitution did not consist of such "clear, indisputable and important truths," he claimed. It interfered with the religious freedom of the people, it excluded many freemen "of the age of twenty-one and upwards" from voting, it concealed "the inhuman, unjust and cruel" institution of slavery, it took away the rights of militiamen to elect their own field

6. *Worcester Town Records from 1753 to 1783*, ed. Franklin P. Rice, *Worcester Society of Antiquity Collections* 4 (1882): 212–52.

officers, and it did not provide for revision within a short enough time. The constitution had been drawn up by a rump convention, he charged, had been before the people for too short a time, and was thus "an unadvised, unconsulted, undiscussed, indigested, tautological, ragged, inconsistent, and in some parts unmeaning, not to say futile plan."[7]

Like the Berkshiremen who believed that power must be taken away from the "great men," Hawley clearly did not see his society as a middle-class, completely democratic one, as some twentieth-century historians have described it, but rather as one in which government, despite a fairly widespread suffrage, had long been controlled by a patronage-ridden Court party and then, with intermittent lapses, by a party of eastern moderate Whigs linked with a few western "aristocrats," who stood firmly in the way of a popular diffusion of political power.[8] In other words, by 1780 Hawley recognized the polarization of Massachusetts society and, contrary to the detached, nonpartisan stance of his former republican colleagues, he openly espoused the side of democratic reform.

On the other side, numerous local "aristocrats" emerged from the Revolution with an equally realistic view of the competitive structure of Massachusetts politics and an equally class-conscious determination to protect "us" from "them." Theodore Sedgwick of Berkshire County wrote to an old Tory friend that he regretted their differences in politics but was pleased that they were still bound by "those sentiments of generosity and true friendship" that distinguished them "from the base— the common herd."[9] "It is my opinion," wrote eastern merchant Jonathan Jackson after the Revolution, that "the people at large, in any numbers together, are nearly as unfit to choose legislators, or any of the more important public officers, as they are in general to fill the offices them-

7. "Joseph Hawley's Protest to the Constitutional Convention of 1780," *Smith College Studies in History*, no. 3 (1917), pp. 31–52.

8. This is not to argue that the struggle pitted the philosophical extremities of aristocracy and democracy against one another. All Americans recognized that the people had a role to play in government and, as John Adams put it, "government more democratical never existed." *Defence of the Constitutions*, in Charles Francis Adams, ed., *The Works of John Adams*, 10 vols. (Boston, 1850–56), 4: 309. But most Americans, Adams included, saw democracy as a continuum: the question was not "democracy or not," but "how much democracy?" Adams agreed with Massachusetts moderates that absolute democracy would be chaos. See ibid., pp. 301–2, 316. They therefore resisted any further extension of the role of the people. Western reformers, on the other hand, argued for such an extension.

9. Sedgwick to Henry Van Schaack, Sheffield, 28 October 1777, in Henry Cruger Van Schaack, *Memoirs of the Life of Henry Van Schaack Embracing Selections from his Correspondence . . .* (Chicago, 1892), p. 78.

selves."[10] The trouble with the people arose from a growing misconception about the nature of liberty, thought Theophilus Parsons of Essex Result fame: "The idea of liberty has been held up in so dazzling colours, that some of us may not be willing to submit to that subordination necessary in the freest states." Jonathan Jackson agreed that "public virtue and good order" had only existed during the Revolution when the people had been governed by their "habits of subordination." The danger facing Americans in the revolutionary aftermath was not the danger of aristocracy, Jackson believed. "The greatest risk they run, is their proneness to an highly democratic government."[11]

Among these men who so sharply drew the line between the people and their "proper" leaders, the tendency ran high to adopt the old Tory interpretation of popular activity. The people, they believed, were mindless and must be led. "Numerous popular assemblies approach nearly to the nature of a mob," wrote Jonathan Jackson, "and are oftentimes more dangerous to general liberty, than any real mobs which may collect in the streets." Such assemblies, he believed, were always controlled by demagogues who "direct the public measures, by influencing the minds of the assembly which is seldom on its guard." Since any "multitude" was ignorant and "must depend upon a few to guide and manage the whole," then clearly traditional leadership must be reasserted. One must go beyond "the bulk of the people, for the greatest wisdom, firmness, consistency, and perseverance," wrote Theophilus Parsons. "These qualities will most probably be found amongst men of education and fortune." "What I shall aim at," agreed Jonathan Jackson, "will be to draw out this *natural aristocracy*, if it must be called so; and bring it into use, disarmed of its malignity, endeavoring to make it a source of the greatest public good, by conveying authority to those and those only, who by nature, education, and good dispositions, are qualified for government." Both Parsons and Jackson agreed that sense and ability could be found among men without property, but generally these were the qualities of "gentlemen of education, fortune, and leisure."[12]

Such was the language of the new politics. By self-consciously identifying their sectional, economic, and class interests, politicians of the late

10. [Jonathan Jackson], *Thoughts Upon the Political Situation of the United States of America* ... (Worcester, Mass., 1788), p. 98.

11. Theophilus Parsons, *Memoir of Theophilus Parsons*, (Boston, 1859), p. 364; [Jackson], *Thoughts Upon the Political Situation*, pp. 131, 55.

12. [Jackson], *Thoughts Upon the Political Situation*, pp. 54–55, 59, 64–65, 109, 57–58, 70–71; Parsons, *Memoir*, pp. 369–70.

and postrevolutionary period separated themselves from the previous generation of leaders and from the language of closed corporatism that had formed the essence of republicanism. While none of them ever put it as succinctly as James Madison, both reformers and conservatives were beginning to share his view that "the most common and durable source of factions has been the various and unequal distribution of property," and that "the regulation of these various interfering interests forms the principal task of modern legislation, and involves the spirit of party and faction in the necessary and ordinary operations of the government."[13] They were beginning to develop the notion, in other words, that politics must be provincial in scope, that it would inevitably involve a clash of values springing from the pluralistic character of their society, and that it would ultimately take partisan forms in defiance of the consensual ideals of an earlier time. In effect, the Revolution had brought political attitudes and practices more closely into line, at least for some men.

For others, however, particularly among the first generation of revolutionary leaders, the rhetoric of republicanism continued to define the point and purpose of the Revolution. And while laying stress on the politics and language of conflict, one must admit that republican ideology, rooted in the partly commercial, partly agricultural towns of the "republican frontier," provides the best explanation of the motives and actions of revolutionaries until 1774. But one must see republicanism for what it was: not an indicator that consensual modes of political behavior still prevailed, but rather that consensual modes were breaking down, that society was fragmenting, economic life was becoming more complex and more diversified, and that political behavior was responding to these new realities. Republicanism, its exaggerated tone aside, represented a determined and at times perceptive attempt to analyze the enormous changes that were taking place in society.[14] Whatever its limitations as a solution to society's ills, moreover, its rhetoric and its ideals were powerful enough to color American political development long after the Revolution.

13. James Madison, "Tenth Federalist," in Alexander Hamilton, James Madison, and John Jay, *The Federalist or, The New Constitution*, ed. Max Beloff (New York, 1948), 41–48, 42, 43.

14. The most promising and most perceptive discourse on this subject is Gordon Wood, "Rhetoric and Reality in the American Revolution," *WMQ*, 3d ser., 23 (1966): 3–32. Unfortunately, neither he nor anyone else has taken up his challenge to use the rhetoric as a key to unlocking the social and economic reality. Wood's book, *The Creation of the American Republic, 1776–1787* (Chapel Hill, N.C., 1969), while brilliant in its elucidation of republican theory, lapses into tired, neo-Whig preoccupation with constitutionalism unrelated to social forces and falls into the consensus trap he had warned against in his article.

Probably its persistence was nowhere more evident than in Americans' attitude towards the development of parties. Their pragmatic formation of political groups and identification of group interests to the contrary, many continued to believe that partisanship was wrong and partisans "unpatriotic"; indeed, something of this feeling has tinged political development right down to the present. While John Adams gravitated towards Federalism in the 1790s and Sam Adams to the Republicans, neither of them ever made a good party man. And it may well have been this reluctance to accept competing parties as a necessary part of things that greatly weakened the Federalist cause in New England and led ultimately to the complete disintegration of the party. "Are we forever to be overawed and directed by party passions?",[15] John Adams wrote in 1797 in the face of the challenge of Alexander Hamilton and the High Federalists. And it is perhaps not surprising that Adams went so far as to blame the "Essex Junto"—the remnant of that hard core of Essex men who led the "eastern party" in the latter 1770s—for many of the problems of his presidential administration. The men were old and powerless by then,[16] but they symbolized for Adams a deplorable tendency among commercial men to put their own private interest first.

Perhaps John Quincy Adams put the antipartisan attitude best in 1802: "A politician in this country must be the man of a party. I would fain be the man of my whole country."[17] There is something at once compelling and terrifying in what he said. It appeals to all of the patriotic emotions in its advocacy of union and unanimity. But at the same time, it ignores the possibility that a man might be both partisan and patriotic; indeed, that partisanship serves the national interest by protecting legitimate differences of opinion among the people. Fortunately, both Adamses came to recognize the inevitability of parties in a free state, and they developed an objectivity and perceptiveness on the subject that was remarkable for the time. But many of their countrymen did not, and they failed to learn that legitimate differences of opinion cannot always be smothered by patriotic emotion or by futile pleas for consensus.

15. Adams to Elbridge Gerry, 6 April 1797, in Adams, ed., *Works*, 8: 538.

16. David H. Fischer, "The Myth of the Essex Junto," *WMQ*, 3d ser., 21 (1964): 191–235.

17. 28 January 1802, Charles Francis Adams, ed., *Memoirs of John Quincy Adams, Comprising Portions of His Diary from 1795 to 1848*, vol. 1 (Philadelphia, 1874), p. 249.

# Appendices

# Appendix A: Partisan Towns and Legislators of Massachusetts in the Late Provincial Period

Table 1. Legislative Voting Records of Massachusetts Towns, 1757–1764, with Correlates

| Town | Court party towns | | | | | | Hall classification[g] | Tax category, 1761[h] | Land Bank investors per 100 of population | Average legislative tenure, 1744–64, in years | Single longest legislative tenure, 1744–64, in years | Population, 1765 |
|---|---|---|---|---|---|---|---|---|---|---|---|---|
| | Should part of militia be employed for defense under New England officers?[a] | Should Agent Bollan receive parliamentary grant?[b] | Should Bollan's name appear first on a commission?[c] | Amendment to bill regulating coinage[d] | Should bill excluding Superior Court Justices from legislature receive 3d reading?[e] | Resolution to excuse Thos. Hutchinson from serving as agent in London?[f] | | | | | | |
| *Suffolk County* | | | | | | | | | | | | |
| Dorchester | 0 | + | + | + | + | + | A | b | 0.93 | 2.5 | 6 | 1,360 |
| Dedham | + | 0 | − | + | + | + | A | b | 0.58 | 3.8 | 10 | 1,929 |
| Chelsea | + | + | + | + | + | + | C | c | 3.40 | 4.7 | 7 | 452 |
| *Essex County* | | | | | | | | | | | | |
| Salem | + | + | + | 0 | + | 0 | A | a | 0.58 | 2.2 | 4 | 4,254 |
| Ipswich | + | + | + | − | + | 0 | A | a | 0.69 | 3.4 | 8 | 3,642 |
| Marblehead | + | 0 | + | 0 | + | 0 | A | a | 0.00 | 3.0 | 7 | 4,954 |
| Almsbury | − | 0 | 0 | + | 0 | + | B | b | 0.00 | 4.0 | 7 | 1,550 |
| *Middlesex County* | | | | | | | | | | | | |
| Cambridge | 0 | + | 0 | + | + | + | A | a | 0.25 | 3.6 | 15 | 1,582 |
| Charlestown | 0 | 0 | + | − | + | 0 | A | b | 0.30 | 5.4 | 14 | 2,048 |
| Woburn | − | − | 0 | + | + | + | A | b | 0.13 | 3.6 | 5 | 1,517 |

| Town | | | | | | | | | | | | | | Pop |
|---|---|---|---|---|---|---|---|---|---|---|---|---|---|---|
| Concord | − | + | + | + | + | + | − | + | A | b | 1.21 | 3.5 | 7 | 1,564 |
| Newton | 0 | + | + | + | + | + | 0 | − | A | b | 0.31 | 5.0 | 12 | 1,308 |
| Sudbury | − | + | + | − | + | + | 0 | + | B | b | 1.72 | 4.7 | 10 | 1,773 |
| Groton, Shirley, Pepperrell[1] | 0 | + | 0 | + | + | 0 | 0 | 0 | B | b | 0.15 | 9.5 | 17 | 1,443 |
| Lexington | − | − | + | + | + | − | − | 0 | A | b | 0.00 | 6.6 | 8 | 912 |
| Chelmsford | − + | + | + | + | + | + | + | − | A | b | 0.20 | 3.8 | 6 | 1,012 |
| Weston | + | + | + | + | 0 | + | − | + | B | c | 0.75 | 3.8 | 9 | 768 |
| Malden | − | + | + | + | + | + | 0 | + | B | c | 1.11 | 3.3 | 9 | 992 |
| Medford | 0 | + | 0 | + | 0 | 0 | 0 | + | A | c | 0.12 | 6.3 | 11 | 790 |
| Westford | 0 | + | + | + | + | 0 | + | 0 | B | c | 0.30 | 4.0 | 6 | 962 |
| Lincoln | + | 0 | + | + | 0 | 0 | 0 | + | B | c | 0.00 | 7.0 | 7 | 646 |
| Hopkinton | 0 | 0 | 0 | 0 | 0 | 0 | 0 | 0 | B | c | 0.40 | 7.0 | 7 | 1,027 |
| *Hampshire County* | | | | | | | | | | | | | | |
| Springfield | + | + | 0 | + | + | + | + | 0 | A | a | 0.00 | 5.8 | 11 | 2,755 |
| Northampton, Southampton[1] | − | − | 0 | + | 0 | 0 | 0 | 0 | A | b | 0.00 | 3.3 | 6 | 1,289 |
| Hadley, S. Hadley, Amherst[1] | − | + | + | + | + | 0 | + | 0 | A | c | 0.00 | 3.3 | 11 | 573 |
| Hatfield | + | + | + | 0 | + | 0 | + | 0 | B | c | 0.00 | 6.3 | 10 | 815 |
| Sheffield, Egremont[1] | + | 0 | + | + | 0 | 0 | + | 0 | B | c | 0.00 | 2.6 | 5 | 1,073 |
| Deerfield, Greenfield[1] | + | + | − | + | 0 | + | + | 0 | A | c | 0.00 | 2.7 | 10 | 737 |
| *Worcester County* | | | | | | | | | | | | | | |
| Worcester | + | 0 | + | + | + | 0 | + | + | A | b | 1.87 | 6.3 | 8 | 1,478 |
| Lancaster | 0 | + | + | + | + | 0 | + | + | A | b | 0.20 | 4.0 | 9 | 1,999 |
| Rutland | 0 | + | + | + | 0 | 0 | + | + | A | b | 0.45 | 13.0 | 13 | 1,090 |
| Oxford, Charlton[1] | + | + | + | − | 0 | 0 | + | − | C | c | 0.31 | 2.8 | 6 | 890 |
| Hardwick | + | + | + | 0 | 0 | 0 | 0 | 0 | B | c | 0.30 | 8.0 | 8 | 1,010 |
| Southborough | 0 | + | 0 | + | 0 | 0 | 0 | + | C | c | 0.43 | 3.3 | 4 | 731 |
| Petersham | 0 | − | + | + | + | 0 | − | + | B | c | 0.00 | 2.0 | 2 | 707 |
| *Plymouth County* | | | | | | | | | | | | | | |
| Plymouth | + | + | − | + | + | + | − | + | A | b | 0.05 | 6.3 | 15 | 2,246 |
| Marshfield | + | + | + | 0 | + | + | + | 0 | A | b | 0.00 | 3.8 | 7 | 1,159 |

Table 1. Legislative Voting Records of Massachusetts Towns (*continued*)

| Town | Should part of militia be employed for defense under New England officers?[a] | Should Agent Bollan receive parliamentary grant?[b] | Should Bollan's name appear first on a commission?[c] | Amendment to bill regulating coinage[d] | Should bill excluding Superior Court Justices from legislature receive 3d reading?[e] | Resolution to excuse Thos. Hutchinson from serving as agent in London?[f] | Hall classification[g] | Tax category, 1761[h] | Land Bank investors per 100 of population | Average legislative tenure, 1744–64, in years | Single longest legislative tenure, 1744–64, in years | Population, 1765 |
|---|---|---|---|---|---|---|---|---|---|---|---|---|
| Duxbury | 0 | − | + | − | + | + | B | c | 0.00 | 5.7 | 11 | 1,061 |
| Bridgewater | − | + | + | + | + | + | A | a | 0.85 | 6.7 | 11 | 3,990 |
| Middleborough | − | + | + | − | + | 0 | A | a | 0.20 | 3.0 | 8 | 3,438 |
| Rochester | + | 0 | + | − | + | 0 | C | b | 0.45 | 4.5 | 5 | 1,985 |
| Pembroke | + | + | − | + | 0 | 0 | A | b | 0.50 | 3.8 | 8 | 1,446 |
| *Barnstable County* | | | | | | | | | | | | |
| Harwich | + | + | + | 0 | + | 0 | B | c | 0.05 | 3.2 | 6 | 1,772 |
| *York County* | | | | | | | | | | | | |
| Wells | + | 0 | − | + | + | 0 | B | b | 0.00 | 4.0 | 9 | 1,569 |
| Biddeford | + | 0 | 0 | 0 | 0 | 0 | B | b | 0.12 | 2.2 | 6 | 753 |
| *Cumberland County* | | | | | | | | | | | | |
| Falmouth | + | 0 | 0 | + | + | 0 | A | a | 0.03 | 2.4 | 6 | 3,783 |
| *Dukes County* | | | | | | | | | | | | |
| Edgartown | 0 | 0 | + | + | 0 | 0 | A | c | 0.00 | 2.7 | 5 | 1,030 |
| *Nantucket County* | | | | | | | | | | | | |
| Sherburne | 0 | + | + | 0 | 0 | + | A | a | 0.09 | 9.0 | 17 | 3,526 |
| *Berkshire County* | | | | | | | | | | | | |
| Stockbridge | 0 | 0 | 0 | 0 | 0 | + | B | c | 0.00 | 2.3 | 4 | 244 |
| Tyringham | 0 | 0 | 0 | 0 | 0 | + | C | − | 0.00 | 2.0 | 2 | 325 |

260

## Country party towns

| | | | | | | | | | | | | |
|---|---|---|---|---|---|---|---|---|---|---|---|---|
| *Suffolk County* | | | | | | | | | | | | |
| Boston (4 reps.) | + | + | 0 | + | − | − | A | a | 0.35 | 4.0 | 14 | 15,520 |
| | | | | | | | | | | | | |
| Milton | − | 0 | 0 | + | − | − | A | b | 0.66 | 3.6 | 8 | 948 |
| Braintree | + | 0 | + | + | + | − | A | a | 0.58 | 3.0 | 5 | 2,445 |
| Weymouth | 0 | + | + | + | + | 0 | A | b | 0.61 | 6.0 | 9 | 1,258 |
| Hingham | − | − | − | 0 | + | 0 | A | a | 0.12 | 5.0 | 10 | 2,506 |
| Medfield | − | + | − | + | + | − | B | c | 0.00 | 2.3 | 5 | 639 |
| Stoughton | − | − | − | − | − | − | B | b | 0.83 | 6.3 | 8 | 2,340 |
| Wrentham | − | − | − | − | − | − | B | b | 0.35 | 2.8 | 7 | 2,030 |
| Medway | 0 | − | 0 | − | − | − | B | c | 0.00 | 3.0 | 4 | 793 |
| Needham | 0 | − | 0 | 0 | − | 0 | B | c | 1.00 | 3.0 | 4 | 945 |
| *Essex County* | | | | | | | | | | | | |
| Newbury (2 reps.) | − | + | − | − | − | − | A | a | 0.28 | 2.9 | 10 | 2,918 |
| | | | | | | | | | | | | |
| Lynn | + | + | 0 | 0 | − | − | A | b | 0.95 | 6.3 | 12 | 2,208 |
| Beverly | − | − | − | − | 0 | − | A | b | 0.64 | 4.0 | 10 | 2,171 |
| Rowley | − | − | − | − | − | − | B | b | 0.33 | 4.0 | 10 | 1,481 |
| Salisbury | − | − | − | − | − | + | B | b | 0.15 | 5.0 | 12 | 1,344 |
| Danvers | − | − | 0 | 0 | 0 | − | A | b | 0.00 | 2.5 | 4 | 2,061 |
| Topsfield | − | − | − | − | − | − | B | c | 0.29 | 3.5 | 5 | 719 |
| Boxford | − | − | − | − | 0 | − | C | b | 0.12 | 3.8 | 7 | 841 |
| Bradford | − | − | − | − | − | + | A | b | 0.33 | 8.5 | 12 | 1,166 |
| *Middlesex County* | | | | | | | | | | | | |
| Reading | + | + | − | − | + | − | C | b | 0.20 | 5.0 | 7 | 1,537 |
| Marlborough | − | − | − | − | − | − | B | b | 0.77 | 6.7 | 17 | 1,287 |

Table 1. Legislative Voting Records of Massachusetts Towns (continued)

| Town | Should part of militia be employed for defense under New England officers?[a] | Should Agent Bollan receive parliamentary grant?[b] | Should Bollan's name appear first on a commission?[c] | Amendment to bill regulating coinage[d] | Should bill excluding Superior Court Justices from legislature receive 3d reading?[e] | Resolution to excuse Thos. Hutchinson from serving as agent in London[f] | Hall classification[g] | Tax category, 1761[h] | Land Bank investors per 100 of population | Average legislative tenure, 1744–64, in years | Single longest legislative tenure, 1744–64, in years | Population, 1765 |
|---|---|---|---|---|---|---|---|---|---|---|---|---|
| Framingham | — | + | + | — | — | — | B | b | 0.77 | 10.0 | 19 | 1,313 |
| Waltham | 0 | — | 0 | — | + | — | A | c | 0.00 | 6.3 | 17 | 663 |
| Watertown | — | — | + | — | — | — | A | c | 0.86 | 6.3 | 8 | 693 |
| Billerica | — | — | 0 | — | + | — | C | b | 0.23 | 4.0 | 10 | 1,334 |
| *Worcester County* | | | | | | | | | | | | |
| Leicester, Spencer[i] | 0 | — | — | — | + | 0 | B | c | 1.78 | 4.3 | 6 | 770 |
| Bolton | 0 | 0 | — | + | — | — | A | c | 0.10 | 4.0 | 10 | 993 |
| Sutton | — | — | — | + | 0 | — | A | b | 0.94 | 5.0 | 8 | 2,137 |
| Harvard | 0 | 0 | 0 | — | — | 0 | B | c | 1.00 | 3.0 | 3 | 1,126 |
| Mendon | 0 | — | — | + | + | 0 | B | b | 1.50 | 3.2 | 4 | 1,843 |
| Westborough | 0 | 0 | — | — | 0 | — | B | b | 0.09 | 3.0 | 7 | 1,110 |
| Shrewsbury | + | — | — | — | 0 | 0 | B | b | 0.14 | 3.2 | 4 | 1,401 |
| Sturbridge | — | — | 0 | — | 0 | 0 | B | c | 0.00 | 7.0 | 3 | 899 |
| Lunenburg | — | + | — | — | + | 0 | B | c | 2.00 | 2.5 | 7 | 821 |
| Dudley | — | 0 | 0 | 0 | 0 | 0 | C | c | 0.57 | 2.0 | 2 | 733 |
| *Hampshire County* | | | | | | | | | | | | |
| Brimfield | — | — | — | + | 0 | + | C | c | 1.00 | 2.4 | 5 | 773 |
| *Plymouth County* | | | | | | | | | | | | |
| Plympton | 0 | 0 | — | — | — | — | C | c | 0.14 | 3.2 | 6 | 1,417 |

|  | | | | | | | | | | | | | | |
|---|---|---|---|---|---|---|---|---|---|---|---|---|---|---|
| Kingston | 0 | 0 | 0 | – | 0 | 0 | 0 | 0 | A | c | 0.12 | 2.0 | 4 | 774 |
| Abington | 0 | 0 | – | + | – | – | 0 | – | A | c | 0.23 | 4.5 | 5 | 1,263 |
| Hanover | 0 | 0 | – | + | – | – | + | 0 | B | c | – | 5.5 | 10 | – |
| *Bristol County* | | | | | | | | | | | | | | |
| Taunton | 0 | 0 | – | 0 | 0 | – | 0 | 0 | A | a | 0.15 | 3.5 | 9 | 2,744 |
| Rehoboth | – | 0 | + | – | – | – | – | – | B | a | 0.30 | 2.5 | 4 | 3,690 |
| Norton | – | – | – | – | – | – | – | – | B | b | 0.84 | 3.0 | 8 | 1,942 |
| Swanzey | 0 | – | + | – | – | 0 | – | – | A | b | – | 3.2 | 5 | – |
| Dartmouth | – | – | 0 | 0 | – | – | 0 | 0 | A | a | 0.06 | 4.0 | 9 | 4,581 |
| Attleborough | – | – | – | 0 | – | – | 0 | 0 | B | b | 0.41 | 2.9 | 7 | 1,739 |
| Dighton | – | 0 | 0 | 0 | 0 | 0 | 0 | 0 | B | c | 0.92 | 2.4 | 7 | 1,177 |
| *York County* | | | | | | | | | | | | | | |
| York | – | – | – | 0 | – | – | 0 | 0 | A | a | 0.00 | 4.0 | 10 | 2,298 |
| Kittery | 0 | – | 0 | 0 | – | – | 0 | 0 | B | a | 0.00 | 2.9 | 8 | 2,368 |
| Berwick | – | – | 0 | 0 | – | – | 0 | 0 | B | b | 0.04 | 3.3 | 7 | 2,374 |
| *Dukes County* | | | | | | | | | | | | | | |
| Chilmark | 0 | 0 | 0 | 0 | 0 | 0 | 0 | 0 | B | c | 0.22 | 1.3 | 2 | 851 |
| Tisbury | 0 | 0 | – | 0 | – | – | 0 | 0 | B | c | 0.00 | 2.0 | 2 | 838 |

Towns with equally divided voting records

|  | | | | | | | | | | | | | | |
|---|---|---|---|---|---|---|---|---|---|---|---|---|---|---|
| *Suffolk County* | | | | | | | | | | | | | | |
| Roxbury | + | – | + | + | + | – | + | + | A | a | 0.40 | 6.3 | 8 | 1,493 |
| *Essex County* | | | | | | | | | | | | | | |
| Andover | – | + | + | + | + | – | 0 | – | A | a | 0.08 | 2.9 | 6 | 2,462 |
| Gloucester | 0 | + | + | + | + | 0 | + | 0 | A | a | 0.45 | 4.0 | 7 | 3,772 |
| Haverhill | – | – | – | + | + | + | + | + | A | a | 0.25 | 4.0 | 6 | 1,992 |
| *Middlesex County* | | | | | | | | | | | | | | |
| Sherburne | 0 | 0 | 0 | 0 | + | 0 | – | – | B | c | 0.50 | 2.0 | 4 | 643 |
| Stow | – | 0 | 0 | + | + | + | 0 | – | C | c | 1.00 | 2.5 | 4 | 794 |
| Littleton | 0 | 0 | 0 | – | + | – | 0 | 0 | B | c | 1.10 | 2.5 | 6 | 773 |

Table 1. Legislative Voting Records of Massachusetts Towns (*continued*)

| Town | Should part of militia be employed for defense under New England officers?[a] | Should Agent Bollan receive parliamentary grant?[b] | Should Bollan's name appear first on a commission?[c] | Amendment to bill regulating coinage[d] | Should bill excluding Superior Court Justices from legislature receive 3d reading?[e] | Resolution to excuse Thos. Hutchinson from serving as agent in London?[f] | Hall classifications[g] | Tax category, 1761[h] | Land Bank investors per 100 of population | Average legislative tenure, 1744–64, in years | Single longest legislative tenure, 1744–64, in years | Population, 1765 |
|---|---|---|---|---|---|---|---|---|---|---|---|---|
| *Hampshire County* | | | | | | | | | | | | |
| Westfield | − | 0 | + | 0 | 0 | 0 | A | b | 0.00 | 3.8 | 6 | 1,324 |
| Sunderland, Montague[i] | − | + | + | − | 0 | 0 | C | c | 0.00 | 2.3 | 6 | — |
| *Worcester County* | | | | | | | | | | | | |
| Brookfield | − | 0 | 0 | 0 | 0 | + | A | b | 0.50 | 3.2 | 6 | 1,811 |
| Uxbridge | 0 | 0 | 0 | − | + | 0 | B | c | 2.91 | 1.6 | 3 | 1,213 |
| *Plymouth County* | | | | | | | | | | | | |
| Scituate | − | + | + | − | − | + | A | a | 0.60 | 5.0 | 11 | 2,501 |
| *Bristol County* | | | | | | | | | | | | |
| Freetown | 0 | 0 | 0 | 0 | − | + | A | b | — | 3.3 | 5 | — |
| *Barnstable County* | | | | | | | | | | | | |
| Sandwich | + | + | + | − | 0 | − | A | b | 0.28 | 4.0 | 7 | 1,449 |
| Yarmouth | − | 0 | + | 0 | 0 | 0 | B | b | 0.00 | 1.8 | 3 | 1,780 |
| Falmouth | + | 0 | + | − | 0 | − | A | c | 0.09 | 1.7 | 3 | 1,125 |
| Barnstable | 0 | 0 | + | 0 | 0 | − | A | b | 0.14 | 5.0 | 15 | 2,146 |
| Eastham | + | + | 0 | 0 | − | − | C | b | 0.38 | 3.8 | 7 | 1,331 |

*Cumberland County*

| | | | | | | | | | | | | |
|---|---|---|---|---|---|---|---|---|---|---|---|---|
| North Yarmouth | 0 | 0 | 0 | 0 | − | + | B | c | 0.09 | 4.0 | 10 | 1,079 |
| Scarborough | 0 | 0 | 0 | − | + | − | A | b | 0.00 | 2.8 | 8 | 1,272 |

NOTE: Only one recorded roll-call vote in the period May 1757 to May 1764 is omitted from this analysis. A vote of February 1, 1764, was omitted because it produced a nonpartisan division on the question of raising troops. + denotes Court party vote, − denotes Country party vote, 0 denotes no vote.

SOURCES: *House Journals*, 1744–1764; tax list of July 9, 1761, ibid.; Van Beck Hall of the University of Pittsburgh provided me with a copy of his classification of Massachusetts towns which is explained in his *Politics Without Parties: Massachusetts, 1780–1791* (Pittsburgh, 1972), pp. 3–22; population statistics are from Evarts B. Greene and Virginia Harrington, *American Population before the Federal Census of 1790* (New York, 1932), pp. 21–30; Andrew McFarland Davis, "List of Partners in the Land Bank of 1740," *CSM Collections* 4 (1910): 165–94.

  a. December 9, 1757.
  b. October 12, 1758.
  c. October 9, 1759.
  d. February 3, 1762.
  e. April 20, 1762.
  f. February 1, 1764.
  g. Van Beck Hall ranked the 343 Massachusetts towns of the 1780s into three groups according to their commercial-cosmopolitan activity. The most commercial and cosmopolitan were designated Group A; the middle group, Group B; and the least commercial-cosmopolitan, Group C.
  h. A tax of £1000 was apportioned among Massachusetts towns on July 9, 1761. The most highly taxed towns paid over £9 and are designated group a; the middle group paid over £4 to £9, group b; the least taxed paid up to £4, group c.
  i. These towns combined to send a single representative. Correlates are for the first named town.

Table 2. Judicial Office-Holding among Partisan Legislators of the 1750s

| Name | Town | County | Office | Date appointed |
|------|------|--------|--------|----------------|
| *Court party* | | | | |
| *From roll calls of 1753 to 1754*[a] | | | | |
| Hon. Samuel Welles | Boston | Suffolk | j.i.c. | 1755 |
| Hon. Thomas Hubbard[b] | Boston | Suffolk | j.p. | 1752 |
| James Bowdoin | Boston | Suffolk | j.p. | 1755 |
| Josiah Quincy | Braintree | Suffolk | j.p. | 1757 |
| William Bowdoin | Needham | Suffolk | | |
| Joseph Williams | Roxbury | Suffolk | j.p. | 1755 |
| Henry Gibbs | Salem | Essex | j.i.c. | 1754 |
| John Tasker | Marblehead | Essex | j.i.c. | 1754 |
| John Hunt | Watertown | Middlesex | j.p. | 1755 |
| Stephen Hall Jr. | Medford | Middlesex | j.p. | 1755 |
| Hon. Chambers Russell[b] | Lincoln | Middlesex | j.i.c. | 1747 |
| Elisha Jones | Weston | Middlesex | j.p. | 1761 |
| William Ayres | Brookfield | Worcester | j.p. | 1754 |
| Gamaliel Bradford | Duxbury | Plymouth | j.p. | 1762 |
| John Winslow | Marshfield | Plymouth | j.i.c. | 1762 |
| *From roll calls of 1757 to 1759*[c] | | | | |
| Thomas Flucker | Boston | Suffolk | j.p. | 1756 |
| Nathanael Hatch | Dorchester | Suffolk | j.p. | 1756 |
| Thomas Goldthwait | Chelsea | Suffolk | j.p. | 1755 |
| John Turner | Salem | Essex | j.p. | 1746 |
| William Stevens | Gloucester | Essex | j.p. | 1761 |
| Charles Prescott | Concord | Middlesex | j.p. | 1759 |
| John Clark | Newton | Middlesex | | |
| John Noyes | Sudbury | Middlesex | j.p. | 1749 |
| William Lawrence | Groton | Middlesex | j.i.c. | 1755 |
| Joseph Buckminster | Framingham | Middlesex | j.p. | 1749 |
| Oliver Fletcher | Chelmsford | Middlesex | j.p. | 1753 |
| Jonas Prescott | Westford | Middlesex | | |
| Luke Bliss | Springfield | Hampshire | | |
| Israel Williams | Hatfield | Hampshire | j.i.c. | 1758 |
| Elijah Williams | Deerfield | Hampshire | j.p. | 1753 |
| Fellows Billing | Montague | Hampshire | | |
| Timothy Pain | Worcester | Worcester | j.p. | 1755 |
| William Richardson | Lancaster | Worcester | j.p. | 1753 |
| George Watson | Plymouth | Plymouth | j.p. | 1754 |
| Thomas Clap | Scituate | Plymouth | j.i.c. | 1743 |
| Daniel Howard | Bridgewater | Plymouth | j.p. | 1749 |
| Ebenezer Sprout | Middleborough | Plymouth | | |
| Josiah Keen | Pembroke | Plymouth | | |
| Roland Cotton | Sandwich | Barnstable | j.p. | 1755 |
| Nathanael Stone | Harwich | Barnstable | j.p. | 1747 |
| Joseph Robinson | Falmouth | Barnstable | | |
| Abishai Folger | Sherburne | Nantucket | j.p. | 1754 |

Table 2. Judicial Office-Holding among Partisan Legislators of the 1750s (*continued*)

| Name | Town | County | Office | Date appointed |
|------|------|--------|--------|---------------|
| | Country party | | | |
| *From roll calls of 1753 to 1754*[a] | | | | |
| Samuel Niles Jr. | Braintree | Suffolk | j.p. | 1757 |
| Thomas Pratt | Weymouth | Suffolk | | |
| Joseph Richards | Dedham | Suffolk | j.p. | 1753 |
| Simon Plympton | Medfield | Suffolk | | |
| Jonathan Adams | Medway | Suffolk | | |
| Benjamin Greenleaf | Newbury | Essex | j.p. | 1762 |
| Joseph Gerrish Jr. | Newbury | Essex | j.p. | 1759 |
| Humphrey Hobson | Rowley | Essex | j.p. | 1759 |
| Isaac Merrill | Almsbury | Essex | j.p. | 1756 |
| Benjamin Milliken | Bradford | Essex | j.p. | 1761 |
| Elijah Porter | Topsfield | Essex | | |
| John Dodge | Wenham | Essex | | |
| Jonathan Foster | Boxford | Essex | | |
| William Brattle | Cambridge | Middlesex | | |
| Enoch Kidder | Billerica | Middlesex | | |
| Samuel Witt | Marlborough | Middlesex | | |
| Edward Walker | Woburn | Middlesex | | |
| Benjamin Hills | Malden | Middlesex | | |
| William Richardson | Lancaster | Worcester | j.p. | 1753 |
| John Haywood | Lunenburg | Worcester | | |
| Nathan Tyler | Mendon | Worcester | j.p. | 1755 |
| John Witcomb | Bolton | Worcester | | |
| Daniel Greenwood | Sutton | Worcester | | |
| Israel Turner | Pembroke | Plymouth | j.p. | 1760 |
| Josiah Edson | Bridgewater | Plymouth | j.p. | 1762 |
| Isaac Bonny | Plympton | Plymouth | | |
| Jacob Porter | Abington | Plymouth | | |
| Benjamin Day | Attleborough | Bristol | | |
| John Bradbury | York | York | j.p. | 1756 |
| Nathanael Sparhawk | Kittery | York | j.i.c. | 1760 |
| *From roll calls of 1757 to 1759*[c] | | | | |
| John Tyng | Boston | Suffolk | | |
| Benjamin Pratt[b] | Boston | Suffolk | | |
| Samuel Heath | Roxbury | Suffolk | | |
| Joshua Hearsey | Hingham | Suffolk | | |
| Peter Coollidge | Medfield | Suffolk | | |
| Richard Bayley | Stoughton | Suffolk | | |
| Timothy Metcalfe | Wrentham | Suffolk | | |
| Benjamin Newhall | Lynn | Essex | j.p. | 1759 |
| John Osgood | Andover | Essex | j.p. | 1761 |
| Henry Herrick | Beverly | Essex | | |
| Thomas Lancaster | Rowley | Essex | | |
| Caleb Cushing | Salisbury | Essex | j.i.c. | 1759 |
| David Marsh | Haverhill | Essex | | |

Table 2. Judicial Office-Holding among Partisan Legislators of the 1750s (*continued*)

| Name | Town | County | Office | Date appointed |
|------|------|--------|--------|----------------|
| John Gould | Topsfield | Essex | | |
| Thomas Perley | Boxford | Essex | | |
| Josiah Johnson | Woburn | Middlesex | j.p. | 1755 |
| John Temple | Reading | Middlesex | | |
| Samuel Livermore | Waltham | Middlesex | j.p. | 1753 |
| Daniel Whitney | Watertown | Middlesex | | |
| Benjamin Tucker | Leicester | Worcester | | |
| John French | Mendon | Worcester | | |
| Henry King | Sutton | Worcester | | |
| Timothy Walker | Rehoboth | Bristol | | |
| Benjamin Akin | Dartmouth | Bristol | j.p. | 1761 |
| Josiah Maxey | Attleborough | Bristol | | |
| Thomas Morey | Norton | Bristol | j.p. | 1761 |
| Benjamin Chadbourn | Berwick | York | j.p. | 1760 |

NOTE: This table concerns justices of the peace and justices of the inferior court appointed before 1763. Plural office-holding is not indicated.

SOURCES: *House Journals;* William H. Whitmore, *The Massachusetts Civil List for the Colonial and Provincial Periods, 1630–1774* (Albany, 1870), pp. 77–152.

a. Legislators present and voting consistently on at least three of the following five issues with no more than one additional inconsistent vote: gold currency act, 13 September 1753; additional grant to the late treasurer, 22 April 1754; excise act, 13 June 1754; question of colonial union, 14 December 1754; question to suspend consideration of report on colonial union, 27 December 1754.

b. Included as a partisan on the basis of external evidence. Hubbard was speaker of the House, Russell was a justice of the Superior Court, and Prat was an acknowledged leader of the Country party by the late 1750s.

c. Legislators present and voting consistently on at least two of the following three issues: militia question, 9 December 1757; whether agent Bollan should receive parliamentary grant, 12 October 1758; whether Bollan's name should appear first on a commission, 9 October 1759. Names from the roll calls of 1753 to 1754 have not been repeated unless they switched parties.

# Appendix B: Response of Massachusetts Towns on the Constitution of 1780

Table 1. A Classification of Massachusetts Towns According to Their Reaction to the Constitution of 1780

Of the many amendments to the constitution of 1780 requested by Massachusetts towns, the ones most frequently requested were thirteen in number. Table 1 shows which of the 207 towns whose votes on the constitution are available requested these amendments. A + denotes whether the town requested the particular amendment. A + in parentheses shows that the town voted for an amendment, but did not put it so strongly as the heading suggests. The towns are listed by county, from west to east with the three Maine counties last. The first ten amendments related directly to the demand for increased democracy in government. The other three were much debated issues, but had no ideological connotation. On the basis of the response of each town to the first ten issues, the emphasis of each return has been noted as "democratic" (D) or "conservative" (C). As Chapter 9 makes clear, this is not to suggest that a town whose return asked for no reform, and hence has been classed as conservative, was in fact conservative. Pittsfield in Berkshire County is an excellent example of a reformist town that did not ask for amendments, reformist or otherwise. The table simply is a general indicator of the western and rural character of the movement for democratic reform. If material in the return of a town was ambiguous or suggested that the town should not be classified as either democratic or conservative, it was listed as unclear (U).

Berkshire County

| Town | Governor, weak or none | Senate, weak or none | Representation favoring rural areas | Pay representatives' expenses | Property qualifications for vote, reduce or eliminate | Property qualifications for representatives, reduce or eliminate | For local registrars or probate courts | Reduce appointive power of governor | For more democratic militia elections | For fixed judges' terms | Article 3, Bill of Rights | Governor's religion | Amendment process | Emphasis |
|---|---|---|---|---|---|---|---|---|---|---|---|---|---|---|
| Adams | | | | | | | | | + | + | + | | | D |
| Becket | | + | | | | | | | | | + | | | D |
| Hancock | + | | | | | | | + | + | | + | + | | D |
| Lanesborough | + | | + | | | | + | + | + | | + | | | D |
| Lee | | | | | + | + | | | | | + | | | C |
| Lenox | | | | + | | + | | | | | | | | D |
| New Marlborough | | | | | + | | | | | | | | + | C |
| New Salem | | | + | | + | | | | | | + | | | D |
| Pittsfield | | | | | + | + | | | | | | | | C |
| Richmond | + | | | | | | | + | + | + | + | + | | D |
| Sandisfield | + | | | | | | | + | | | + | + | | C |
| Stockbridge | | | | + | + | + | + | + | + | + | + | | | D |
| Tyringham | + | | | | | | | + | + | | | | + | D |
| Washington | | | + | | | | | | | | | | | C |
| West Stockbridge | + | | + | | | | | + | + | | | + | | D |
| Williamstown | | | | | | | | | | | | | | C |
| Windsor | + | | | | | | | + | | + | + | | | D |

Totals of emphasis: 13 democratic, 4 conservative

270

| Town | | | | | | | | | | | | | | | | Class |
|---|---|---|---|---|---|---|---|---|---|---|---|---|---|---|---|---|
| Ashfield | + + | | + | + + | + | + + | + | + + | + | + | | + | + + | | | D |
| Belchertown | + + | + | | + + | + | + | | + + | + | + | + | + | | | | D |
| Bernardston | | | | | | | | | | + | | | | + | | | C |
| Brimfield | | | | | | | | | | | | | | | | | C |
| South Brimfield | | | + | + | + | + | + | + | + | | | | | | | | D |
| Charlemont* | | | | | | | | | | + | + | | | | | | D |
| Chesterfield | + | + + | + | + | | + | + | + + | + | + | | + | | + | | | D |
| Colrain | | + + | + | | | | | | + + | + | | | | | | | D |
| Conway | | + | | | | | | | | | | | | | | | D |
| Cummington | | | | | | | | | | | | | | | | | D |
| Granby | + | + | + + | | + | + | | + | + | | | | + | | | | D |
| Granville | + | | + | | + | | | + | | | | | | | | | D |
| Greenfield | | + | | | + | + | + | | + | | | | | | | | D |
| Greenwich | + + | + | | | + | | | + | | | + | | | | | | D |
| Hadley* | | | | | | | | | | | | | | | | | C |
| South Hadley* | | | | | | | | | | | | | | | | | D |
| Hatfield | + | + | + | + + | | + + | + | + + | | | | | + | | | | D |
| Leverett | | | | | | | | | + + | | | | | + + | | | D |
| Ludlow | + + | + + | | + + | | + + | + + | | | | | + + | | | | | D |
| Monson | | | | | | | | + | | | | | | | | | D |
| Montague | | | | + | | | + | | | | | | | | | | D |
| Northfield | + | + | | | | | | | + | | | | | | | | D |
| Northampton | | | + | | | | | | | + | | | | | | | D |
| Norwich | + | + | | | | + | + | | | + | | | | | + | | D |
| Palmer | | | | | | | | | | | | | | | | | D |
| Pelham | + + + + | + + + + | + + | + | + + | + + | + + | + | + + | + | + | + + | + + | + | | | D |
| Shelburn | | | | | | | | | | | | | | | | | D |
| Shutesbury | + | + | | + | | + | | | + | | + | | | | | | D |

Table 1. A Classification of Massachusetts Towns According to Their Reaction to the Constitution of 1780 (continued)

| Town | Governor, weak or none | Senate, weak or none | Representation favoring rural areas | Pay representatives' expenses | Property qualifications for vote, reduce or eliminate | Property qualifications for representatives, reduce or eliminate | For local registrars or probate courts | Reduce appointive power of governor | For more democratic militia elections | For fixed judges' terms | Article 3, Bill of Rights | Governor's religion | Amendment process | Emphasis |
|---|---|---|---|---|---|---|---|---|---|---|---|---|---|---|
| Southampton | + | | | | | | | | | | | + | + | U |
| Southwich | | + | + | + | | | | + | + | | + | + | | D |
| Springfield | + | + | + | + | | | | + | | | | + | + | D |
| Sunderland | | + | + | | | | | + | + | | | | | D |
| Ware | + | | | | | | | | | | | + | + | D |
| Westfield | + | + | | | | | + | + | + | | + | + | | D |
| Warwick | + | + | | | | | | + | | | | | | D |
| Westhampton | + | | + | | + | + | | + | + | | | + | | D |
| West Springfield | | + | + | | + | | | | | | + | + | + | D |
| Wilbraham | + | + | + | | + | + | | + | + | + | | + | | D |
| Williamsburgh | | | | + | | | | | + | | | | | D |
| Totals of emphasis: 31 democratic, 3 conservative, 5 unclear |

Worcester County

| Town | Governor, weak or none | Senate, weak or none | Representation favoring rural areas | Pay representatives' expenses | Property qualifications for vote, reduce or eliminate | Property qualifications for representatives, reduce or eliminate | For local registrars or probate courts | Reduce appointive power of governor | For more democratic militia elections | For fixed judges' terms | Article 3, Bill of Rights | Governor's religion | Amendment process | Emphasis |
|---|---|---|---|---|---|---|---|---|---|---|---|---|---|---|
| Ashburnham* | | | | | | | | (+) | | | | | | C |
| Athol | + | + | + | + | + | + | | | | + | | | + | D |
| Barre | | | | | | | | + | | | | + | | D |
| Bolton | | | | | | | | | | | | | | C |

272

|  | |
|---|---|
| Brookfield | C |
| Charlton | D |
| Douglass | D |
| Dudley | C |
| Fitchburg | D |
| Grafton | D |
| Hardwick | C |
| Harvard | D |
| Holden | C |
| Lancaster | C |
| Leicester | C |
| Leominster | D |
| Lunenburg* | D |
| Mendon | D |
| Milford | D |
| New Braintree | D |
| Northborough | D |
| Northbridge | C |
| Oakham | C |
| Oxford* | D |
| Paxton | C |
| Petersham | D |
| Princeton | C |
| Royalston | D |
| Rutland | C |
| Shrewsbury | D |
| Southborough | D |
| Spencer | D |
| Sturbridge | D |
| Sutton | D |

273

Table 1. A Classification of Massachusetts Towns According to Their Reaction to the Constitution of 1780 (*continued*)

| Town | Governor, weak or none | Senate, weak or none | Representation favoring rural areas | Pay representatives' expenses | Property qualifications for vote, reduce or eliminate | Property qualifications for representatives, reduce or eliminate | For local registrars or probate courts | Reduce appointive power of governor | For more democratic militia elections | For fixed judges' terms | Article 3, Bill of Rights | Governor's religion | Amendment process | Emphasis |
|---|---|---|---|---|---|---|---|---|---|---|---|---|---|---|
| Templeton | + | | | | | | | | | | | + | | C |
| Upton | | + | | | | | | + | | | + | + | | D |
| Uxbridge | | | + | | | | | | | | + | | + | D |
| Ward | | | + | | | | | | | | | + | + | D |
| Westboro | + | + | + | | | | | + | | | | | + | D |
| Westminster | | + | + | | | | | | | | | | + | D |
| Winchendon | | | | | | | | | | | | + | | D |
| Western | | + | + | | | | + | | | | + | | | D |
| Worcester | | | + | + | | | | | | | | | | D |

Totals of emphasis: 29 democratic, 13 conservative, 1 unclear

Middlesex County

| Town | Governor, weak or none | Senate, weak or none | Representation favoring rural areas | Pay representatives' expenses | Property qualifications for vote, reduce or eliminate | Property qualifications for representatives, reduce or eliminate | For local registrars or probate courts | Reduce appointive power of governor | For more democratic militia elections | For fixed judges' terms | Article 3, Bill of Rights | Governor's religion | Amendment process | Emphasis |
|---|---|---|---|---|---|---|---|---|---|---|---|---|---|---|
| Acton | | | | | | | | | | | | | + | U |
| Ashby | | | | | | | | | | | + | | | C |
| Bedford | | | | | | | | | | | | | + | U |
| Billerica | | | | | | | | | | + | | | | U |
| Cambridge | | | | | | | | | | | | | | C |
| Charlestown | | | | | | | | | | | | | | C |

274

| | Chelmsford | Concord | Dracut | Dunstable | East Sudbury | Framingham | Groton | Holliston | Lexington | Lincoln | Littleton | Malden | Marboro | Medford | Natick | Newton | Reading | Sherburn | Shirley* | Pepperrell | Stoneham | Sudbury | Stow | Tewksbury | Townshend | Waltham | Watertown | Westford | Weston | Woburn |
|---|---|---|---|---|---|---|---|---|---|---|---|---|---|---|---|---|---|---|---|---|---|---|---|---|---|---|---|---|---|---|
| | C | D | C | D | D | D | C | D | D | C | D | D | C | C | C | C | D | C | C | C | C | C | C | C | C | C | C | C | C | D |
| | | | + | + | | + | | + | + | | + | + | | + | + | + | | | | + | + | + | | | | + | | + | | |
| | + | + | | + | | | + | + | + | + | | | | + | | | | | + | + | + | | | | | + | | | | |
| | | | + | | + | | + | + | + | | + | | | + | | + | | | | | | | | | | + | | | | |
| | | | | | | | | | | | | | | | | | | | | | | | | | | | | | | |
| | | | | | | | + | | | + | | | | | | | | | | | | | | | | | | | | |
| | | | | | | | | | + | | | | | | | | | | | | | | | | | | | | | |
| | | | | | | | | | | | | | | | | | | | | | | | | | | | | | | |
| | | | | | | | | + | | | | | | | | | | | | | | | | | | | | | | + |
| | | | | | | | | | | | | | | | | | | | | | | | | | | | | | | |
| | | + | | | | | | + | + | + | | | | | | | | | | | | | | | | | | | | |
| | | | | | | + | | | | + | | | | | | | | | | | | | | | | | | | | |
| | | | | | | | + | | | + | | | | | | | | | | | | | | | | | | | | |

Table 1.  A Classification of Massachusetts Towns According to Their Reaction to the Constitution of 1780 (*continued*)

| Town | Governor, weak or none | Senate, weak or none | Representation favoring rural areas | Pay representatives' expenses | Property qualifications for vote, reduce or eliminate | Property qualifications for representatives, reduce or eliminate | For local registrars or probate courts | Reduce appointive power of governor | For more democratic militia elections | For fixed judges' terms | Article 3, Bill of Rights | Governor's religion | Amendment process | Emphasis |
|---|---|---|---|---|---|---|---|---|---|---|---|---|---|---|
| Wilmington | | | | | | | | | | | (+) | | + | U |
| Totals of emphasis: 6 democratic, 23 conservative, 8 unclear | | | | | | | | | | | | | | |
| **Bristol County** | | | | | | | | | | | | | | |
| Attleborough | + | | | | | | | + | | | + | + | | D |
| Berkley | + | | | | | | | + | + | | | + | | D |
| Dartmouth | | | | | + | | | | | | + | | | D |
| Dighton | | | | | | | | | | | + | | | C |
| Easton | | | | | | | + | | | | + | + | + | D |
| Freetown | + | | | | | | | | | | + | | | D |
| Mansfield | + | | + | | + | | | | | | | + | | D |
| Norton | + | + | + | | + | | | | | | | + | | D |
| Rehoboth | | + | | | | | | | | | + | | + | D |
| Raynham | | | | | | | | | | | + | | | C |
| Swanzey | | | | | | | | | | | + | | | C |
| Taunton | | | | | | | | | | | + | | + | C |
| Totals of emphasis: 8 democratic, 4 conservative | | | | | | | | | | | | | | |

## Suffolk County

| Town | | | | | | | | | | | | | Class. |
|------|---|---|---|---|---|---|---|---|---|---|---|---|--------|
| Bellingham | + | + | | | | + | + | | | + | | | D |
| Boston | + | | | | + | + | + | | | + | | + | C |
| Braintree | | | | | | | | | | | + | | C |
| Brookline | | + | | + | | | | | | | | | D |
| Chelsea | + | + | | + | | | | | | + | | | C |
| Cohasset | | | | | | | | | | + | | | C |
| Dedham | | + | + | | | | | | | + | | + | D |
| Dorchester | | | | | | | | | | | | + | D |
| Foxborough | | | | | | | | | | | | + | C |
| Hingham | | | | | | | | | | | + | | C |
| Medfield | + | | | | | | + | | | + | | | D |
| Medway | + | | + | + | | + | + | + | | + | | | C |
| Milton | + | | | | | | | | | | | | D |
| Needham | | | | | + | + | + | | + | + | + | | C |
| Roxbury | | | | | | + | + | | | + | | | D |
| Stoughton | | + | | | | + | | | | | | | D |
| Stoughtonham | | + | + | | | + | | | | | | | D |
| Walpole | | + | + | | | + | + | | + | + | | | D |
| Wrentham | + | | | | | | | + | | | | | D |
| Weymouth | | | | | | | | | | | | | C |

Totals of emphasis: 7 democratic, 10 conservative, 3 unclear

## Essex County

| Town | | Class. |
|------|---|--------|
| Almsbury* | + | C |
| Beverly* | | C |
| Bradford* | + | C |
| Haverhill* | + | C |
| Middleton* | | C |

Table 1. A Classification of Massachusetts Towns According to Their Reaction to the Constitution of 1780 (*continued*)

| Town | Governor, weak or none | Senate, weak or none | Representation favoring rural areas | Pay representatives' expenses | Property qualifications for vote, reduce or eliminate | Property qualifications for representatives, reduce or eliminate | For local registrars or probate courts | Reduce appointive power of governor | For more democratic militia elections | For fixed judges' terms | Article 3, Bill of Rights | Governor's religion | Amendment process | Emphasis |
|---|---|---|---|---|---|---|---|---|---|---|---|---|---|---|
| Newburyport* | | | | | | | | | | | | | | C |
| Salisbury* | | | | | | | | | | | + | | + | C |
| Totals of emphasis: 7 conservative | | | | | | | | | | | | | | |
| **Plymouth County** | | | | | | | | | | | | | | |
| Abington | | + | | | | | | | | | + | | | U |
| Bridgewater | | | + | | | | | | | | | | | C |
| Halifax | | | | | | | | | | | | | | C |
| Kingston | | | | | | | | | | | | | | C |
| Marshfield | | | | | | | | | | | | | + | C |
| Middleborough | + | + | + | | + | + | + | + | | | + | | + | D |
| Pembroke | | | | | + | | | | | | | | + | D |
| Plymouth | | | | | | | | | | | | | | C |
| Plimpton | | + | | | + | | | | | | | | | D |
| Rochester | | + | | | | + | + | | + | | + | + | | D |
| Scituate | | | | | | + | + | | + | + | + | + | + | D |
| Wareham | | + | | | + | + | + | | + | | + | + | | C |
| Totals of emphasis: 5 democratic, 6 conservative, 1 unclear | | | | | | | | | | | | | | |

## Barnstable County

| Town | | | | | | Class |
|---|---|---|---|---|---|---|
| Barnstable | | + | + | + | + | D |
| Eastham | + | | ++ | ++ | | D |
| Falmouth* | | | | + | ++ | C |
| Harwich* | | | | + | ++ | C |
| Wellfleet* | | | + | + | | C |
| Yarmouth | | | + | + | ++ | C |

Totals of emphasis: 1 democratic, 4 conservative, 1 unclear

## York County (Maine)

| Town | | | | | | Class |
|---|---|---|---|---|---|---|
| Arundel | + | + | | | | C |
| Berwick | | | | + | | C |
| Biddeford | | | | + | | C |
| Buxton | | | (+) | + | + | D |
| Kittery | | | ++ | ++ | | C |
| Wells | | | ++ | ++ | + | C |
| York | | | | | | C |

Totals of emphasis: 1 democratic, 6 conservative

## Cumberland County (Maine)

| Town | | | Class |
|---|---|---|---|
| Cape Elizabeth* | + | + | C |
| New Gloucester* | | | C |

Totals of emphasis: 2 conservative

## Lincoln County (Maine)

| Town | | | Class |
|---|---|---|---|
| Edgecumb | + | + | C |
| Georgetown* | | | C |
| Newcastle* | | | C |

Table 1. A Classification of Massachusetts Towns According to Their Reaction to the Constitution of 1780 (*continued*)

| Town | Governor, weak or none | Senate, weak or none | Representation favoring rural areas | Pay representatives' expenses | Property qualifications for vote, reduce or eliminate | Property qualifications for representatives, reduce or eliminate | For local registrars or probate courts | Reduce appointive power of governor | For more democratic militia elections | For fixed judges' terms | Article 3, Bill of Rights | Governor's religion | Amendment process | Emphasis |
|---|---|---|---|---|---|---|---|---|---|---|---|---|---|---|
| Pownalborough* | | | | | | | | | | | | | | C |
| Vassalborough* | | | | | | | | | | | | | | C |

Totals of emphasis: 5 conservative

Sources: Mass. Arch., 276, 277; Samuel E. Morison's file in MHS (indicated by asterisks).

Table 2. A Summary of the Number of Massachusetts Towns Calling for Democratic Amendments to the Constitution of 1780 (counties listed from west to east with three Maine counties last)

| County | Total number of towns replying | Governor, weak or none | Senate, weak or none | Representation favoring rural areas | Pay representatives' expenses | Property qualifications for vote, reduce or eliminate | Property qualifications for representatives, reduce or eliminate | For local registrars or probate courts | Reduce appointive power of governor | For more democratic militia elections | For fixed judges' terms |
|---|---|---|---|---|---|---|---|---|---|---|---|
| Berkshire | 17 | 7 | 1 | 4 | 2 | 5 | 4 | 2 | 7 | 6 | 4 |
| Hampshire | 39 | 15(1) | 10(4) | 13 | 7 | 14 | 8 | 6 | 13 | 18 | 6 |
| Worcester | 43 | 19(4) | 17(5) | 15 | 4 | 8 | 4 | 7 | 16 | 4 | 6 |
| Middlesex | 37 | 2 | 2 | 4 | 0 | 2 | 0 | 1 | 2 | 1 | 0 |
| Bristol | 12 | 5(1) | 2(1) | 2 | 0 | 3 | 0 | 1 | 2 | 1 | 0 |
| Suffolk | 20 | 3 | 6 | 5 | 0 | 5 | 1 | 8 | 3 | 1 | 2 |
| Essex | 7 | 0 | 0 | 0 | 0 | 0 | 0 | 0 | 0 | 0 | 0 |
| Plymouth | 12 | 1 | 4 | 2 | 0 | 4 | 3 | 3 | 1 | 2 | 1 |
| Barnstable | 6 | 1 | 0 | 0 | 0 | 1 | 0 | 0 | 1 | 1 | 0 |
| York | 7 | 1 | 1 | 0 | 0 | 0 | 0 | 0 | 0 | 0 | 0 |
| Cumberland | 2 | 0 | 0 | 0 | 0 | 0 | 0 | 0 | 0 | 0 | 0 |
| Lincoln | 5 | 0 | 0 | 0 | 0 | 0 | 0 | 0 | 0 | 0 | 0 |
| Total | 207 | 54(6) | 43(10) | 45 | 13 | 42 | 20 | 28 | 45 | 24 | 19 |

NOTE: Numbers in parentheses indicate the number of towns in addition to those already noted which addressed this issue but not precisely as the heading suggests.

SOURCES: Mass. Arch., 276, 277; Samuel E. Morison's file in MHS.

281

Appendix C: County Representation in Selected Massachusetts Legislatures, Provincial Congresses, and Constitutional Conventions (counties listed from west to east with three Maine counties last)

| County | General Court May 25, 1774 (1) | First Provincial Congress October 1774 (2) | General Court July 19, 1775 (3) | General Court May 29, 1776 (4) | General Court May 28, 1777 (5) | Constitutional Convention September 1779 (6) |
|---|---|---|---|---|---|---|
| Berkshire | 8 | 7 | 7 | 11 | 20 | 27 |
| Hampshire | 11 | 39 | 25 | 27 | 41 | 51 |
| Worcester | 20 | 56 | 38 | 34 | 62 | 65 |
| Middlesex | 24 | 75 | 34 | 44 | 30 | 47 |
| Bristol | 11 | 16 | 15 | 15 | 19 | 20 |
| Suffolk | 17 | 34 | 20 | 43 | 24 | 36 |
| Essex | 18 | 27 | 23 | 48 | 32 | 50 |
| Plymouth | 13 | 18 | 12 | 19 | 17 | 17 |
| Barnstable | 7 | 8 | 11 | 8 | 9 | 2 |
| Nantucket | 1 | 0 | 0 | 0 | 0 | 0 |
| Dukes | 1 | 2 | 3 | 3 | 0 | 0 |
| York | 5 | 6 | 6 | 6 | 6 | 5 |
| Cumberland | 3 | 5 | 5 | 8 | 6 | 2 |
| Lincoln | 1 | 0 | 7 | 0 | 0 | 2 |
| Total | 140 | 293 | 206 | 266 | 266 | 324 |

SOURCES: The Journal of Each Provincial Congress of Massachusetts in 1774 and 1775, ed. William Lincoln (Boston, 1838), pp. 7-15; House Journals; Journal of the Convention for Framing a Constitution of Government for the State of Massachusetts Bay . . . , [1 September 1779–16 June 1780] (Boston, 1832), pp. 8-19, 34–35.

Bibliographical Note

Index

# Bibliographical Note

The considerable number of comprehensive bibliographies listing the standard literature on eighteenth-century Massachusetts make yet another unnecessary. Particularly valuable comprehensive bibliographies are those found in Robert E. Brown, *Middle-Class Democracy and the Revolution in Massachusetts, 1691–1780* (Ithaca, N.Y., 1955), and Richard D. Brown, *Revolutionary Politics in Massachusetts: The Boston Committee of Correspondence and the Towns, 1772–1774* (Cambridge, Mass., 1970). The latter is excellent for town records. Students may also wish to consult the extensive bibliography in my doctoral dissertation, "A History of Political Parties in Revolutionary Massachusetts, 1770–1780" (University of Wisconsin, 1968). This bibliographical note, therefore, will assess the value of the more important sources and will comment on some of the most recent secondary literature.

The student of Massachusetts history is confronted with a wealth of resources, perhaps more extensive than for any other state in the Union, much of it still untapped or at least underexploited. Many standard collections, as a matter of fact, still retain their hidden reserves and await only the careful scrutiny of the determined scholar. For the late provincial period, I found the Israel Williams Papers at the Massachusetts Historical Society essential in establishing the link between local and provincial politics and in following the course of Court party politics. The Correspondence of Thomas Hutchinson, found in the State Archives of Massachusetts and appearing as Massachusetts Archives, vols. 25, 26, and 27, carries the official and Court party view down to 1774. There are no equivalent collections for the opposition or Country party point of view, although the Thacher Papers and the Ezekiel Price Papers in the Massachusetts Historical Society provide insights into the role of merchants and the link between Boston and country towns in the early 1760s.

For the 1770s, correspondence to and from John and Samuel Adams represents the most significant body of material. Samuel Adams, unfortunately, destroyed many of the letters he both wrote and received so that we are left chiefly with his public papers and the few letters retained by his correspondents. Harry A. Cushing edited the best selection of these as *The Writings of Samuel Adams*, 4 vols. (New York, 1904–8). The Samuel Adams Papers in the New York Public Library contain a number of excellent letters relating to the mid-1770s. I am indebted to Professor Merrill Jensen of the University of Wisconsin for the use of his microfilm copy of these papers. An excellent exchange of political information among the Adamses and their friends James and Mercy Warren is to be found in the *Warren-Adams Letters*, 2 vols. (Boston, 1917–25), edited by Worthington Chauncey Ford. Other correspondence of John Adams is most extensive and is found chiefly in the Adams Papers in the Massachusetts Historical Society. In the microfilm edition (State Historical Society of Wisconsin), I used especially reels 89, 90, and 344–47, which provided rich detail on the relationship between state and continental politics and the disintegration of the old Popular party in the mid to late 1770s. Some of this same material may be found in Lyman H. Butterfield, ed., *Adams Family Correspondence*, 2 vols. (Cambridge, Mass., 1963); and in Charles Francis Adams, ed., *The Works of John Adams*, 10 vols. (Boston, 1850–56), and *Familiar Letters of John Adams and his wife Abigail Adams, During the Revolution* (Boston, 1875). Also of value for the late 1770s is Butterfield's edition of the *Diary and Autobiography of John Adams*, 4 vols. (Cambridge, Mass., 1961).

Several smaller collections have special merits. Among collections at the Massachusetts Historical Society, the Andrews-Eliot Papers are excellent for day-to-day life in Boston in late 1774, while the papers of Elbridge Gerry, Robert Treat Paine, Josiah Quincy, Jr., Theodore Sedgwick, James Sullivan, and John and Timothy Pickering provide numerous details on the ebb and flow of provincial and state politics. The Paine Papers are excellent for details on the last session of the General Court in June 1774. The Sedgwick Papers provide a unique window on the internal revolution in Berkshire County in the late 1770s and should be read in conjunction with Henry C. Van Schaack, *The Life of Peter Van Schaack, LL.D., Embracing Selections from his Correspondence* . . . (New York, 1842), and *Memoirs of the Life of Henry Van Schaack Embracing Selections from his Correspondence* . . . (Chicago, 1892). The Sedgwick-Van Schaack connection illustrates the closeness of conservative revolutionaries and Tories. Three collections in the New York Public Library also illuminate the politics of the 1770s: Letters and Minutes of the Boston Committee of Correspondence, in the George Bancroft Collection; the Joseph Hawley Papers; and Autograph Letters of Joseph Warren.

For purposes of political analysis, the various journals of Massachuetts legislative bodies are essential. The *Journals of the House of Representatives* and the *Journals of the Council of Massachusetts* are available on microfilm in the Records of the States of the United States, State Historical Society of Wisconsin. A reprinting of the *House Journals* from 1715 to 1766 has been undertaken by the Massachusetts Historical Society, most recently under the editorship of Malcolm Freiburg. The picture is not complete without *The Journals of Each Provincial Congress of Massachusetts in 1774 and 1775*, edited by William Lincoln (Boston, 1838), and *Journal of the Convention for Framing a Constitution of Government for the State of Massachusetts Bay* . . . , *1779–1780* (Boston, 1832). Extracting significant material from the parsimonious prose of legislative journals is something of an art, but there are important subsidiary materials for the late 1770s that establish the primacy of state over local politics. Among these are the following in the Massachusetts Archives: Journal of the Constitutional Convention of 1777–1778, vol. 156; Petitions of Massachusetts Towns respecting Treasury Notes, vol. 156; Returns of Massachusetts Towns on the Constitution of 1778, vols. 156 and 160; and Returns of Massachusetts Towns on the Constitution of 1780, vols. 276 and 277. Much of the material on the 1780 constitution appears in Oscar and Mary Handlin, eds., *The Popular Sources of Political Authority: Documents on the Massachusetts Constitution of 1780* (Cambridge, Mass., 1966), although their arrangement of the material fails to impose upon it any analytical rigor whatsoever. Of more value in determining the patterns of constitutional argument are the selected materials in Robert J. Taylor, ed., *Massachusetts, Colony to Commonwealth: Documents on the Formation of Its Constitution, 1775–1780* (Chapel Hill, N.C., 1961).

In recent secondary literature, three themes are of particular interest to the student of revolutionary Massachuetts: the nature of political groups or parties, the political role of the towns, and the role of popular forces or crowds. While agreed that provincial and state politics were something less than partisan, recent historians of Massachusetts have not achieved consensus in their view of the political structure. John J. Waters, Jr., has emphasized the role of leading families in *The Otis Family in Provincial and Revolutionary Massachusetts* (Chapel Hill, N.C., 1968), and, with John A. Schutz, in "Patterns of Massachusetts Colonial Politics: The Writs of Assistance and the Rivalry between the Otis and Hutchinson Families," *William and Mary Quarterly*, 3d ser., 24 (1967): 543–67. In many respects, however, this emphasis on personal and family rivalries carries us very little beyond the interpretation of Thomas Hutchinson in his *The History of the Colony and Province of Massachusetts-Bay*, a three-volume edition of which appeared under the editorship of Lawrence Shaw Mayo (Cambridge, Mass., 1936). Robert Zemsky's *Merchants, Farmers, and River Gods: An Essay on Eighteenth-Century American Politics* (Boston, 1971) suggests that Massachusetts legislatures in the period 1740 to 1756 were characterized by a united leadership and a rank and file that cast their votes without reference to the leaders' position. Where Zemsky stresses personalities and issues as the bases of shifting alignments, Van Beck Hall provides us with much clearer determinants of political action in his sophisticated analysis of the towns in the 1780s, *Politics Without Parties* (Pittsburgh, 1972). As the title suggests, political alignments lacked the organizational structure that Hall believes mark proper political parties, but he nonetheless demonstrates a high level of voting consistency among the state's most commercial and cosmopolitan centers as opposed to the small, chiefly agricultural communities. Hall, however, does not consider the theoretical constraints on partisan organization, as does Richard Hofstadter in his *The Idea of a Party System: The Rise of Legitimate*

*Opposition in the United States, 1780–1840* (Berkeley, Calif., 1969), a work that would have benefited from an examination of the late colonial period as well.

The large number of recent studies of New England, particularly Massachusetts, towns has caused some anxiety in the profession. What do they all mean? Can one generalize for all Massachusetts upon the evidence of a single town study? Was there a provincial politics apart from the combined politics of the towns? And if there was, which was the more important? Hall's *Politics Without Parties* shows us finally that many town studies, excellent though they may be, at best describe the forces at work in some kinds of towns, not all. Thus the valuable work of Kenneth Lockridge, of which his *A New England Town, the First Hundred Years: Dedham, Massachusetts, 1636–1736* (New York, 1970) is the best example, provides us with details of the changes taking place among established, eastern agricultural communities in the early eighteenth century, and his work is reinforced and extended by Edward M. Cook, Jr., "Social Behavior and Changing Values in Dedham, Massachusetts, 1700 to 1775," *William and Mary Quarterly*, 3d ser., 27 (1970): 546–80, and by J. M. Bumstead, "Religion, Finance, and Democracy in Massachusetts: The Town of Norton as a Case Study," *Journal of American History* 57 (1970–71): 817–31. James A. Henretta provides evidence of a widening gap between rich and poor in his "Economic Development and Social Structure in Colonial Boston," *William and Mary Quarterly*, 3d ser., 22 (1965): 75–92. Again, however, we might assume that his findings have application in other large, commercial-cosmopolitan centers (although even in this class, Boston was unique), but how they may be generalized beyond that is problematical.

Two studies take a more general approach to the towns. Michael Zuckerman's *Peaceable Kingdoms: New England Towns in the Eighteenth Century* (New York, 1970) poses the thesis that the towns shifted from a consensual to an accommodative politics, and that the towns became and remained the focus of political action down to the Revolution. There is much of value here, particularly in Zuckerman's delineation of changing political styles and the persistent attachment to ideals of harmony and peace, but his conclusions about the Revolution, made with no significant examination of provincial politics, clearly outstrip his evidence. Allen David Grayson has particularly criticized Zuckerman for his claim that eighteenth-century towns were virtually autonomous from the provincial government and for overgeneralizing the experience of a few towns: "The Zuckerman Thesis and the Process of Legal Rationalization in Provincial Massachusetts," with a rebuttal by Michael Zuckerman, *William and Mary Quarterly*, 3d ser., 29 (1972): 442–68. More directly focused on the Revolution, Richard D. Brown's *Revolutionary Politics in Massachusetts* provides useful detail on the exchange of revolutionary ideas and rhetoric by Committees of Correspondence, but his emphasis on the role of the towns, particularly in the period after June 1774, obscures the role of county conventions and other popular gatherings, sometimes of a class nature, and carries us little beyond the view put forth by Harry Alonzo Cushing in his *History of the Transition from Provincial to Commonwealth Government in Massachusetts* (New York, 1896) which emphasized the stability provided by the towns.

The revolutionary character of the American Revolution has been more apparent in those studies not so preoccupied with the role of the towns, many of which have placed new emphasis on the role of popular forces or crowds. Again, however, there is disagreement as to how best to interpret that role. Hiller B. Zobel presents a rather traditional view of the Boston crowd as a trained and directed mob in his *Boston Massacre* (New York, 1970). This account fails to penetrate the frame of reference of his elite (not only Tory) sources, but is suggestive of the mobility of crowds from town to town. Jesse Lemisch's work has provided a fresh perspective on inarticulate, revolutionary crowds, and has called for a more sympathetic understanding of popular motives which he sees as distinct from those of the leadership. His "The American Revolution Seen from the Bottom Up," in *Towards a New Past: Dissenting Essays in American History*, edited by Barton J. Bernstein (New York, 1968) is perhaps the best statement of his hypothesis. Pauline Maier, however, has suggested that crowds were not born with the Revolution and that they were often concerned with restoring order or righting injustice: "Popular Uprisings and Civil Authority in Eighteenth-Century America," *William and Mary Quarterly*, 3d ser., 27 (1970): 3–35. In all three of these works, there is an overconcern with urban crowds and a continuing need to explain how crowds numbering in the thousands could appear in small rural towns as in Berkshire in 1778. We need to know more about how popular forces from various towns interacted, not only as spontaneous crowds but also in militia organizations, county conventions, and partisan meetings, for these were the novel structures of the Revolution and the proof that the times were truly revolutionary.

# Index

Adams, Abigail: reports local conditions, 104, 157, 160, 162, 175; on split in congressional delegation, 133; on conflict among representatives, 169

Adams, John: political views of, 6, 8–9, 15, 31, 32, 48, 63, 145, 149–50, 155, 168, 216–17, 219–27, 255; on Tories, 6, 71; "Dissertation on the Canon and Feudal Law," 15; republicanism of, 32, 63, 64, 176, 219–27, 255; on patronage, 48; on provincial and state politics, 50–51, 138, 155, 160, 168, 170, 176, 180, 186, 197, 216–17; and Boston politics, 55, 71, 83; biographical sketch of, 58; in Congress, 126, 130–31, 170, 186; as chief justice, 128, 138; on Independence, 140–41; and constitution of 1780, 216–17, 219–27, 247; *Defence of the Constitutions*, 220, 222; mentioned, 24, 27, 33, 238, 255

Adams, John Quincy, 255

Adams, Samuel: on partisanship, 9, 31, 145, 149; republicanism of, 32, 60, 63, 90, 145, 149, 203, 224, 255; biographical sketch of, 57–58; as political organizer, 57–58, 60, 69, 73, 75, 77, 90, 93; and nonimportation (1769), 67; and Hancock, 72–73, 131, 132, 134, 200; opposed by merchants, 81, 82, 83–85; and Tea Act,

86–87; described by Hutchinson, 89; designs against, 93; in Congress, 98, 108, 170, 200; and Provincial Congress, 111, 114–15, 120–21; and constitution, 120–21, 126, 219, 224; and state politics, 128, 131, 142, 164, 170, 197, 203, 255; and Independence, 142

Admiralty court: opposed, 53–54; defection of Otis from, 54

Agriculture: problems in, 27, 39–40; linked with commerce, 39; in Country party towns, 45, 46; political emergence of farming towns, 61. *See also* Farmers

Allen, Rev. Thomas, 137

Almsbury, 41

Amory, John: as Boston merchant, 76, 84

Andover, 147

Andrews, John: as moderate merchant, 81, 83–84, 85, 87, 111, 114; describes Boston town meeting, 83–84; on rural spirit, 101, 102, 105; and Provincial Congress, 111, 114

Appleton, Nathaniel, 76

Articles of Confederation, 183

Ashfield: constitutional views of, 163, 164

Athol, 242

Attleborough, 165

Austin, Benjamin, 146

291

DESIGNED BY GARY GORE

MANUFACTURED BY IMPRESSIONS, INC., MADISON, WISCONSIN

TEXT LINES ARE SET IN CALEDONIA, DISPLAY LINES IN OPTIMA AND CALEDONIA

Library of Congress Cataloging in Publication Data
Patterson, Stephen E                1937 —
Political parties in revolutionary Massachusetts.
Includes bibliographical references.
1. Political parties — Massachusetts — History.
2. Massachusetts — Politics and government — Colonial period.
3. Massachusetts — Politics and government — Revolution.
I. Title.
JK103.M4P37      329'.02      72-7991
ISBN 0-299-06260-0